THE SHINING PATH

THE
SHINING
PATH

LOVE, MADNESS, AND
REVOLUTION IN THE ANDES

ORIN STARN AND
MIGUEL LA SERNA

W. W. NORTON & COMPANY

INDEPENDENT PUBLISHERS SINCE 1923

NEW YORK   LONDON

Copyright © 2019 by Orin Starn and Miguel La Serna

For information about permission to reproduce selections from this book, write to Permissions, W. W. Norton & Company, Inc., 500 Fifth Avenue, New York, NY 10110

For information about special discounts for bulk purchases, please contact W. W. Norton Special Sales at specialsales@wwnorton.com or 800-233-4830

Manufacturing by Sheridan
Book design by Daniel Lagin
Production manager: Lauren Abbate

Library of Congress Cataloging-in-Publication Data

Names: Starn, Orin, author. | La Serna, Miguel, author.
Title: The Shining Path : love, madness, and revolution in the Andes / Orin Starn and Miguel La Serna.
Description: First edition. | New York : W.W. Norton & Company, [2019] | Includes bibliographical references and index.
Identifiers: LCCN 2018054651 | ISBN 9780393292800 (hardcover)
Subjects: LCSH: Sendero Luminoso (Guerrilla group) | Peru—Politics and government—1968–1980. | Peru—Politics and government—1980– | Revolutions—Peru—History—20th century. | Guerrilla warfare—Peru—History—20th century. | Terrorism—Peru—History—20th century. | Guerrillas—Peru—Biography. | Revolutionaries—Peru—Biography. | Communists—Peru—Biography.
Classification: LCC F3448.2 .S73 2019 | DDC 985.06/3—dc23
LC record available at https://lccn.loc.gov/2018054651

W. W. Norton & Company, Inc., 500 Fifth Avenue, New York, N.Y. 10110
www.wwnorton.com

W. W. Norton & Company Ltd., 15 Carlisle Street, London W1D 3BS

1 2 3 4 5 6 7 8 9 0

CONTENTS

PART II

PART III

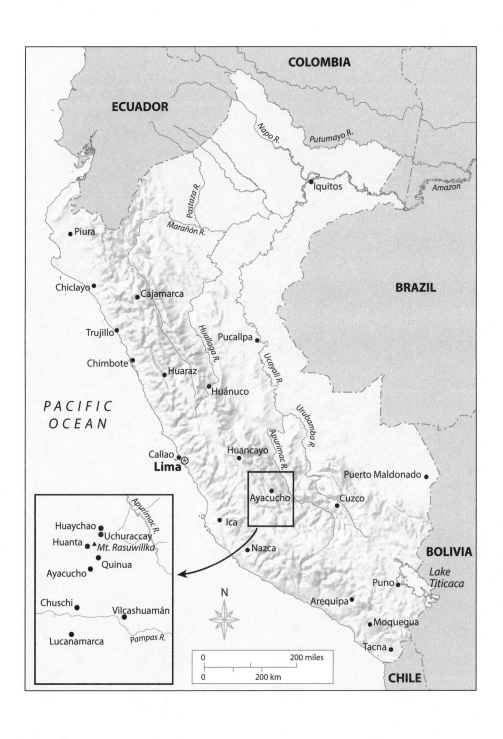

THE SHINING PATH

Prologue

The old man had dozed off in front of the television.

He woke to the sound of keys in his steel door. *One, two, three, four* . . . one by one, the deadbolts clicked open.

"Good evening, Guzmán," said the policeman. The old man sat on his cot. He reached out to shake the proffered hand. Three others, two women and a man, crowded into his tiny cell. A man with a video camera trailed behind.

The police officer said they'd come to search the cell. "We have a judicial order from the Third District National Court."

The old man listened, then chuckled. "Are you joking?"

"No problem, laugh if you want," the policeman said.

The old man had been locked away for more than two decades. He was kept mostly in solitary confinement, but he hadn't lost his sparring skill. And it annoyed him to be awoken by late-night visitors.

"Ladies and gentlemen," he said, "as usual, you don't know what you're doing." He'd been a lawyer once. He waved and gestured, evidently taking some pleasure in the fray.

"We'd be thankful," the policeman pleaded almost as if the prisoner himself, "if you'd allow us to proceed with our work."

"At this hour?" the old man snorted, looking at his watch for effect.

And then, surprisingly spry for a man soon turning eighty, he sprang up, almost lunging at the officer.

"No, sir!" he said. "No, you won't!"

He was not just anyone, after all. As maximum leader of a lethal guerrilla insurgency, he had once issued the orders for assassinating government leaders and assaulting military bases. His followers sang anthems exalting his name. The government built this concrete prison just to hold him.

The old man knew his countrymen hated him. When the newspapers reported his hospitalization for gastrointestinal troubles, readers took to the comment sections wishing him a terrible death. *Make this traitor Communist piece of shit drink his own diarrhea. Cut him to pieces. Dump them in Lake Titicaca.* Most people considered him a mass murderer.

It did not bother the old man. He had dedicated his life to fighting for a new world. He took heart that Miriam, his wife and fellow revolutionary, remained steadfast as she, too, grew old in her own prison cell far across the sleeping city.

"Miriam, my only one," he wrote, "however bad the times, no matter the distance or circumstances, you live in me."

The old man acquiesced to the police search at last, helpless to stop it. "You'll get all my things out of order," he could only grumble. He had always been orderly in everything.

"Thank you, thank you, sir," one woman said. She was a prosecutor. "We'll be quick."

They went to work.

There wasn't much to find—a little Santa Claus figurine, an empty Coke can, a self-help book, *Getting Old Doesn't Mean Slowing Down.*

Then his visitors filed out, locking the old man down again.

He usually slept well, despite a bad hip. Heads split open by a machete? A woman blown to bits before her two little boys? A country in flames? The old man believed their war had been just despite its ugly costs. He did not fear dying alone in his windowless cell. A true revolutionary kept his spirits. "I've got an almost built-in optimism," he told an interviewer once.

He was penning his movement's history.

He'd be at it early the next morning.

PART I

CHAPTER ONE

The Train to Machu Picchu

The train from Cuzco left early so as to get back the same day.

It was the only way to one of the world's great wonders, Machu Picchu. The fabled Lost City of the Incas lay three hours away down a twisting whitewater canyon where no road reached. A shuttle bus brought tourists the last few miles to the stone ruins perched so gloriously high above the Urubamba River.

Susan Bradshaw had always wanted to see Machu Picchu, ever since coming across a *National Geographic* spread about it. "I know a guy who can take you," a friend told her. Susan had just split up with her lawyer husband, and, still only in her late thirties, wanted an adventure.

She'd gone to meet Buz Donahoo, the man her friend recommended. Buz ran his own travel company, Condor Adventures, but he struck Susan more like some mythical alpha male from a Hemingway novel than any ordinary tour guide. As a young man, he'd bummed from San Francisco to Santa Fe and Belize with stints in the Coast Guard and as an apprentice

architect to Frank Lloyd Wright. ("Be an integer," the great man had cryptically counselled, "One thing throughout.") It was 1986 by now, Buz almost
fifty. He remained a great storyteller, ladies' man, and the life of every party.
Susan signed up for his next Peru trip.

"Pack your sun dress!" Buz told her. "Get ready for some fun." Recent
troubles in Peru did not bother Buz at all, even reports about a malignant
guerrilla insurgency, Shining Path. "Avoid visiting places where they are
particularly active; they have no love of foreign tourists," counseled one
guidebook. Susan's parents wanted her to cancel. Seven others did drop out,
shrinking Buz's group to four. They flew into Lima, the Peruvian capital,
before heading up to Machu Picchu.

It was hard to imagine a gloomier city than Lima, hardly the place for a
sun dress. Hungry kids hawked penny candies between rubble and garbage.
Tanks and soldiers guarded government buildings. *This looks like Dresden*,
Susan thought. The Spanish viceroy's splendid seat had been famous for its
gilt, gardens, and courtly processions back in colonial times. Susan could
barely imagine it.

It was a relief to get to Cuzco, the Machu Picchu departure point. Until
the early sixteenth century, when the bearded Spanish conquerors stormed
into the Andes, the city had been the Inca empire's capital. Its streets still
showed the magnificent pre-Columbian masonry, boulders fitted so tightly
you could not slide a knife between them. Steaming coca tea helped Susan
and the others acclimate to the thin mountain air. Buz had reserved rooms
at a fleabag hotel; the clerk paid no attention when Susan and Rebecca, a
Hewlett-Packard engineer, complained about a *muy grande Señor Rata*,
a very big Mr. Rat, poking around their room. They still enjoyed seeing
ancient Cuzco's sights.

The Machu Picchu train left at seven o'clock in the morning. It dawned
frosty blue, and, by the station, the open-air city market was already bustling with local shoppers. The crowded stalls there sold fruit and vegetables,

kitchen utensils, and uniquely Andean wares like dried llama fetuses for curing ceremonies. Buz warned everyone about the thieves at the station. They could razor-slit a wallet from a gringo's backpack without anyone realizing it until much later. Susan and the others held tight to their things.

Theirs was the direct tourist train, half-empty on this morning. Younger Americans, Israelis, and Europeans on the hippie backpacking circuit took the cheaper local train, squeezing in between Andeans with their animals, packages, and kids. A pilgrimage to Machu Picchu had long been obligatory for modern-day seekers of every kind. "Mother of stone / condor's foam / High reef of the dawn of man," wrote the Chilean poet Pablo Neruda. An awestruck Ernesto "Che" Guevara described the citadel as indigenous civilization's highest expression, a call to purifying Latin American revolution. Less politicized travelers found it a good place to drop acid.

And then, just as Susan sat down, the bomb exploded. It rocked the train like a great Andean earthquake. "It's only an airplane! It's only an airplane!" a man across the aisle shouted. Screams came from the next car up.

Buz gallantly jumped over to shield Susan and Rebecca from the blast. Susan raised her head to see. "No," Buz said, "get down." He feared gunfire or more explosions.

At last, they got up from the floor. Smoke and dust filled the car, blood streaking the windows. Stunned passengers stumbled down the aisle trying to get out. One man held his intestines in his hands.

Susan learned later that the blast had killed eight people.

She got off the train with the others as a news photographer snapped her picture.

That shot of a blonde American woman appeared on *Time* magazine's cover a few days later. Smoke streaked Susan's face, the mangled train behind her.

The biggest Peruvian news magazine, *Caretas*, put the attack on its cover too. It reported that the bomb had been in a red backpack. A young man, pretending to be a passenger, left it in the luggage rack before descending from the train. Wounded tourists had to find taxis to the hospital in the disorganized confusion following the blast.

Yet more "bloody, indiscriminate terrorist aggression by Shining Path," *Caretas* concluded.

———————

The train bombing did not surprise Gustavo Gorriti at all.

Gorriti was a *Caretas* reporter, assigned to cover Shining Path. This fierce rebel group wanted to impose a Communist government in Peru. A former lawyer and philosophy professor, Abimael Guzmán, led the growing insurgency. His followers called him Chairman Gonzalo and, worshipfully, "the Fourth Sword of Marxism" after Marx, Lenin, and Mao. They had massacred villagers, dynamited government offices, and killed some other tourists in a self-declared "people's war" to seize power. "Violence is a universal law," Guzmán declared, explaining that without it "an old order cannot be overthrown to make way for a new one." No journalist had yet interviewed the fugitive leader in person.

The dogged Gorriti hoped to be the first. He was a latecomer to journalism, taking an unlikely pathway to *Caretas*. He'd been raised between his parents' Lima house and their farm down the desert coast. At twenty, Jewish and curious about the place, he'd gone off to Israel in 1967. He studied philosophy at Jerusalem's Hebrew University.

It had been an exciting time to be young in Israel. Rock music, drugs, and coffeehouse-philosophizing—this was the late 1960s—accompanied the country's smashing victory in the Six-Day War. Gorriti stayed almost four years, and had a child with an Israeli-born Mexican woman in a short love affair. He returned to Peru in 1971, a single father with his baby daughter in tow. There he helped his parents with the farm, and fell in love with Esther Delgado, the daughter of a neighboring farm owner. They soon married, but

Gorriti grew restless. He wrote some freelance newspaper essays, and wondered about a full-time writing career. That would mean moving to the big city of Lima for good.

He had been uncertain, especially about the finances. "Gustavo," Esther told him, "we'll make it work. And you'll regret it if you don't try." They left for the city. Gorriti tried drafting a novel. Then, the family savings almost exhausted, he looked for a journalism job. That might be the best way to write for a living.

He landed an interview with *Caretas*. The magazine's offices sat at the corner of Camaná and Emancipación in the dilapidated Lima downtown. Enrique Zileri, the owner-publisher, was a burly man with a legendary temper. "I don't publish your excuses. I publish news," he'd yell at the unfortunate reporter who failed to get a story. Gorriti waited for the publisher without much confidence about his chances.

Zileri strode in at last. He appeared in a good mood, humming a Spanish Civil War ditty. Two different military dictators had tried to shut his magazine down, but Zileri always stood his ground. Nor was he afraid to hire talented people from unorthodox backgrounds. Before him now stood a Jewish cotton farmer who, improbably enough, happened also to be a judo expert. (As a teenager, Gorriti trained with a top sensei, becoming a six-time Peruvian and also an Israeli university champion.) And Zileri saw, leafing through his freelance articles, Gorriti was a talented writer. He offered him a job, a trial period at first.

Gorriti covered assorted stories in his first *Caretas* months. A shadowy guerrilla insurgency had appeared seemingly from nowhere in the Andes, and, early in 1981, the news editor wanted someone to investigate. The magazine's senior reporters preferred the Lima political beat. "We're going to have you go, Gustavo," the editor told Gorriti.

Gorriti had followed reporting about the rebels. They called themselves the Peruvian Communist Party, but had become better known as *Sendero*

Luminoso, Shining Path. The name came from a passage by the country's early-twentieth-century socialist leader, José Carlos Mariátegui, about the revolution's bright way to the future. Their stronghold lay in Ayacucho, a poverty-stricken region in Peru's south-central Andes, although the *senderistas* also carried out attacks in Lima and other cities. They robbed dynamite from mines to make bombs and raided police stations for guns and ammunition. Despite the homemadeness of their revolution, Shining Path was gaining strength in the mid-1980s. Its leader, Abimael Guzmán, had gone underground before the war started. He'd become Peru's most wanted man.

No one had a clue as to Guzmán's whereabouts. "A master of disguise," waxed a British reporter, who claimed that Andean villagers thought the rebel chieftain could "fool his hunters by transforming himself into a stone." A cloud of secrecy and fear surrounded Shining Path along with wacky theories. A crazy cult? A millenarian Indian rebellion? Foreign fighters helicoptered in from an aircraft carrier? Gorriti doubted that Shining Path was altogether a breed apart. The rebels were Communists, after all, and in that sense no novelty in the Latin America of Fidel Castro's Cuban Revolution and so many more guerrilla movements. They left their hammer-and-sickle flag next to the bodies of executed informers splayed on the dusty roads.

Gorriti knew plenty about Marxism and its many permutations. He was a red diaper baby himself. His mother, Dora, had been a teenage Communist activist in her native Czernowitz, today in Ukraine. The city was a center of arts and literature until a thuggish Romanian dictatorship took over after World War I. When the Siguranţa Statului, the regime's secret police, began rounding up dissidents, Dora went into hiding. She fled to Palestine, but the British deported her back to Czernowitz for being a Communist. By then, the Siguranţa Statului had assassinated many of Dora's activist friends. The Nazis eventually occupied the city, overseeing the mass deportations of Jews, Communists, and others to labor and death camps, Auschwitz among them. "It was sheer luck I got out alive," Dora told her boy.

Dora fled to New York, then Peru. There she met and married Gorriti's father, Gustavo Sr. He was a prominent Communist congressman and former journalist, who had lived in Chile before being expelled for anti-government reporting. After the US-backed Manuel Odría military dictatorship banned Marxist parties in 1949, Dora and Gustavo Sr. left Lima. They took their toddler son and two daughters to start a farm in a desert irrigation project down the Pacific Coast. An optimist and adventurer, Gustavo Sr. thought they would make enough money there for their children to pursue careers in the arts and politics. Dora, while far from convinced, agreed to the plan.

It had been a primitive life at first. They had to truck in water, and, with no indoor plumbing, Dora bathed the children in an iron tub outside. Little Gustavo and his sisters clopped to school on the family donkey. His parents did have a big library, though. The young Gorriti curled up with adventure classics like Jules Verne's *Fifty Thousand Leagues Under the Sea* and Alexander Dumas's *The Three Musketeers*. He liked best the Italian writer Emilio Salgari, whose swashbuckling pirate hero, Sandokan, the Tiger of Malaysia, crossed swords with arrogant British admirals and sinister criminal sects. "Reading is traveling without the bother of baggage," Salgari supposedly declared.

There, in that same family library, Gorriti found Marx, Engels, Lenin, and a doorstop of a book, the Soviet Academy Dictionary of Philosophy (which, in high Soviet fashion, gave Stalin a longer entry than Descartes, Spinoza, or Kant). This was not exactly pleasure reading. Even so, Gustavo, a teenager by then, enjoyed learning about the Paris Commune and the Bolshevik Revolution. He read some Marx as well, absorbing the bearded prophet's brilliant social analysis, complex technical language, and absolute certainty about the coming storm. The task for philosophy, as the young Marx wrote in his *Theses on Feuerbach*, was not just to "understand society but to change it."

So, when his editor assigned him to Shining Path, Gorriti understood something about Marxism's mindset. He was unsure about everything else. Where was Abimael Guzmán? Could he find a way to interview the rebel chief? How big was Shining Path? And what threat did it pose beyond a few mountain attacks? Gorriti hoped his trip would supply answers.

He climbed out of bed in Lima's dreary dawn to head for the airport.

It was a short hop to Ayacucho with the plane climbing up the whole way.

Gorriti stared down at the dawning peaks. They towered over the great green carpet of the Amazon jungle that widened beyond across the continent. In its way, Gorriti knew, his own Peru could sometimes seem as make-believe as Salgari's proverbial exotic locales—its mountains spiking the sky like the Himalayas; its deserts as scorching as the Sahara; its marvelous ancient civilizations with their crumbling pyramids and golden tombs. There was corruption, poverty, and filth along with a rainbow mountain of seven colors, Vinicunca, and countless unbelievable sights. Gorriti enjoyed his young years in Israel and later lived for stretches in Boston, Washington, DC, and Panama. He had always been drawn back home.

This was the new journalist's first trip to Ayacucho. The city lay in a mountain valley cut by red rock and cactus canyons, two hundred miles north of Cuzco along the spine of the Andes. Its cobblestone streets, sandstone churches, and arid climate gave Ayacucho the spare beauty of a run-down Santa Fe. This was also the apparent ground zero of Shining Path's armed rebellion.

Gorriti had made the trip with Óscar Medrano, a *Caretas* staff photographer and an Ayacucho native. "*Allinllachu taytay,*" Medrano greeted the waiter at the old hotel. The ancient Incan language, Quechua, was still widely used in Ayacucho, especially by the region's villagers. Medrano, a country boy who made good in Lima, grew up speaking the expressive native tongue. He doubled on this assignment as photographer and interpreter, since Gorriti, like most white Peruvians, did not know any Quechua. The affable Medrano called his brawny pale colleague *el gringo* without much thinking about it.

Gorriti got his first look at Ayacucho from the taxi into town. He did not see the tanks, helmeted troops, or antiaircraft guns he recalled from Israel's war zones, and, in fact, no obvious signs of war at all. Chattering high schoolers promenaded under the plaza's archways by elderly newspaper vendors, chap-cheeked shoeshine boys, and the hurrying suited lawyers of any Andean city. Gorriti also saw mountain villagers—the men in ponchos and rude rubber sandals cut from discarded tires; the women in puffy wool skirts and bowler hats. They were descendants of the ancient Andeans and numbered in the millions across the highlands. "Peru owes its misfortune to the indigenous race, whose psychic degeneration has taken on the biological rigidity of a being that has definitively stopped evolving," an early-twentieth-century ideologue wrote. Some superior Limans still complained about the so-called *mancha india*, the "Indian stain," as the main obstacle to the country's progress and modernization. Most villagers called themselves *comuneros*, community members, or simply *campesinos*, peasants, and they eked out a bare living from their small plots. Their impoverished hamlets scattered back into the elevations around the city of Ayacucho.

The main police commander did not appear especially worried by Shining Path. His name was Carlos Barreto, a civil guard general, and a special anti-terrorism unit, the *sinchis*, had recently arrived to reinforce his regular officers. Barreto was staying at his hotel and Gorriti talked to him several times. The guerrillas did not amount to much, Barreto claimed, and his men were forcing Shining Path's retreat. He did not expect the insurgency to survive for much longer.

Only at night did Gorriti realize that, in fact, something was very wrong. The police had imposed a curfew, and, when the sun sank over the moun-

tains, the streets emptied instantly. "It turned scary quiet in the night," a
rare visiting American traveler recalled, "just like before a big storm."

Gorriti read a Milan Kundera novel for a bit in bed, then fell asleep.

———————

"*Vamos*, Óscar, let's go," Gorriti told Medrano the next day.

Gorriti wanted to investigate reports about the police torturing captured Shining Path prisoners.

Medrano led the way to the investigative police headquarters near their
hotel. When the two men presented their *Caretas* credentials they were told
to wait for the commander.

Time dragged, and, since no one paid them any mind, they went down
a stairway to the holding cells.

As Gorriti and Medrano descended, a teenager was being brought up by
two policemen. His face was bloody and swollen as if he'd just been beaten.

And then, in a patio by the cells, they saw a single prisoner seated on a
chair, loosely guarded by some younger policemen.

Gorriti introduced himself.

"Journalists are liars," the young woman said, turning away. She had
olive skin, ebony hair, and a proud curved nose.

"Have you been mistreated?" Gorriti asked.

He'd heard that police gang-raped captured female guerrillas.

Then, Gorriti wrote later, the woman raised her face, and looked at him
"from a well of sadness, distant, profound, with her drowned in it."

"All I can tell you," she said, "is that until my arrest, I believed that Hell
only existed in the afterlife."

An older officer noticed Gorriti and Medrano at last.

"What are you doing? This a restricted area!"

Gorriti was not one to back down. He asked if they were torturing
prisoners.

"No, we don't torture," the officer said, suddenly weary. "We'll hit them some, or hang them up, or submarine them, but that's not torture."

"*Señor,*" Gorriti said, "that's torture."

"Look, we don't do them any harm. When the doctor examines them, everything's fine. And they tell us what we need to know. So we can save lives."

The policeman paused, looking at Gorriti.

"These people kill. Did you know that?"

————

Gorriti wrote a story back in Lima about his trip.

A sidebar excerpted his interview with Barreto and the general's optimism about putting down the rebellion.

Yet Gorriti also remembered the tired police captain's words. *These people kill.* It was as if he understood the cruel truth, namely that the war had only just begun. His own men were being gunned down and they'd themselves sunk to brutalizing captives.

Even the police captain did not guess what lay ahead. By Christmas 1982, a year after Gorriti's visit, the rebels would virtually control Ayacucho, the police cowering in their barracks. Fernando Belaúnde, the Peruvian president, placed Ayacucho and neighboring regions under military rule. Patrolling soldiers broke down doors to drag away suspected *senderistas*. The soldiers fanned out to rape, kill, and massacre in mountain villages, too. Shining Path answered with its own stunning brutality across the Andes, the cities, and into the jungle. "People killing each other / *Mamacha de las Mercedes,* Mother of Mercy, what's happening here?" an Andean ballad lamented. Nearly 70,000 Peruvians would perish before the fighting ended. The war cost an already poor country over two billion dollars in damages, and forced more than 600,000 villagers to flee their homes. Their blackened farmhouses became an antique land's newest stone ruins.

The war changed many lives. Gustavo Gorriti would become a *New York Times* contributor and best-selling author, among Latin America's best-known journalists, as well as a wanted man, a prisoner, and an exile himself. A pair of skilled police detectives, Benedicto Jiménez and Marco Miyashiro, gained fame for heading the hunt for Abimael Guzmán. Then, too, there was the mercurial shantytown activist, María Elena Moyano, and a mountain boy, Narciso Sulca, who took up stones and sling to stop the fierce-eyed *senderistas* from invading his village. A world-famous novelist, Mario Vargas Llosa, ran for president to end the bloodshed, corruption, and his native Peru's freefall into the void. The Shining Path rebellion inspired a John Malkovich film, *The Dancer Upstairs*, while providing Vargas Llosa, a future Nobel Prize winner, with material for three novels. It was a war frightening, deadly, and wrathful enough to have been sworded to life by a jungle sorcerer's curse.

Everything began with praiseworthy, even noble intentions. That great Communist longing to redeem humanity from misery and injustice motivated Shining Path to its war. When the gaunt Franciscan friars came ashore in Peru with the Spanish conquerors, they offered salvation in the next life. The *senderistas* and their Communist faith promised the more immediate earthly heaven of a new socialist order. They would mobilize the masses to destroy the rotten capitalist system with its hunger, inequality, and oppression. In the shiny new world, as Marx somewhat vaguely imagined it, a liberated humankind would renounce profit's unhappy pursuit. The evolutionary destiny of our species lay in Communism's blessed state of mutual responsibility and the common good.

This cosmology once appealed worldwide. An "untranscendable philosophy for our time," an admiring Jean-Paul Sartre described Marxism in 1960. Marx's followers split into warring sects, but the common appeal of his teachings lay in a compelling theory of history and society, and a stern yet glorious prophecy about a new order. The revolutions in Russia in 1917 and China in 1949 went forward in Marx's name. Many among the twentieth century's most gifted people embraced, at one time or another, the revolutionary Communist creed: Charlie Chaplin, Frida Kahlo, Albert Camus, W. E. B. Dubois, Woody Guthrie, Robert Oppenheimer, Simone de Beauvoir. A promising university student, Abimael Guzmán, fell under that spell too. So did his first wife and fellow revolutionary, Augusta La Torre, a Communist landowner's bright-eyed daughter, as well as her dear friend, Elena Iparraguirre, Comrade Miriam by her nom de guerre, who married Guzmán after La Torre's mysterious death. "The future lies in guns and cannons," Guzmán told his followers in 1980, "the oppressors will be irretrievably smashed." They went to battle in the Andes weeks later.

As much as it might be portrayed as a mysterious primitive rebellion, Shining Path would prove a quite ordinary Marxist insurgency in most regards. The *senderista* exaltation of their party as quasi-divine entity never to be questioned followed earlier twentieth-century Communist precedents. So did their obsession with rooting out "revisionist" enemies of the revolution. The apotheosis of Abimael Guzmán as the all-seeing Chairman Gonzalo resembled Dear Leader cults typical of state socialism everywhere. Shining Path terror and mass killing also had abundant Marxist antecedents. "There are times when the interests of the proletariat demand the ruthless extermination of its enemies," Lenin insisted in 1918. (His Bolsheviks shot, bayoneted, and clubbed to death the tsar's family, including the five children, and butchered Cossack peasants by the thousands.) The *senderistas* likewise scorned mercy as a luxury that could not be afforded to real and imagined opponents. *Forgiveness did not exist in the party*, a former Shining Path fighter said.

Their revolution faced long odds from the start. A "dwarf star," the anthropologist Carlos Iván Degregori described Shining Path. The party burned tremendously hot, and yet was small in size with a maximum force of perhaps 5,000 fighters at its high point. Although a learned man and meticulous organizer, the venerated *senderista* chieftain, Guzmán, could not see beyond the suffocating dogma of his quite crude brand of Marxist philosophy. His Gonzalo Thought was hardline Communist boilerplate with only minor adaptations to Peruvian realities. (Guzmán exhibited no interest in more original Marxist thinkers like the Italian philosopher Antonio Gramsci and the Hungarian critic Georg Lukács.) Shining Path ultimately failed to muster any lasting support like Ho Chi Minh's Vietminh or Castro's 26th of July Movement. Even the poorest peasants wanted the *senderistas* gone by the war's end.

Nor could the timing of Shining Path have been any worse. In the 1980s, exactly as Guzmán launched his war, the planet lost patience with Communism's broken promises. Red China went capitalist; the Berlin Wall came down; the Soviet Union fell to pieces. Only some stubborn radical intellectuals and a few remnant Marxist insurgencies could convince themselves that the world proletarian revolution would be occurring anytime soon. To soldier into the 1990s under Marxism's banner made the *senderistas* into a doomed anachronism, at once pathetic and deadly. They fought the Peruvian army, but also a more formidable force, the bull rush of history itself. Augusta La Torre and Elena Iparraguirre read Russian novels for relief from the war. Their revolution's defeat had been foretold as much as Anna Karenina's train track leap or any tragic epic's ending.

Perhaps global Communism would have crumbled on its own over time. The denunciations of class oppression and imperialist domination could lose their novelty, and the flagship Marxist country, the Soviet Union, hollowed out to dour old men on the May Day parade reviewing stand. But to ensure Cold War victory, the United States employed its own brutal means: CIA torture, napalmed villages, and secret coups. Abimael Guzmán and his followers loathed the American imperialists, but they also detested the latter-day Soviet leadership and post-Maoist Chinese reformers. (And none more than the "imperialist lackey" Deng Xiaoping for steering China into the global capitalist economy.) In the eyes of Shining Path, the two great Communist powers had betrayed the masses by parleying with the

United States and compromising their commitment to revolutionary ideals. The *senderistas* believed themselves summoned to uphold the uncorrupted Communist creed. They accepted no aid from abroad besides some penny donations from a few tiny Maoist solidarity groups in the United States and Europe.

Their fervor made them prepared to do just about anything. "She sacrificed everything," as the brother of the dead Augusta La Torre remembers it, "for her love of the people." The *senderista* thirst to see the Andes dawn red led them to frightful cruelty and mad illusions of victory. Their path ended in blood, death, and an old man in a prison cell.

The elderly Guzmán did not like to dwell upon personal details. A good Communist should stay focused on the struggle for socialism, he believed. He did recall meeting his first love, Augusta, when she was still a teenager. "An Ayacucho afternoon in April, the hallway of a big old house, a stone patio, and a jasmine scent: blue blouse, and the beautiful woman emerging from the girl." They married less than two years later to seal a revolutionary partnership. Elena Iparraguirre would soon join their war to smash the decaying old order.

What did Marx say?

They had nothing to lose.

And a world to win.

CHAPTER TWO

A Tree Can Be a Weapon

It was raining early in 1962 when Abimael Guzmán descended from the bus at the Ayacucho terminal. A local landowner and government functionary, Carlos La Torre, welcomed him. La Torre headed Ayacucho's Communist Party. He'd been alerted about Guzmán, a rising leader who had just been appointed as a philosophy professor at the local San Cristóbal University, the UNSCH. Guzmán's arrival, Carlos La Torre hoped, would energize Communist organizing in town. There were few card-carrying party members in Ayacucho as yet. They dined together once a month more like a Rotary Club than real revolutionaries.

That day La Torre's wife, Delia Carrasco, went into labor with their fifth child. The couple gave their children Russian nicknames in homage to Stalin's Soviet Union: Boris, Sacha, Nika. This new boy, Humberto, became Yuri after the cosmonaut who had recently become the first man in space. Guzmán chatted with La Torre on the way to the hospital, before saying goodbye. The young professor struck Carlos as a formidable intellectual and staunch Communist. He invited him to dinner at their house off Ayacucho's main plaza when Delia and the baby returned from the hospital.

Guzmán became a frequent caller. "He was polite, courteous, a little disoriented until he found a place to live," Delia recalled. Once classes started after winter break, Guzmán sometimes invited students over to the La Torres's house. He'd discourse about philosophy and world affairs, pausing occasionally for questions. The oldest La Torre girl, Augusta, was just a high schooler, and no co-eds came anyway in this conservative Catholic town. She would lean over the balcony to listen to the interesting speaker.

One time the young professor grew thirsty, and requested a drink. Augusta slipped downstairs to find the family's servant. "Don't my parents have money to buy him something?" she asked. When told that they had gone out, Augusta pulled off her sweater. She handed it to the servant with instructions to give it to the shopkeeper for a soda on credit. Her father, Carlos, chided her afterwards. "You shouldn't worry about such things, *hijita*," he said. "I could have bought it when we came back."

Their new family friend made other acquaintances. Guzmán joined an informal reading group that included a mathematician, an agronomist, an archaeologist, and an education specialist. They were all newly hired San Cristóbal professors, the former seminary having reopened in 1959 with ambitions to become a top university. Guzmán and his friends agreed on a text to read, then discussed and often argued over it for hours in a local bar. "We thought we were geniuses," said Luis Lumbreras, who would become among Peru's most prominent archaeologists. He found the well-read Guzmán to be Marxist in orientation, yet considerate and open to debate. In his Lima sitting room decades later, the elderly Lumbreras could still not quite believe that his friend had allowed himself to be apotheosized as the world's greatest living Marxist-Leninist, Chairman Gonzalo, much less that he had directed a hateful war. "I can't explain it," the archaeologist puzzled sadly over his coffee.

———————

It was no novelty for Guzmán to arrive a stranger in a new place. His father, Abimael Guzmán Silva, an accountant, ran Hacienda El Arenal, a plantation in the Tambo Valley along the southern Peruvian coast. An incurable womanizer, the married Guzmán sired various illegitimate children, among them one with a local woman named Berenice Reinoso Cervantes. She baptized the boy Abimael after his father, although the older Guzmán initially refused to recognize his paternity. Berenice decamped a few years later for Sicuani, a small town near Cuzco, then to the smelly fishing port of Chimbote, and back to Sicuani again. "Something of the Andes surely stayed inside me," Guzmán believed. He had his first exposure there to highland poverty, and the precariousness of rural life. One day, when Abimael was seven, he saw an Andean peasant woman begging passersby for money to bury her daughter. The little corpse lay besides the distraught mother. That image stayed with Abimael for years, although the news from overseas also grabbed his imagination. He sat next to his mother's wood-box radio to follow Stalin, Hitler, Roosevelt, and the great battles of World War II.

In 1948, after Abimael turned twelve, Berenice left him with her brother's family in Callao, the port by Lima. She did not say why, only leaving an awkwardly worded letter: "My son, take care of your mother's child. You're the only who can." Leaving children with relatives was quite common in Peru, so Abimael made the best of it. He liked Callao, where the fishing boats brought in their squirming silver catch of grouper and sea bass. Then, after only a year, he moved yet again, this time to his father's house. By then, the older Guzmán had relocated to Arequipa, a stately Andean city beneath the snow-capped volcano of El Misti. Abimael had barely known his father and half-siblings, but he soon felt at home in their big house near the city square. His stepmother, Laura Jorquera, a kind Chilean woman, treated her husband's illegitimate child like one of her own. Abimael studied at Arequipa's most exclusive high school, La Salle. The local Spanish-descended aristocracy sent its children to be schooled by the Christian brothers there.

Some future biographers would claim Abimael had an unhappy childhood. His mother abandoned him, after all, which supposedly left the young boy embittered and unstable. A half sister of Abimael's described him angrily smashing a mirror after a love interest's rejection. Heartbroken rage had left the teenage Abimael out to destroy the country, by her account. But most others who knew Abimael remembered a well-adjusted, even-tempered young man, albeit reserved. He harbored no resentment towards his mother, although wistfully kept a Parker fountain pen she gave him before leaving. "While it had its disadvantages," he would write, his childhood gave him "multiple and diverse experiences" and an outward-looking view of the world. Abimael found solace in books, counting *Don Quijote* and the *Iliad* among early favorites. "He was introverted," one friend recalled, "but he had a great sense of friendship, unpretentious and sincere." The bookish boy assisted others with their homework.

Abimael excelled in high school, even in the required military training class. Its instructor, a lieutenant, expected everyone to rise at attention when he entered. One day, early in the semester, the chattering students neglected to get up from their desks.

The annoyed officer picked a random boy.

"You there!" he said, calling on Abimael. "Name?"

"Student Guzmán."

"Now listen to me," the teacher said. "What's my rank?"

"Lieutenant."

"Well, then, answer correctly. What's your name, student?"

"Abimael Guzmán, Lieutenant, *Sir!*"

"Very good," the officer said. "Now, Student Guzmán, I'm going to come in again."

"Yes sir, Lieutenant, *Sir!*"

This time Abimael jumped up, calling out his classmates:

"*Atten-tion!*"

The students rose in unison. The teacher let them stand there for an awkward moment before calling on Abimael once again.

"Student Guzmán!"

Abimael didn't dare get it wrong again. "Yes sir, Lieutenant, *Sir!*"

"Before next class, you should gargle with a bag of pins. We need to talk like men, not in a little sissy voice. This isn't a co-ed school. It's for young men. Do you copy?"

There was snickering laughter from the classroom.

Abimael was relieved to have passed the test.

"Copy that," he repeated, "Lieutenant, *Sir.*"

———

The graduating Guzmán briefly considered a military career, but decided to become a lawyer. He enrolled in 1953 at Arequipa's San Agustín University, where he found his higher calling as a revolutionary. His memory of the village poverty he'd seen in the Andes had always left him wanting to do something about it. He began college at a moment of new unrest, too. A military dictator, General Manuel Odría, ruled Peru then; Arequipa became a center of opposition to his regime. Police shot down three protestors in one street battle. Many San Agustín students joined the protest movement. It impressed Abimael to witness the senior students' readiness to risk everything in the good fight against the dictatorship.

At the university, Abimael encountered the Communist classics for the first time. They included *The Communist Manifesto*, Lenin's *One Step Forward, Two Back*, and books by Stalin, who was still largely held in high Communist regard. (Picasso painted the Soviet dictator's portrait upon his death.) The materialist theory of history, Abimael thought, persuaded in every way. Didn't a society's way of organizing its economy indeed determine everything else about it? Wasn't class struggle between workers and owners the core contradiction in capitalist societies? And didn't the laws of dialectical materialism assure the bourgeoisie's ultimate overthrow? Abimael paid little attention to Marx's more humanistic early writings. He hewed instead to the conventional Soviet-style "scientific socialism" prevalent in 1950s Peru. There would be little room for doubt, chance, or irregularity in the young revolutionary's worldview to the very end.

By graduation day, Abimael had become a convinced Marxist believer. His tract-like law thesis "The Bourgeois-Democratic State" predictably derided "lyrical affirmations" about democracy and liberty as a camouflage for exploitation. The state was only the "executive committee of the bourgeoisie," according to Marx and his occasional collaborator, Friedrich Engels. After Communism's victory, a so-called dictatorship of the proletariat would rule until the institutions of law and government were no longer necessary. Abimael studied philosophy too, and for that degree wrote a somewhat more nuanced thesis about Immanuel Kant's theory of space. It displayed impressive familiarity, especially for a provincial university student, with Thomas Hume's empiricism, Einstein's theory of relativity, and post-Euclidean geometry. The argument remained conventionally Marxist by attributing primacy to material reality to challenge Kant's claim about space as the mind's invention. "Physical science and geometry," Abimael wrote, prove that "space has a material reality independent of our subjectivity."

His new convictions led Abimael to join the Peruvian Communist Party in 1956. It took some persuading to overcome objections about his insufficiently proletarian origins, but the serious young man convinced the local leaders about his revolutionary commitment. The party was pro–Soviet Union in orientation, as Mao's Red China was only beginning to exercise global influence. It operated in high bureaucratic socialist fashion with reports, plenaries, and committees aplenty. That suited a young man who had always been punctilious about planning and hierarchy. "At the head of each group there will be a leader," Abimael detailed a plan for his high school newspaper. "The group leader will appoint four assistants . . . there will be a central committee made up of nine members." Abimael might have been reserved, but he could go on for hours when his turn came to speak. He was a good orator, speaking fluidly while sometimes slashing the air to drive home points. At twenty-six he became the party's youngest regional committee member. Abimael would forever be a "dedicated Communist" by his own description.

In 1961, after graduating, Abimael took a few law cases, and taught at San Agustín for a bit. Then he heard about a philosophy opening at Ayacucho's university, a twenty-hour bus ride farther up the Andes. He applied and got the job, but then wondered about going. By contrast to Arequipa, a center of politics and commerce, Ayacucho was a backwater. It had no telephones, just one movie theater, and fewer than 30,000 people. A former professor of Abimael's, however, vouched for the reopened Ayacuchan university, San Cristóbal, and, more than that, the necessary experience of *Perú profundo*, the deep Peru, the Andean heartland in its wrenching poverty and indigenous traditions. *You can't understand Peru unless you go*, he said. Abimael packed his professor's dark suit, tie, and navy blue shirts for the trip.

San Cristóbal's administrative building abutted the town cathedral on the main plaza. An ancient fig tree in its porticoed seventeenth-century court-yard gave the building its name, *la higuera*, the figgery. There the dean of arts and letters, Efraín Morote, greeted his newest hire. A tiny man from a prominent local family, Morote was a noted folklorist with leftist sympathies. His assistant showed Abimael to his office in the modern classroom complex around the corner, where Guzmán met Luis Lumbreras and other faculty. Recruiting efforts attracted some younger foreign scholars to San Cristóbal, among them the Dutch anthropologist, R. T. Zuidema, who was decoding the ancient Incan system of ritual pathways, the *ceques*. Many students at this tuition-free public university came from relatively humble village families. These brown-skinned kids had often grown up speaking Quechua, and, or so their peasant parents hoped, would become *profesionales*, lawyers and doctors. "Their families made big sacrifices for them to come," as one professor said.

It did not take Abimael long to become a star professor. He'd walk into the lecture hall, set down his books, and chalk the day's subject matter on the board. Then, turning to the class, he'd pose a question: Does God exist? That was a heretical thought in Catholic Ayacucho, exciting the class to debate. Eventually, Abimael took over. He would make references to Plato, Spinoza, Hegel, Nietzsche, and Schopenhauer as well as to Marxist thinkers like Engels, Lenin, and Peru's great homegrown socialist, José Carlos Mariátegui. His lectures were not dogmatic, but they always returned to Marxist first principles. God, Abimael explained, was a human invention, not an objective reality. Hadn't Marx called religion the opiate of the masses? Curious townspeople hung at the windows to hear these lectures. There was little else to do in provincial Ayacucho anyway.

The young philosopher never seemed too concerned about his popularity, or with charming students. After finishing a lecture, he usually walked alone to his next engagement. Some co-eds, behind his back, called Guzmán "Dr. Armpit," since he always carried a book under his arm. (His other nickname became "Dr. Shampoo" for a supposed ability to brainwash impressionable students.) Guzmán cut a polite yet distant, somewhat mysterious profile around town, at least when not debating Heisenberg's uncertainty principle with Lumbreras and the others over one too many piscos. "He was serious and occasionally amiable, always very correct and baronial," a San Cristóbal student said. His new friend Carlos La Torre sometimes invited him for the weekend to the La Torre country house over in the pretty Huanta Valley.

Abimael did not plan to remain a professor forever. His post was a temporary means to advancing Communism's cause. The university provided a pulpit for preaching Marxism's virtues and a recruiting ground for young militants. He threw himself, simultaneously, into revitalizing Ayacucho's moribund Communist Party. That might mean a one-to-one with a high-ranking Lima comrade; a meeting with a party-allied student organization; a planning session about the next steps. Guzmán had no time for hobbies or distractions. "He has no personal interests, no business affairs, no emotions, no attachments, no property," the Russian anarchist Sergei Nechayev described the true revolutionary. "Everything in him is wholly absorbed in the single thought and the single passion for revolution." That description already fit Guzmán by the early 1960s.

His life revolved around *el partido*, the Communist Party, the holy instrument of revolution. A philosopher before anything else, Marx left the nitty-gritty of strategy and organization more to others. His friend and sometime financial supporter Friedrich Engels formed Communist parties across Europe after Marx's death. It was Vladimir Lenin, however, who established the blueprint for successful revolutionary organizing. (The Italian socialist Antonio Gramsci called the Russian leader Marx's St. Paul for his institutionalizing role.) His Bolsheviks became the great twentieth-century model for a proper Communist party. Members would be the revolution's priestly elect, the vanguard, the guides shepherding the less ideologically advanced proletariat to the red dawn. At once a bureaucratic political organization and, like the US Marines or the Jesuits, a mythologized sacred entity, the Party could never be wrong. A member had to sacrifice everything at its command. The Leninist conviction about the Party's indispensable role guided Vietnam's Ho Chi Minh, China's Mao Zedong, and other mid-twentieth-century Marxist leaders. "Without a Communist Party—that axis, that factor that energizes, leads, guides, nothing will be done," Abimael affirmed.

His arrival to Ayacucho coincided with the widening schism between the planet's two Communist giants, the Soviet Union and China. After Stalin's death in 1953, the reform-minded Nikita Khrushchev became Soviet premier. Mao sharply objected to Khrushchev's more conciliatory attitude to the West, among other disagreements. The Chinese leader wanted to unite the world's poor countries to smash, as his propagandists had it, "the paper tiger of Yankee imperialism." ("If we can promise the people nothing more than revolution," Khrushchev supposedly retorted, "they will scratch their heads and say 'isn't it better to have good goulash?'") In 1961, Mao's government officially designated the Soviet leadership as "revisionist traitors." The antagonism between Moscow and Beijing forced Marxists worldwide to choose sides. A country lawyer, Saturnino Paredes, led the so-called Red Flag faction's 1964 split from the pro-Soviet Communists. His Maoists claimed to be the one real Peruvian Communist Party.

There was no doubt in Abimael's mind as to the right choice. His opinion was that the reform-minded Khrushchev had sold out Lenin and Stalin's more uncompromised Communist rule. It was Mao, Abimael believed, who stood for real revolution. (And he adopted the Red Chinese convention to place "sinister" before just about any mention of Khrushchev's name.) Abimael established his own Maoist "Red Fraction" in Ayacucho, a subgroup of Red Flag with some independence. His student followers soon controlled the Federation of Revolutionary Students. Abimael won appointment to the University Council, the oversight body for campus affairs. It had taken him only a year in Ayacucho to become a figure to be reckoned with. He was ready for a first test of will.

That opportunity came with the arrival to Ayacucho in 1963 of four fresh-faced American Peace Corps volunteers. The program had only just been established by John F. Kennedy to, by his explanation, help liberate the world's poorest nations from "the bonds of hunger, ignorance, and poverty." The more self-interested agenda was winning hearts and minds in America's Cold War campaign to block further Communist advances worldwide. In Latin America, of course, the United States had long played the region's bully. What the late-nineteenth-century Cuban independence leader José Martí famously described as the "monster of the north" occupied Cuba, Haiti, Mexico, Puerto Rico, the Dominican Republic, and Nicaragua at various points. It also secretly sponsored the ugly 1954 military overthrow of a left-leaning Guatemalan president. The Ayacucho volunteers were there to demonstrate good will and assist with modernizing a "backward" Peru. One was a recent Stanford graduate, another from Princeton; all were in their early twenties. They had been assigned to teach English at San Cristóbal.

The four volunteers faced considerable mistrust. When Kennedy authorized the failed Bay of Pigs invasion in 1961 to overthrow Fidel Castro's new socialist government, it suggested the Americans had not given up their imperializing habits. Many Latin American leftists wondered whether the Peace Corps might be a cover for spying or worse. In *Blood of the Condor*, a Bolivian film, creepy American volunteers with horrendous Spanish accents conspire to sterilize Indian women. Then, too, a foreigner could be a *pishtaco,* or, in Quechua, a *ñakaq.* The legend of these pale-skinned, marrow-sucking human vampires dated back to Spanish conquest and its extractive empire. In late-twentieth-century versions, the marrow powered NASA's Space Shuttle or was used to manufacture expensive Italian perfume. At best, a gringo seemed an odd creature to many Andeans, always snapping pictures and eating raw vegetables, among other strange habits. Nevertheless the young Americans worked dutifully at gaining local trust.

It went well at first. The volunteers—three men and a woman—made some local friends. A town basketball team recruited one, David Scott

Palmer, as its player-coach. He had lettered in basketball at Dartmouth, and, at 6'6", stood a freakish foot taller than the Ayacuchan average. His new team, the Huamanga Arrows, had the advantage of the city's 9,000-foot altitude, which left opponents gasping for air. "After a day or two the Lima teams would get acclimated," Palmer recalled. "And then they'd destroy us."

Then came the first trouble signs. A few Peruvian professors, the volunteers heard, complained that the Americans intended to "take over" the San Cristóbal languages department. When some students came over for a party, they had been criticized as "gringo lovers." Nor did the Americans receive invitations to a big university reception. The recent Cuban Missile Crisis, and Kennedy's military blockade of the island, inflamed anti-American sentiments. When a Peace Corps administrator visited Ayacucho, students picketed his hotel. "Cuba, yes! Yankees, no!" they chanted. The volunteers noticed these "foreboding signs," Palmer wrote later. (He became a prominent political scientist at Boston University.) They did not understand how precarious their position had become.

Nor did the Americans realize that Abimael Guzmán was stage-managing it all. The gangly Palmer had his office down the same university floor. Curious about why Guzmán's lectures drew crowds, he stopped by once to listen. He found the bespectacled professor "very charismatic and verbally articulate," and, at the same time, less a brilliant thinker and "more a big fish in a small pond." Guzmán always greeted Palmer with polite *buenos días*, but appeared to "want to avoid having anything to do with gringos." Palmer heard that Guzmán was a radical and left it at that.

Then, one day, everything exploded. The volunteer who taught a night class, Jane Wilson, had trouble keeping her students' attention, between the late hour and distracting power outages (a frequent occurrence in Andean towns back then). While explaining test answers during a post-exam review session, she asked one to stop talking with her friends. The young woman, a chatterbox, paid no mind; an exasperated Wilson told her to leave. She ushered the girl to the door and, not wanting to seem too severe, gave her an encouraging pat on the bottom on her way out. The other students laughed and gasped at their classmate's expulsion until Wilson restored order. She trudged back home without thinking more about it.

That little butt pat gave Guzmán his chance to chase the Americans from town. His followers in the Federation of Revolutionary Students circulated flyers charging Wilson with insulting her student's "physical and moral integrity" and violating her human rights. Wilson resigned to avoid further trouble. After more charges and debate, the student assembly voted to strike if the other volunteers did not also leave Ayacucho. Efraín Morote, the former dean, had become the rector. He found Guzmán an impressive man, and, sympathizing with his radical views, would not stand up for the Peace Corps volunteers. The University Council, where Guzmán held sway, formally ordered Palmer and the two remaining others to leave the university. They turned in their grades and departed Ayacucho within the week.

The affair gave Guzmán a first victory. He and his supporters claimed to have faced down American imperialism and its proxy volunteers. Radio Habana, the Cuban state station, approvingly reported the Ayacuchan expulsion of probable spies from the "misnamed Peace Corps." For Guzmán, the incident proved that his Red Fraction activists could "defeat a powerful enemy." Nobody cared that their great victory amounted to chasing out four young Americans on an almost comically exaggerated charge. "[We] felt strong and capable of great achievements," Guzmán wrote.

Some weeks later, David Scott Palmer returned to Ayacucho, this time with a Peruvian-administered reforestation project. His former Huamanga Arrows teammates came to see him one evening. Could he rejoin the team? Some of the players, Palmer knew, had participated in the anti–Peace Corps protests. He could not resist asking if they really wanted an evil gringo imperialist on their squad. "That was just politics," one explained. "This is sports." Palmer went back to anchoring the middle for the Arrows.

A trip in 1965 gave Abimael a chance to see Mao's new socialist China for himself. The Chinese government had begun inviting young Communist leaders from Africa, Latin America, and Asia for revolutionary training. Lenin had written extensively about imperialism's evils, and, influenced by his views, Mao regarded the developing world as the great hope for world revolution. His successful 1949 liberation war showed how Communism could triumph even in a poor agrarian country. The Chinese hosted more than three thousand visitors in the mid-1960s, among them various Peruvians. Getting to Beijing took Abimael almost three days, requiring plane changes in Zurich and Prague before a final Moscow stopover. He had hoped to visit Lenin's tomb only to be told that travelers in transit could not leave the hotel.

That was only a momentary disappointment. When Guzmán arrived in Beijing at last, his official guide brought him to Tiananmen Square. There he admired the forest of red flags, and the giant portrait of Mao, the Great Helmsman, mole and all. The Chinese leader then ranked with Pelé, Martin Luther King Jr., and the Beatles among the world's most famous faces, inspiring Andy Warhol's half-mocking, half-flattering silk screens. His so-called Great Leap Forward, modeled on Stalin's brutal policies, had ended in 1962, only three years before Abimael's visit. That catastrophic forced march to industrialization and collectivization triggered a famine that historians believe killed as many as eighteen million people. It included absurdities like a "Kill a Sparrow Campaign" as part of eliminating the "Four Pests": rats, flies, mosquitos, and sparrows. (Exterminating the birds and the resulting ecological imbalances eventually led Mao to declare bedbugs the fourth pest instead.) Few among Mao's many global admirers cared to see his rule's dark side.

The Chinese developed a whole special curriculum for their visitors. In the sessions about guerrilla warfare techniques, Guzmán and the others in his group heard from experts—veterans of Mao's Long March and the war against the Japanese occupiers—about how to recruit and train a rebel army, and the classic Maoist strategy of mobilizing peasants to encircle the cities. Their teachers emphasized opportunistic thinking and inventiveness.

"Take a weapon!" one ordered. Guzmán and the others were puzzled. They had no guns or other arms.

"We don't have any," one man said at last.

"False!" the instructor said. "Open your eyes! A tree is a weapon—a shield. A rock is a club. A pen is a dagger."

In that improvisational spirit the students learned to make bombs and grenades from dynamite. As poor as it was, Peru had plenty of that. Its many coal, copper, and gold mines went through explosives by the barrel, a giant munitions supply in the right hands. "A humble weapon of the people," Abimael later said.

Other courses focused on politics and theory. "Power comes from the barrel of a gun," went the Maoist saying. Nevertheless, their teachers underlined that a Communist's all-important weapon was always ideology, or, as the Maoist jargon had it, a "correct political and ideological line." That meant upholding anti-revisionist, anti-imperialist principles at all times. "Not to have a correct political point of view is like having no soul," Mao wrote. Only a properly prepared cadre could lead the masses to victory. Abimael delighted in these "masterful courses," as he described them, and in visiting schools, hospitals, and factories that showed Mao's accomplishments. He made a last trip before leaving to see the lovely lake gardens in the ancient imperial city of Hangzhou.

The young Peruvian, barely thirty, boarded the plane back home late in 1965. He was eager to get back to party organizing in Ayacucho and countrywide.

His only regret was not meeting Mao in person. The Great Helmsman sometimes appeared to shake hands with visiting socialists, but Abimael only saw him speak at a Tiananmen Square rally. Mao did greet some other visiting Latin Americans. "It's not hard to start a revolution," he said. "You just have to make up your mind."

Abimael had already made up his mind. He would go to war.

It was just a matter of when.

CHAPTER THREE

Comrade Norah

"My life is my own," declares Eleanora West, "I want to live as I choose." The glamorous newspaper publisher in Constantin Virgil Gheorghiu's *The Twenty-Fifth Hour* rejects an unsavory American lieutenant's offer to free her in exchange for marrying him. This dystopian fantasy novel, a literary sensation when published in 1950, unfolds in the twenty-fifth hour of its title, a grim new world governed by bureaucrats and machines. Eleanora, a Jew, flees the Russians and Germans during a semi-fictionalized World War II, only to fall captive to the Americans and the creepy officer. She had earlier compromised to save her newspaper and life, but will do so no longer. "Don't take it too hard, Mr. Lewis," Eleanora says. "But I just couldn't spend twenty-four hours under the same roof with you."

It was hardly surprising that Augusta La Torre enjoyed *The Twenty-Fifth Hour* so much. The book was an interesting read, and, besides that, it validated her teenaged impatience with the state of the world. A dark hour of unpleasant reckoning surely awaited modern humanity if something was not done soon. Augusta identified with the plucky Eleanora, the pragmatist who bought her way out and then, finally, refused to run any longer. "I am ready to surrender my life at any time," Eleanora announces. That decision was not mock melodrama for Augusta. She had also thought about dying for her beliefs.

Everything began for Augusta on her family's estate in the Huanta Valley. Until relocating to Ayacucho in the early 1960s, the La Torres made their home at Iribamba, a few miles outside the pretty town of Huanta. The locals prided their valley as a land of *eterna primavera*, eternal spring, and its sunny orchards bore avocados, oranges, and *limones*, the key limes necessary for ceviche. Augusta and her friends played *zampay*, hide-and-seek, along the rocky hills above the river pasture. They retreated to the big manor house when the heavy afternoon rains rolled down from the heights above the valley.

The La Torres belonged to the valley's landowning elite. They employed poor Quechua-speaking laborers under the semi-feudal system still prevalent in the Andes back in the 1950s. Along with these *peones*, or "peons," for the farm work, the La Torres kept black house servants. A novelty in the Andes, they came from the faraway desert coast, the descendants of slaves who cut cane there in colonial times. It might have seemed strange for a plantation owner to be a Communist, but Carlos La Torre did not see it that way. Several local *hacendados* belonged to the Communist Party or to the APRA, a populist party also outlawed for a time. Carlos's mother, who held title to Iribamba, shared her son's Communist sympathies. "If you're such a Communist," a friend once asked her, "then why don't you give away your land?" The aristocratic family's radical convictions did not go that far. "Don't touch what's mine!" she shot back with a smile.

The girl Augusta was known for her kind heart. She went to the María

Auxiliadora Elementary School in the town of Huanta, where her parents also owned a house, winning gold ribbons for best academic performance. When other girls forgot their homework, Augusta gave them hers to copy. Once, when she was about nine, Augusta invited her entire fourth-grade class to Iribamba for the weekend. The trip was a great adventure for the little girls, many from modest means, with games and horse riding. At dinner, they sat primly at the manor house's long table like a scene from *Madeline*. Then the black servants brought out the meal. Perhaps embellishing some, one girl would recall them as garbed in matching white blazers, blue slacks, and bow ties—and the serving dishes being solid silver. Augusta and her friends didn't do much sleeping that night, of course. They whispered and giggled on their cots into the early hours.

As a teenager, Augusta left to study in Ayacucho, which lay an hour away on the dirt highway. Her parents moved there too, although the family went back to Iribamba on weekends and holidays. Carlos got a job in the Social Security administration, while Delia taught at a preschool. Augusta enrolled in an all-female Catholic high school. Her friends there considered her something of an innocent for her unassuming ways. They bought makeup kits and primped their hair like good adolescent girls, but Augusta rolled from bed, threw on her blue skirt, beige blouse, and royal blue kerchief, and went to class without a second look. Once, she tied a shoestring around the sole of her shoe when it came loose. When Delia, her mother, asked what had happened, Augusta shrugged.

"Oh, nothing. My shoe just split, that's all."

Augusta could be stubborn sometimes. Once a nun at the high school noticed her skirt's hem line. "It's too high for a respectable lady," she said, proceeding to rip down the stitching to lengthen the skirt. Until then, Augusta paid no attention to her hemline, but she did not like being bullied. "I'm going to complain to my parents and the education ministry," she said. The nuns sent Augusta to silent meditation during recess, and, even so, the rebel girl wore the same torn skirt for weeks in a silent protest. Some other girls tore out their hems in solidarity with their classmate.

After graduating, Augusta entered a teacher training institute, a boarding school near her parent's house. She had grown into a beautiful young woman with light-olive complexion, elegant eyebrows, and black hair. When pressed by the other girls, however, Augusta confessed that she had not yet kissed a boy. She could not dance either. When her friends smuggled in a bottle of vodka and pulled out a record player for one girl's birthday, they taught Augusta the male steps for a bolero. She stumbled around at it in her pajamas.

Her good looks drew attention from Ayacucho's young men. One was Alberto Morote, a nephew of the San Cristóbal rector, Efraín Morote. He was a classmate of Augusta's older brother, Carlos Jr. Augusta needed help in physics, and Carlos Jr. hoped Alberto, a science whiz, might tutor her. He brought him over one day.

"Hey, Alberto," Augusta said casually. "Nice to meet you."

Alberto stared at the lovely girl.

She had *misiñawi,* "cat eyes" in Quechua, a kind of hazel that seemed to change colors between brown, green, and yellow.

Alberto stood there stunned. He was momentarily tongue-tied only then to address Augusta, who was still just seventeen, by the formal *usted* reserved for elders and superiors.

"Enough formalities!" Augusta said. "All my friends know you. They say you're the best in your class at physics."

This brought Alberto back down to earth. The two began talking, first about physics, then everything. Alberto, only eighteen himself, saw that Augusta was better read than he in most subjects.

"Which do you think came first, the material or the spiritual?" she quizzed Alberto.

When Alberto, a good Catholic boy, said the spirit, Augusta chuckled.

Her father had inculcated her in a Communist's atheism.

"Why are you laughing?" Alberto asked, slightly offended.

"I'm sorry, it's not your fault. That's what they've taught you. But would you like to explore the issue further?"

"Sure, great!" Alberto said, eager to see Augusta again.

Augusta dug out a book, handing it to Alberto.

"Read it, then we'll talk again."

Alberto looked at the text. He had never heard of Georges Politzer's *Elementary Principles of Philosophy*, but said he would try it.

Alberto went home and devoured the book. A French-Hungarian Marxist who was executed by the Nazis, Politzer advocated questioning authority. The best philosophers had to be "enemies of god, enemies of the state, and corrupters of youth." Morote found himself in agreement with Politzer—and Augusta. He wanted to debate more philosophy with her, to look again into those eyes, and, because he was very serious about such things, to tell her that he had changed his position about the universe's motivating principles.

His answer satisfied Augusta, and they met more often. They would discuss the problems of Peruvian society, which Augusta had seen firsthand in the Huanta Valley. She knew how Peru's peasants lived, the hunger and misery of daily life, and with her mother's encouragement learned the native Quechua tongue. Augusta and Alberto read various books together, including Lin Yutang's epic *The Vermillion Gate* about love and turmoil in early-twentieth-century China. Alberto tried to resist becoming infatuated with Augusta, but had fallen in love anyway. He was entering San Cristóbal that year and thought they might marry at some point.

Then one day Alberto met a friend in the street.

"Hey, guess who got hitched today?" the friend said.

"Who?"

"Augusta La Torre."

Alberto was shocked. How could that be? He had seen Augusta the night before and she hadn't said anything about an engagement.

"To whom?" Alberto asked.

"To Abimael Guzmán."

Alberto stood there confused, then angry. How could Augusta have kept such a secret from him? They had never spoken directly about their feelings, and, even so, the wishful Alberto had wanted to think that Augusta shared his hope for their friendship leading to romance and a future together. He went to see her straightaway.

"How could you do this?" Alberto demanded. "You can't just play with people's feelings like that!"

Augusta was unperturbed, her mind made up already. She could not help it if Alberto had fallen so heavily for her.

"I can't be the wine that quenches your thirst," she said.

What, Alberto wondered, did that mean?

"So our relationship, where does it stand?" he demanded.

"Look, Alberto, let's be clear. Our task is transforming the country. That needs to be our focus. Abimael is the man who will lead the revolution. That's what we need right now."

"You've played me for a fool," he said. "You could have at least told me."

Augusta tried to keep their friendship going after that. They met some years later by the fountain in Lima's Plaza de Armas. She wanted to recruit Alberto for the revolutionary cause.

He decided to have nothing more to do with her.

———————

Augusta kept her engagement secret from her classmates, too. Younger San Cristóbal professors, including Guzmán, sometimes stopped by the teacher training institute to visit the lively young women there. One of Augusta's friends noticed her surreptitiously reading books about Cuba and the Soviet Union in class.

"What are you doing, Augustita?" Gisela whispered, using the intimate diminutive for her friend. "They'll catch you!"

Augusta paid no mind. She kept reading with the book hidden under the desk so the teacher couldn't see.

"I need to read these," she explained after class. "Abimael gave them to me."

Then it came out that she would be marrying Guzmán.

The other girls were surprised, even a little horrified. "But he has a moustache," one said. "And it's yucky how he greases down that wiry hair." "He's so old," another added. Their friend's husband-to-be was not exactly elderly at twenty-nine, but eleven years older than Augusta.

The new couple had known each for almost two years before marrying, often chatting at the La Torre house. It had not taken Abimael long to see Carlos's daughter as a potential wife. He was hardly immune to female charms, and could be an old-fashioned, almost mushy romantic. ("Woman is the most beautiful creature who walks the earth," he once wrote.) Augusta's disdain for makeup and fashion fit the ideal of the good Communist woman who did not primp along the road to revolution. She came from a loyal Communist family besides. Abimael introduced Augusta to his favorite Marxist texts and instructed her in philosophy and history. She gave him the chance to sculpt his own revolutionary Galatea to life. They would lead the coming war.

The match thrilled Augusta's parents. Carlos saw his younger friend as a future leader, and, influenced by their conversations, abandoned his pro-Soviet beliefs for Abimael's Red Fraction and its Maoist line. "An extraordinarily lucid man, very likeable, with an agreeable manner," the approving Delia described her future son-in-law. She and Carlos hosted the marriage ceremony at their house.

And what about Augusta? She had certainly admired Abimael's intellect from her balcony listening post. As a Communist's daughter, she believed in a revolution's necessity, and even as a young girl wanted to right injustices. Once, when Augusta was about eight, she burst in to tell her mother about a peasant family's dying baby. (Delia's family had their own hacienda not far from Ayacucho.)

"They have twins," Augusta said, angry and trembling. "They're letting the baby girl starve; they say girls aren't good for working the fields. I have to bring them milk."

Delia had no cow's milk. She suggested goat's milk instead. Augusta raced back to the peasant hut with a bottle. The little girl survived.

"Augusta suffered when bad things happened," Delia explained years later. "She wanted to fix them immediately." Her daughter occasionally suffered from anxiety and mood swings through her girlhood. A childhood friend remembered Augusta's smile giving way to tears for no apparent reason.

Marrying Abimael allowed Augusta to turn full-time to political work. She had never been interested in romance for romance's sake, or been carried away by teenage dreams about movie star hunks. Whistling catcalls, or *piropeos*, from admiring men both embarrassed and irritated her. ("She was a beautiful woman who was uncomfortable being beautiful," the archaeologist Luis Lumbreras said.) It was not as if Abimael was a smelly old man, either. Other girls might laugh about his wide-hipped walk and wiry hair, but he cleaned up well enough. He had square features and a warm smile, when not distracted by his books. His looks probably did not matter much to a young woman so keen to give herself over to the fight for a new social order.

They wed on February 3, 1964, in the living room of the La Torres's house. Only Augusta's family and a few friends attended the ceremony. A city clerk did the honors—no priest for the Communist couple. The eighteen-year-old Augusta did not wear any jewelry, styling her hair in a simple dark bob. She did concede to a cream-colored dress with three-quarter-length sleeves, a cinched waistline, and a flair skirt—and kitten heels to match. Her husband sported a dark single-breasted suit over a white dress shirt and his usual black-rimmed glasses. He wore the relaxed smile of a man aware of his good fortune.

Everyone seemed happy, and yet, as the wedding photographer recalled it, the occasion lacked any giddy exhilaration. He took pictures of Abimael and Augusta taking their vows, and then sitting on the couch with Carlos, Delia, and a few friends. It was as if the match had been foreordained, a revolutionary matrimony in the making. The new couple honeymooned at Machu Picchu before returning to Ayacucho for the new university semester.

Some weeks later Augusta ran into Gisela near the market.

"*Hola*, Augustita!"

"Hi, Gisela!"

They hugged.

"How was your summer?" asked Gisela. "I was in Lima, and Ica. Have you enrolled yet?"

"No," Augusta said. "I got married."

"To whom?" This was the first Gisela had heard about it.

"To Abimael. I'm not coming back to school either."

The two girls parted, somewhat awkwardly. Gisela had also grown up in the blue-green Huanta Valley, and, sometimes she and Augusta ran into each other there or along Ayacucho's hilly streets. They promised each time to get together, but never did.

The newlyweds moved to Lima after Abimael's return from China in 1965. They stayed for a bit with Carlos and Delia, who had moved to the capital, before renting their own apartment. Abimael took some law cases and taught at La Cantuta University, winning new followers there. He remained a member of Saturnino Paredes's Red Flag, the lone Peruvian Maoist Party for the moment, although he continued to lead his Red Fraction as well. Augusta received her own invitation to China for a training course in 1967, joined by Abimael at the end. Mao had just launched the Cultural Revolution to rid the country of "bourgeoisie" elements. Young Red Guards massed to shout anti-imperialist slogans from the Great Helmsman's Little Red Book. They paraded shamefaced "revisionist" traitors in dunce caps. The Cultural Revolution's organized hysteria brought arbitrary persecution, mob lynchings, and mass executions, but many leftists worldwide saw an inspiring mobilization. (It meant "more active involvement in local politics," one American political scientist asserted, and "aroused revolutionary ideals.") An enthused Abimael went so far as to describe the Cultural Revolution as the "greatest political movement of the masses in history." When he and Augusta dined with the La Torres back in Lima, they told stories about the new revolutionary China. Augusta's five-year-old brother Humberto was more interested in the presents his older sister brought for him and her other younger siblings.

That trip to China increased Abimael's optimism about their own revolutionary prospects. If he and his followers wished to be true to Mao's model, they must begin the battle from the countryside. The Chinese Communists made remote Yan'an their headquarters after the Long March. Why couldn't the Ayacuchan mountains become the stronghold for a Peruvian people's war? The region prided itself on a periodic rebelliousness dating back to the mythologized revolt of its Chanka people against the Inca empire. "The Ayacuchan can't be bought," a ballad boasted. "When there's danger, he offers his life." Recent land occupations demonstrated the downtrodden Quechua-speaking peasantry's impatience with big landlords. Here, Abimael wrote, the indigenous villagers "drown[ed] in exploitation and oppression," yet showed signs of accepting it no longer. They lacked only guidance from better-educated Communists armed with Marxist-Leninist thought. He and Augusta returned in 1970 to Ayacucho to begin that work.

Abimael seemed even more confident and purposeful than before. "He was energized by China," a San Cristóbal colleague believed, "and extremely focused." As the university's director of personnel, Abimael placed his loyalists everywhere. His friend and fellow professor, the agronomist Antonio Díaz Martínez, became student affairs director. Martínez and some others belonged to the growing Red Fraction under Abimael's command. They circulated Beijing's official newspaper, *Peking Daily,* published in often comically bad Spanish translations, and screened the latest Chinese propaganda movies. Sometimes Abimael delivered public lectures in the city's movie theater to attract more recruits to the cause.

Nobody outmaneuvered Abimael, at least at the university. A young sociologist, José Coronel, occasionally tried. He was a former student leader and a leftist, but disliked Mao and the Cultural Revolution. "Burning books?" he said. "Banning Beethoven as Western decadence? Not for me."

Once Coronel took on Abimael at a university council meeting. The council was considering the appointment of an avowed Maoist named Murillo. Abimael wanted another faculty ally, and expounded about the candidate's academic qualifications. That all but sealed the matter, given Abimael's influence.

Coronel raised his hand anyway.

"What is your objection to Professor Murillo?" Abimael asked.

San Cristóbal, Coronel said, already had a literature professor with similar credentials. Their university had other faculty needs, he insisted.

Abimael was unperturbed. He listened calmly to his young colleague, letting him finish. When Coronel sat down, Abimael dismissed the objections in a few words and put the appointment to a vote. Just as he knew they would, the other faculty members approved Murillo's appointment. Abimael ruled the university for the moment.

Coronel noticed Augusta by the doorway. When he had been a student leader earlier in the 1960s, Augusta had tried unsuccessfully to convince him to join the Red Fraction. He found her a warm and pleasant young woman, though also controlling, almost neurotic. She'd once demanded that he take down a Che Guevara poster at the student union. (The Argentine-born revolutionary icon was a misguided romantic adventurer in hardline Maoist eyes.) Now, at the university council meeting, Augusta monitored the proceedings. "She looked anxious, biting her nails as if the revolution depended on the vote," Coronel said. He saw Augusta as the young wife in the domineering Abimael's shadow.

It was not so simple as that. Abimael might be the older "doctor," the philosopher, and the leader in the very male political world. As much as Augusta still played the supporting wife, her time in China and cosmopolitan Lima gave her new confidence. She threw herself into organizing neighborhood committees, women's groups, and street vendor associations under the Red Fraction's control. Her father noted the change in a 1966 birthday poem. "From your first timid steps," Carlos wrote, "[you have become] strong and brave . . . holding high those red flags with which I invited you into the world." Augusta was still sweet and friendly, and yet, leaving her teens behind, no longer the bobby-socked schoolgirl. She had become a leader.

Sometimes she and Abimael dined with Luis Lumbreras and his wife. "Very intelligent, very affectionate," the archaeologist remembered Augusta. "A unique person." It may have been an exaggeration, as some claimed later, that Augusta ordered her older husband around, but she did sometimes poke fun at his seriousness. The couple maintained old-school proprieties in public. They never kissed or held hands in the street, and yet everyone saw that Augusta and Abimael adored each other. Lumbreras viewed Augusta as the more compelling personality. "If you told me that one of them would lead a revolution, I would have said it would be Augusta."

Augusta made Ayacucho's city market into a recruiting ground. She'd maneuver between the trotting porters, clothes peddlers, and the food carts where a peasant laborer could sit down for a bowl of soup or an *emoliente*, a sweet barley tea. The market was a good place for getting out word about the latest Red Fraction event.

Here, Augusta was in her element, flashing her inviting smile. She knew the market women and chatted them up in their native tongue as she passed out flyers. Her leaflets brimmed with regulation Maoist sloganeering about "reactionary" laws and the "proletarian line." It was Augusta's likeability that made the best selling point.

"Hey there, *mamita*!" Augusta would say, using a favorite Andean endearment. "Listen, we are having this rally and you just have to go! Everyone has to go! It's for the good of the people."

The women would smile and nod. Some might come, most not. Even the uninterested did not like to disappoint Augusta, whom everyone had known for years and who had such a good way with people.

"Yes, *mamita*," they'd say. "We got the flyers. We'll be there!"

———

Everything seemed in flux in the wider world. It was 1968, the year of the Prague Spring, the Paris uprisings, and marches against the Vietnam War, not to mention acid trips and the Summer of Love. Even Ayacucho was slowly changing, with San Cristóbal quadrupling to over three thousand students. A few more cars and motorcycles rattled down the streets and, as always, the town gamboled through its well-known Carnival celebration with costumed dancers, flute-playing villagers, and drunken revelry. "Hey, Ayacuchan girl!" one song proposed, "don't take me to mass. Let's go skinny-dipping in Aguas Pampas."

One night in October, down in Lima, army generals seized power in a coup. They trundled the elected president, Fernando Belaúnde, from the presidential palace in his pajamas. The new president, General Juan Velasco, came from a slum family in the desert city of Piura. His "Revolutionary Government of the Armed Forces" surprised many Peruvians by implementing a quasi-socialist agenda. It nationalized foreign oil companies while abolishing the old hacienda system and giving the land to villagers. "Peasant, the Master will no longer feed off your poverty!" Velasco promised.

All this left radicals scratching their heads. A military junta for the poor? That came as a novelty in a Latin America more accustomed to jackbooted anti-Communist, pro-American dictators like the Dominican Republic's Rafael Trujillo and Nicaragua's Anastasio "Tacho" Somoza. ("He may be a son of a bitch," FDR supposedly described Somoza, "but he's our son of a bitch.") The pro-Soviet version of the Peruvian Communist Party threw in with Velasco's new government. That was only more evidence for its "corrupt" revisionism, Abimael believed, and he insisted that Velasco was continuing the collusion between the state, capitalists, and landlords to exploit the masses. This "bureaucratic capitalism with semi-feudal, semi-colonial characteristics," as Abimael labeled it, must be destroyed completely. Only a year back from the China of the Cultural Revolution, Abimael shared the vehement Red Guard spirit and its contempt for compromise. His *senderistas* would dynamite the "fascist" Velasco's tomb early on in their war.

An unpopular 1969 decree gave the military junta's opponents their opportunity. If a high schooler failed a certain number of classes, he or she would have to pay a fee to continue their studies. The measure meant to tighten lax standards, but it struck a nerve. Ever since the conquering Spaniards claimed the Andes for their own more than four centuries before, a special symbolism had attached to the ability to read and write. One legend described a Spanish lord commanding his Indian servants to carry some melons to a Lima friend. He also gave them a letter to his friend detailing the gift, and warned the Indians not to eat any of the succulent orange fruit. The men, hungry and thirsty, stopped to cut open a few melons, carefully hiding the letter so it would not witness their transgression and report it to anyone.

The story ended with the recipient, after reading the letter, telling the stupefied Indians exactly how many melons they had eaten, then flogging them. Ancient Andeans had been highly accomplished in the arts of ceramics and smithing, but they had no writing system. (Except for knotted strings, or *quipus*, apparently for record-keeping.) The new Spanish empire made the written word a sign of authority, an instrument of power, and a dividing line between colonizer and colonized.

The fight for education would become among Peru's most cherished popular causes. By the early 1900s, many Andean villagers began to build adobe schools with an eye to the future. They'd petition the authorities for a teacher, then sell a sheep or pig to buy pens, notebooks, and textbooks for their children. As the Peruvian anthropologist Carlos Iván Degregori explained, these poor farmers regarded schools as the "black box" of modernity and progress. Education offered their children, at least in theory, an escape from a peasant's life to an office job in the city. The new continuation fee for laggard students would be 100 soles, or about two dollars, as much as ten times more than what a field hand earned in a day planting potatoes or digging ditches. Almost immediately, the decree sparked protests across the Andes, and also in Lima. Several hundred *Asociaciones de Padres de Familia,* Parent Associations, petitioned Velasco to rescind the fee.

Abimael wanted to take on the military government, and, as with the Peace Corps six years before, he saw his chance. His supporters denounced the supposed effort to end free education, even though Velasco had not proposed anything nearly so sweeping. A few thousand people assembled in Ayacucho's main square on June 17, 1969, to shout anti-government slogans. "The largest rally ever in the city's history," Abimael asserted later. Riot police set up barricades and a machine gun nest for fear of things getting out of hand.

The situation turned ugly a few days later. When some Red Fraction–supporting students threw stones at the police, the officers chased them into the market. They waded into the crowded stalls, clubbing down anyone in their way. The police brutality led to running battles between angered locals and patrolling officers, especially in the poorer neighborhoods of San Juan Batista and Magdalena. Tear gas choked the alleyways, and the police shot and wounded several people by nightfall. A mutiny might start elsewhere, an old saying went, "but when it spreads to Ayacucho the matter is serious." The city had mostly rejoiced when General José Antonio Sucre's army ended Spanish rule by defeating the viceroy's army at nearby Quinua in 1824. Now everyone seemed to be rising up against Velasco's government.

The generals down in Lima, hoping to restore order, flew in heavily armored anti-terrorism forces, the *sinchis*. They had intelligence reports about, as one newspaper put it, "the pro-Peking agitator Abimael Guzmán Reynoso," and ordered the arrest of Guzmán and other protest leaders. Just before sunrise, the *sinchis* pulled Abimael from bed, taking him and about forty other activists to the airport. The sociology professor José Coronel, Abimael's sometime adversary in university politics, had been arrested too. Policemen commanded their handcuffed prisoners to line up on the runway.

"Do you think they'll shoot us?" Abimael asked Coronel.

"I doubt it," Coronel guessed, correctly.

An army cargo plane flew the prisoners to Lima.

The arrest of protest leaders inflamed passions still further. Roving bands chucked bottles, Molotov cocktails, and more rocks at the police, who now shot and killed four protestors down one street—a bricklayer, a university student, and two boys. In Augusta's hometown of Huanta, only an hour away, the situation turned into open warfare. Hundreds of Andean villagers stormed down from the heights. They wore their ponchos, woolen hats, and a grim look ready for a fight. The country people joined other protestors to torch a police station and take the subprefect hostage. A peasant woman fronted a surging mob around the outmanned police. To prevent the government from sending reinforcements, the protestors had blockaded the highway to Ayacucho. Only the arrival on foot of two hundred *sinchi* commandos rescued the besieged officers. They opened fire indiscriminately, killing more than fourteen people. "The blood of the people has a rich perfume," a ballad recalled that day in the defiant Ayacuchan manner. "It smells like jasmine, violets, geraniums, and daisies."

A state of emergency prevailed over the next few days. Even as the Ayacuchan authorities declared a day of mourning for the dead, police helicopters buzzed over the red-tile rooftops of the angry city. Air force jets crossed the mountain sky, while police broke down doors to detain more protest leaders. One San Cristóbal student, Zenaida Gógora, heard shots outside, and found a boy bleeding in the street. She and some market women flagged down a doctor, but he fearfully refused to help. The women brought the boy to the hospital. He died before the emergency room team could do anything to help him.

That evening in the twilight, Augusta climbed the winding stairs up near Zenaida's house. She had drawn a shawl over her hair for disguise. An intelligence service report already identified her as a "provocateur" and "Communist agitator" some years before. The younger Zenaida had admired Augusta ever since hearing her deliver a speech one day about "The World Reality." (She had become a regular public speaker by then.) Augusta wanted to see Zenaida now.

"Quiet!" she warned. "They're looking for me. I've heard you're helping the wounded."

She gave Zenaida some money.

"It's not much, but use it for what you need."

Then Augusta vanished down the dark stairway.

A day or so later, Augusta learned that the city morgue had delayed releasing the bodies of those killed in the protests. Apparently, the authorities feared the funerals would fire more anti-government sentiment. Risking arrest, Augusta led a march to the morgue. "The masses headed by Norah and other comrades seized the corpses from the morgue and led a giant funeral march that left the city deserted," Abimael wrote afterwards, using Augusta's nom de guerre. She had gone by "Comrade Sara" at first, but chose Norah later in a nod to the heroine of *The Twenty-Fifth Hour*. Her adoring husband likely exaggerated the size of the march, and, according to others, the morgue voluntarily relinquished the bodies without anything having to be "seized." The morgue story nonetheless became part of Comrade Norah's legend many years later.

The protestors carried the day in the end. As a result of so much negative reaction to the fee decree, Velasco repealed it. Now, still only twenty-four, Augusta came away with her first taste of war—the blood price, the sweetness of victory, the anxiety of the struggle. Her urgent new task was to get Abimael out of prison. According to another of the novel's characters, the Nora of *The Twenty-Fifth Hour* looked sometimes like a Picasso portrait with "eyes, a nose, a mouth, and ears, but each isolated and made independent by suffering." Perhaps Augusta believed that her revolutionary convictions gave her immunity to any such weaknesses. She boarded the propeller plane down to Lima on a bright Andean morning, ready for whatever had to be done there.

CHAPTER FOUR

The Great Rupture

Augusta La Torre walked down the stairs from her plane into the terminal at Lima's Jorge Chávez Airport.

A female supporter was supposed to meet her Ayacucho flight. Augusta had no idea what this woman looked like or even her name, since, even more so after the riotous Ayacucho protests, their Red Fraction limited communications to make things harder for the police intelligence services. It would soon organize itself into cells, a tactic of Lenin's Bolsheviks in the Russian Revolution. Each militant knew only the ten or so other members of their cell to limit damage if any of them fell captive. Augusta had been told only to look for a young woman dressed in black holding a magazine in her hand. But she didn't even make it that far. As soon as she entered the terminal, airport security police stopped her, then took her into a back room for questioning.

Elena Iparraguirre saw what was happening from the waiting area. Picking up Augusta was her first assignment for *Socorro Rojo*, Red Aid, a

Maoist solidarity group, and it had already gone wrong. Iparraguirre, trying not to panic, calculated her options. If she left, she would be abandoning her charge, leaving Augusta alone in police custody. If she stayed, she might get arrested herself, since the authorities seemed to have good intelligence about Augusta's arrival. As Iparraguirre tried to make up her mind, Augusta reappeared from the security room, and came out towards her. Iparraguirre's heart was still racing, but Augusta seemed calm, relaxed even. Iparraguirre guided her out to her car and the two women headed into the city.

Augusta had flown down to work for Abimael's release from prison. She was soon able to visit him in El Sexto, the decrepit jail in downtown Lima, bringing food and blankets. The Velasco government, wanting to maintain its progressive profile, did not press charges against the Ayacucho protestors. Abimael would soon be freed, none the worse for the experience. He had already been jailed once before as a student in Arequipa.

That week in Lima changed Augusta's life forever. She and Elena Iparraguirre, the new recruit from the airport, became close friends, helping Abimael prepare for the coming revolution. When Augusta died late in the war, Elena replaced her as Abimael's wife and the *senderista* second-in-command. The police would claim that Augusta had been murdered in a conspiracy of love, power, and ambition.

————

Elena grew up in the sunny seaside town of Huacho, the daughter of a pharmacist mother and a farm equipment salesman father. Her mother, a protofeminist in 1950s Peru, urged her four children, all girls, to study, study, study. "It's the only way for a woman to become independent," Blanca said. Little Elena liked going with her father, Alberto, to retrieve their blue DeSoto from the parking lot for family excursions. Her name, he explained, came from Helen of Troy, because she was the world's most beautiful girl in his eyes. Alberto belonged to the APRA, the left-leaning populist party. He told

Elena about the APRA's great failed revolt in 1932, just up the coast in the city of Trujillo. Sometimes Blanca recounted stories about Micaela Bastidas, the warrior wife of the eighteenth-century rebel Túpac Amaru, and María Parado de Bellido, a heroine of the Peruvian Independence War. Her parents taught Elena to admire anyone who fought for a noble cause.

All Peruvian roads, then as now, led to Lima, the center of everything, and by far the country's biggest city. When Elena was still a child, her family moved there to the middle-class Jesus María district. She'd inherited her father's interest in politics, and, as a teenager, she followed the news about the Cuban Missile Crisis and the Indochina wars. But traveling was the young Elena's big dream back then. She especially wanted, as a movie lover enchanted by Hollywood hits like *Ben Hur* and *Casablanca,* to visit the United States. After finishing high school in 1963, she guided American tourists around Machu Picchu as a way to improve her English while earning some money. She applied to various fellowship programs in the United States, and, to her surprise, won an award to pursue an education degree in Philadelphia. Her parents did not want her to go. They subscribed to the APRA's credo of anti-imperialist Latin American solidarity. The charismatic *aprista* founder Víctor Raúl Haya de la Torre called for the "helpless and balkanized Disunited States of the South" to unite against the "increasingly powerful United States of the North." Elena paid little mind, thrilled about the prospect of an adventure abroad.

About that time, Elena met Javier Blas Verástegui, an engineer with a degree from Lima's San Marcos University. They fell in love and wanted to stay together. Javier had lined up a fellowship too, but in France. Why, he asked, didn't Elena come with him to Paris? Elena thought it over for a few days. Then she made a counteroffer.

"I'll go, but I don't want to give up my scholarship. I'll come if you can get me one in France."

Javier took it from there. He found Elena, who had a Montessori credential, a French government fellowship in a training program for children with special needs. Elena was required to learn French before going. Every day, she rose before dawn, heading for a morning language course and then her job as a kindergarten teacher. She worked afternoons at her mother's pharmacy (after overcoming her squeamishness about giving shots). She was also pursuing a graduate degree in education at La Cantuta University and, in the evenings, went to class there. This punishing schedule did not bother Elena, who had grown into a smart, determined, and well-organized young woman. Her parents were relieved that their daughter would go to cultured France rather than vulgar America.

At La Cantuta, Elena found herself drawn to radical politics. In Peruvian universities by the late 1960s, especially the public ones, most students professed to being Maoists. Both Red Flag and a new Maoist splinter group, Red Homeland, organized regular rallies to sloganeer about national liberation and revolutionary warfare. A Trotskyite group attracted some supporters, advocating, as Trotskyites did, for a less bureaucratized, more internationalized struggle. (Their leader, Hugo Blanco, led Cuzcan peasant land invasions early in the 1960s.) The pro-Soviet version of the Peruvian Communist Party had a small campus presence. What Freud once called the "narcissism of minor differences" often left Communists everywhere to hate rival socialist parties even more than the bourgeoisie. A Stalinist agent bludgeoned the exiled Trotsky to death with an ice axe in his Mexico City study for his supposed treachery to the Soviet cause. The competing Peruvian Communist groups fought constantly over the best way to achieve the goal of socialist revolution.

Elena did not join any group just yet. But she read about the 1969 Ayacucho school fee uprising, and its radical spirit impressed her. When the opportunity arose to work for the release of the prisoners, she eagerly volunteered, including that first assignment of meeting Augusta at the airport.

Elena was star struck by Augusta at first. At twenty-two, Elena was just two years younger, and yet, besides the movie-star looks, Augusta seemed far more mature and wise. She had been to China; apparently read every novel ever published; and discoursed about Marxist-Leninist texts with practiced authority. Elena tried to be helpful by driving Augusta to meetings with lawyers and party activists around the city. Afterwards, the two young women would go out for coffee and a corn tamale. They'd talk until three o'clock in the morning about books, movies, and revolution. It flattered Elena that so glamorously intriguing a person wanted to be her friend.

Elena began to think about becoming a full-time activist too. Should she really go to France? Didn't Peru need committed Communists to advance the revolution? Augusta urged Elena to stick with her plan. The trip, she counseled, would give Elena precious knowledge and experience, and she'd bring that back home to the struggle. Blanca and Alberto, meanwhile, demanded that their daughter marry Javier before going to France with him. Elena loved her parents, even if they belonged to what most Marxists dismissively labeled as the "petty bourgeoisie." She married Javier in absentia, a complex bureaucratic procedure, since he had already left for Paris. For a good-bye present, Augusta gave Elena the complete works of their party founder José Carlos Mariátegui, who in addition to his political activism was a fine essayist. She boarded the plane with the books in her suitcase.

Being abroad at last was exciting. Elena and Javier had busy school schedules and almost no money, but that did not stop them from seeing the sights. In her free time, Elena walked around the Luxembourg Gardens, or stopped at the Musée d'Orsay to gaze at the Degases and Monets. She and Javier traveled on the cheap everywhere around Europe—to Rome and the Sistine Chapel, Spain's Alhambra, and the Swiss Alps. One weekend expedition took them to Prague, where the Soviet Red Army tanks had recently crushed the 1968 democratic reform movement. According to Mao, the Soviets had become "social imperialists" who ruled their satellite countries by force. ("Socialist in words, imperialist in deeds," the Chinese leader said.) What Elena saw in a fearful, depressed Prague seemed to confirm Mao's negative opinion about the Soviets. Some weeks after that trip, back in their Paris apartment, Elena discovered that she was pregnant. While she did not care too much about the gender, she hoped for a girl. "*Serás mujercita*," she'd whisper to her growing stomach. The baby was indeed a girl. Blanca, Elena's mother, came from Lima to help around the house.

Her two Paris years fortified Elena's increasing radical convictions. She and Javier lived in a run-down apartment complex in Massy, a landing place for students, exiles, and refugees from everywhere. They met another Javier, a Mexican Marxist who had escaped the 1968 Tlatelolco Square massacre in Mexico City. Others in the Massy complex had fled Algeria, the Belgian Congo, and Haiti with more tales of terror and struggle. Here Elena saw that revolution was a global ambition, and began to appreciate the price it could exact from those who joined the cause. That the world's injustices demanded action seemed obvious enough in France itself. "I saw how African immigrant kids got nothing for shining shoes and sweeping streets," Elena recalled. She watched a big protest march down the Champs-Élysées against America's war in Vietnam. Only fear about losing her fellowship and being deported kept her from joining.

Elena found Red China's stock high in Paris. "You could buy Chinese newspapers and magazines everywhere," she said. Reports about Stalin's labor camps, purges and executions, and brutal collectivization policies left many French leftists disenchanted with the Soviet Union. By contrast, Mao's Red China gave new Third World chic to the old Communist cause. Intellectual superstars such as Jean-Paul Sartre, Julia Kristeva, and Michel Foucault praised Mao, and, much like Abimael Guzmán and other Peruvian leftists, they asked no questions about his government's abuses. Some young French Maoists formed communes to model an egalitarian post-capitalist life. That Maoism enjoyed such favor seemed to Elena more verification for Augusta's opinion about revolution, namely that Red China should be Peru's model. She returned to Lima in 1973 to throw herself into the fight.

It took Augusta a few hours to update the jet-lagged Elena on the night of her return. After Elena's departure for Paris, she explained, she and Abimael had led Red Fraction in breaking away from Red Flag, forming their own new Peruvian Communist Party. They believed Saturnino Paredes, the Red Flag leader, had gone astray by embracing the obscure Albanian Maoist model. A bitter Paredes charged Abimael with "false Marxism-Leninism," "opportunism," and other deviations from the correct proletarian line. (Abimael answered in kind by dismissing Paredes as a "rightist liquidationist" and "last thick root of the old revisionist tree.") Now no less than four rival groups claimed to be the true Peruvian Communist Party—the old pro-Soviet one, Red Flag, Red Homeland, and Abimael and Augusta's new party, Shining Path. They had only about fifty members, but, Augusta told Elena, all of them absolutely committed to the revolutionary cause. Hadn't the Bolsheviks begun with only a fistful of followers? Their new party would lead the coming people's war for Communism in Peru.

Augusta brought Elena to a party function the day after her return. It was unlike anything Elena had ever seen: a room of women—black, brown, and white—all dedicated to revolution. They belonged to the *Movimiento Femenino Popular*, or Women's Popular Movement, a party-controlled group established by Augusta in the late 1960s. A wide-hipped, somewhat chunky man in his early forties rose to speak. He delivered a long, yet, Elena thought, compelling speech about Marxism's history in Peru. The struggle for Communism had gone astray over the last decades, but their new Peruvian Communist Party would base itself in what the man described as the "irrefutable scientific principles" of "dialectical materialism" and "Leninist-Marxist-Maoist Thought." Elena liked how he addressed the young female

audience without the usual sexist condescension or leering from male political leaders. Hers was the first hand raised in the question period.

"If, as you say, the Peruvian Communist Party has such rich experience
and theoretical foundation, then why hasn't it taken up arms yet?"

The speaker smiled slightly from his square-framed glasses. "We didn't
revolt because we didn't have people like you," he told Elena. "Now we do."

When the session ended, Elena wanted to know who the speaker had
been. Others addressed the man only as *el Profesor*, the Professor. Elena went
over to Augusta's mother, Delia, also there.

"Who was that speaking just now?"

"That," Delia smiled, "is the future president of Peru."

Elena stood there, not quite following. Delia clarified, "He is Professor
Guzmán. He's Augusta's husband."

Elena found an Education Ministry job to support herself. Her activism
became the real focus of her formidable energies. She was a pleasant yet
forceful woman with strong shoulders, a prominent nose, and a commanding gaze. Their new Peruvian Communist Party wanted to take over SUTEP,
the national teacher's union, already radical in flavor. Elena organized
marches and recruited teachers into the party. She fled down the street with
other protestors when the riot police moved in with tear gas and water cannons. In retribution, Elena believed, for her political activities, the Education Ministry reassigned her to Sicuani, coincidentally the same backwater
town where Abimael spent a boyhood year. Undaunted, Elena organized
party activities there too. When they were both in Lima, she and Augusta
compared notes. Augusta went to the hospital for the birth of Elena's second
child, a boy this time.

Few outsiders would have guessed at the two young women's militant
views. When chatting with the hospital nurses or a store clerk, Elena and

Augusta came across simply as gracious women. They switched at party meetings into unsmiling Maoist-speak about the "mass line," "rightist opportunism," and, of course, "world proletarian revolution," the Communist holy grail. Both Red Flag and Red Homeland, the two other Maoist parties, advocated armed struggle to destroy the oppressors. A Red Homeland leader, Hector Ceballos, waved a wooden rifle at rallies to shout about seizing power at gunpoint. He and the other Marxist groups were not actually ready to make the leap from bluster to real war.

It was hard for Elena to leave Lima often because of her children. To spread the gospel of armed revolution, Augusta traveled constantly in the 1970s. Even though she and Abimael disliked being apart, he encouraged her to go—the party always came first. That meant long trips on the rickety trucks that plied the rutted mountain tracks with their cargo of goats, chickens, crates of fruit, and sacks of cement. On top perched the dust-streaked passengers in ponchos and blankets. They would bump through steamy valleys, rocky gorges, and over mountain passes to reach some forsaken town. An exhausted yet determined Augusta would jump down from the truck ready to get to work. She might speak at a union meeting, meet peasant activists, or visit a few villages before moving to the next stop.

Once Augusta appeared in the mining town of La Oroya. She had come for a big mineworker meeting in this sooty, freezing mountain outpost of almost post-apocalyptic ugliness. A young man, Gilberto Hume, there with some other Lima leftists, recalled a white woman among the brown miners. She was a "beautiful woman" of about thirty, even with her "hair austerely tied up in a bun" (as Augusta often did to avoid unwanted male attention). Meeting organizers assigned Augusta to the "Feminine Sub-Committee," but she attended other group meetings anyway. The mystery woman would "listen attentively to the speeches and debates and then at the end, only at the end, ask to speak," according to Hume. Then Augusta would give a little speech, always the same, about "exploitation, the peasant-worker alliance, and the war from country to city." She was as dogmatic and uncompromising as Abimael in her public presentations, perhaps even more so. Hume and the other Limans nicknamed Augusta "the Evangelist" for her missionary devotion. They noticed that she won followers. Augusta arrived alone, only to have recruited some twenty tough mineworker unionists to her side by the end.

Augusta and Elena went together to Ayacucho in 1975. It was Elena's first visit to the old colonial city with its bougainvillea cloisters, gilded altarpieces, and the strong Andean flavor to the culture and street life. One peasant woman had laid some *olluco* out for sale on the sidewalk. (A favorite Peruvian dish, *olluquito con charqui*, combines that little tuber with dried llama meat.) Elena chatted with the woman, whose broken Spanish had a heavy Quechua accent.

"How old are you?" Elena asked.

"Thirty-three, *mamita*," the woman replied.

Elena was shocked. She would have guessed at least sixty, but the Ayacuchan countryside's poverty exacted its price in years. *Cuzco is opulent by comparison*, Elena thought.

She had come with Augusta for a meeting of the Women's Popular Movement, which, although ostensibly independent, was a front organization under party control. Both women had been raised by strong mothers to believe in women's rights. As a girl, Elena especially liked a storybook about Anne Boleyn, who, after her husband, Henry VIII, had her beheaded, became a heroine for the English Reformation. She and Augusta scorned "bourgeoisie feminism" and its canonical texts like Simone de Beauvoir's *The Second Sex*. Their Marxist orthodoxy taught that modern-day sexist oppression originated with capitalism (a view famously advanced by Friedrich Engels in *The Origins of the Family*). Only a Communist revolution could liberate women and all subjugated people. "The struggle of Peruvian women belongs to the struggle of the oppressed and exploited masses and they are fighting the same enemy," the founding statement of the Women's Popular Movement explained. Early Marxist heroines like Rosa Luxemburg and Liu Ju-Lan showed the way. Elena and Augusta also admired a contemporary radical icon, the American Angela Davis, a Black Power advocate and a Communist like them. Closer to home, as the Women's Popular Movement reminded its members, Micaela Bastidas, the anti-colonial leader, proved that "Peruvian women have been and are popular combatants." They only had to join the revolution under party leadership to win freedom.

These recruitment efforts had been paying off. It helped to have a magnetic woman, Augusta, selling the party to potential female members. Their leader, Abimael, might be a man, and also their totemic icons Marx, Lenin, and Mao. That Augusta was second-in-command, however, showed that a woman could become a party leader. In Elena and early activists like Osmán Morote's first wife, Teresa Durand, the party had other strong women as well. The delegates at the Ayacucho meeting of the Women's Popular Movement agreed to expand its activities nationwide. Their party would become the first Latin American guerrilla movement to draw so many women into its ranks.

Family was becoming a problem for Elena, however. Her domestic duties made it hard to find enough time for her party organizing. (She still worked at the Education Ministry, too.) One evening, Augusta stopped by to visit. The two women chatted in the kitchen after Elena put her two little children to bed. Elena asked her friend if she wanted children one day.

"I don't have time for kids," Augusta said. "I have to dedicate myself to the revolution."

A real Communist gave up everything for the fight. Elena agonized, then decided. One night, she told the astonished Javier that she was leaving to dedicate herself to the party and the coming revolution. "You'll have to raise our kids now," she said. And, with that, she walked out the door.

Elena, the true believer, never returned. "The political work couldn't wait," she explained years later. "I had to respond to the demands of the people, of the party." It still pained her to think about it. "My children lost their mother to the war," Elena said, "and I lost them."

––––––––––

A secret meeting of the party's Central Committee convened early in 1978. Abimael, Augusta, and about thirty other high-ranking militants sat on this main oversight body. Elena was not yet a Central Committee member, but she had been invited together with some other midlevel militants. It took some time for everyone to arrive at an isolated desert house just outside Lima. Their meetings could go on for days, even weeks. No one would be allowed to leave until it was over. Everyone brought sleeping bags.

Their gatherings followed the party's regulation conventions. They addressed each other by their pseudonyms in the expected Communist way—Comrade Norah, Comrade Nicolás, and, the name Abimael went by then, Comrade Álvaro. (Elena eventually chose Comrade Miriam, after the strong-willed sister of Moses, a character she recalled from Cecil B. DeMille's *The Ten Commandments* of her movie-going girlhood.) There would be at minimum one lengthy Abimael speech, of course. After days or sometimes weeks, the party ratified final agreements, and, once the war had begun, some new campaign with an ungainly Cultural Revolution–style title ("Shaking Up the Countryside with Guerrilla Actions," "Great Plan to Conquer Bases in Function of Conquering Power in the Whole Country," "Culminating by Brilliantly Establishing a Historic Milestone"). Each meeting was its own little passion play of an orthodox Marxist variety.

It was still not especially unusual to be planning an armed revolution. "If you go carrying pictures of Chairman Mao / You ain't gonna make it with anyone anyhow," the Beatles already warned in 1968. That message, however, arrived slowly to Peru and other poor countries across the postcolonial world. Starry-eyed Western radicals often remained infatuated with the Great Helmsman and guerrilla warfare as well. Whether the Black Panthers, the Nicaraguan Sandinistas, or the Palestinian Black September Organization, many rebels brandished their rifles for the cameras through the 1970s. It remained what journalist Vijay Prashad has called "the time of the gun" for the global left's romance with armed freedom fighters.

That 1978 plenary meeting occurred at a moment of doubt for the Peruvian left. The country's military leaders had recently announced their intention to return to the barracks. Peruvians would elect a new president. Other leftist parties, after much debate, decided to participate. That was a dreadful mistake, Abimael now explained. They must not fall prey to what the Shining Path leader dismissed as the "constitutionalist illusions" of electoral democracy. Voting was bourgeoisie trickery to fool the masses into believing they had a voice. According to Lenin in *State and Revolution*, "The oppressed are allowed once every few years to decide which particular representatives of the oppressing class shall represent and repress them in parliament." The task was smashing the state, which served the ruling classes. (Abimael had drawn heavily on Lenin in his law thesis to advance this argument.) Only revolution could liberate Peru and the planet at last.

Abimael knew that some at the meeting did not yet want war. According to their self-declared principles of "democratic centralism," every party member had a say, albeit with the leaders given the last word. In reality, Abimael increasingly controlled everything, and both he and Augusta would brook no more delay. A few Central Committee members questioned their preparedness, but Abimael went on the offensive before long. He lit into the doubters as "rightist opportunists, revisionists from head to tail." One insulted "revisionist" moved to remove Abimael as the party's leader. Abimael knew that the Central Committee majority would side with him. He agreed to a vote, and, as he wrote later, the Central Committee "immediately and swiftly repudiated" the motion. Three dissidents would be expelled from the party. Several more only escaped by admitting their errors in a "self-criticism" session after the fashion of the Red Guard's public shamings, and, before that, Stalin's show trials. To doubt their party leader and the urgency of armed struggle had been a terrible counterrevolutionary error, they confessed. Only a few last matters remained for consideration after six exhausting weeks in the farmhouse.

One was reorganizing the Central Committee. Abimael wanted the party's governing body trimmed to twelve members. It would be easier to control that way. Some younger party members would also be promoted to the committee, among them Óscar Ramírez, better known as Comrade Feliciano, an Arequipan from a military family. Abimael also advanced another name: Comrade Miriam.

Elena was surprised. She had gotten to know Abimael in the past few years, but not especially well. Had Augusta brought her name to Abimael's attention? "I accept the call," Elena said.

Now Abimael called his new Central Committee to vote.

"All for armed struggle?"

The ayes had it. A unanimous vote.

He had what he wanted.

Only the final planning remained. To centralize the revolution's management, Abimael established a Permanent Committee later in 1978, the party's highest authority. He, and, of course, Augusta, would belong, and Elena became the third and final member. She had earned Abimael's confidence as the most effective Lima organizer. (And it pleased Augusta to see her best friend join them in the party's new triumvirate.) Augusta and Elena admired the older Abimael's dedication and intellect, but they had also become seasoned leaders with strong opinions of their own. They followed an agenda at meetings of their new Permanent Committee, and its members, all three of them, addressed each other as "Comrade" to keep things official. The junior member, Elena, mostly observed at the start, later having her say, too. Their first task was to agree upon strategy and tactics for the coming war.

Eventually they reached consensus. Their war would stick to the consecrated Maoist strategy of revolution from the countryside. The father of Communism, Karl Marx, dismissed poor farmers as backward conservatives, or, in his words, "a sack of potatoes." It had been Mao's innovation to insist that peasants could become revolutionaries. "Countryside as center, city as complement," went the saying. Some eight million Peruvian villagers farmed tiny plots at starvation's edge. Surely, it seemed, they would rally to rebellion under the party's leadership. Urban guerrillas lately had been crushed—Argentina's Montoneros, Brazil's MR-8, Uruguay's Tupamaros. "Lima had the military garrisons and police stations," Elena said. "We were only able to do hit-and-run attacks there." The remote Andes could become "liberated zones" under their own more permanent control.

It was decided to make Ayacucho the center for guerrilla action. There, thanks to Abimael and Augusta, the native daughter, they had contacts, experience, and knew the lay of the land. A previous Peruvian insurgency, the Revolutionary Leftist Movement, had been hunted down back in 1965. (Carlos La Torre, Augusta's father, was briefly arrested for belonging.) Its leaders followed the focalist model, *foquismo*, namely the idea that a little guerrilla band could spark the brushfire of revolution. That strategy had worked for Fidel Castro and his bearded fighters in their Sierra Maestra campaign to seize power in Cuba, but nowhere else. In Bolivia, late in 1967, Che Guevara was hunted down, with CIA help, after failing to ignite a revolt there. Abimael scorned *foquismo*. Only sustained organizing by a traditional Leninist party, he believed, could lay a revolution's groundwork. Spontaneity and freelancing guaranteed failure, and Abimael once dismissed Che as a "chorus girl." They should not expect quick victory. The "battle will be cruel, long, difficult," Abimael warned.

Abimael's faith in their success was absolute, almost messianic in its certainty. He might dismiss belief in God as folk superstition and yet, in truth, his Communism and Christianity had some notable similarities. Each possessed sacred texts and chosen prophets together with missionary impulses, doctrinal obsessions, and the promise of human salvation. As a Catholic schoolboy, Abimael read the Bible, and he retooled the Book of Genesis in a 1979 speech about Mariátegui's founding of the Peruvian Communist Party. "Light that melted earth, and that mud turned to steel. Light, mud, steel: the Party arose in 1928," Abimael began. More recently, he continued, they had been "enlightened by a more intense light, Marxism-Leninism, Mao Zedong Thought." Now "we are on the inevitable path toward Communism, to arrive at full and absolute light." Historian Yuri Slezkine terms the Bolsheviks a "millenarian sect" for their inbred tribalism, apocalyptic certainty about capitalism's day of reckoning, and self-appointed role as the instruments of transfiguration and redemption. Guzmán and his acolytes saw themselves as summoned to blessed revolutionary duty in the same way.

The Shining Path leader predicted that the government would do everything to crush their revolt. They must maintain secrecy to avoid infiltration and betrayal. In Russia, the Bolsheviks, who became the Soviet Communist Party, had turned conspiracy and misdirection into advanced revolutionary art—the cell system, the pseudonyms, the "front organizations" puppeteered by the party from behind the scenes. "If the party isn't clandestine, it will be nothing at all," Abimael said. Their secrecy would give fearsome mystique to the revolution.

To begin the war meant going underground. Abimael resigned his post at San Cristóbal in 1975. By the late 1970s, he seldom appeared at public meetings, and someone surreptitiously removed his photo from university files. After the police briefly arrested Abimael at the La Torres's Lima house in 1979, Augusta explained to her parents that they were moving out for good to take up arms. "She said that we all die of something," Delia recalled, "and that their work was very beautiful." Elena had already cut ties with her family. No one paid much attention to any of them dropping from sight. They had lost influence at San Cristóbal in the 1970s. Their little Maoist group seemed to have disbanded for failing to win enough supporters.

It was quite the opposite. The disappearance of the party's three top leaders marked a final preparation. Their last step was a so-called First Military School in late 1979. Fifty-one party members gathered secretly at a house in Chaclacayo, a placid Lima district where the highway begins to wind up into the Andes. The invited militants were mostly in their twenties, and, as was the *senderista* way, about half were women. They received training in weapons, explosives, and propaganda. At the final ceremony in April 1980, each graduate was awarded a diploma and a green beret bearing a red star, bronze button, and the inscription: *1 Cia. Del EGP*, 1st Company of the Popular Guerrilla Army. Then the room fell silent for Abimael's closing speech. His call to arms anticipated the coming battle's ferocity:

> Comrades, we are entering the great rupture. . . . the Party provides the masses of the world with their long-desired liberator . . . it will not be easy: the sinister black hosts will come for us, mount powerful assaults, great offensives. We will respond, we will ravage them . . . the people will rear up, arm themselves, rise in revolution to put the noose around the necks of imperialism and the reactionaries. They will be strangled, necessarily, necessarily. The flesh of the reactionaries will rot away, converted into ragged threads, and this black filth will sink into the mud. . . . The future lies in guns and cannons! The armed revolution has begun! Glory to Marxist-Leninist-Mao Zedong Thought! Let us begin the armed struggle!

A sympathetic interviewer would later suggest that this speech had been a "beautiful political poem of war." Truly, Abimael admitted, "sometimes in politics you have to let yourself go, so that the passion, the deep feelings, can strengthen our determination." He modestly averred from saying anything more. "What literary value it might have I couldn't really say."

His loyalists had no such doubts. There was a pause after Abimael finished as if the young fighters wanted to take in the moment. They would have to die and kill for the cause. "Conquering bases we will make that New State," went a party hymn. "Constructing the future with our blood."

"*Salud,* Cheers!" someone finally shouted.

Everyone lifted their glass to the war.

CHAPTER FIVE

First Blood

Benigno Medina owned the Ayzarca farm down the Pampas Canyon. It lay in the sandy bottomland of this magnificent gorge ten hours by horseback from Ayacucho. Medina grew sugar cane there, hiring local Indian laborers. Most farmers still employed a donkey-powered medieval wood press, a *trapiche*, to squeeze out the cane juice. A shed at the somewhat more modern Ayzarca housed a gas-powered mill for the job. Medina's farmhands poured the splintery brown syrup through a hot coiled snake of copper pipe. Dripping out came the *aguardiente*, cane liquor, the elixir of the mountain party. It begot forbidden sex, sad ballads, and the occasional deadly knife fight.

Medina liked to drink. A big man whose mutton chop sideburns gave him a resemblance to Peru's naval hero, Miguel Grau, he belonged to the mestizo landlord class. Medina seems to have been generally well-liked despite his rumored weakness for the market women who sold his cane liquor. He organized school fundraisers and road improvements. Various village parents asked him to be the godfather, *padrino*, for their babies, the customary peasant way to form ties with a local notable. They could expect minor future patronage like a few coins for a child's school uniform.

This night was Christmas Eve 1980. Few villagers knew anything about trimmed trees, presents, and Santa Claus except as a vague rumor about far-away countries. Medina, the local catechist, led evening prayers in Ayzarca's chapel. His family and some friends dined afterwards on duck soup to mark the night before Christ's birth.

Then the alarm sounded. Medina heard explosions and shouting out-side, and, suddenly, some thirty shadowy figures burst into the room. "Men and women carried homemade spears, shotguns, and dynamite bombs," his daughter Betty told a Lima newspaper. The guerrillas, shouting down Betty's plea for her father's life, blindfolded and beat her, then dragged Medina to the chapel. Her fourteen-year-old brother, Alfredo, hid in a tree.

All night Betty listened to her father's screams. Only when the police arrived the next morning did the guerrillas flee, and Betty go to the chapel. "When I went to my father, I found him horribly mutilated. They had cut off his tongue and testicles, and sliced open his stomach." The attackers killed a farmhand and wounded five others who tried to save their master.

The guerrillas left a painted message across the farmhouse.

"Long Live the People's War."

Benigno Medina became the first to die in the new war. It had begun six months before in another village, Chuschi, a half day away by a peasant's sturdy walk over the steep trails. There on the evening of May 17, 1980, the day before the first presidential elections in twelve years, five masked men stormed the village clerk's office. One put a gun to Florencio Conde's chest, and, after tying the bewildered registrar to a chair, the men gathered the paper ballots and wood urn. They piled the voting materials outside, and set them ablaze in the mountain night. That day became the *Inicio de la Lucha Armada*—ILA for short, the "initiation of the armed struggle," and a Shining Path holiday. (Some Peruvian girls would be named "Ila" later in the 1980s.) There could be no truck with what party flyers denounced as the "electoral farce" and the attempt to deceive the masses into accepting any solution besides overthrowing the system. The *senderistas* had begun the great battle to which Abimael had called his followers at the First Military School only weeks before. The detachment at Chuschi left their red hammer-and-sickle banner flying over the village square before vanishing into the dark hills after midnight.

A police helicopter touched down the next day. The police detained the village schoolteacher, Bernardino Azurza, a young San Cristóbal graduate and a *senderista* organizer. Radical teachers like Azurza played a vital role in spreading the revolutionary message in the countryside. The police told the Chuschinos that Azurza was a *terrorista*, a terrorist, the first time they had heard the word, but he was soon released. Azurza reappeared in Chuschi some months later. One day, he and some local supporters seized the village governor, paraded him naked around the square, then banished him for good. Azurza's subsequent speech about "Marxist-Leninist-Maoist Thought" and "Chairman Gonzalo" left Chuschi's peasants puzzling over what he might have been talking about.

Azurza and other party members took orders from the Ayacuchan regional commander, Comrade Norah, Augusta La Torre. She left Lima after the First Military School to take charge in the mountains. As the Ayacucho native, Augusta had the advantages of Quechua fluency and familiarity with village customs like the *pachamanca*, a feast of roast potatoes and guinea pig, and the coca leaf offerings to the *wamanis*, the spirit masters of the peaks and lakes. Her people skills allowed her to connect with the peasants. She felt at home in the great mountains.

Their war plans prioritized the Pampas River and its twisting valleys. "We picked the area because it had the highest concentration of poor peasants," Elena explained later. In villages like Chuschi little cornfields and mud hamlets clung to the mountainside, and babies, *angelitos*, perished from hunger and disease with the nearest doctor many hours away. Many peasants spoke only Quechua, and they had no running water, electricity, or hope for the future. The more daring had begun, as early as the 1930s, to abandon their neglected hamlets for Lima's slums. According to Mao, the poorest villagers would embrace the revolutionary message because they had so little to lose. That seemed to make the Pampas Valley the right place for Augusta to concentrate her efforts at the start.

She directed some early raids herself, including one on the Ayrabamba farm some weeks after the Chuschi ballot-burning. Her fighters broke into the owner's farmhouse before dawn and, as the man fled in his pajamas, tied up his nephew and the nephew's wife. Their baby began screaming and, mercifully, a *senderista* found a bottle for it. Later in the day, Augusta held a "people's trial" to judge the landlord's family. (She was "green-eyed" and a *gringa*, a white woman, according to a later court report.) These community tribunals would become common in the party's "liberated zones." Under the supervision of *senderista* militants, villagers weighed the crimes of a landowner, thief, or corrupt official. They usually ended in an *ajusticiamento*, a "bringing to justice," with a whipping or, later in the war, a bullet in the head or stoning to death. Carlos, the landlord's nephew, was lucky. He would only receive a warning.

Before her fighters retreated, Augusta was approached by a peasant woman. Her husband, the woman said, was a *peón*, a day laborer. He had worked at Ayrabamba for three months without yet being paid. Could the *Señorita* do anything? Augusta led a small crowd over to sack the company store. She was always meticulous, and formed three lines to ensure orderly looting. Her fighters would distribute the tools, clothes, medicine, and other dry goods to the laborers. The impatient men broke ranks almost immediately. They pushed in to empty the store shelves into their burlap sacks. Augusta decided not to try to stop them, and gave a few bills from her leather satchel to every hired man there afterwards. Only then did the *peones* mount their horses and mules, many munching crackers from the looted store, and ride away home. Augusta's fighters tied up Carlos and his wife in a storage shed. *You and your uncle have forty-eight hours to vacate the farm,* they told him.

The government sent in the anti-terrorism police commandos, the *sinchis*, to hunt the guerrillas. They swept through the valley after Benigno Medina's murder, randomly detaining villagers along the way. At the police station in the nearest town, Vilcashuamán, the *sinchis* interrogated Giorgina Gamboa, a fifteen-year-old from near Ayzarca. "Talk!" the *sinchi* commander screamed, "You saw it! You're a *terruca*, a terrorist!" His men stuffed a rag in the teenager's mouth, then seven or eight policemen beat and raped her repeatedly. The bloodied, traumatized girl was held for four more months, and, when finally released, found herself pregnant. "I wanted to kill myself," Gamboa said. "So many had raped me I thought I had a monster inside." She kept the baby, and, at sixteen, left for Lima to work as a house maid. The *sinchis* also took away Gamboa's brother. He was never seen again, among the war's first *desaparecidos*, or "disappeared ones." The battle in the Andes was becoming Latin America's latest so-called dirty war between Marxist insurgents and anti-Communist counterinsurgency forces in the mold of Argentina, Guatemala, and Chile. Both sides would commit many more terrible atrocities before it ended.

Augusta's fighters soon controlled the Pampas Valley. Only the larger towns had police stations. They were understaffed, and the officers seldom ventured far into the countryside. Policemen in the *Guardia Civil,* the main national force, made the equivalent of about fifty US dollars a month, small incentive to risk their lives. Some officers abandoned their posts, a few selling their guns to the guerrillas. Rebels stormed banks, police stations, and government buildings elsewhere across the Andes. "Shining Path Leads to Death," reported a *Los Angeles Times* story.

No one seemed to agree on just what to call the growing rebellion. The government and the Lima newspapers typically described the *senderistas* as "terrorists" or "subversives" (and sometimes, more colorfully, as "demented criminals," "murderous assassins," "fanatical hordes"). By contrast, the rebels invariably referred to themselves as the Peruvian Communist Party, shortened sometimes to *el Partido*, the Party. Foreign correspondents preferred Shining Path, a label with more exotic mystery. "Shining Path tells the Indians that one day they will rule again as the Inca did," *The Observer* speciously claimed. Abimael never discussed Peru's ancient kingdoms in his monologues about class struggle and the history of imperialism. His fighters taught villagers about Marx, Mao, and Chairman Gonzalo, not Manco Inca as the *Adventures of Tintin*–style reporting sometimes had it. It made for less colorful copy to relate that Shining Path was only a quite generic Communist insurgency.

Elena supervised Lima operations. Unlike the country-born Augusta, who could handle a gun, she had never held one before the war. Now she inventoried firearms captured from the police: a Smith & Wesson .44 caliber revolver; a MGP 8 mm automatic pistol; a FMK-3 submachine gun. When Abimael and Augusta went to China in 1967, they were told that a liberation movement should not seek weapons or other help from abroad. They did not want aid anyway from the "social imperialist" Soviet Union, which assisted other insurgencies in Latin America and Africa. That meant that those commandeered guns and their plentiful dynamite supply remained their only weapons. (One 1980 mine raid alone netted 1,520 dynamite cartridges.) Elena met with sympathetic electrical engineers who gave advice about vulnerable points in the power grid. The former Montessori teacher was becoming a self-taught expert in guerrilla warfare's tradecraft.

Their first action in Lima came only weeks after the Chuschi ballot-burning. In the twilight on June 13, 1980, about two hundred militants, all belonging to a Shining Path front organization, the Movement of Classist Workers and Laborers, set fire to the municipal building in the run-down San Martín de Porres district. They left leaflets announcing that the Peruvian Communist Party had begun its "brilliant people's war." A few days later, Elena's fighters hijacked a cargo truck near Lima's wholesale market. They distributed more flyers and, Marxist Robin Hoods, passed down cartons of food to the eager crowd. "Our people were long gone before the police got there," Elena said later.

A more unusual action drew attention, too. One morning late in 1980, Limans awoke to find mangy dead dogs dangling from lamp posts around the city. "Teng Tsiao Ping [Deng Xiaoping]: Son of a Bitch," read the sign tied to one poor mongrel. After Mao's death and the defeat of hardline Communists headed by the so-called Gang of Four, Deng had become China's new leader. He halted the Cultural Revolution and its crazed fervor, and was beginning to open his country to the market economy and an eventual future of Starbucks, Apple stores, and exploited migrant factory workers. Treachery to collectivizing socialist principles made Deng, in Shining Path's Maoist parlance, a "running dog of imperialism." In all likelihood, the Chinese leader cared little or nothing what some obscure Peruvian rebels thought, and mystified Limans had no clue about such Communist doctrinal disputes. The dead dogs did give the tabloids a grisly oddity to report, alongside a soap opera diva's latest fling and new evidence for an imminent extraterrestrial invasion.

The senderistas began bringing down the power lines in Lima and other cities. "To sabotage the electricity is very important," Abimael explained, because it "strikes hard at the Peruvian economy." His fighters wanted to destabilize everything so as to topple the state. A far-off boom and the ensuing city blackout, an *apagón*, would mark the war years in Lima like the droning Nazi warplanes over London during World War II. When the lights went down, they sometimes lit torches in the shape of a giant hammer and sickle above the darkened metropolis. An unimpressed rock band, the I Don't Know Who and I Don't Know How Manys, remixed a familiar Latin American lullaby about elephants on a spider web to poke fun at the blackouts. "*Un terrorista, dos terroristas,*" they sang, "*se balanceaban sobre una torre derrumbada*" ("one terrorist, two terrorists, balanced on a knocked-down electric tower").

The new Peruvian president, Fernando Belaúnde, downplayed the rebel threat at first. An aging architect and career politician with bushy white eyebrows, Belaúnde mistrusted the military, which had overthrown his first government back in 1968. He did not want to call out the troops. Instead the president tried to dismiss Shining Path as juvenile bomb-throwers or maybe a band of cattle rustlers. Hoping they might go away, he left the fight to the overmatched police. Newspaper cartoonists, never lacking for material in Peru, drew Belaúnde in a cloud, a distracted old man beyond the material world. His interior minister, José María de la Jara, assured Peruvians that Abimael Guzmán's capture "was imminent."

The murder of Benigno Medina announced Shining Path's readiness to spill blood. Its fighters would hang, machete, strangle, stone, and shoot many thousands more people in the coming years. How could a former philosopher professor and two intelligent, cultured women captain such a murderous rebellion? That exclusive Permanent Committee—Abimael, Augusta, Elena—did not themselves light the fuses or pull the triggers. Yet the party's governing troika issued the death orders. Augusta approved the Medina murder, and may have been there that night. The "masses demanded" the landowner's death, claimed Osmán Morote, the San Cristóbal rector's son and a Central Committee member. Medina had been tortured and killed for "repeated oppression of the people."

That Shining Path went to war showed their conventional Communist convictions. The coming socialist paradise would be worth the dreadful yet temporary bloodshed, reasoned Marxism's granite monument icons and now the *senderistas*. "We are prepared to sacrifice 300 million Chinese for victory of the world revolution," said Mao on a 1957 Moscow trip. That extreme carnage may sometimes be necessary to achieve greater goals was hardly a concept unique to Communism. When Abraham Lincoln, for example, sent thousands of young Union troops to the trenches at Petersburg, he knew most would die, and yet believed it to be the only way to defeat the Confederacy. (He supposedly spoke about the "awful arithmetic" of such decisions.) Lincoln's decision to escalate the war led to the end of slavery and lasting peace. The tragedy of Communism was that its bloodletting failed to produce the promised nirvana of prosperity and equality for humankind.

No weakness could be shown in the fight for socialism. When Shining Path firebombed a municipal building or killed a policeman, they were following the instructions of the most consecrated Marxist revolutionaries. "We can't expect to get anywhere," Lenin warned in 1918, "unless we resort to terrorism." The *senderistas* fully embraced the Cultural Revolution's exuberant Manicheanism to describe "crushing," "smashing," "strangling," "garroting," "pulverizing," and "annihilating" foes. To scrub away the pestilential vermin and black filth like Benigno Medina cleared the path to victory. "There was a point in my rebellion," the ex-Communist Italian activist Ignazio Silone wrote in 1950, "where hatred and love coincided." Didn't Augusta's brother say she fought for the love of the people? To overthrow the hated system would be her revolution's beautiful gift to the poor and the downtrodden.

Their war might not have happened had it not been for Augusta and Elena's passion for the revolution. Some wonder whether Abimael might have remained just another male leftist leader endlessly pontificating about a people's war in the abstract had it not been for his wife. "Augusta was the key person," says Carlos Váldez, an Ayacuchan who knew them both in the 1960s. "Without her Abimael would have just been a theoretician. She was a woman with charisma, which was needed to convince people. And she had two fundamental things Guzmán didn't: she knew Quechua and knew the local identity." Elena complemented Augusta with her organizational skills and aggressive conviction in armed revolution as the only path for Peru and the world. Both Elena and Augusta were doers. Once the war had begun, they would not be distracted by doubt, mercy, or second thoughts. Their decisiveness stamped itself on the insurrection in an irreversible way.

None of the top *senderista* leaders came from the oppressed classes themselves. The Central Committee was composed mostly of light-skinned, city-bred people like the party's ruling triumvirate. Even the one who knew the countryside best, Augusta, held to outdated Maoist caricatures about exploited serfs and evil landlords. A more feudal regime had indeed existed in the mountains as late as the 1960s. Some *hacendados* owned whole valleys and kept indigenous villagers in semi-indentured servitude. By the 1980s, though, peasant land invasions and Velasco's 1969 agrarian reform broke up most big estates. Benigno Medina, exploiter? His Ayzarca "estate" barely topped sixty acres. The *senderistas* tortured Medina to death for belonging to a "feudal oppressor landlord" class that mostly no longer existed in the highlands.

The party's foot soldiers did largely issue from more humble origins. As was true of Chuschi's Bernardino Azurza, many fighters had been recruited from San Cristóbal or area high schools. They came from copper-complexioned, Quechua-speaking families: the children of construction workers, tradesmen, and peasants. Becoming revolutionaries allowed these young militants to join a momentous cause in a postcolonial Peru where provincial origins and an Indian-looking face were no passport to advancement. "By joining Abimael's movement, young people became better than white; they went instantly from the bottom to the top of the social pyramid," journalist Robin Kirk explains. Having weapons gave new recruits a feeling of power and adventure in the bargain. According to one *senderista*, they sometimes set off explosions "just for the sake of blowing [something] up." Nobody seemed to notice how much their glorious party's organization replicated the hoary colonial hierarchies of the system it intended to destroy. A coterie of leaders from the more privileged Spanish-descended echelons of society gave marching orders to a poor brown army.

Young rebels received training from Augusta and other high-ranking cadre. When they headed to the *campo*, the countryside, the *senderistas* could communicate in Quechua with the locals. One peasant described their message:

> *Laqatam qapisun, llapa autoridadmi tukunqa llapa apum chink-anqa. Manam sallqa runapaq despreciokuna kanqachu.* ("The guerrillas and peasants will take the city and all its authorities and the rich will disappear. There will no longer be contempt for the high country peasants.")

Earlier twentieth-century political movements, as historian Jaymie Heilman notes, failed to remedy the neglect and disdain for Ayacuchan villagers. (That included the populist APRA party, the modernizing Popular Action party, and Velasco's military government.) Why not give the *senderistas* a chance? They promised justice for the poor—and seemed so confident in their triumph. Many villagers joined the "furious mob" at Ayzarca on Christmas Eve, according to a newspaper account.

The readiness to take life extended to animals. There had been the lamp post dog hangings, and an assault in 1982 on Huamanga University's All-pachaka farm, an hour outside Ayacucho. Allpachaka bred improved cattle to make cheese for export, which made it a tool of market capitalism in *senderista* eyes. According to Antonio Díaz Martínez, a San Cristóbal agronomist and a friend of Abimael, the farm "follow(ed) the Prussian junker road" (a reference to Lenin's theory about capitalism's route to supplanting feudalism). The rebels would destroy Allpachaka to hand the land over to peasants.

One day in August 1982, the *senderistas* descended upon the farm. They plunged knives into the heads and necks of the panicked cattle. "We killed as many as we could," one young fighter said. Some village women wept at the sight. "*Waqcha animalkuna*—the poor animals," they pleaded in Quechua. "Why kill them that way?" At last, the *senderista* recalled, "we stopped, but we had already killed one-fourth of them, about eighty." They set fire to the farm buildings before leaving.

The most famous Peruvian writer, still in his early forties, read about the attack. Mario Vargas Llosa had just published a six-hundred-page novel, *The War of the End of the World*, about a wild-eyed nineteenth-century rebellion in Brazil's own backcountry. Was something like that now arising in his native Peru? Vargas Llosa based a scene in his later *Death in the Andes* on the Allpachaka slaughter. He described the cattle going "mad, stampeding, running into each other, falling, getting in each other's way, blinded and stupefied by panic."

––––––

Few could deny Shining Path's successes by 1982. By then, the rebels had executed over 1,800 actions between burned municipalities, toppled electrical towers, and raided police stations. They had the police on the run not only in Ayacucho, but in Huancavelica, Andahuaylas, Apurímac, and Junín, the neighboring regions. Their party-run "Popular Committees" governed liberated villages. A war of national liberation, Mao warned, could take decades to wear down the enemy enough to claim victory. The *senderistas* were advancing much faster than Abimael imagined at the start. After only two years at arms, his fighters controlled a big swath of the Andes.

These successes emboldened Abimael to think big for himself. The highest promise of Communism was equality, and yet, paradoxically, the victory of revolutionaries always resulted in the rule of a single strong man. In *Animal Farm*, the most famous work of anti-Communist satire, George Orwell portrayed Stalin as the pig Napoleon, and lampooned the justificatory reasoning at work. "No one believes more firmly than Comrade Napoleon that all animals are equal," Napoleon's lieutenant, Squealer, explains to the other farm animals. "He would be only too happy to let you make your decisions for yourselves. But sometimes you might make the wrong decisions, comrades, and then where should we be?" In death, the great Communist leader was laid to rest like a Catholic saint in his own mausoleum. Both Lenin and Mao's embalmed bodies lie in state even today. Lesser Communist leaders like Cuba's Fidel Castro, North Korea's Kim Il Sung, and Albania's Enver Hoxha enjoyed their own personality cults in life and death.

That Abimael had such ambitions became evident at the party's Second National Conference in May 1982. The Central Committee and fifty other party members gathered at a Lima house, arriving separately to avoid suspicion. These meetings usually began by everyone standing to sing "The Internationale," the Communist anthem. "We will become brothers over the conception of the proletariat; over revolutionary violence," Abimael said in his opening welcome.

Every party assembly reserved some hours for a *balance*, a stock-taking to assess the war's progress. Only a few weeks before, they had mounted a successful assault to free imprisoned comrades from the Ayacucho prison. There were supposed to be simultaneous jailbreaks in Jaén, a jungle town, and several other places. But the Jaén Shining Path commander deemed it too risky. The Ayacucho *senderistas* went ahead anyway, making a first try on the night of February 28. Their plan broke down when the getaway pickup truck failed to arrive in time. Four *senderistas* died. Abimael gave the Ayacucho commander, Comrade César, new orders by phone the next day. *Do it again, right away. The same plan, the same fighters. At whatever price.* The police would not expect a second attack so soon after the first one, Abimael correctly guessed. César and his detachment freed seventy-eight *senderistas* in less than half an hour, and the escape made national headlines. Two policemen died in the assault. Their fellow officers took revenge the next day by shooting three wounded *senderistas* in their hospital beds, and, finding a fourth about to go into surgery, ripping out his IV to strangle him with it. The jailbreak and its ugly aftermath forced the resignation of Belaúnde's interior minister.

Freeing the prisoners had not been enough for Abimael, who faulted César for not succeeding on the first try. "When Comrade César reports," he said now at the meeting, "he presents himself as the hero, a knight in shining armor rescuing damsels in distress." In reality, the "failure to annihilate the enemy forces" from the start "betrayed the basic principles of war." An outgoing college dropout from the southern town of Tacna, César stammered explanations, but others denounced his "vacillation," forcing the young commander into the expected self-criticism. "I was wrong to disagree with our wise secretary general," César admitted. He seemed genuinely distraught about failing to meet party expectations.

Then Abimael turned to Comrade Alberto, a Central Committee member and the man who ignored the order to storm the Jaén jail. Alberto claimed there had been no good way to retreat from the town. Abimael accused Alberto of "individualism," placing personal over party interests. During a break, a few *senderistas* complained among themselves about Abimael being too harsh. When Abimael discovered this, he grew still more annoyed. It breached discipline to discuss party affairs out of session—and even more to criticize him, the secretary general, behind his back. He called the unhappy Alberto and his defenders to account when the conference readjourned.

"These [comrades]," Abimael said, "have ridiculous body language. They even look upset when you serve them a cup of coffee."

Facing resistance never surprised Abimael. The correct proletarian line, Mao taught, would always be threatened by dark rightism in its "opportunist," "revisionist," and "reactionary" manifestations. Those who fell into counterrevolutionary error had to admit to their mistakes, and, afterwards, prove repentance through self-criticism (and be expelled from the party as a last resort). Abimael moved now to put down the deviationists.

"I'm tired of this!" he said. "[Alberto and his backers] should speak frankly and without antagonism. They should put their hand to their chest and not confuse weakness for fighting resolve."

Abimael was only getting going. "The struggle is just and correct and the party, as its organizing body, is even more so." There could be nothing more holy than the party. "Some people don't know what the party really is. The reactionaries speak despotically against the party and its Guiding Thought, and four idiots do the same. Our first obligation is defending the party."

Abimael went a step farther. "I've been intentionally patient, [but] no one can deny that the Leadership is what directs the Armed Struggle." There was no mistaking the message: Abimael *was* the party. Any dissenter would be branded a rightist opportunist or worse. No one dared to question his leadership again, at least in meetings like this.

Now Abimael went in for the kill. "They want to go against the secretary general. They think he's alone," he said, speaking about himself in the third person. "Is the secretary general alone? The Political Committee is with him. The Political Bureau is with him. Two-thirds of the Central Committee and the party's left [the truest Communists] are with him." The dissidents could only bow down before Abimael and his revolutionary stewardship.

The groveling began with Alberto. He vowed to "learn from Comrade Gonzalo" and renounce individualism. Before the war, Abimael had been "Comrade Álvaro," but he then chose Gonzalo, a German name for "warrior" in etymology. "Learning from Comrade Gonzalo is key. It guarantees the triumph of the Revolution," Alberto submitted.

His repentant supporters repeated the same nostrums.

Elena jumped in too.

"I criticize my comrades who have committed errors," she said. "Our struggle is clear, firm, and correct. We must fulfill our role." The meeting continued for some time, the criticizing and self-criticizing, without Abimael saying a word. Then he moved on to the next agenda item at last.

"We must never tire," Abimael said, "of learning and teaching."

That day heralded Abimael's elevation to full cult status. Until then, he had been "Comrade Gonzalo," but from then it would be "Chairman Gonzalo," the infallible party leader. Their guiding ideology, once "Marxist-Leninist-Maoist Thought," became "Maoist-Leninist-Gonzalo Thought"—or simply "Gonzalo Thought." Abimael's two commanders, Augusta and Elena, endorsed and even encouraged his deification. They recognized his founding role in the party, and, pragmatically, felt their revolution could benefit from having a mythologized chieftain. "Abimael wasn't more intelligent than us," Elena said. "But every movement needs a representative, a face—

it's a law of history." Augusta apparently coined the phrase *Pensamiento Gonzalo*, Gonzalo Thought—and the new slogan, "Learn from Chairman Gonzalo." Hadn't she told the disappointed Alberto Morote that her new husband was "the one to lead the revolution?" She believed that still almost two decades later.

The Gonzalo cult enshrined Guzmán as the greatest living Communist. He was the new prophet, it declared, and had been chosen to lead the world proletarian revolution towards its inevitable victory. The "social imperialist" Soviets had long ago shown their black revisionist colors. Following Mao's death, the *senderistas* had hoped the so-called Gang of Four, led by Mao's widow Jiang Xing, would rule China, staying faithful to the Cultural Revolution's missionary radicalism. Instead, the "running dog" Deng initiated his market-oriented reforms and China's opening to the West. That left Abimael as Mao's true successor, or, as his followers described him, the "Fourth Sword of Marxism," after Marx, Lenin, and the Great Helmsman. The *senderistas* began to make paintings, wall hangings, etchings in the best hagiographic Dear Leader tradition. (By one estimate the Chinese Communist Party printed more than a billion Mao posters over the decades.) These official images slimmed Abimael and smoothed his skin. He was the great warrior-professor in his coat and glasses. One pamphlet showed a gigantic Abimael—the validating visages of Lenin, Marx, and Mao in the top corner—standing over the globe to plant the flag in Ayacucho. The iconography indicated unsubtly that Chairman Gonzalo was going from the Andes to captaining the Communist movement worldwide.

It remained Abimael's absolute conviction that the laws of history and reason assured their triumph. "Marxism is an ideology and [also] a science," he said. In truth, clearly enough, the *senderistas* had been swept up in the madness of their mounting illusions. Castrating a dead farmer? The quivering cattle carcasses? The invincibility of Marxist-Leninist-Maoist-Gonzalo

Thought? They could boast advances, but, because President Belaúnde did not want to call in the army, the government had not really begun to fight. Their small army faced long odds even in its fringe country. To think that Abimael would lead the planet's oppressed masses to revolutionary victory was hallucinatory in the extreme. A growing "New Left" in Latin America was embracing peaceful organizing and the ballot box as the path to social democracy. (And dissident British Marxists had already by the late 1950s challenged Stalinist orthodoxies after the Soviet invasion of Hungary and new revelations about the gulags and labor camps.) Abimael and his fighters had committed themselves instead to an unreconstructed Marxist ideology of armed struggle that would be obsolete within a decade. Their country would pay the price.

Nothing cooled their burning convictions in the war's first years, not even imprisonment. After the Ayacucho jailbreak, the government reopened El Frontón to house captured rebels. This was Peru's Alcatraz, an ocean rock prison just off the coast of Callao. That did not stop the *senderistas* from converting their cellblock into a recruitment center and training ground, collectivizing chores like washing and cooking to model a miniature social- ist utopia. They supplemented their diet by netting fish off the rocks, and, when a sea lion mistakenly waddled into the cellblock, clubbed it to death for stew. The *senderistas* at El Frontón looked like Peru itself—Indian, fair- skinned, mestizo, a few blacks, some old and most younger, many in their teens. Every morning, they rose to chant and sing with thunderous preci- sion. "Gonzalo is armed struggle," one anthem announced:

> *Gonzalo! The masses roar*
> *And the Andes shake.*
> *They express the burning passion*
> *A sure and steeled faith.*

One morning late in 1982, a journalist came across to El Frontón on the police boat. It was *Caretas*'s Gustavo Gorriti, and, as he watched, two hundred Shining Path prisoners lined up in formation for breakfast. They raised fists to chant more party slogans, and, afterwards, toured Gorriti around the cellblock. A group of the men surrounded Gorriti afterwards. "At this moment," a young militant said, "we are the vanguard, the lighthouse of the world revolution." Gorriti was struck by their discipline and their stony fervor. *These people kill*, that Ayacucho policeman had told him. Gorriti sounded a warning in his report about El Frontón. A democracy could "successfully defend itself against a fanatical minority," he wrote. "But now the worst mistake that could be made would be to underestimate them."

CHAPTER SIX

The Lynching

Gustavo Gorriti was fifteen when his older sister fell sick with cancer. Edith was serious and kind-hearted, with a gift for the sciences. She won a scholarship to Moscow's Lomonosov University in 1961. Gustavo Sr. and Dora were nervous about sending their teenage daughter halfway across the world. As old-school Communists, however, they placed their trust in the Soviet Union and the reported advances in science and technology there. The whole family went to see Edith off on her great journey. Gustavo Sr. and Dora could not hold back a few tears. It was a long, expensive trip to Moscow. They did not expect to see their daughter again until she finished her degree.

But Edith's stay in the Soviet Union lasted little more than a year. She had been diagnosed there with cervical cancer. The Moscow doctors performed a hysterectomy, but Edith returned to Lima weak and pale. She was scathing about the Soviet system. "It's a bunch of corrupt old men, Gustavo," Edith told her younger brother. "They drive around eating caviar in black limousines while there's no food in the stores." Lomonosov was a run-down, second-rate university by Edith's description. She would not go back under any circumstances.

Her health improved back home. The doctors declared her cancer in remission, and, encouragingly, Edith put on new muscle at the gym. She wanted to resume her medical studies, this time at Montreal's McGill University. Just a few weeks before her scheduled departure, she went in for the university's required medical exam. A scan revealed a new tumor. The doctors operated, but the cancer spread anyway. Edith died at nineteen.

Gustavo Sr. and Dora never recovered from their daughter's death. The Soviet specialists apparently botched Edith's care, and, after that, Dora, the teenage Communist resistance fighter, wanted no more to do with leftist politics. Gustavo Sr. had lost his daughter, but he would not give up on the Soviet Union. The former congressman kept his membership in the pro-Soviet Peruvian Communist Party. He explained away Edith's bad experience as an exception. *Hadn't Stalin's Red Army kept the Nazis from world domination?* Gustavo Sr. said, rightly enough. That became his last good argument as the Soviet Union's corrupt tyranny gradually eroded its credibility at home and abroad.

Edith's bad experience left her younger brother skeptical about state socialism's shiny promises. As a student, Gustavo admired Che Guevara and Cuba's young fighters, and yet he never joined the regulation Marxist groups. When he began reporting on Shining Path in 1981, he saw that the *senderistas* fought, as his parents once had, for a better society. Gustavo also understood, after Edith's cynical tales about the Soviet system, how far wrong that fight could go. Clearly, Shining Path was a dangerously fundamentalist example of old-school Marxist bellicosity. At El Frontón Gustavo had seen firsthand how the insurgency had metastized into dogmatism, violence, and cultishness under its fugitive cynosure's commanding eye.

By late 1982, the *senderistas* had gained yet more strength in Ayacucho, the launching point for their rebellion. Many locals sympathized at least some with the rebels, Gustavo had noted on his trip there. Their uprising, after all, possessed a homegrown flavor—an army of local youth led by a former San Cristóbal professor. When the anti-terrorism police commandos, the *sinchis*, arrived in 1981, they only alienated Ayacuchans by raping, shooting, and terrorizing. The 1982 funeral of Edith Lagos—a young *senderista* militant killed in a highway shootout—became a massive rally. A crowd of over 10,000 people shouted anti-government slogans behind the red flag–draped coffin. "The armed people will win! The people will never forget spilled blood!" The *senderistas* seemed to capture the city's self-avowed spirit of rebellion and independence. "An Ayacuchan can't be bought," a ballad said. "He bares his breast when danger arrives."

Gustavo received his editor's approval, early in 1983, for a second Ayacucho reporting trip. Only a few weeks before, President Belaúnde had finally sent in the troops, placing the city and surrounding mountains under military law. Army platoons stomped down the cobblestoned streets:

> *Yes sir, here we are!*
> *Little terrorist*
> *if I find you*
> *I will eat your head.*
> *One. Two.*
> *Three. Four.*

The brown-skinned young soldiers were scrawny, scared, and ill-trained, despite their bravado. (Wealthy families bought their sons exemptions from Peru's military service requirement.) That they had been trained to fight a conventional war against the hated Ecuadorians placed them at further disadvantage. Here the troops faced an elusive guerrilla insurgency with the Andean peaks for a fortress.

Once more, Gustavo boarded the dawn flight to Ayacucho. He was again accompanied by the Ayacuchan-born *Caretas* photographer, Óscar Medrano, who had also gone with Gustavo to El Frontón. (A Medrano picture of captive *senderistas* on a dock there became one of the war's most haunting images.) A *cholo*, Medrano proudly called himself. That label described poor migrants with some Indian blood. Medrano had risen from darkroom assistant to well-known photographer at Peru's biggest magazine. A likeable and talented man in his mid-thirties, he had a country boy's comfort in the highlands. He paused sometimes on mountain hikes so Gustavo could catch his breath, although, mindful of the former judo champion's pride, pretending to be the one needing the rest. Medrano made friends everywhere, among them with his high school soccer teammate, Osmán Morote, the future *senderista* leader. "I was just a poor boy but a good player, so Osmán asked me to be on the team," Medrano recalled.

It so happened that Medrano had struck up a friendship with Ayacucho's top general. Clemente Noel held the title of "Military-Political Commander" for the big mountain zone under military rule. When Medrano was in Ayacucho on an earlier assignment, he brought the general a courtesy copy of the latest *Caretas* (not mentioning that he'd also brought one for his *senderista* friend Osmán Morote). The older general was the prototypical career officer, with a barking voice and a drinker's bulbous nose. He invited Medrano to stay for a whiskey, apparently lonely for company. They smoked, drank, and played cards.

Now that acquaintance would come in handy. After he and Gustavo checked into their hotel, Medrano received a phoned invitation from Noel to come over for a visit. "*Sí, mi general,*" Medrano said, "Yes, my general. I'll be there right away." He brought Gustavo, and they took a taxi to Los Cabitos, the army base near the airport. Noel offered the men a drink, and, after a bit, told the two *Caretas* reporters that his men would be helicoptering the next morning into Huaychao. This hamlet in the heights above

the Huanta Valley had been in the news. According to reports, the villagers there had killed seven *senderistas*. President Belaúnde, desperate for
good news, acclaimed them as brave patriots. Now Noel wanted to airlift in
food and medicine for the Huaychainos. He needed a Quechua translator
to communicate with villagers. Would Medrano do it? "You can take pictures," the general said.

There was only one problem. "You," Noel told Gustavo, "can't come."
There wouldn't be room on the helicopter, the general said, although Gustavo suspected it had more to do with the military man's mistrust of journalists. Medrano could make magic with his camera, but he did not want
to face the burly *Caretas* publisher, Enrique Zileri, if they came back only
with pictures and no story. "It'd be better, my general, if the gringo goes
too," offered Medrano. A *Caretas* story, Gustavo added, would show how
poor peasants had rebuffed the *subversivos*, the subversives, to side instead
with government forces. When Gustavo went to the bathroom, Noel smiled
conspiratorially at Medrano.

"OK," the aging general said. "The gringo can go. Just make him sweat
a little by not telling him until the last minute."

At four o'clock the next morning, Medrano roused Gustavo from his
hotel bed.

"Noel said ok, and to come early to Los Cabitos."

They headed over to board the helicopter.

———

Narciso Sulca had spent his whole life—all twelve years of it—in Huaychao.
A talkative and adventurous boy by nature, he waited some nights until his
parents fell asleep, then shook his little brother Leandro awake. The boys
would slip out of the family's hut into the enveloping dark. It was usually
too foggy to see the stars from Huaychao, so Narciso and Leandro headed
farther up into the mountains. Their village and some fifty other hamlets

scattered over the moors of Iquicha above 12,000 feet. Nowhere else in the hemisphere did human beings live at such high altitude. Narciso and Leandro, only ten, wore peasant sandals, ponchos, and *chullos,* the ear-flapped Andean woolen caps. They barely noticed the oxygen-deprived cold in the black night.

At a promontory the two boys lay back to gaze at the twinkling sky. "*Mayu,*" Leandro said, pointing out a constellation that meandered like a river. His brother traced the Big Dipper with his finger—"*Wisslla,*" he said. Sometimes the boys spotted an airplane's lights crossing above. Their parents had explained that these were *latapisqokuna,* "tin birds" in their native Quechua. Where were they going? Did people stand in them like on buses? Narciso made a toy airplane from the clay by the creek.

Sometimes, however, the older Narciso left his brother at home. He would join other teenage Huaychainos at *pakapaka,* a sort of spin-the-bottle game where girls hid in caves and boys headed out to find them. It was usually innocent enough, but sometimes a boy tried to force himself upon a girl. That had happened to Juana, Narciso's aunt, who could not fight off a young man from a nearby village. When Juana told her family, she had to marry her rapist to hide the shame of premarital sex. She left him eventually, to raise her small daughter alone.

Narciso stayed out of trouble. He was the oldest among Isidro Sulca and Francisca Rimachi's four children. A peasant boy had to help out at an early age, and, at seven, Narciso was out herding the family's llamas and sheep. When he and Leandro got a little older, they rose before dawn to help their father pack the llamas for the weekly outdoor market across the moor. The two boys and their father set out under the silent peaks. Their beasts carried sacks of purple, yellow, and white potatoes as well as the shriveled freeze-dried ones for soup, *chuño* (which Huaychainos made by leaving the tubers overnight in the cold). "Five hundred distinct varieties of potato flower on the terraces above the abyss," the mid-twentieth-century Peruvian novelist

José María Arguedas wrote. The tuber was apparently first domesticated in the area around Lake Titicaca about eight thousand years ago. Every french fry owes its existence to ancient Andean farmers.

At the outdoor market down in a canyon village, Narciso would go around to see the peddler's wares and perhaps buy a hard candy. One Friday, a few strangers appeared. They wore peasant garb and spoke Quechua, and, quite suddenly, one loudly demanded the attention of the marketgoers. They belonged to the Peruvian Communist Party, the young man announced. "We will destroy the government of the rich and make a government for the poor." Most people ignored him, but Narciso listened for a bit. He decided it wasn't worth his time, drifting off towards some local girls. They had brimmed their bowler hats with the scarlet primrose of the unmarried.

The strangers showed up again a few weeks later. Narciso had heard stories around Huaychao, whispers really. The strangers supposedly roamed the cliffs with guns and knives, sometimes coming to farmhouses to ask for food and shelter. So this time, Narciso paid closer attention.

"The rich, the villagers who are in favor of the government, the authorities," the same young man said, "we will remove and finish them all off."

A little crowd of villagers had gathered to listen now. The strangers asked if they had encountered any soldiers yet. No one said a word. Well, the leader said, if a patrol arrived, the villagers should be on guard, not giving any help. But no one should worry, he added. The party would protect the poor and shoot the soldiers. Their leader, Chairman Gonzalo, was the "Teacher of Teachers, the Eagle of the Andes." He guaranteed victory.

Guns? Soldiers? Shootouts? It sounded too far-fetched to believe. Then, another Friday, the strangers came again. But rather than more long speeches, they dragged out one villager, forcing him to face the crowd. This "traitor," one said, had "badmouthed the Party." The strangers ripped off the man's shirt and whipped him with a *chicote*, a blunt rawhide whip. Narciso learned that they executed him later.

Narciso didn't quite know what to think. Who wouldn't want justice? Everyone knew that the rich had chests of gold coins, while poor villagers went hungry if the rains did not come. A revolution, as much as the twelve-year-old understood the word, sounded appealing, but Narciso was unsure about its specifics. It had been rumored that the strangers wanted to remove their village leaders, including the *varayoq*, or staff carriers, whose silver-capped wooden canes symbolized their authority. Narciso's father was Huaychao's clerk, and an uncle, Lucas, was the lieutenant governor, the villager appointed by the government as its local representative. What did they ever do except keep Huaychao safe? No, Narciso thought, best to keep his distance from the fierce strangers and their Chairman Gonzalo.

The *senderistas* under Augusta La Torre's command already controlled the Pampas Valley a hundred miles to the south. Only now, late in 1982, had the guerrillas deployed north into Narciso's Iquichan highland area. According to the plan agreed upon at their Second National Conference, they would *batir el campo*, or "churn up the countryside." That meant "cleansing the countryside, incendiarizing it, removing all the political authorities and landlords, eliminating all government functionaries," Abimael explained. The *senderistas* had not made much headway in Iquicha's cloud villages so far. Townspeople might look down upon them as *chutos*, or savages, but the Iquichans did not like being ordered around. They could turn ferocious, in fact, when pushed too far. A century and a half before, after the Spanish Viceroy's forces had been defeated at Quinua in 1824, the Huaychainos and other contrarian Iquichan peasants revolted against the new creole government. With "only Stones and sticks," according to one account of their short-lived yet bloody rebellion, the peasants "have several times defeated those who called themselves invincible, leaving us the field covered with arms and cadavers." The Iquichans had been among the enraged villagers who slung rocks at the police in the 1969 anti-government protests.

The arriving *senderistas* found some support in Iquichan hamlets.

But Narciso's Huaychao had resisted overtures. "They were ignorant about everything," a *senderista* commander complained later. "The only thing they wanted was to be left alone. They never received us well, didn't like being asked for clothes or blankets." But the *senderistas* persisted. Narciso and his family heard stories about the rebels elsewhere strangling recalcitrant villagers to death. They feared trouble soon.

One night early in 1983, the Huaychainos assembled to discuss how to deal with the *senderistas*, or *tuta puriqkuna*, nightwalkers, as they called them. Narciso's father Isidro and the others crouched around by kerosene lamplight in the village assembly hall. Many villagers chewed coca leaf, an ancestral mountain tradition, and, now and then, spit out green juice like baseball players do their chaw. After some preliminaries, an old man, Santos Quispe, rose to speak, and got to the matter at hand: the growing rebel presence. "Nothing good will come of this," he said. "But we must try to stop them." Several *varayoq* spoke in agreement, and so did Lucas Ccente, the lieutenant governor, and other village leaders. Each man and woman signed, or, since most could not write, placed a thumbprint on an agreement to keep out the *tuta puriqkuna*. The villagers headed home through the fog that welled up from the jungle day and night. *Yakusiki*, wet-asses, other Iquichans called Huaychainos.

Some days later, a rebel detachment descended towards Huaychao from the ridge. The *senderistas* had about fifty fighters camped in the peaks, but, not expecting any trouble, their commander sent only eight fighters to do some preaching about the revolution that day. The rebels were thin, dirty, and ragged, yet also tough-looking with the hollow eyes of ascetics. They carried guns, knives, and a few dynamite bombs. One *senderista* held up their party's red flag. A young woman led them.

Narciso was in the fields with the animals.

He saw the *senderistas* head into the village.

"Long live the armed struggle and Chairman Gonzalo!" they shouted.

Narciso ran home to sound the warning. His father, Isidro, had them bar the door. Then he left to join other villagers down by the chapel. Strangely, even as a toddler, Narciso had never been able to cry. He wanted to now. "I was sure I wouldn't see my father again," he recalled.

A few Huaychainos greeted the rebels.

"*Yaykukamuy, yaykukamuy*—Welcome, welcome!"

One woman brought them some sugary tea.

It was a stalling tactic, allowing villagers time to arrive from their farmhouses. Then they would have the numbers to take on the *senderistas* as had been pacted at their assembly. At last towards afternoon, Huaychainos and the *senderistas* gathered in the assembly hall.

The woman leader spoke first.

She was seventeen, but assured and unsmiling.

"Comrades," she said, "the masses led by President Gonzalo will be victorious." The party would appoint a "Popular Committee" to oversee village affairs in the meantime. "There will be no more thieves, witches, or fathers abandoning their families."

Santos Quispe, the old man, rose to reply.

"Our village already has its own authorities."

"You are with the reactionaries," the young *senderista* said coldly, "an enemy of the revolution."

"Remember who you are talking to," someone replied. "This is our village."

The Huaychainos were tiny people, really, none taller than 5'4" or so. They lived on little besides boiled potatoes and some shredded mutton and guinea pig. Their calloused hands had a farmer's dirt under every fingernail. The men wore *chullos* under their felt hats for extra protection against the cold.

"You're just *suwatakuna,* thieves!" one man shouted. "You're not the real law."

The *senderistas* reached for their weapons. They could not permit such defiance. But the Huaychainos pounced first. Several picked up the stones they had been sitting on to fling at the nearest rebel. One villager pinned down the teenaged commander. She was trying to light a bomb, ready to blow up herself and everyone else rather than surrender.

One rebel escaped back into the hills. The Huaychainos dragged the other seven outside to the *juez rumi*, the "rock of justice," the place for discipline and punishment. Men tied their scrawny captives to the oblong rock.

The atmosphere turned ugly. It was too much, the harangues, the bomb, the *senderista* threats. Now men shouted to kill the *suwatakuna*, the thieves, and others crowded fiercely around the *juez rumi*.

Not everyone wanted the prisoners to die.

"Killing isn't easy," pleaded Juana Cabezas, Narciso's aunt. "People die hard!"

"Don't kill them," said Isidro, his father.

They were a minority.

Other villagers grabbed ropes. They strangled the *senderistas* one by one between blood, vomit, and screams. "Surely now, they will kill us all!" a woman cried when it was done at last.

Some men dug a hole to dump the bodies. Everyone recognized, once the atmosphere calmed some, their perilous predicament. How long before Chairman Gonzalo's wrathful warriors returned for revenge? The Huaychainos knew that no one would come to their rescue, at least any time soon.

"The police, the army didn't care what happened to us," Narciso said later.

Feeling alone in the world was nothing new for Huaychainos. "Let me cry through this rain," pleaded a vicuña, the llama's wild relative, in a village ballad. Until 1975, the Huaychainos had been serfs, *peones*, who labored for a big landowner, Juan Juscamaita. The land belonged to them now, but little else—no money, no road, no clean water, and, when drought or blight struck, no food. Few even spoke good Spanish. It was hard to imagine a more unforgiving place than this neglected village at the roof of the world.

Their only hope lay in banding together. They had horsewhips and wooden spears, and, of course, their *huaracas*, the peasant slings of the kind with which David slew Goliath at Hebron. Men used them to hunt vizcachas, a mountain chinchilla with a small mouthful of meat on it. They could whirl the rock to its target at over a hundred miles an hour. And now, too, the villagers had an old Winchester rifle and a shotgun, captured from the *senderistas*. One Huaychaino, an army veteran, knew how to handle the weapons. On his advice, the villagers agreed not just to sit back, vulnerable to assault at any time. They would send out men to patrol the village fields and mountains. Narciso, age twelve, followed behind them some nights. He was becoming a child soldier of a kind.

The villagers also sought help. A delegation went to Huanta, eight hours away on foot, to ask for police protection. Other Huaychainos headed off to seek support from area villages: Carhuahurán, Purus, Chaca, Upaiccpampa. In one hamlet, Uchuraccay, an hour away, the villagers had already pacted to fight the *senderistas*. Their letter to Huanta's subprefect explained that decision in peasant Spanish. "Sir Subprifecture of the Probinc of Huanta," it read, "Wee have accorded in Geniral Assembly and every community meber have rose not to agree with the tirrorists." Each village was its own little universe, and yet Iquicha had united in the last great war, the revolt to restore the Spanish king. The Huaychainos hoped that other Iquichans would rise against the *senderistas*.

The rebels, meanwhile, regrouped, readying new assaults. They camped in the heights, in the rocks beneath Mt. Rasuwillka. At over 15,000 feet, its peak knifed above the moors, the region's tallest mountain and its most potent spirit divinity. *Apu Rasuwillka,* Lord Rasuwillka, Narciso's father called it. Although they might say prayers to the Virgin Mary and sometimes attend Catholic mass in Ayacucho, most villagers still saw the peaks, rocks, and lakes as living beings. A medicine man, the *qampiq*, might summon *Apu Rasuwillka* to heal a sick child, or, for the right price, to cast a malevolent spell on an enemy. The *senderista* camped in Mt. Rasuwillka's heights for the commanding view, but their menacing presence fed the perception of the *apu's* power. An earlier tale about *Apu Rasuwillka* supposedly bringing down an airplane circulated once again. The passengers' cries still echoed in the rocks, the story said.

One day, some *senderistas* ambushed patrolling Huaychainos, flinging another crude bomb at them. It detonated so loudly that Huaychao, more than two miles away, "*katatatarunku*—trembled," as one villager put it. The twenty patrollers, startled yet unharmed, chased the *senderistas* up a mountainside, where the outnumbered rebels dug in behind some rocks.

Narciso had been tending his livestock not far down the mountain. He grabbed his *huaraca* and, abandoning his animals, scrambled up to join the men. The older ones yelled at the boy to go back home. In the old days, his father had once told him, Huaychao's *yakusiki*, "wet-asses," sometimes faced off in drunken ritualized warfare against Uchuraccay's *rumi maki*, "stone-throwers." Back then a villager might suffer a bloody nose or a broken bone. Now it might be a bullet in the head.

"Get down, boy!" yelled the patrol leader. "You're going to get yourself killed."

Narciso looked around and saw that all the men had taken cover, many behind boulders.

"Miserable plate-lickers of Belaúnde. You will be pulverized, miserable dogs," the *senderistas* shouted.

"Delinquents. Criminals. Pig shit spawn," the Huaychainos yelled back.

At last a patroller, the army veteran, wounded a *senderista* with the captured Winchester rifle. The others fled, carrying their injured comrade back up Mt. Rasuwillka.

Several days later, the village delegation returned from Huanta. They brought with them a platoon of the anti-terrorism police, the *sinchis*. On the way to Huaychao, other Iquichan peasants had come out to meet the commandos, who warily gripped their automatic rifles. The villagers offered potatoes and broad beans, and, even though the *sinchis* did not understand their Quechua, pled for protection from the *tirrukukuna,* the terrorists. Once the *sinchis* arrived in Huaychao, the village leaders made welcoming speeches, then invited the *sinchis* to eat. They had some men dig up the putrefying corpses of the dead *senderistas* to show the police after the meal.

The *sinchis* had killed plenty.

"Well done!" the *sinchi* commander congratulated the Huaychainos. "That's the way to defend yourselves."

But the *sinchis* left before nightfall. They did not especially want to tangle with the *senderistas*, and peasant lives did not matter much to them anyway. The villagers would have to find a way to protect themselves.

The Huaychainos had no choice but to keep up defenses. A few days later, village patrollers captured six teenage boys and, ominously, brought them to the *juez rumi,* the justice rock. "*Tuta puriq suwata wañuchiy—* kill the thieving terrorists!" several men shouted. They were drunk and the air thick with danger and dread about a new attack.

Only a coincidence saved the teenagers. Narciso's uncle, Fortunato, saw that one was his godson Mardonio, the child of friends in a village some hours away. Why not keep the boys prisoner until they got the facts straight? Fortunato said. It was agreed to spare their lives for the moment.

No one knew what to think now. Could the six boys be *senderistas*? Had they been advance scouts? Green military helicopters circled Huaychao some days, though without landing. One fired down some machine-gun rounds, probably mistaking the villagers for *senderistas*. The only certainty seemed to be the nightwalkers' return, sooner or later. They had killed three Huaychainos in hit-and-run raids over the last few weeks.

Then, finally, a helicopter landed. Narciso had never seen anything like the Bell 212 and its roaring rotors bending back the grass in their gale. He watched two soldiers, rifles at the ready, jump down from the *cachi-cachi*, or "dragonfly," as villagers had dubbed helicopters. An Andean-featured man with a camera followed, then a burly white one with pen and notepad at the ready: Óscar Medrano and Gustavo Gorriti. They had come to report the story.

The villagers streamed in from their fields to greet the arriving journalists. They carried sticks and slings, a white banner, and several Peruvian flags, declaring allegiance to the government. Their faces, as Gustavo wrote after-wards, "bore the obvious signs of extreme poverty and privation, as well as suspicion and anxiety." Did these isolated peasants know what a journalist was? The Huaychainos pressed around their city visitors with their fears, stories, and cries for protection. Medrano took pictures with his Nikon F3, and, before long, had posed the *varayoq*, the staff holders, by the grave of the *senderistas* for some shots. The two soldiers unloaded a machine gun tripod from the helicopter as a precaution should the *senderistas* choose to attack. An army medic set up a table. He attended to many villagers, mainly handing out aspirin, though rehydration salts for a shrunken baby brought forward swaddled like a mummy in wool wraps.

The villagers produced one of their teenage captives. It was Mardonio, Fortunato's godson, who was wretched and blinded by the sunlight after having been kept prisoner in a muddy hole. Gustavo saw that the boy had been beaten with "a terribly bruised and swollen face." The scornful army medic did not want to treat a possible terrorist, but Gustavo urged him to check for broken ribs. A few villagers, brandishing their whips, murmured again for Mardonio to be put to death. Gustavo and the soldiers told the vil-lagers to instead bring all their captive boys down to Huanta to hand them over to the authorities, which they did some days later. (Eventually Mardonio returned to lead anti-*senderista* patrols.) His report from Huaychao and Medrano's photographs would headline the next week's *Caretas*.

Gustavo pondered the significance of Huaychao. If other Andean hamlets turned against the *senderistas*, it could ruin their plan to encircle the cities from the countryside. Few signs yet existed of more widespread peasant backlash against Shining Path, as far as Gustavo was aware. Then again, a band of unknowns had ridden into these same mountains out of nowhere on peculiar four-legged animals almost half a millennium before. Francisco Pizarro's men garroted the Inca Atahualpa and seized his empire. It sometimes seemed as if anything could happen in the Andes.

For Gustavo, getting out of Huaychao remained the more immediate matter. The fog had cloaked the village once more. They would have to stay the night unless it lifted, the commanding air force officer warned. Gustavo perceived a blackening mood among the Huaychainos. He had accidentally kicked the ball down a gully in an impromptu soccer game, then smiled at some watching villagers to acknowledge his clumsiness. They stared back stonily. "Something had changed from the morning," Gustavo said later. Various villagers had been leaving and arriving across the moors through the day. What was happening, he had Medrano ask one man in Quechua? A Huaychaino waved sullenly to the south. "There's a *guerrita*, a little war," he said, "at Uchuraccay."

It worried Gustavo to hear about the trouble. He knew that eight other reporters had headed on foot the day before to investigate the Huaychao *senderista* killings. Their left-wing newspapers had extensively reported army abuses, and, likely for that reason, General Noel refused them safe-conduct passes. The men decided to go anyway. They planned to drive to where the road petered out, and, after spending a night at their guide's house, make the hike up into Iquicha. The group had not yet arrived in Huaychao. Did they meet trouble in Uchuraccay? It was a dangerous moment between the *senderistas*, army patrols, and aroused villagers.

Their own predicament presented its own concerns. Gustavo wondered uneasily about the Huaychainos. Perhaps, he thought, they had decided it unwise to share their story about lynching the *senderistas*. Did the Huaychainos intend to prevent them from leaving the village? Gustavo was not eager to have his skull smashed in by peasant rocks. And then, too, the *senderistas* might have gotten wind of their visit. They were only six—Gustavo, Medrano, the army medic, the two soldiers and the helicopter pilot (Jorge Barboza, an air force major and the commanding officer). The *senderistas* would hack them up without mercy.

"Let's talk about this," Gustavo told Barboza. "When it gets dark, I think we should form a defense perimeter."

The commander agreed, and ordered his men to set up the submachine gun. They heaped some stones for a guard post. One soldier lit a campfire from dried manure for some comfort from the cold. If anyone other than Huaychao's lieutenant governor approached their camp that night, they would only receive one warning. *After that, shoot to kill*, Barboza said.

Then, unexpectedly, the sun cracked through the mist.

It was enough for the helicopter to lift off.

The pilot banked towards the city of Ayacucho. Could they stop in Uchuraccay, Gustavo shouted over the rotors? "It's too late," Barboza yelled back from the pilot's seat. "We won't find our way to the base in the dark." Gustavo peered down for a glimpse of Uchuraccay. The terrible events there that day would soon become Peru's biggest news story, and a decade of death and madness was only beginning for young Narciso and the Iquichans. "This crazy world is painted in hypocrisies," an Ayacuchan carnival song warned. "Men sharpen spears to make hearts bleed."

PART II

CHAPTER SEVEN

Inquest in the Andes

"Lend me the new boy!" Luis Becerra shouted across the newsroom. He was the police editor at *La Crónica*, a Lima tabloid. "I don't have anyone and there's a big crime downtown." The new boy wasted no time in grabbing his coat and straightening his tie. Mario was only fifteen, although tall enough to pass for older, at least at a distance. His father was Peru's Hearst Corporation representative and had influence with the newspapers. He had gotten young Mario a job at *La Crónica*.

The teenage reporter and his photographer, Ego Aguirre, hurried to the crime scene a few blocks from their office. The policemen recognized Aguirre, waving him into the boarding house room. A young woman's dead body lay there covered by a sheet. Aguirre yanked off the cover, and, the practiced tabloid photographer, pulled down her top to snap pictures of the knife wound across her small breasts. Mario had barely ever seen a woman's breasts before, much less ones smeared with blood. ("To me," he wrote years later, "seeing a naked woman in bed has always been the most disquieting and most disturbing of experiences.") He was momentarily paralyzed by fear and a nausea at the dreadful sight.

Mario gathered himself to take detailed notes, and, as the bored policemen took no notice, collected letters and photographs from the dead woman's drawer. Back at the office, he drafted his story with help from the police editor, Becerra, a legendary drunk and tabloid melodramatist. It ran the next morning, January 19, 1952, accompanied by a gruesome photograph of the half-nude victim, who had been knifed by a jealous boyfriend. Mario's story claimed that the dying girl had begged her murderer to end her misery. He supposedly complied by suffocating her with a wet towel even as "the blood from her wounded breast stained her brown body and her life slowly extinguished."

That gangly cub reporter, Mario Vargas Llosa, grew up to become one of the world's most famous writers. At twenty, he left Peru for Paris, where he published his first novel, *The Time of the Hero*. This gritty, tortured, raunchy tale about a Lima military boarding school (where Vargas Llosa had been a student) became an international bestseller. Vargas Llosa soon churned out more acclaimed books, among them *Conversation in the Cathedral*, a dizzying concoction about fear and apathy under dictatorship. The dashing Peruvian—a literary celebrity already in his twenties—socialized in Left Bank cafés with Jean-Paul Sartre, Susan Sontag, and Albert Camus. He led the so-called boom generation of celebrated Latin American writers along with his friends Gabriel García Márquez and Julio Cortázar. His novels melded that generation's magical realism with a talent for plot, pacing, and character. They were smart books and good reads too.

The young Vargas Llosa left his impoverished, corrupt Peru with no desire ever to return there. "I have promised myself hundreds of times," he wrote, "to live a long way from Peru forever and not write anything more about it and forget its aberrations." Vargas Llosa had a London flat, later moved to Barcelona, and jetted around the world. But he could not help returning home to Peru almost every summer. There were friends and family to visit. And his country always supplied him with marvelous, sordid, and spellbinding stories. What writer could abandon such a trove? Vargas Llosa set novels in a brothel in the desert city of Piura; a native village in the Manu jungle; and in Lima coffee shops and movie theaters. (He described people in the capital as moving around "like fish in dirty water.") Vargas Llosa and his wife Patricia kept an apartment in the seaside Barranco district for their visits. There the famous writer walked his dog in the Lima mist, the *garúa*, greeting neighbors with a polite nod.

And now, early in 1983, Vargas Llosa would be drawn into the war. He read about Shining Path with increasing revulsion. By this time in his midforties, the novelist had long since abandoned the Marxist leanings of his student days. He was dismayed by the terrible failings of state socialism and the Soviet Union's brutalization of its own people (which included jailing fellow authors like Aleksandr Solzhenitsyn and Lev Kopolev). "You cannot be a modern man and Marxist," Vargas Llosa declared. The writer was almost the same age as Abimael Guzmán, the Shining Path leader. Both men grew up partly in Arequipa, but they had never met. The former philosophy professor, Vargas Llosa believed, was a bloodthirsty believer in a retrograde dogma. Marxism-Leninism-Maoism-Gonzalo Thought? Vargas Llosa saw the conventional Western pathway of elections and free markets as the best answer for Peru and the world.

The latest war news especially horrified the novelist. According to newspaper stories, a party of eight reporters had been massacred in a remote village called Uchuraccay. They had been on their way to investigate the Huaychao lynchings of *senderistas*, and, although the details could not yet be verified, the initial reports said that villagers surrounded and stoned the reporters to death. This, apparently, was the *guerrita*, the little war, which

Huaychainos had mentioned to Gustavo Gorriti and Óscar Medrano. Policemen and soldiers hiked in some days later to investigate the killings, exhuming the bodies. A television news crew filmed the corpses of the dead journalists laid out like bruised mannequins across the village green.

The deaths sparked national uproar. Did the villagers really kill the reporters? If so, why? Or, as some leftist critics charged, could army troops have been the real killers? The skeptics believed the government might be fabricating the whole story of a Huaychaino revolt against Shining Path. According to this theory, General Noel's troops had massacred some innocent villagers, afterwards claiming they were *senderistas*. Then Noel supposedly had the reporters killed to prevent them from reaching Huaychao and reporting on the supposed cover-up. It was not unreasonable to suspect the worst about the military. Early reports indicated, after all, that soldiers were raping, looting, and killing in the Ayacuchan countryside. They suggested that the Peruvian military had adapted the murderous Guatemalan counterinsurgency model where government troops slaughtered Mayan villagers to crush leftist rebels.

The Peruvian president, Fernando Belaúnde, wanted to calm the outcry. He named an independent investigatory commission, inviting his country's most acclaimed intellectual, Mario Vargas Llosa, to head it. Belaúnde had known Vargas Llosa for years. He once offered him the ambassadorship to Great Britain, but the novelist declined. "I can serve my country best through my profession as a writer," he replied. He trusted that "Fernando," as he addressed the president, would understand his reason for "turning down your generous offer."

This time, Vargas Llosa accepted Belaúnde's invitation. He disliked preachy fiction and placed his vocation for writing above everything else. "I belong to this notebook and pencil," he explained in an essay about Hemingway's discipline that might have been about his own. His conviction was nevertheless that literary creation expressed freedom and rebellion by its very nature. "Literature is fire," Vargas Llosa wrote. "Its mission is to shake, disturb, alarm, keep us constantly dissatisfied with ourselves." When he condemned Fidel Castro for jailing a dissident Cuban writer, many leftists attacked him as a traitor to socialist ideals. Vargas Llosa spoke out just as strongly, however, against the US-backed Latin American military juntas of the 1960s and 1970s. He worried that the furor over the murdered journalists threatened Peru's fragile democracy. His country had only just returned to civilian rule with Belaúnde's election three years before.

Vargas Llosa flew to Ayacucho on February 8, 1983, to begin his investigation. Also aboard were the two other members of what became known as the Vargas Llosa Commission, a journalism school dean and a law professor. As much as he had traveled the world, Vargas Llosa was, by his own admission, only acquainted with the rural Andes in a "superficial, touristic" fashion. The writer therefore recruited two anthropologists, a social psychologist, a linguist, and two Quechua translators. He hoped that they could help to solve the mystery of the dead journalists.

———

The mood in Ayacucho had been growing darker and more fearful by the day. The city had been under military rule for six weeks when Vargas Llosa and his commissioners arrived there, and, as historian Alberto Flores Galindo put it, General Noel's troops behaved like an occupying "colonial army" by treating all Ayacuchans as likely terrorists. Soldiers broke down doors to search for weapons and propaganda. They dragged suspected *senderistas* away to Los Cabitos, the regional army base. Whispered stories described nighttime executions, gang rapes, and target practice with live prisoners. Many of those detained by the troops never reappeared. When their families made inquiries, they were told that no record existed of their son or daughter ever being in army custody. "Someone from Ayacucho has disappeared," mourned a song, "Where could she be? Perhaps under the stony ground becoming earth or among the thorns budding like wildflowers."

Vargas Llosa and his team set up in the old hotel off the town square. It was the state-run *Hotel de Turistas*, and yet Ayacucho was never a big tourist destination, and hardly any came now that the war had begun. Only a few police officials and the stray visiting journalist, like Gorriti and Medrano, stayed at the hotel. "It is sad to see it deserted," Vargas Llosa wrote in his journal. One man talked his way past the soldiers at the hotel's entrance to approach the writer. He pled for help, showing Vargas Llosa a handwritten death threat from Shining Path. Vargas Llosa explained to the man that he had no power to protect him. In Ayacucho, he wrote in his journal, a feeling prevailed of *zozobra*, a Spanish word for something between anxiety, foundering, and vulnerability.

Their investigation demanded a trip to Uchuraccay to meet with the villagers. At dawn four days after arriving in Ayacucho, Vargas Llosa pulled on his jeans, a checkered shirt, and a sheepskin cowboy jacket. An armed convoy of black cars and army jeeps transported the writer and his party to Los Cabitos. General Noel had received orders from President Belaúnde to cooperate with the commission. He had mustered four helicopters for the eighteen-minute trip up to Uchuraccay. (By land, the journey took two days, first by car and then on foot.) Vargas Llosa did not yet know the full story about Los Cabitos and the horrors behind its guard towers and barbed-wire fence. He chatted with Noel on the way over to the helicopters without realizing that his host was turning the base into a black-site killing center.

———

The choppers touched down on a mountainside close to Uchuraccay. Because this was the heart of the war zone, soldiers and anti-terrorism police had marched in to secure the area beforehand. It was the rainy season. Vargas Llosa and the other commissioners picked their way down the muddy path between the bare grass and black stone. They had been told that *senderistas* camped up towards Mt. Rasuwillka, and were perhaps even now monitoring their arrival from an overlook. The young rebel fighters, like the Trojans taunting the Greeks across their walls, occasionally raised red flags on promontories above Uchuraccay. Their *vivas* to Chairman Gonzalo and the people's war echoed over the farmhouses below.

Uchuraccay looked much like other Iquichan hamlets, a tumbledown chapel, one-room school, and some stone houses. Vargas Llosa had learned that about two hundred peasant families scratched a living from their plots there.

But where had they gone?

The village was empty. It appeared that the Uchuraccainos had fled at the sound of the helicopters. An uncertain Vargas Llosa asked his advising anthropologists what to do. Juan Ossio and Fernando Fuenzalida, both professors at Lima's Catholic University, were prominent scholars experienced in Andean villages. The affable Ossio had gotten his doctorate at Oxford University. He befriended Vargas Llosa when his fellow Peruvian taught at St. Anne's College as a visiting professor.

"Let's ring the chapel bell, Mario," Ossio said. "It's how they call village meetings."

He and Fuenzalida found the village sacristan. The little man set the iron bell clanging across the mountains. The Uchuraccainos came down in clusters from the hills.

They greeted their visitors in the customary village manner, which consisted of a mumbled welcome, averted gaze, and a light brush of a handshake. About a hundred had shown up all told, mostly men with a few women and children. The Uchuraccainos wore the same battered hats, woolen garments, and crude sandals as the neighboring Huaychainos and other Iquichan peasants. Many villagers had the "scarred cheeks and swollen lips of those who live exposed to the cold of the uplands," Vargas Llosa wrote afterwards. One old woman wore no shoes. Their appearance reminded a later visitor of characters in a Breughel painting. Vargas Llosa looked almost like a pale extraterrestrial among them. He was a head taller and three shades whiter than any Uchuraccaino. They circled somewhat warily on the village green to hear what their visitor had to say.

The novelist began with an offering to the *apus,* the mountain spirits. This had been suggested by his anthropologists, Ossio and Fuenzalida, to pay respect to local traditions. As they had instructed, Vargas Llosa performed the *tinkay*, a ritual offering of some coca leaves and a few drops of *aguardiente*, cane liquor. He said a little prayer to Mt. Rasuwillka, the highest Iquichan peak, for his linguist to translate into Quechua for the villagers.

Here the anthropologists did not have it quite right. The *tinkay* was only performed in Iquicha at specific times, among them the planting season, which was weeks away. "*Será su costumbre*—it must have been his custom," an Uchuraccaino puzzled later over Vargas Llosa's offering. The writer and his party also distributed cookies, crackers, and coca leaf. They found the villagers glad enough to receive those goods.

Vargas Llosa rose to explain the purpose of his visit. He was, uncharacteristically, a little nervous before the village crowd. His words had the stilted precision of a Spanish king's emissary landing on some foreign shores. "*Comuneros* of Uchuraccay: We come in the name of the President to bring peace like the water that courses through the veins of the *apus* to give you life." Vargas Llosa added what he probably imagined to be an Indian-sounding flourish by calling the village uchu-RAJAY. The proper stress was only on the last syllable. Some Uchuraccainos may have wondered if this government emissary was talking about their village or some other one.

"A few days ago," Vargas Llosa continued, "there were problems in the community resulting in the death of eight *forasteros*, strangers. This occurrence has caused great worry to the president."

He meant the stoning of the journalists.

"Nobody," he added, "should kill anyone in our country or should make justice with their own hands." Here the writer betrayed a white coastal Peruvian's condescension about supposed Andean backwardness. The Uchuraccainos knew full well that Peruvian law banned murder.

Vargas Llosa finally got to the point.

"I want to hear from your own mouths what happened."

———

Vargas Llosa did not yet know what to believe. "I had many doubts," he said afterwards, "about whether the villagers had done it." Always intrigued by police investigations, the future writer devoured pulp mysteries as a boy. He wrote two literary detective novels himself, *Who Killed Palomino Molero?* and *Death in the Andes.* The murdered journalists gave him his chance to solve a real-life mystery.

His deeper interest lay in the human psyche's dark places. Vargas Llosa admired the French writer Georges Bataille, who was obsessed with evil and eroticism (including incest, necrophilia, cannibalism, and human sacrifice). His own romantic life had edged towards the unconventional pleasures of intrafamilial intimacy. He had been briefly married, at nineteen, to a much older aunt (a romance he memorialized in his novel *Aunt Julia and the Scriptwriter*). When Vargas Llosa was a boy, his father abandoned the family for years at a time. Ernesto beat Mario regularly when he did come home, leaving the boy in bruised tears. The adult Mario was calm and confident, though his childhood left him prone to occasional anxiety, mistrust, and angry outbursts. He once punched out his former friend Gabriel García Márquez for supposed meddling in his personal life.

The Uchuraccay killings exhibited human wrath in the extreme. They recalled Shirley Jackson's "The Lottery," a classic horror story about an American farm community stoning. Vargas Llosa wondered about the villagers circled around him now at the village green. Could they really have ganged up to kill the reporters in such gruesome fashion? He soon had his answer from the villagers themselves—and with no mystery novel suspense.

Yes, the Uchuraccainos freely admitted, *we killed the journalists.*

Various village men stepped forward to explain, all telling the same story. The *puriqkuna*, the nightwalkers, had been raiding for months, stealing livestock and killing. When the *sinchis,* the anti-terrorism police, passed through the village, they instructed the Uchuraccainos to kill any stranger who came on foot from then on. Some days later, the reporters walked up from the valley, carrying a red flag and shouting *vivas* to the people's war. Being "ignorant people," as the Uchuraccainos excused themselves, they mistook the journalists for terrorists. They killed them, exactly as the *sinchis* instructed. Their concern now was protection from guerrilla reprisals. Would Vargas Llosa help? The Uchuraccainos wanted the "Honorable Mr. Government," as they referred to President Belaúnde, to send rifles to defend themselves, and establish a village army post.

Their story was not convincing in its every aspect. A red flag? Vargas Llosa suspected that the villagers fabricated this detail to justify their mistaken killing. He asked them more about it through his translator. Here the Uchuraccainos shut down questioning. "*Bandera roja! Bandera roja!* Red flag! Red flag!" they murmured angrily. And the journalists yelling revolutionary slogans? That sounded like more invented justification for the murders. When one villager volunteered that the *sinchis* had never actually ordered them to kill anyone, he was shouted down by the others. Was the story of the kill order still more exculpatory embellishment? The fate of the reporter's guide raised more questions. He had vanished that day. Vargas Llosa asked the Uchuraccainos if they knew anything about his disappearance. A sullen chorus rose again: "*Chayllam, chayllam*—enough, enough."

"Change the subject, Mario," Juan Ossio whispered.

These tough country people had stoned eight people to death.

It did not seem wise to press them now.

Actually the villagers were concealing even more than Vargas Llosa suspected. Far from marching in with a red banner, the reporters had waved a white handkerchief in surrender. They begged the peasants for mercy, never chanting guerrilla slogans. Some villagers, already fearful about more *senderista* attacks, had drunk their share of cane liquor that day, further blackening their mood. When eerie last photographs were later recovered from the camera of one of the dead reporters, they showed the eight men kneeling before grim farmers. *We are journalists, not terrorists*, the reporters pled. The Uchuraccainos could have marched their captives down to the valley police station. Instead they sent the rocks flying. (They were the *rumi maki*, after all, the "stone-throwers," especially known for prowess with their slings.) One reporter crawled around a wall, only to be cornered and bludgeoned to death there. The villagers did not want to admit to such cruelty, much less to expose themselves to possible murder prosecution. Their story about a regrettable yet unavoidable mix-up provided cover for their actions.

Nor did the villagers wish to acknowledge their own divided loyalties. By contrast to neighboring Huaychao, the *senderistas* found support in Uchuraccay at first. A younger village man, Severino Morales, established a People's Committee there. "Among our combatants in the [Uchuraccay] zone was Comrade Severino," a party official reported. "From there our fighters went down to shake up the lazy sleeping enemy in the Civil Guard [the police] posts in Huanta and Tambo." But when the *senderistas* executed a village leader, Alejandro Huamán, late in 1982 for pulling down a red banner, it set a revolt in motion. The great majority of Uchuraccainos signed the declaration "not to agree with the tirrorirsts [*sic*]." They coordinated with other Iquichan villages like Cunya, Macabamba, and neighboring Huaychao to expel the rebels. Only a few hours after killing the journalists, some Uchuraccainos tied Severino Morales, the village *senderista* leader, behind a donkey, dragged him through the dirt, and then beat him to death. They strangled the reporter's guide, believing him also to be a *senderista*. (He came from a settlement just down the mountain.) The villagers buried Morales and the guide in secret graves, and threatened Morales's widow to keep her quiet. Admitting to killing two more men would have left them in even greater legal jeopardy. Then, too, the army might take reprisals if it learned that their hamlet had ever harbored guerrilla sympathizers. So the Uchuraccainos fashioned themselves as a single loyal community seeking "Mr. Government's" protection from the terrorist thieves.

The basics of their account remained accurate enough, however. Most Uchuraccainos indeed had little concept about what a journalist might be and, besides that, having a reputed *senderista* for a guide made the reporters even more suspect. (In reality, the newspapermen apparently had no idea about the guide's sympathies.) The slaughter of the reporters had been cold and cruel, but, as Vargas Llosa later wrote, it was unsurprising given his native country's "abandonment" of its impoverished Andean villagers. In the heights of Iquicha, the peasants had been besieged, terrified, and completely unprotected by the government before a ferocious insurgency. It was little wonder that things turned ugly when the unfortunate reporters came puffing up from the valley.

The atmosphere lightened towards the assembly's end. It was carnival time, the biggest Ayacuchan holiday. Even in wartime, villagers headed down to the city to dance, drink, and sing their way through the streets. One Uchuraccaino drew a *pingullo*, a wood flute, from under his poncho. A girl sang a high *qarawi* celebrating fertility and the rainy season. The barefoot old woman pulled Vargas Llosa out to dance. "*Futu, futu,*" the Uchuraccainos cried. They wanted pictures to commemorate the visit. Then the helicopters roared away, leaving the villagers alone in the bloodied mountains once again.

It remained for Vargas Llosa to complete the report. To make certain General Noel had not plotted to kill the reporters, the writer interviewed troop commanders, the Uchuraccay schoolteacher, and others. Vargas Llosa knew that he, unlike the dime-novel detective, could not tie up every loose end. His own literary sensibilities, as his translator John King observed, exhibited a tension between "a will to define stark clarities, and an awareness, from a pluralist sensibility, that such clarities are necessarily elusive and contingent." That the villagers killed the journalists in a dreadful mistake seemed to be the one certainty in this case.

Back in Lima, Vargas Llosa presented his commission's report to President Belaúnde. His findings stirred immediate controversy. The more restrained critics, among them several anthropologists and historians, faulted the writer for exaggerating Uchuraccay's primeval backwardness. The villagers maintained an "ancient, archaic" lifeway in an "almost absolute" isolation, Vargas Llosa claimed. This portrayal betrayed a predictable outsider's exoticism about the Andes as a land of "untouched" villages, millennial traditions, and tantalizing mystery. ("Mario was very preoccupied," as Juan Ossio delicately put it, "by the contrast between barbarism and civilization.") Vargas Llosa did not notice—or chose not to see—that Uchuraccainos owned radios, jeans, rubber boots, and record players despite the undeniable remoteness of their moors. Several villagers were army veterans; some had worked construction in Lima; and others migrated between the highlands and tropical Apurímac Valley homesteads. (And indeed what ethnohistorian John V. Murra famously called "vertical archipelago" trading systems connected the Andes to the desert and jungle for centuries before the Spaniards.) It demanded the novelist's writerly liberties to depict the Uchuraccainos as quite such the marooned primitives of his report.

More rabid critics stuck to the military conspiracy theory. A left-wing newspaper, *El Diario de Marka*, which employed three of the dead journalists, suggested that an unidentified "light-skinned stranger" directed the Uchuraccay massacre. The newspaper repeatedly made this claim despite abundant evidence that the villagers acted alone. Its editorialists charged Vargas Llosa with abetting a government cover-up. He was a liar, a stooge, a puppet of Belaúnde and the military, they and others claimed. Another critic denounced Vargas Llosa for "making money over the dead bodies of the murdered journalists." The Uchuraccay case gave Peru's leftist intellectual classes an opportunity to settle scores with a fellow writer who had dared to criticize Fidel Castro and Marxism, and then go on to become more famous than any of them.

Later investigations would vindicate Vargas Llosa and his report. He had quite accurately reconstructed the events on that bloody January day. "Vargas Llosa exoticized some and missed some things," historian Ponciano Del Pino has said, "but he had the basics right." That was no small accomplishment between barriers of language, culture, and the war's upheaval. It was also unfair to charge Vargas Llosa with excusing military abuses. His report noted the difficulty of fighting the *senderistas* ("an immense territory" and "an enemy that strikes and dissolves into the rural population"). Vargas Llosa nonetheless partly blamed for Uchuraccay on Noel and his troops. Their brutality "contributed to creating the context of abnormality, suspicion, panic, and hate that led to the slaughter of the journalists."

A furious Vargas Llosa lashed back at his critics. He insisted, plausibly enough, that one reason why leftist commentators questioned his report lay in the "incurable romanticism of their revolutionary dreams." They could not comprehend that peasant villagers might reject Marxist guerrillas—and unwind their *huaracas* to stone men they believed to be insurgents. It was much easier to think that General Noel orchestrated the killing like nasty right-wing military men elsewhere in Latin America. Although Noel had indeed begun a deadly dirty war in Ayacucho, he did not order Uchuraccay. The attacks over his report, Vargas Llosa indignantly complained, were "the worst offense I've experienced in my life."

Still more trouble awaited the writer. He was summoned back to Aya-cucho in 1984 for a court hearing. A local judge intended to prosecute him for concealing the supposed military order to kill the journalists. His questioning quickly veered into the absurd:

Judge: You have yourself confessed that you are a person subject to convictions of a hedonist character.

Vargas Llosa: Hedonism is a philosophy that considers pleasure to be the reason for life. I am not a hedonist.

Vargas Llosa had to stand for fifteen hours of this sham interrogation. His attempt to do his civic duty had shrunk down to a sweaty courtroom packed with reporters, photographers, and curiosity seekers. Nothing ever came of the judge's investigation.

The trials of Vargas Llosa hardly compared to those of the Uchurac-cainos. When presenting their report to President Belaúnde, Vargas Llosa and Juan Ossio, the anthropologist, conveyed the village request for an army post. Belaúnde nodded vaguely without following through. That gave vengeful *senderista* bands freedom to attack Uchuraccay repeatedly over the next months—and kill more than a hundred villagers. "We have swept out those shit savages," a Shining Path commander reported. Surviving peasants fled to valley towns. They sought solace in the late-night sermons by evangelical pastors about suffering, fire, and shimmering salvation in the end times. "Our suffering in those years was like when Jehovah expelled Adam and Eve from Eden," one man explained. Uchuraccay became a ghost village.

A disheartened Vargas Llosa returned to Spain.

His role in the war was not yet over.

CHAPTER EIGHT

Shouting in the Rocks

The guerrillas moved by twos, each pair about a half mile apart. *If the miserable reactionaries ambush they won't kill us all,* someone explained to the peasant boy. Lurgio Gavilán had recently joined the rebels, leaving his family's farm in the Apurímac Valley. Their band kept alert despite hunger, cold, and exhaustion. When a helicopter gunship flew above, they ducked under rocks for cover. Nights, four kept fixed guard while a fifth patrolled the perimeter. They camped in high spots, preferably with a view.

As this day dawned early in 1983, the clouds lay heavy across the sky. It was only a few weeks after the Uchuraccay massacre, and Lurgio's band had bivouacked about fifty miles farther along the mountains. The boy sipped some soup, then passed the bowl to the next fighter. One comrade read from Marx and from Mao's *Five Essays on Philosophy.* They sang a hymn to Chairman Gonzalo:

Gonzalo brought the light,
taking from Marx, Lenin, and Mao
he forged the purest steel.
Tearing down old walls
dawn breaks optimistic
And overflowing with enthusiasm.

They would split up to search for food, the leaders said. Lurgio and his companion, Rosaura, talked on their way down the canyon. She was seventeen, a gentle young woman five years older than Lurgio, who was twelve. In the countryside, where childhood was always short, the very young sometimes joined the *compañeros,* the comrades, as some called Shining Path. Lurgio's big brother, Rubén, had become a local commander. Lurgio left home to follow his brother, and also because, as much as he understood it, the guerrillas wanted to end poverty and injustice. It seemed a better option than his parents' dirt-farming life.

The rains came heavy in this El Niño year. Swollen streams bulled down from the high country, sending waterfalls frothing over the canyon walls. When Lurgio and Rosaura came to a farmhouse, the dogs barked, and an old man and two barefoot children emerged. *Greetings in the name of the People's War and the Peruvian Communist Party,* the young guerrillas said. The elderly peasant gave them some beans and potatoes. Lurgio and Rosaura went on along the path, and a flock of little parrots swerved by under the warming sun. Small birds appeared often in peasant ballads, a symbol of mountain life's loveliness and fragility. ("My little dove, where are you? Do you find love in the cold? Does the wind caress you?") *There are always reasons to keep on living,* Lurgio knew.

Their forty fighters would move to a new camp that night. They slept until early evening, before picking their way down the trail by moonlight for several hours. Their leader suddenly halted. "We're going to attack that house and kill the miserable bastards," he said. They surrounded the house, several fighters rushing in with revolvers. Lurgio heard shots. A wounded man stumbled out, a woman screaming behind him. He pleaded for his life, for his children's sake. The leader handed a rifle to a comrade, Sandra, who shot him dead. "This man is a rat, a traitor," the leaders said. He had supposedly betrayed their whereabouts to the army.

From the outside, Shining Path could appear to be an invulnerable force. A war machine, some called it. Lurgio and his fellow fighters had no such illusions in their stone shelters. They came mostly from peasant families, a ragged band of children and teens, who had just a few rifles and not many more bullets. As General Noel's troops swarmed into the Andes early in 1983, *senderista* units faced a ten-thousand-man military force. Lurgio and his little detachment could be hunted down at any time. They faced a good chance of being shot on the spot if any of them fell captive to pursuing soldiers.

The peasant boy took comfort in his friend Rosaura's company. They sometimes whispered about deserting, and yet tried to keep faith. "We continued to believe in our Chairman Gonzalo," Lurgio wrote years later. They had no idea where Chairman Gonzalo might be, or much of anything about him besides the drawings of a stern yet wise and benevolent man in their leaflets. That did not keep Lurgio from hoping that their great leader "might appear in a helicopter at any moment and do away with the soldiers. But no, he never arrived, he remained invisible."

Many others wondered about Abimael's whereabouts, too. The red-painted *vivas* to Chairman Gonzalo covered walls, but the man himself had vanished into hiding. Neither the police nor the army intelligence services had any good leads, lacking even a recent photograph. The US ambassador, Alexander Watson, believed Abimael might be running the revolution from another country. His attachés and the small Peruvian CIA station had been keeping an eye on Shining Path, especially after the rebels bombed the North American–Peruvian Cultural Institute and Sheraton Hotel to demonstrate their distaste for Yankee imperialism. Others speculated that Abimael had a highland village or jungle hideout, or that he had died. The Incas venerated their mummified rulers, provisioning them with corn beer, human sacrifices, and granite palaces. Perhaps the *senderistas* were worshipping a dead man too, while concealing his death from outsiders. One tabloid reported Abimael being sighted shopping at Harrods.

The truth was more prosaic, namely that the *senderista* leader was holed up in Lima. It would have been difficult to direct nationwide operations from a remote Andean hamlet, and Abimael had never been a bush fighter anyway. He did not have picky tastes, but he had grown up middle-class, accustomed to a comfortable bed and his morning cup of Nescafé. Nor did his health allow him to stay long in the mountains. He suffered occasional headaches, dizziness, and fatigue from polycythemia, a rare blood disorder, and high altitude worsened his symptoms. A hideout in some Lima shantytown would bring others too close, besides lacking comforts. So Abimael directed the war from rented houses in more upscale areas of the capital like Miraflores, San Borja, and San Isidro. A well-dressed party member, perhaps a lawyer or engineer, pretended to be renting the house for him or herself. The owner had no idea that the real occupant was going to be the hemisphere's most wanted terrorist leader.

These garden district houses suited *senderista* purposes in multiple ways. Most people still thought of Shining Path as a rural rebellion in the distant Ayacuchan highlands. Abimael's police pursuers would be unlikely to suspect that he was residing in an exclusive district like San Isidro with its tennis clubs and pricey boutiques. The houses in wealthier neighborhoods typically had the added advantage of walls to deter thieves, which provided privacy and some defensive possibilities. To avoid being captured together in a single police raid, Abimael, Elena, and Augusta stayed at different houses. They moved every so often as a further security precaution.

Their one early close call occurred almost by accident. Thanks to a sympathetic janitor who had the keys, party leaders sometimes convened in an office building near the Gutiérrez Oval, a busy roundabout in San Isidro. They did so only on weekends when the building was empty, but one day in 1982 their lookout rushed into the conference room. The whole Central Committee was there that day, Abimael included. *The police have cordoned off the whole block*, the lookout said. *We're surrounded*. Fernando Belaúnde, Peru's president, had arrived for some engagement along with his big security detail. The *senderista* commanders left the building in staggered groups, walking by the police outside without attracting notice. That Abimael had grown a beard gave him some cover in a pinch. Every Peruvian pictured him as clean-shaven from the old photographs. Their party propaganda kept up the fiction by showing him beardless as well.

It was still possible for Augusta to make long trips to the Andes. She led those early attacks in the Pampas Valley, and, as late as 1982, a police intelligence report placed her in the nearby Apurímac mountains. Her high school friend, Gisela Huamán, saw her on the street in Huanta about then, hurrying somewhere. "Don't tell anyone you saw me," Augusta said. By that time, the *senderistas* effectively controlled the town, and, if a fighter snuck behind a policeman to shoot him in the head, no one would come to the dying man's aid for fear of reprisal. Another of Augusta's childhood friends, Sonia Meneses, had a policeman boyfriend. He never had any trouble; Sonia attributed that to Augusta's command in the area. Her childhood playmate was looking out for her.

It did not pay to anger Augusta, always the rigid revolutionary. One day in the late 1970s, before the war began, she visited her cousin Adriana and Adriana's husband Eduardo Spatz, a German expatriate with a *Hogan's Heroes* accent. The couple's farmhouse lay outside Huanta only a few miles from the La Torres' former Iribamba estate. Contrary to local rumor, Spatz was not a wanted Nazi war criminal, but he did have guns. Augusta wanted them. The German said no. He was an avid hunter who did not want to relinquish his firearms.

"You're one of the first we'll burn!" Augusta shouted.

Her fighters made good on that threat. After Spatz defied an ultimatum to leave, the *senderistas* attacked during a big rainstorm one night late in 1982—dynamite, gunshots, rebel yells through the downpour. But Spatz had fortified his farmhouse into a bunker. It had barbed wire, cemented windows and, creepily, a thick adobe perimeter wall topped with human skulls from an ancient graveyard. While his wife fed him ammunition, Spatz fired away into the black downpour. The *senderistas* retreated, but the couple decided to leave some days later. Nobody would rent to them, fearing rebel retribution. They escaped to Germany, where Spatz found work as a night watchman.

The army's occupation forced Augusta to abandon the Andes by early 1983. She had to stay mostly inside, even in Lima, for being so well known to the government intelligence services. When Augusta and Elena left the capital to give secret training sessions for new recruits, they went only to Arequipa, Ica, and other places away from the main war zones. The police would not be looking for them there. Augusta and Elena renewed their old custom, reading together. New choices included Balzac's *The Human Comedy* and, appropriately enough for wartime commanders, Tolstoy's *War and Peace*. Augusta liked Russian novels, but found the French existentialists too wishy-washy for her hardline Marxist tastes. Joyce's *Ulysses* elicited a more generic complaint. "I don't like it," Augusta told Elena. "Too hard to follow."

Her family remained under constant surveillance. Although they retained title to Iribamba, Carlos and Delia had been living in Lima for more than a decade. The police raided the house several times searching for some clue to Abimael's whereabouts. Augusta's parents, fearing worse, fled to Sweden in 1982. Their youngest son, Humberto, eighteen, drove them to meet Abimael and Augusta for a good-bye party. A proper Peruvian *despedida* meant many pictures, but Humberto realized afterwards that they could not keep them. He stripped the film from his camera to expose it. Augusta's baby brother eventually opened a popular *tapas* restaurant in downtown Stockholm. Her brother-in-law, Javier Esparza, became the party's point man in Europe. Army troops torched Iribamba in reprisal against the La Torres and their rebel daughter. A few goats from neighboring farms sometimes strayed in to graze in the fields along the riverbank.

It worried Augusta to be cut off from the countryside. To maintain party discipline, she helped to arrange for so-called "retransmission" meetings for communicating the latest plans from Lima to the provinces. More than a hundred Ayacucho *senderistas* were summoned to a farmhouse for one such assembly on a mid-1982 night. It had been readied with the usual photographs of Marx, Lenin, and Mao on the walls and some hammer-and-sickle decorations. As loyal peasants stood guard outside in the shadows, Comrade Clara, Augusta's replacement as area commander, oversaw the proceedings. The likeable, forthright Clara, whose real name was Elvira Ramírez, had been a psychology major at Lima's Federico Villarreal University. Like many students, she found her way into the party, and was eventually named to the Central Committee for her effectiveness and loyalty. Her task on this night was to "retransmit" the Second National Conference, the meeting some months before where Abimael had been definitively enshrined as a Marxian demigod. She put on the hard *senderista* mask to inaugurate the meeting after the customary opening rendition of "The Internationale."

"Comrades," Clara began. "In the name of the Peruvian Communist Party, and under the authority of the Central Committee, I open the

Retransmission of the Second National Conference. And I do so with my unconditional submission to our leader, the Chairman of the party, Comrade Gonzalo." Expressing subjection to Abimael had become a required party ritual.

It took Clara hours to "retransmit" the conference. The party leadership had reviewed their considerable advances in "shaking up" the countryside, she reported, and towards "destroying all vestiges of the Old State to establish the Popular Committee of the New Power." Along the way, Clara read long quotations from Marx and Mao, which she informed the others Chairman Gonzalo had recited by memory. Then, finally, she described how Alberto and his supporters had been exposed as a "petty bourgeois nucleus" for doubting the prison escape plan. Their Chairman Gonzalo, she confessed, had also found fault with her. She had encouraged César to "vacillate" before the second successful Ayacucho prison raid. Chairman Gonzalo had been entirely correct about her "lack of Communist resolve," she said. Almost always, as journalist Ricardo Uceda noted, the *senderistas* attributed failures to ideological weakness. It could never be bad luck, not enough bullets, or, in this case, the apparent engine trouble of the escape pickup truck. Clara's expressions of remorse cued a lower-ranking party member, Héctor, to acknowledge his cowardice during the prison attack. His repentance did not seem sincere enough. "Class traitor!" "Liar!" "Coward!" "Hypocrite!" the cries came. The *senderistas* always obsessed over the filth of mistaken ideology and its threat to the party's pure light. "Dust will accumulate if a room is not cleaned regularly, our faces will get dirty if they are not washed regularly," Mao explained. Only vigilance and the purifying rituals of self-criticism could "prevent all kinds of political dust and germs from contaminating the minds of our comrades and the body of our Party."

"Yes, comrades, I fled the action," Héctor wept. He was a schoolteacher with small children. "It seemed like suicide. I thought about my family. . . . My place was there, in action, comrades, but now I swear to you that I will be a more courageous combatant from now on. I want to be at the front line in the next attack. I will show with my own blood that what I say is true."

"Look at him," cried Carlotta Tello, the fiery little military commander. "He's weeping like Mary Magdalene."

"Comrades," Clara cut her off. "We have discussed this point sufficiently. The two-line struggle has drawn us together."

She hugged the miserable Héctor at the meeting's end.

He died weeks later in an assault on the Tambo police station.

Only the leaders of Lurgio and Rosaura's band attended that retransmission meeting. They rejoined the others afterwards, and, one dreary afternoon, the area commander made an announcement at a big outdoor assembly. "We have among us *compañeros* who have betrayed the Party and sold out. For this reason tonight they will die." Lurgio's heart thumped crazily. Had his whispered conversations with Rosaura been overheard? The party had a thousand eyes and thousand ears. To desert the revolution was an unforgivable crime. Loyalty or death, Lurgio knew. The only honorable way for a Communist to leave the party was dead on his shield like a Spartan warrior.

Instead the leader pointed to eight other young fighters, three women and five men. Traitors, he said. Their crimes had been keeping food, money, and medicine meant for the party, and overstaying leave time. That night, Lurgio and some others took their condemned comrades to be shot in a gorge. "We pulled roughly on their ropes, as they tried uselessly to break free," he wrote later. They shot the traitors one by one. Some cried and shook the hands of their former fellow fighters. Others still shouted "Viva Gonzalo! Viva Mao!" Lurgio and his companions stacked the corpses in a stony grave by moonlight.

The quiet, reliable Lurgio earned a promotion after a year, becoming a *compañero,* a party member. One night, he went alone to see some villagers. He was supposed to tell them to be at a certain place at a certain time, although his commanders had not explained for what purpose. Lurgio found the peasants chewing coca in a farmhouse. He spoke nervously in Quechua about Chairman Gonzalo and social justice, trying to sound like a real Communist. "How could they send a child?" Lurgio overheard his hosts murmur afterwards. He was three months shy of fourteen.

The army's troops pursued guerrilla units ever more closely. One day in 1983, a patrol arrived in Incaraccay, close behind the *senderistas.* The troops grabbed an old man. *Where did they go?* the sergeant asked. *I don't know, papay* (little father), the man replied. The sergeant cut off the man's ear. When he threatened to cut off the other one, the man pointed towards a path, the blood dripping from his head.

"They went that way, *papay,*" the old man said.

"You knew the whole time, you fucker," the sergeant said. "You're going to eat your fucking ear."

The old villager had to cut his ear in two to choke it down.

This monstrous cruelty could sometimes backfire. It fostered hatred and resentment towards the soldiers, sometimes aiding guerrilla recruitment, and yet some peasants did not like the *senderistas* any better. More village militias had formed to keep out the rebels. Despite their repeated attempts to smash the *yanaumas,* or "black-heads" as the *senderistas* called them, they had failed so far. The *yanaumas* captured many *senderistas,* sometimes lynching them just as the Huaychainos did on their judgment rock. "These militias are tough," one of Lurgio's comrades said.

His own company became increasingly desperate. The young fighters had only a few beans and potatoes left, and, coming across a bony horse one day, they butchered it for stew. Lurgio assisted Tania, the company's nurse, who had no antibiotics and not enough bandages. Their party anthems no longer warded off growing despair around the camp. "We were human, children, peasants shouting among the lifeless rocks with no one listening," Lurgio wrote.

Every regional commander had to send regular reports for Abimael's review. He had been expecting and, in fact, wanted Belaúnde to send the troops to Ayacucho. It was an axiom of Mao's theory of protracted war, after all, that a liberation struggle must draw the stronger enemy into the hostile countryside (as Chinese Communist forces did with the occupying Japanese imperial army). The invading soldiers would thunder murderously into peasant villages, and many party fighters would have to give their lives in the escalating battle. They would persist, however, and the demoralized enemy would eventually retreat. The expanding guerrilla insurgency would go on the offensive to final victory. A "river of blood," as Abimael described it, would flow before it was over. He was the Red Moses who would guide the masses to the Communist promised land.

Now the army had been drawn into the Andes. To plot next steps, the Shining Path Permanent Committee gathered early in 1983, namely Abimael, Augusta, and Elena. They might be husband, wife, and longtime friend, but, always the good party bureaucrats, kept notes and wore their blue Mao uniforms. Theoretically, the *senderistas* only reached accords after Central Committee debate in their "democratic centralist" system. Actually, Abimael and his two chief advisors decided most next steps in advance in their Permanent Committee meetings. They were the "reddest of them all," he once said.

It took several sessions to decide about responding to the army's counteroffensive. Elena was becoming more assertive about offering opinions. She proposed a temporary retreat from the Ayacuchan countryside. They were suffering too many losses there.

"We should pull back," she said. "There's too much force."

Abimael agreed. They could redeploy elsewhere.

"That's not the right move," Augusta said. Most peasants still backed them, she insisted, and they could pick spots to avoid directly confronting the military and its superior firepower. When Augusta's eyes sparked like this, she usually had her way. They agreed to stay, and, formalizing their military structure, established the *Ejército Guerillero Popular*, the People's Guerrilla Army. They were merely renaming their existing undermanned bands yet reaffirming commitment not to back down from the intensifying battle.

The other urgent matter had become the village militias. As a devoted reader of Peruvian history from her girlhood, Elena was not surprised that some peasants had turned against them. Hadn't the Spanish puppet, Manco Inca Yupanqui, at first helped the colonizers to consolidate their rule? And hadn't some Indians later joined the royalists to crush Túpac Amaru's anticolonial rebellion? Some villagers would always side with the oppressors, she reminded Abimael and Augusta. A "feudal-fatalist mentality" persisted in the countryside, after all, or so Abimael had asserted in a 1973 university lecture. The Huaychao revolt against their fighters indicated that the moor dwellers remained mired in backward thinking. "[The] Huaychainos were ignorant about everything," reported the party's local commander, Comrade Juan. "When we talked to them about Communism, they just said 'they're atheists, devils. We don't want them. Get out, we don't want you.'" All the peasants wanted, Juan said, "was to be able to live without being bothered by anyone." That such unenlightened farmers would oppose the revolution did not seem surprising at all.

Something had to be done. The army was encouraging and sometimes forcing peasants to form militias even in party strongholds like the Pampas Valley. In one hamlet, Lucanamarca, the inhabitants had old feuds with *senderista*-supporting villages down the mountain. That made the Lucanamarcans quite willing to form an anti-guerrilla militia, or "Civil Defense Committee," as the army called them. In the early hours of March 22, they captured a *senderista*, marching him into the square. He begged for mercy, but village women showered him with stones and Quechua curses. Men held his head up by the hair, clubbing him with sticks. They placed the *senderista*'s body on a straw bed, doused him in kerosene, and lit him on fire. The blackened corpse lay on the church steps for a day.

What to do about the growing militias became an agenda item at the Central Committee's Third National Conference. The meeting lasted over multiple sessions in early 1983, this time in a safe house in Lima's Chaclacayo suburb. Their guide, Mao, often said that Communists should live among, listen to, and learn from peasants (although his disastrous Great Leap Forward left more than five million villagers dead from famine and overwork). Augusta and other party members had spent much time in the Ayacuchan countryside during the 1960s and 1970s. But their preconceptions about its "semi-feudal" character prevented much real learning or even listening. They still mistakenly saw the post-agrarian-reform Andes as a land of evil landlords and exploited serfs (and paid little attention to the great migrations of villagers to the cities, among other more recent complexities). That peasants might want to be left alone or, say, join an evangelical church was explained away as ignorance, that "fatalist-feudal mentality."

The Central Committee members listened attentively to reports from provincial commanders about the village militias and Lucanamarca. Abimael, Augusta, and Elena had agreed beforehand to take tough action. After the European revolutions of 1848 had been crushed, Marx himself advised future socialist organizers that the "only way to ensure the old society's death . . . [is] revolutionary terror." Keeping the Lucanamarcans and other peasants in line meant that "in every village, quite frankly, a brief period of terror is necessary," Abimael affirmed in a party document. They must make Lucanamarca pay for defying the revolution, especially since the heights of the Pampas Valley had strategic value. The *senderistas* risked being hemmed in by the army if they could not move freely across the mountaintops.

Their readiness to act had to do with customary privileges, too. Both Abimael, a sugar plantation administrator's son, and Augusta, the daughter of landowners, descended from the old mestizo ruling class. Their self-appointed right to decide what was best for poor villagers derived from hereditary habit in addition to their advanced Marxist science. Anthropologist Carlos Iván Degregori described *senderista* leaders as the *nuevos mistis*, the new mestizos (in the pale-skinned Abimael and Augusta's case with little or no mixed ancestry at all). They fought to free the indigenous peasantry without relinquishing the big landlord's prerogative to dictate life and death. The Central Committee authorized action against Lucanamarca and two other hamlets.

"Lucanamarca, Huancasancos, Sacsamarca will be ashes!" shouted the massed *senderistas* early in the afternoon of April 3, 1983.

They had received the order from Lima.

Some were regular fighters, others peasants from lower in the valley. They wielded machetes, knives, and at least one AK-47 captured from the army, while raising their red flag with its golden hammer and sickle. After killing some villagers along the way, they arrived at Lucanamarca, which clung to the mountainside like an Italian hill town. Some Lucanamarcans fought back with slings and stones, but they had no chance. The *senderistas* went door to door, searching for money and hidden villagers. They found one man's life savings, perhaps twenty dollars, wrapped in a cloth. The villager seemed oblivious to his danger.

"Give me back half," he insisted. "I can't survive without it."

An annoyed *senderista* shot the man in the head. (Remarkably, he survived to tell the tale.)

The *senderistas* separated men and women in the village plaza. They lined up the men, hacking them down with machetes and pickaxes to save ammunition. Those who didn't die right away received a bullet from the AK-47 at last. When the rebels finished with the men, they lined up the women. The *mamitas* cried, pleading in shrill Quechua as the rebels brought out the kerosene. They would burn the women alive in retribution for the Lucanamarcans having done the same to their comrade.

Suddenly, a child lookout called from the church bell tower.

"The army's coming!"

The commanding rebel ordered his fighters to torch the hamlet. They set buildings on fire before vanishing, the smoke rising into the blue Andean sky. The army platoon arrived to find piled bodies and weeping villagers, a scene out of a woodcut from Germany's sixteenth-century Peasant Wars. Some analysts would later attribute the war's carnage to peasant brutality or latent Indian resentment about oppression. It was exactly the opposite. There had been little Andean killing before Shining Path. The main cause of the escalating carnage was the importation of Marxism in its most rigidly orthodox form. An order from the party's Lima commanders left sixty-seven peasants dead in Lucanamarca. "The poor were exterminated," a *huayno* mourned. "Abimael Guzmán and his people killed my *paisanos*."

It did not trouble Abimael that so many people died at Lucanamarca. Although acknowledging some "militarist excess," he believed the massacre delivered its intended message. "We showed that we were a tough bone to gnaw, that we were ready to do anything, anything." (Here Abimael seemed to be channeling Lenin's well-known assertion that "we must stop at nothing . . . to save Communism.") Why? "To serve them [the masses], that is what we want." A further attempt at justification would become that the Lucanamarcans had been "army auxiliaries." That made the penniless farmers into legitimate targets for armed attack, Elena claimed later.

The army's arrival completely changed the war in the countryside. In the first two years, when Augusta roamed the Pampas Valley, many hamlets welcomed the *senderistas,* with some exceptions like Huaychao. The rebels did not have to hack people apart to keep the peasantry in line. Their terror tactics set villages like Lucanamarca against the revolution for good. It had been one thing, too, for a villager to give food and shelter with no real consequences, and another now to see it could mean being shot by an army patrol for doing so. Some peasants kept faith with the *cumpas,* the comrades, especially those who had family brutalized by the army. Never again, however, would the *senderistas* enjoy the wider acceptance of their first two years. Their plan to encircle the cities from the countryside was beginning to run aground. They would have to find another way to win.

The Lucanamarca news reached Lima's *Caretas* office. Óscar Medrano, the *Caretas* photographer, happened to be in Ayacucho just then. He raced over to the city hospital to photograph massacre survivors. Medrano saw police guards at the door, barring reporters, and quickly made a plan. He borrowed a *portaviandas,* a metal lunchbox, from a market woman. After double-wrapping his camera in plastic bags, Medrano put it in the lunchbox, then covered it with soup. *I'm bringing lunch for an injured friend,* he explained to the police. They waved him into the hospital.

Medrano found a wounded Lucanamarcan in his bed. The peasant had a white bandage over his head.

Medrano greeted him, explaining he was from *Caretas.* "*Urquy kay vendaje,*" he asked. "Can you remove your bandage?"

The man complied. Medrano snapped pictures of the hideous machete slash from various angles, and took several more with the bandage on. Like every good photojournalist, he shot plentifully in hopes of capturing the moment's essence. Medrano circled an image from his contact sheets later in the darkroom. That picture of the villager staring sorrowfully into the camera would become the Peruvian war's most iconic photograph.

The death toll rose sharply with the army's intervention. At least 2,255 people were killed in 1983, almost triple the combined total from the war's first three years, and the majority of the victims poor villagers like the Lucanamarcans. "Most [deaths] are caused by the reaction," a 1984 *senderista* document claimed. "They fill lakes [with blood] while we only soak our handkerchiefs." By contrast, the army blamed the rebels for most of the bloodshed. According to the later government-sponsored Truth and Reconciliation Commission, the *senderistas* bore responsibility for 46 percent of the approximately 70,000 war dead; government forces for 30 percent; and village militias the remaining part. Both sides slaughtered at will by the time of the Lucanamarca massacre, whatever the exact numbers. It was hard even to guess at the carnage in some isolated provinces.

Those stories about the army's atrocities proved true. According to an investigation by journalist Ricardo Uceda, General Noel and his military intelligence officers established secret prisons to torture and execute captives. They baptized one camp near Ayacucho as *La Isla de la Fantasía,* "Fantasy Island." Here, the military joke went, captured guerrillas could fulfill their dream of dying for the revolution. At another detention center, the *Casa Rosada,* the "Pink House," counterinsurgency officers entertained themselves by using a prisoner for target practice. (He fell dead after a few rounds of fire.) Noel had executed captives buried in the shooting range by the Los Cabitos army barracks.

It was the war's hardest moment for Shining Path. "The army came like a hurricane," Elena said. At training meetings with new recruits, she tried never to show any fear or doubt. *You must wear the face of victory to go to war,* the party taught. Augusta kept up the same confident front. "We are turning from novitiates to veterans," Abimael told them.

Their difficulties could not be denied. One afternoon in 1984, Clara's Ayacucho committee held a meeting outside the city. It included the standard self-criticism session, and, upset at being targeted, one local commander walked out. Clara and the others assumed the man, Fedor Aucapuccla, would return, but he was tired of fighting. He reported the *senderista* meeting at a police checkpoint.

"Aucapuccla's been gone a long time," said Carlotta Tello, the area military chief. "We'd better go."

It was too late. The police had radioed Los Cabitos, and troops surrounded the house. A firefight left six *senderistas* dead. The army captured six more alive, including Clara, Carlotta, and a third woman. They took their prisoners to Los Cabitos. A new general, Adrián Huamán, had become the military commander, but the army compound remained a black hole that swallowed up captive guerrillas. Amnesty International had received over one thousand reports of disappearances there and at a navy-run detention center in Huanta's soccer stadium by late 1984.

The army did not realize that Clara was the top Ayacucho commander. Their interrogator focused on Carlotta.

"Do you understand that you still have hope if you give information?" the major asked.

"I'm a dead woman," the brash young Ayacuchan reportedly replied. "But the Party will never die. When I'm dead, the Party will destroy you. I'll die knowing that we will win. You'll die not knowing why."

The army held the women for almost a week, raping them by one account.

Then one night the soldiers hooded the rebel prisoners, marching them down a hill to be shot. Clara reportedly showed no fear, in the expected *senderista* manner. She had not expected to see Communism's dawn herself, although she was pregnant and had hoped her baby would. Clara and Carlotta, neither yet thirty, were shot in turn. Soldiers dumped the bodies in a mass grave at the firing range.

The end seemed near for Lurgio Gavilán, too. A patrol surrounded his band a little after Clara's death, shooting at Lurgio and his friend Rosaura as they clambered across the rocks. A bullet shattered Rosaura's arm, but she kept running. Then another bullet pierced her in the back. She bled to death in the dirt, while Lurgio stumbled forward. He made it back to their camp near Mt. Rasuwillka. The surviving *senderistas* cooked some potatoes and horsemeat, while Lurgio tended the wounded. "It is not serious," he told them as he'd been taught. "We will go down in history as heroes."

The next morning, the soldiers closed in. Their bullets, mortars, and grenades shook the ground. Lurgio lay face down on a rock, pretending to be dead. A soldier noticed the boy. He pointed his gun at Lurgio's head to finish him off.

"Stop, don't shoot!" someone said.

His captors brought Lurgio to their commander. The lieutenant interrogated him, village militiamen translating. Lurgio sobbed blindly, a boy reduced to tears.

The soldiers and villagers laughed. "Kill him already," the villagers said. "Even ones as small as he have burned our villages." The lieutenant ignored them. He brought lost boys back to live at the base. There Lurgio received some schooling, learned to speak Spanish, and helped with chores. The soldiers kept a caged eagle for a pet. Lurgio liked talking to animals, a habit from his peasant boyhood. "Here's a bit of intestine," he would tell the eagle. One day it escaped into a eucalyptus tree. It pleased Lurgio to watch the great bird take flight, winging away towards the peaks.

CHAPTER NINE

The Queen of Villa

A pickup truck carried Eugenia Delgado and her six children down the road out of Lima one morning. Eugenia was a single mother. She did not earn much as a washerwoman in the oceanfront Barranco district with its decaying mansions and tropical gardens. Her three boys, Carlos, Eduardo, and Raúl, brought in a few more coins peddling toothpaste and cigarettes along Lima's streets. Eugenia sometimes couldn't pay the rent for their rooms a few blocks from the San Francisco Church. Now, finally, they would have their own house. Eugenia had signed up for a lot in a new settlement, Villa El Salvador, a half hour south of Barranco. They were moving that morning.

Her middle daughter, María Elena, gazed out from her perch on the pickup's flatbed. She was twelve, gap-toothed and willowy, bearing her father's last name, Moyano. The asphalt turned into a dirt track passing by a pig farm's ramshackle sties. Then, a little farther along, María Elena saw shacks clustered across the desert. Their straw-mat walls were wired to wooden posts. Some had no roofs, but it never rained in these Peruvian deserts anyway. (Herman Melville, who visited Lima as a sailor in 1844, lamented the sad city's "tearless" sky in *Moby-Dick*.) Eugenia found their patch of sand: Sector 3, Group 18, Block P, Lot 2. María Elena helped to unload their clothes, a table, and some kitchen utensils.

This, Eugenia announced, would be their new home. The trials of a new life in the desert did not seem to worry her. She pointed to one corner of the sand. "Your room will be there," she told the boys. "You girls," she waved to Narda, Martha, and María Elena, "will be here." Eugenia motioned to another corner. "Here's my room! And, *carajo*, goddamit, we'll have a spiral staircase to the second floor!"

The boys fought for the honor of going to buy the straw mats, the *esteras*, and other necessary materials. By evening, as darkness fell across the desert, Eugenia and the children had put up their shack. The wind blew through the straw and kept extinguishing their candle. A family one lot over, the Carrillos, shared hot chocolate. That was dinner for María Elena and the others that night. She went to sleep in the bed that Eugenia shared with her three daughters.

It was 1973, and the news from abroad included the Arab oil crisis, the Watergate scandal and a television viewership of over a billion people for Elvis Presley's *Aloha from Hawaii Via Satellite*. A little-known philosophy professor, Abimael Guzmán, and his wife were only just then beginning to prepare their armed insurrection. The young María Elena Moyano would grow up to become a well-known leader herself. She would risk everything to front the opposition to Shining Path. A bronze statue in Villa would celebrate María Elena's life. The skinny black girl lay in her crowded bed with that future still far away. She fell asleep to the ocean surf's distant rumble across the bare hills.

The life of María Elena Moyano would be bound to her new desert home. Those shacks in Villa El Salvador marked the latest unexpected chapter in Lima's almost five centuries of existence. The Incas had been a mountain people, ruling from Cuzco, a thin-aired Rome. Their empire stretched more than two thousand miles from modern-day Chile to Colombia in its fifteenth-century heyday. By contrast, the conquering Spaniards required a port city, a way to keep connected to their Iberian home base and the other colonies. Their commander, Francisco Pizarro, founded Lima in 1535, by the Rímac River north of the ancient desert shrine of Pachacamac. The so-called City of Kings became the gilded seat of Spain's South American empire until Peruvian independence in 1821. Invading Chileans occupied Lima during the War of the Pacific (1879–1883). The capital had barely a hundred thousand residents at the turn of the century, and orchards and farms lay just a short carriage ride from the city center. Only in 1903 did the first car bump down the Paseo Colón, to great excitement.

Everything changed over the next decades. Many villagers abandoned the Andes for Lima in a *Grapes of Wrath*–style exodus to match the flight from the Dust Bowl in the United States. The migrants erected their shacks in a giant half circle of *pueblos jóvenes* ("new towns"), around Lima's old districts, which fronted the Pacific Ocean. "On the way to Arabia," a street comic described sandy shantytowns like Villa El Salvador. Elderly Lima *señoras* blamed the "uncivilized" highlanders for the dirt, crime, and traffic, while more forbearing observers wondered at the city's new face. "Lima, air with a light patina of courtly mold / ancient lamp that I recognize in the dark, what are you?" wrote the poet and essayist Sebastián Salazar Bondy. The capital grew to four million people by 1980 towards a place among the biggest and most chaotic megalopolises in the hemisphere.

The new home of María Elena Moyano had a somewhat special history. In 1971, three thousand people illegally camped on a vacant Lima hill, and, after the police killed a man in a failed eviction attempt, the military government intervened. An agreement gave the squatters land for a new settlement, Villa El Salvador, in the Lurín desert down from Lima. Several thousand needy others were also able to sign up for a rectangle of sand there, among them María Elena's mother, Eugenia. The leftist dictator General Juan Velasco wanted Villa to model progressive urban development. His planners arranged lots there by sector, group, and block, loosely inspired by Cuba's socialist design and the experimental Brazilian capital, Brasilia. In contrast to the more haphazard layout of other shantytowns, the Villa grid left room for roads, parks, schools, factories, and health clinics. Having grown up in a city slum, Velasco took a special interest in Villa. He and his wife went out some Sundays to inspect progress.

It remained one big sweaty campout at first. María Elena and her family had to buy water from tanker trucks and dig a hole in the sand for a toilet. There were no Villa high schools yet. So María Elena and Narda, her older sister, finished their education back in Barranco. At daybreak, the girls walked a mile down to the bus stop. They crowded onto the rattle-trap *micro*, as everyone called the buses, along with bricklayers, gardeners, and street peddlers on their way up to work in the city. It took the two Moyanos an hour and a half to make the opening bell. Each girl carried a single buttered roll to last the day.

Everyone in Villa was some kind of poor. One night, soon after María Elena and her family arrived, a woman asked Eugenia to borrow her table. Her baby had just died and she had nowhere to lay out the little coffin for the wake. "Up, everybody!" ordered Eugenia. The woman and her relatives carried away the table. The children ate evening soup squatting on their shack's dirt floor.

Most families improved their lot with time. They held chicken barbecues, *polladas*, to raise money for school projects, and, eventually, the government came through with sewage, running water, and electricity. A dearth of good factory jobs led Villans to set up their own juice stands, shoe-repair stalls, garages, welding shops, and corner stores. (What sociologists called a small-scale unregulated "informal economy" grew rapidly every-where across an expanding Lima.) Somehow Villans cobbled together a liv-ing between their little family enterprises, and, as often as not, at least one household member holding down a job as a dishwasher, housecleaner, or security guard. Eugenia never got her spiral staircase, but she did build a two-story house with a little garden and a television. The empty sectors in Velasco's master plan filled to make Villa into a bustling district of almost 150,000 people by 1980.

It was made to match for a free-spirited teen like María Elena. She went to neighborhood parties where the loudspeakers blared the latest shanty-town hits. "Dance! Dance! Dance!" enjoined *El Chacalón*, "The Big Jackal," who godfathered a new part-cumbia, part-Andean musical genre called *chicha*. María Elena paired with Narda to lead a youth volleyball squad. Her application was accepted by the sociology program at Lima's Garcilaso de la Vega University.

And she fell in love, too. Gustavo Pineki, a friend of María Elena's broth-ers, lived down the street. He was a calm, good-looking man with moist brown eyes and a graceful way about him. María Elena had been working in a community-run day care center. A cabinetmaker by trade, Gustavo charmed her by fashioning a little table and chairs for her classroom. They had been together for three years when, at twenty-one, María Elena became pregnant. The devoutly Catholic Eugenia was incensed. An illegitimate grandchild? Gustavo and María Elena placated Eugenia by marrying at her former Barranco church.

But the newlyweds had no place to live. Gustavo heard that an apart-ment complex in the affluent Miraflores district needed a caretaker. They would get a little apartment and a bit of money for sweeping, doing repairs, and keeping an eye on things. He and María Elena moved in along with their new baby, Gustavo Jr.

That experiment did not last long. María Elena, trying to help, would mop the stairs between cooking and caring for the baby. One day, a woman accused her of stealing clothes from the rooftop line. María Elena was furious. It was bad enough that she had recently been forced to drop out of the university, lacking the tuition fees. She would not be treated like a shuffling brown housemaid. Gustavo knew he could not coop her in Miraflores any longer.

There was a knock at Eugenia's door later that same day. It was María Elena, Gustavo, and the baby with their things in a borrowed truck. María Elena explained to her mother that they would be moving back in until they found their own place. She was back in Villa to stay.

———————

That was when María Elena grew serious about politics. She had been exposed as a teenager to the ideals of social justice and the gospel of the poor through a Catholic youth group. (A Peruvian Dominican priest, Gustavo Gutiérrez, coined the concept of "liberation theology" for the new activist Latin American Catholicism.) She read Marx, Lenin, and the founding Peruvian Marxist father, José Carlos Mariátegui, before dropping out from the university. When María Elena moved back to Villa with Gustavo and their baby in 1978, she attended Maoist study sessions. The organizers claimed to belong to the one true Peruvian Communist Party, but others just called them Shining Path. Their leader, Abimael Guzmán, sometimes came to Villa meetings, although María Elena never met him. Her study group organizers told her that the former philosophy professor was Peru's greatest revolutionary.

One night in 1979, María Elena surprised Gustavo with an announcement. They had a little house close to Eugenia's by then. "I'm going to the mountains to fight. I'll be leaving in a few days," María Elena said. The Peruvian Communist Party, she explained, would soon go to war. She intended to join the revolution.

A shocked Gustavo tried to talk her out of it. He was a leftist himself, although not an activist by nature. After leaving school in the sixth grade to help at his father's carpentry shop, he'd read on his own, even parsing Marx's doorstop trilogy, *Capital*. He had his own theories about race, revolution, and their fellow Peruvians.

"Malena," Gustavo said. That had been her nickname from girlhood. "Peru is not like Russia with Lenin or Mao in China. They're one race, more united. We're a mixture of races. Besides, Peruvians are *envidioso*, envious people. They only look out for themselves. Nothing will change here, maybe just get a bit better."

Gustavo added a practical angle.

"You're from the coast. You're a *negra*, a black woman. You're not made for the mountain cold. Leave the fighting to *serranos*."

María Elena was unmoved.

Gustavo grew angry. He had to go the next morning to help at his father's shop in Lima's Pueblo Libre district.

"I'm going tomorrow," he said. "If you've gone to Ayacucho when I get back, then don't come back."

Gustavo returned that weekend to find María Elena still there. She hadn't ruled out joining Shining Path, but told Gustavo she would wait. They talked for hours about politics, revolution, and Peru's future.

That year, 1980, Abimael Guzmán's revolutionaries went to battle. Although the *senderistas* showed their contempt for elections by burning ballots, the country voted anyway. Other socialist groups did not share Shining Path's disregard for democracy as a sham capitalist diversion. In a rare show of Peruvian leftist pragmatism, they formed the United Left coalition. Their candidate, Alfonso Barrantes, a diminutive man nicknamed

El Frejolito, the little bean, won the Lima mayoralty in 1984. He became the first socialist mayor of any Latin American capital city. An expatriate Spanish schoolteacher, Michel Azcueta, another United Left candidate, was elected as Villa El Salvador's mayor that same year.

Armed revolt, by then, no longer seemed necessary to María Elena. She joined the United Mariateguista Party, the largest United Left coalition member, and threw herself into community organizing and local politics. Her dimpled smile, outgoing personality, and forceful manner made her a natural leader. The United Mariateguista Party backed a new women's group, the Popular Federation of Women of Villa El Salvador, or FEPOMUEVES, which grew to several thousand members. María Elena worked in its breakfast program and other activities. She was elected FEPOMUEVES president in 1984 at the age of twenty-five.

That María Elena was a *negra,* black, made her somewhat exceptional in Villa. Her father, Hermógenes, came from Chincha, the Afro-Peruvian heartland down the coast. He and Eugenia had three children together before splitting. Other black families lived in Villa, as well as some *chinos,* the generic Peruvian word for immigrants from China, Japan, or anybody with narrow eyes. But most Villans had migrated there from Ayacucho, Ancash, Cuzco, Junín, and other mountain states, or "departments," as Peruvians called them. The tallish, Afro-wearing María Elena did not look much like the short Andean women who picked her to lead FEPOMUEVES.

That mattered little. It was true that Peru's ugly system of color and money bore similarities to apartheid South Africa, as one anthropologist noted. A wealthy white minority secured itself behind walls and watchmen in enclaves like San Isidro and Las Casuarinas. But there was also a certain relaxed feel, at least in Lima's *pueblos jóvenes*, about race relations and bodily appearance. A Villan might hail a friend or even a stranger as *negro* (black), *gringo* or *colorado* (white), *chino* (Asian), *gordo* (fatty), *flaco* (skinny), or *chato* (shorty). Perhaps the most common designation, *cholo*, the catchall for poor brown Peruvians of provincial origin, flew thick in street banter. Adding a diminutive marked friendship and even endearment. (*¿A dónde vas negrita linda?* "Where are you going pretty black girl?" a plaintive ditty asked.) Poverty had a way of overriding racial designations in the shantytowns. "Neither black nor Indian can assume we're superior here in the desert," María Elena once told a friend. She loved to drink, smoke, joke, argue, pontificate, laugh, and push her way to the dance floor, no matter who was there.

Many black Peruvians excelled at salsa, merengue, and cumbia. María Elena had little aptitude for these tropical beats, though it never kept her from a party. She was better at the syncopated Andean *huaynos*.

"Am I really black?" she asked Gustavo, half seriously. He, an expert *salsero*, had noticed María Elena's bad rhythm. He was far too wise a husband to say anything about it.

María Elena frequently commanded the microphone as *animadora*, the mistress of ceremonies, at community events. There'd be speeches, socializing, food, a clown act, and dancing between the marauding toddlers, paper streamers, and beer crates. María Elena would call out an old couple to dance a *huaylash* or a *huayno* from their native Andes. "*¡Arriba, jóvenes, arriba!*" she'd laugh. "Go to it, youngsters, go to it!"

The festivities sometimes ended with a Villa anthem.

María Elena closed her eyes for the chorus.

In Villa I was born; in Villa I will die.

The hopeful energy in Villa drew admiring attention from abroad. It was a self-proclaimed *comunidad auto-gestionaria*, a self-made community, a model of poor people's democracy in action. The late 1970s and early 1980s marked a high point for international leftist solidarity with Latin America between church groups, human rights activists, and the idealistic *brigadis-tas* who headed down to support Nicaragua's 1979 Sandinista revolution. Various foreigners arrived to lend a hand in Villa.

A young Italian couple moved in near María Elena. Guido Sattin, a doc-tor, and his wife Marina Rodinó came from Venice, and, committed leftists, left the Grand Canal and the Doge's Palace behind to volunteer in a desert shantytown. María Elena quickly befriended the couple in her gregarious way. One night, Sattin and Rodinó heard a rapping at their door. María Elena carried a bruised little bundle in her arms. It was a baby, only months old, and its mother had just been killed in a car crash. María Elena wanted Sattin to examine the infant because the local health clinic had already closed. "She was always caring for people," Sattin remembered.

It paid to have María Elena in your corner. One day, a Spanish health worker, Charo Torres, heard a rumor—some locals believed her to be a *sacaojo*, or eye-snatcher. A cousin to the *pishtaco*, the legendary Andean vampire, a *sacaojo* cut out poor children's eyes for transplants. They some-times assumed a white person's form, and, the stories said, cruised poor neighborhoods in Mercedes-Benzes and other luxury cars scouting for new victims. (Various sociologists argued, reasonably enough, that *sacaojo* tales captured anxiety about war, poverty, and more Peruvian children being adopted abroad.) Residents in one Lima shantytown, Huaycán, nearly lynched a suspected eye-snatcher.

María Elena acted quickly. She cornered some women who were spread-ing the story about Torres, the Spaniard. "Who saw a *sacaojo*?" she asked. "*Vamos*, c'mon, tell us all about it!" The embarrassed rumor-spreaders did not dare reply. The stories stopped. Torres and María Elena's other foreign friends noticed that no one ever broke into their house or bothered them on the street. They enjoyed protection from the young woman who was such a force in Villa.

That María Elena had become a leader measured the changing times.

friends included the two Dianas, Cecilia Blondet, and Charo Torres, the Spaniard. They drank together at Barranco's watering hole, Juanito.

Even her unkindness about the older Floras was revealing in its way. María Elena had no patience for the expected Peruvian deference to whiteness and the moneyed. "She was exactly the same with a Miraflores millionaire and a Villa mother," Cecilia Blondet recalled. Her boldness was part of her charm.

Once María Elena went to a reception with Blondet. She had borrowed her mother's favorite white suit without permission. "Don't hug me!" María Elena ordered everyone. "In fact, don't touch me! I can't get stains on my suit." Blondet made a joke about her friend's fastidiousness. María Elena did not want to hear it. She had to get that suit back into Eugenia's closet with no telltale clues to her unauthorized raiding. Little scared María Elena besides her mother.

The war was reaching Villa by the mid-1980s. Unlike the mountains, where Shining Path had its "liberated zones" until the army's arrival, the *senderistas* operated covertly in Lima and its shantytowns. They killed a policeman and bombed a few government offices in Villa, but otherwise carried out few armed actions at first. Occasionally, the district went black when the rebels brought down the power lines once again, a hammer and sickle flickering up in the hills. By now some local restaurant owners had bought generators to stay open during blackouts.

María Elena and her friends made the best of it. When the government imposed a curfew, a *toque de queda*, her Italian neighbors, Guido and Marina, hosted parties. These affairs attracted local activists, church workers, foreign volunteers, Lima feminists, and random Villans. María Elena was a regular. The parties lasted until curfew's end at five o'clock in the morning. Only then could everyone leave without danger of getting in trouble with a police patrol. No one paid much attention to the far-off boom of the occasional rebel bomb.

It could have been María Elena lighting the fuses. Hadn't she been about to abandon her husband and baby to head for the Andes? In contrast to that other charismatic young leftist leader, Augusta La Torre, María Elena decided against the plan for a revolution at gunpoint. She was too pragmatic, freethinking, and unbound by convention for *senderista* orthodoxies. Her childhood questions about God's existence had always irritated her mother. *If He did exist, why did He allow so many children to die from hunger?* María Elena asked. Gustavo's counterarguments had led her to question Shining Path's inflexible ideology and, once the war began, she grew increasingly distressed by its carnage. The *senderistas* seemed to be retreating from the Andes anyway. Her faith lay in dignity and social justice through local organizing now.

Even so, Gustavo was right about the *envidia*, the jealousy and backbiting. There always seemed to be squabbling between María Elena's United Mariateguista Party and other leftist groups. Some Villa women believed that María Elena had deserted them for her fancy Lima friends. That did not keep her, in 1986, from easily winning reelection as president of FEPOMUEVES, the Villa Women's Federation. "She was an extraordinary young woman," remembered Guido, the Italian doctor, "and starting to fly."

Anything seemed possible. María Elena had ambitions for herself as well as for Villa and her country. Mayor of Villa? A congressional seat? One night with Gustavo, she wondered out loud if she might be president some day. Her curiosity took her to a tarot reader once. The woman dealt María Elena's cards on the table. "You'll be famous," she accurately divined, but said nothing about the cost.

CHAPTER TEN

The Shining Trench

Narciso Sulca sat at his desk after recess, holding in the rage.

"*¡Serrano chuto!*" the other boys had been taunting him on the playground. "Indian hillbilly!"

It had been more than a year since Huaychao villagers strangled the seven *senderistas* at the judgment rock. The rebels responded with deadly surprise attacks, once late in 1983 hacking a Huaychaino and his son to death after surprising them alone in their fields. Narciso and his family slept in caves many nights. It was muddy and freezing, but they could not light a fire for fear of giving themselves away. Their sheep bedded down in the hollows as well; the lowing, fleas, and stinky manure made things even more miserable. *Utaq uywakuna qinan kausanchik*, Narciso thought. "We are living like beasts."

Many Huaychainos fled to Carhuahurán, a slightly bigger village with a military post for protection. Narciso's family finally moved there too, but Narciso was sent to Huanta for middle school. His father, Isidro, feared that the soldiers would force his oldest son into the village militia and also wanted him to get an education. Isidro had migrated to Lima for a spell as a young man, learning Spanish and to read and write. He warned his thirteen-year-old about the treatment of Iquichans before sending him on his way.

"When you get to Huanta, the kids are going to call you *chuto*, dirty Indian. You give it back. Tell them they're the dirty ones."

His father had been right about the insults. The kids at his town school were also poor and mostly from country families, but they looked down on the "backward" Indians far up in Iquichan villages like Uchuraccay and Huaychao. Even for an Iquichan, Narciso was a tiny boy, of the kind who gets picked on in any school. The other boys teased him about his chapped cheeks and his ill-fitting clothes. Narciso returned furious from every recess.

One day at lunch, a valley boy knocked over his bowl of chicken soup. It was too much for Narciso, who jumped up to push his persecutor away. "Whatever, hillbilly!" the boy scoffed. "Where are you from, *chuto de mierda*, highland motherfucker? I'll rip off your balls and—"

Little Narciso pounced on his tormentor before he could finish. He tripped the bigger boy, pummeling him until a teacher pulled them apart. After that, no one bothered Narciso, but his parents couldn't afford to keep him in Huanta beyond that first year. He went back up to live in his family's mud shelter in Carhuahurán.

The war had become a stalemate by the mid-1980s. Refugees like Narciso's family settled around Carhuahurán and its military base. The army's arrival put the *senderistas* on the defensive, although they still raided unprotected farmhouses. Some couples stopped having sex; they did not want to bring babies into so terrible a world. That Carhuahurán had secret *senderista* sympathizers made the atmosphere even more fearful, a war "*entre prójimos*," or between neighbors, as anthropologist Kimberly Theidon described it. Boys like Lurgio Gavilán and Narciso had few options besides joining the *senderistas* or fighting them as village militiamen. Narciso became a *ron-*

dero, as Isidro had feared, and at fourteen was out with the soldiers hunting rebels, the *malafekuna*, the people of bad faith. The *senderistas* traveled with the devil himself, village pastors said.

Narciso's family had no land in Carhuahurán. He rose early to hike with his brother Leandro and Isidro over the *jalca*, the moors, to their Huaychao fields. They walked silently across the grassland between the giant volcanic outcroppings folded at strange angles by primeval fires. Little else but tubers grew at this altitude, and Narciso used his *chakitaklla*, the traditional foot plow, to dig furrows. He and his brother stopped midday to eat some cold boiled potatoes, peeling them with their mud-encrusted fingers and tossing away the red and purple skins. By midafternoon, Isidro would yell for his boys to pack up. They had to get back to Carhuahurán before the *tuta puriqkuna*, the nightwalkers, descended from the heights to raid some new village in the black hours before the dawn.

Gustavo Gorriti wondered sometimes about Huaychao and its villagers. His reporting kept him so busy that his helicopter trip there two years before already seemed long ago. The *senderistas*, Gustavo knew, maintained a presence across the Ayacuchan countryside. One Sunday in 1985, some rebel sympathizers tethered an unfortunate donkey at Huanta's open-air market. It was a *burrobomba*, packed with explosives and pamphlets, and soon detonated to shower shoppers with paper and shredded flesh. Down in Lima, a few weeks before, four guerrillas opened fire at a bus stop by Lima's navy headquarters, killing three people. The rebels once more strafed the US ambassador's residence, and, showing their equal opportunity disdain for foreign powers, bombed the Chinese and Soviet embassies for betraying true Communist principles. "Conquering power everywhere across the country," the latest red wall graffiti declared.

Even the archaeologists had to decamp from this land of a million ruins.

A Stanford archaeologist, John Rick, ran a project studying an ancient hunting site in a high *puna* region beyond the mining town of Cerro de Pasco. One evening, *senderistas* appeared out of the frigid darkness. The commander quizzed Rick about his research, then, as a "contribution" to the revolution, asked to siphon gas from his four-by-four. Rick and his team could stay, the man said, maybe even come back for next year's field season. "Here in Peru there is a class struggle going on," he said. "When you return Chairman Gonzalo will be president." The *senderistas* wanted to shut down a nearby government-administered cooperative farm, which, like Allpachaka, they viewed as an instrument of evil capitalist development. They shot the farm administrator; set the buildings ablaze with gas; and slit the throats of two hundred sheep. Rick wisely decided to close down operations. He had told the *senderista* commander he was Canadian, and, if the guerrillas discovered he was an American, a potential Yankee spy, that might mean a bullet in the head. Almost every dig shut down by the late 1980s.

By now Gustavo had become Peru's best-known war reporter. Enrique Zileri, the *Caretas* publisher, also assigned him to investigate a drug kingpin, Reynaldo Rodríguez López, or *El Padrino*, The Godfather. Rodríguez López kept a rare liqueur collection and paid for English classes so his *burros,* drug-runners, could learn the language. His Lima cocaine lab exploded in 1985, leading to his arrest. Gustavo wrote a long story about the drug lord and his payoffs to corrupt police, but he knew that *El Padrino*'s fall would not slow Peru's multimillion dollar cocaine trade. His country was growing more dystopian by the day.

Even with his late start in journalism, Gustavo was still young, thirty-seven, and sometimes lifted weights to stay in shape. His tenaciousness made him the prototype of a war reporter, and, a fine writer as well as a hard-driving investigator, his stories related the facts with occasional literary flourishes like a reference to Hannah Arendt or a French novel. Gustavo had some tough Israeli swagger from his years in the Mideast, which rubbed some rival reporters the wrong way. That nobody had known him until Zileri gave him a job at *Caretas* added a bit of mystery, too. So did Gustavo's being a Jew, a relative rarity in Catholic Peru, even though his father was a gentile and their family had never been observant. One rumor said the star *Caretas* reporter was an undercover Mossad agent.

No one realized that Gustavo had come into possession of some unique source material. One day in 1982, Felipe MacGregor, a Jesuit philosopher and the former rector of Lima's Catholic University, had invited him over to his residence. MacGregor confided that he had been given clandestine Shining Path documents. He did not say who had given him the material, but he wanted to be rid of it. A leading churchman could not be found with rebel papers. The white-haired Jesuit admired Gustavo's reporting. He offered him the documents.

Gustavo thumbed through the manila files.

He saw leaflets, handwritten notes, and much more.

"Interested?" MacGregor asked.

"A little," Gustavo smiled at the old priest.

It had already been in Gustavo's mind to write a book about Shining Path. His new trove of *senderista* material would anchor the project, but he had no time for it with his weekly *Caretas* deadlines. When, somewhat to his surprise, Harvard University offered him a fellowship with time to write, Gustavo talked it over with his wife, Esther. She liked the idea of escaping chaotic Lima for a bit. Gustavo packed his Shining Path papers into a steamer trunk, but spent the year in Cambridge attending lectures, giving several himself at area universities, and taking in Boston's sights with Esther and their teenage daughter. His book would have to wait a little longer.

Back in Peru again, Gustavo found some new optimism. A new president, Alan García, was finishing his first year in office. He was a Latin Kennedy, only thirty-six, a spellbinding speaker with Spanish film star looks. García declared that Peru would unilaterally reduce its debt payments to international creditors. His priority, he said, would be raising living standards for his country's struggling majorities. The outgoing Belaúnde administration had not only mismanaged the war, but left the Peruvian economy in shambles. There were some recovery signs at first under the new García presidency.

The young president promised a more effective counterinsurgency. By 1985, over half the country had been placed under military command to combat Shining Path and the Túpac Amaru Revolutionary Movement (MRTA), a smaller guerrilla group. The government forces and *senderistas* sometimes seemed intent on outdoing each other in grisly bloodletting. Almost every week brought some new report about military torture, massacre, and rape. (The *senderistas* seldom raped, lacking the macho military culture with so many women in their ranks.) The counterinsurgency's savagery was an international embarrassment for the Peruvian government. García wanted this to change. He would not, he claimed, sanction combatting "barbarism with barbarism."

It surprised Gustavo to discover that his boss, Enrique Zileri, had an almost teenage crush on the young president. "I think he may be the answer," the *Caretas* publisher said. The magazine did not much report on García's extravagant deficit spending, or how the new chief executive was packing his administration with corrupt hacks from his APRA party. Instead it ran a flattering spread about García's skill at crooning creole standards on the guitar.

Gustavo was less hopeful, especially about the war. Only two weeks after García's inauguration, army troops marched into Accomarca. This Andean village lay in guerrilla heartland around the Pampas River. The soldiers herded weeping villagers into the chapel. They shot them one by one and burned the bodies. The story reminded Gustavo of My Lai, the 1968 American massacre during the Vietnam War. In Accomarca, the troops also killed the children, seven small bodies among the corpses. The carnage made for a mirror image of Shining Path's Lucanamarca massacre two years before. A distressed García promised an inquiry. His power to rein back the military was proving limited at best.

The latest Ayacucho general, Wilfredo Mori, wondered about the possibility of a government investigation. What if García ordered an inquiry into Los Cabitos? It had been Clemente Noel, the first commander there, who secretly authorized his men to execute captives and bury the bodies at the base. That practice continued after Noel left Ayacucho in 1984. More than two hundred bodies lay in a mass grave in the firing range a stone's throw over the cactus mesa from the city airport. To prevent any remains being found, General Mori hurriedly had his soldiers build an adobe shack, powered by a gas flame thrower. They dug up the corpses and, over several weeks, cremated them at night. Farmers down the canyon smelled the human smoke. It was as if a little secret Auschwitz had appeared in the Andes. There would be no inquiry until decades later.

The biggest wartime bloodbath of all was about to take place. On the morning of June 18, 1986, Gustavo received a call from a government contact, letting him know that Shining Path prisoners had staged a synchronized mutiny at three Lima jails. They held three guards hostage at El Frontón, the island prison Gustavo and Óscar Medrano had visited early in the war. At Lurigancho, a jail in a working-class Lima district, the *senderistas* had another hostage. Rebel women seized control of their Santa Barbara jail in Callao. The *senderistas* issued twenty-six demands, among them to be recognized as prisoners of war. They wanted blankets, soap, cots, mattresses, speedier trials, and improvements to Peru's jails. The "nefarious policy of disappearance" by the counterinsurgency must end, the statement said.

It had become the Shining Path way to treat the prisons as another front in the war. "The political and military activity of a Communist cannot end on the day of his arrest," Abimael explained. Hadn't Lenin and Stalin, both jailed various times under the tsar, kept working for the revolutionary cause from their cells? The *senderista* leader enjoined his followers to transform the "black reactionary dungeons" into "Shining Trenches of Combat." Prisoners decorated cellblock walls with revolutionary murals. A more educated party commissar would tutor the others in Marxist-Leninist-Maoist-Gonzalo Thought, and sometimes, as some rebels had little schooling, how to read and write with greater proficiency. No guard dared to interrupt or even enter the cellblock without permission. Whenever the authorities tried to regain control, they met resistance. About thirty prisoners died in a fire after one confrontation at Lurigancho. The rebels exacted revenge by gunning down Miguel Castro, the El Frontón superintendent, who had already earned their ire for limiting visitors and other measures. They left their usual sign by his body before fleeing: "This is how scoundrels die. The armed people will avenge its martyrs." Castro's small son watched his father bleed to death.

Now the government faced three prison mutinies at once. The *senderistas* had planned the action to coincide with the International Socialist and Social-Democratic Conference, which Lima was hosting that year. Foreign journalists and some well-known politicians like the former West German chancellor Willy Brandt were arriving. The ambitious Alan García wanted to showcase his young administration's supposed achievements for these visitors. By timing their uprising for that weekend, the *senderistas* hoped to place the president in an impossible position. He would look weak by doing nothing—or be forced into a bloody battle for the prisons. A massacre to put down the uprisings during the big international conference would expose the regime's "genocidal" nature to the world, Abimael believed, and increase sympathy for the revolution and its red dawn. (He had ordered the uprisings after the customary rubber stamp from a Central Committee plenary two months before.) "The forces of reaction are dreaming when they try to drown the revolution in blood," the Shining Path leader said, reaffirming party principles. "They should know that they are nourishing it."

Alan García had no patience for more trouble from Shining Path. The rebels had killed two policemen earlier that week, along with bombing offices of the president's APRA party and gunning down a top navy admiral in broad daylight. García summoned his cabinet and military commanders for an emergency meeting. It did not take long to reach a decision. *No negotiations. Take back the prisons.* The order was apparently transmitted from the Presidential Palace by early afternoon on the day of the uprising. To guarantee enough firepower, the armed forces took over the operation. Explosions and gunshots were heard at Lurigancho until after midnight, then nothing. The navy launched an assault at El Frontón. Its commanders intended to crush the revolt and also avenge their admiral's recent murder. ("The subversives should know," a vice admiral warned, "that they have awoken a lion.") The navy helicopter gunships and rocket fire that day made Lima's bay look like a scene from *Apocalypse Now.*

President García announced the next morning that the riots had been put down. The operation "has demonstrated to the country that authority has been imposed," he said. But what, exactly, had occurred at the three prisons? Gustavo, working with three *Caretas* colleagues, learned that the navy had bombed El Frontón to rubble. They killed at least 120 prisoners. At Lurigancho 124 died along with two more *senderistas* at the women's prison. By comparison, the infamous 1968 uprising at New York's Attica Correctional Facility left 43 dead. More than five times that many people, over 240, had just been killed in the three Lima prisons—and that was not all. Gustavo and his colleagues found a wounded Lurigancho prison guard in his hospital bed. He related that more than a hundred rebels had been executed there after surrendering.

The full details came out slowly. An army team had blasted a hole in the cellblock, and a police anti-terrorism unit rushed in through it. They were met by rebels armed with slingshots, spears, and crossbows. The war cries rang through the dust: "Long Live the People's War," "Long live the Shining

Trench of Combat," "Long Live President Gonzalo." Thirty *senderistas* perished in the gunfire and exploding grenades before the others surrendered.
The police commandos forced the men to lie face down in the prison yard.
"Eliminate them," their commander reportedly said. His men went through,
shooting the surrendered prisoners in the back of the head. "Where is President Gonzalo?" a commando screamed at Antonio Díaz Martínez, the
former San Cristóbal agronomy professor and a high-ranking party official. "Where is Gonzalo hiding?" Díaz Martínez did not reply. He was shot,
too. A single *senderista*, Efrén Ticona, saved himself by playing dead in the
strewn corpses. He recalled the commandos looking for anyone still breath-
ing. "At that point they no longer fired, just used their knives."

Gustavo and his colleagues went to Zileri. They had good evidence that
the police had slaughtered surrendered inmates, they explained. The big
Caretas publisher, who once worked in advertising, always included society
pages and half-naked pinup girls in the magazine to sell more copies. But he
maintained his old commitment to publishing the truth no matter the consequences. The Lurigancho massacre story ran in the next issue. (Zileri did
walk over to the Presidential Palace to warn Alan García beforehand that
the damning report would soon appear.) "No immediate parallels in our
country's history exist for the primitive brutality of the deliberate atrocity
committed at Lurigancho," Zileri wrote in an editorial.

There was little outcry about the prison atrocities otherwise. The big
socialist conference had already ended—and the visiting foreign dignitaries and reporters left town—before the whole story of the post-surrender
executions had been revealed. Many Peruvians thought the *senderistas* got
what they deserved for wreaking so much death and destruction. "Those
who mutinied are the ones who violated the law," even Lima's leftist mayor
said. The biggest concern for poor Peruvians was getting by from day to
day. Wealthy Limans could avoid the war altogether except for inconvenient
blackouts and indignant cocktail conversation. Most killings occurred in

zonas periféricas, the poor outlying districts like Puente Piedra and Villa El Salvador. Some white families stopped hiring Ayacuchans for fear they might be *terrucos,* terrorists.

Alan García's presidency soon collapsed into rubble as well. After the news about the Lurigancho and El Frontón massacres, García promised to punish the responsible officers. ("Either they leave," he said, "Or I do.") His big promises and operatic balcony speeches were wearing thin, especially amid new danger signs. Prices were rising, and, by the late 1980s, inflation would skyrocket above 7,000 percent, leaving the Peruvian sol as worthless as Confederate bank notes after the US Civil War. Unemployment, poverty, and hunger led to increasing despair in an already war-torn country. García left office in 1990 among Peru's most hated men and a favorite target for dark humor. One crude joke involved his mother giving anal birth to a piece of shit.

Not even the *senderista* leaders anticipated such a ferocious crushing of their prison uprising. "It was a hard blow," Elena said. She and Augusta shed tears afterwards away from the others. (Abimael supposedly never cried, perhaps as a defensive mechanism from his difficult childhood.) They designated June 19 as the "Day of Heroism," a holy day for the party to recall its martyrs. "By sacrificing their lives," a party statement claimed, the prisoners had "conquered a great political, military, and moral triumph for the proletariat and the Communist Party of Peru." In truth, they had died for nothing, the prison slaughter generating no upswell of Peruvian support for Shining Path and garnering scant attention abroad. The government did not return the remains of dead prisoners to their families until more than three decades later.

It was grueling to cover both the drug trade and the war. Gustavo stayed up past midnight every Sunday to meet the weekly *Caretas* deadline. Was journalism any different from his old farm life, he wondered sometimes? He had once met Seamus Heaney at Harvard, and, in one poem, the future

Nobel Prize winner compared writing and farming. *(Between my finger and my thumb / The squat pen rests. / I'll dig with it.)* Reporting demanded its own spadework between the cold calls, cultivating contacts, and chasing down leads. The competitive Gustavo wanted to beat everybody else to the story. He truly believed, more idealistically, in journalism's righteous role in exposing wrongdoing and corruption. Other Peruvian reporters were also risking their lives to bring back the truth from the jungle and mountains. Their work brought many *senderista* and military atrocities to light for the first time.

News about yet another possible mass execution of Andean villagers reached Gustavo a few months after the prison massacres. A military communiqué announced that an army patrol had fought and killed thirteen "criminal subversives" near a town called Vilcashuamán, a day's drive from Ayacucho. The troops captured "arms, munitions, homemade grenades, subversive propaganda." But Ayacucho sources told Gustavo that the soldiers had actually killed unarmed villagers. The army concocted the guerrilla firefight story to cover up its latest peasant massacre.

Gustavo headed to Ayacucho again. The military command now forbid journalists from leaving the city. According to Los Cabitos, this was for their own safety. The real reason was to keep journalists from investigating the latest rapes, executions, and massacres by the counterinsurgency forces. Military death squads hunted down reporters who probed too far. A correspondent for Lima's *La República* newspaper, Jaime Ayala, disappeared from the navy detention center at the Huanta stadium. His body was never found. Twenty reporters had already been slain in the war, among them the eight at Uchuraccay.

The willful Gustavo was undeterred. Accompanying him to Ayacucho was Nick Asheshov, a British journalist who edited the English-language *Lima Times.* He was good company and offered some protection besides. At least in theory, the army would not harm Gustavo if he was traveling with a foreign reporter. Gustavo also recruited a local Ayacucho reporter, Hugo Ned Alarcón, who had an old VW Bug. His customary photographer, Óscar

Medrano, came too, all the more indispensable for his Quechua fluency. Early in the morning, the four men packed into the Bug, which sputtered up over some Mongolia-like steppes before descending into more cultivated farmland. They talked their way through an army checkpoint with a story about visiting friends in a village aid group. A cloudburst turned the mountain road to slop, and the mud-spattered Bug bumped into Vilcashuamán at dusk.

The town straddled a little hill. It had been a magnificent ceremonial center in pre-Columbian times, and the Spanish conquistadores, as was their way, constructed a church directly over the Inca's Temple of the Sun to show their mastery. Now Vilcashuamán was another sad little Andean town. An army base guarded against *senderista* assault.

Some soldiers appeared to ask Gustavo and his companions for their papers. Óscar Medrano, the native Ayacuchan, dealt with the young sergeant.

"We're here to see some friends, *jefe*," Medrano said. "It's late. We're tired. We'll come first thing tomorrow to register with you."

The sergeant let them go. They found a place to stay in the town clinic, and agreed to head out at daybreak for Pomatambo. That was the village where the supposed army confrontation with the guerrillas had occurred. They would be back in Vilcashuamán by midmorning to check in at the army base before returning to Ayacucho.

Their plan worked, to a point. It dawned sunny and blue, and the VW bumped by little lakes, the peasant fields of green and gold, and stands of eucalyptus. The road shrank into a faint track, but they made it to Pomatambo, where the journalists found distraught villagers eager to tell their story. An army patrol, they said, burst into the community assembly hall on the evening of October 22. They had been brewing *chicha*, the native Andean corn beer, for an upcoming fiesta. The troops seized seven men, marching them through the night to another village, Parcco. There they kidnapped five more people, including the eighty-two-year-old village sacristan and a woman with her two small children. Several days later, the villagers discovered the charred remains of their loved ones on a nearby hill. A peasant woman held up a skull fragment and some poncho shreds.

Qusaypata llapa imantan tarirqaku, she said.

"It's all they found of her husband," Óscar translated.

Gustavo did not always trust war stories. This area had been sympathetic to Shining Path, and, in fact, was not far from Ayzarca, where the *senderistas* had tortured Benigno Medina to death in the war's first killing. When the army came looking for rebels, they sometimes had reason. Many young soldiers had seen their friends' limbs blown off by a *senderista* bomb, or shot down in an ambush. Fear and anger could spur them to slaughter villagers for suspected complicity.

That did not lessen the obvious horror of what had occurred at Parcco and Pomatambo. The military had failed to wipe out the *senderistas* after almost two years of savage warfare. A victorious counterinsurgency, Gustavo knew, demanded more aid to peasants, better intelligence, and a strategy based on well-reasoned operations rather than indiscriminate massacres. Some generals realized this too, among them Adrián Huamán, who had succeeded Noel as the Los Cabitos commander. He had still authorized the secret executions, but also faulted the Belaúnde administration for not funding village public works to win over the peasantry. Huamán was dismissed for his dissenting views.

By then it was almost noon. The local schoolteacher, whom Gustavo guessed had guerrilla ties, became increasingly nervous. "I'm leaving," he said. "The army will come. They'll kill us all." He disappeared into the hills. Gustavo and Nick Asheshov interviewed more villagers. Not until after lunchtime did the VW pull back into Vilcashuamán.

The soldiers were waiting for them.

"Where have you been?" the sergeant demanded. "You were supposed to register."

Then he noticed Óscar's cameras and saw the truth. "*Carajo,* goddamit, you're reporters!" he shouted. Gustavo feared the worst. The soldiers were teenagers, undisciplined, some with wild eyes. They might well have been among the ones to massacre the villagers from Parcco and Pomatambo.

Fortunately, the base commander turned out to be a pleasant young captain. He allowed Gustavo to telegram Enrique Zileri that they had been detained, and, happy for some conversation, escorted them to see a stone Incan throne with a valley view. Óscar snapped pictures of Gustavo and Nick seated there.

The unexpected hospitality hardly meant that the reporters were in the clear. An army helicopter buzzed down to transport them to the Los Cabitos base. What orders did the crew have? A thought came to Gustavo: *I wonder if they'll push us from the helicopter.* The Argentine military death squads back in the 1970s disposed of prisoners that way.

Their helicopter made the short flight without incident. The colonel at Los Cabitos guessed, correctly, that the captive journalists had been investigating the Parcco and Pomatambo massacres. He knew Gustavo and Óscar from a previous trip, but regarded them now with silent fury. It was too risky, however, to "disappear" a British citizen and Peru's best-known journalist. (Some years later, an army death squad did murder another *Caretas* correspondent, Hugo Bustíos.) The colonel turned the reporters over to the police, hoping at least to see them jailed for a bit.

At the station, Gustavo and Nick refused to give statements. The more pragmatic Óscar wanted to get back to Lima. He proposed a compromise to the police commander. "What if I give a declaration for the three of us?" That sufficed. The men were set free, though they were required to leave Ayacucho within twenty-four hours.

There was one thing the authorities did not know. Just before the reporters had been detained in Vilcashuamán, Óscar hid his film rolls in Hugo Ned Alarcón's VW. They had powerful shots, like the woman with her husband's remains. The soldiers had allowed Alarcón to drive back to Ayacucho since there wasn't room for him in the helicopter. When Alarcón pulled in late that night, Óscar pulled the rolls from their hiding place in the wheel well. Now he and Gustavo had everything they needed for their report. They boarded the first Lima flight the next morning.

What Gustavo wanted next was to interview Abimael Guzmán. He had located the *senderista* chieftain's medical records. They revealed his polycythemia, which kept him from the Andes. The fugitive rebel, Gustavo guessed, must be in the jungle or Lima. Latin America's other most-wanted man, the drug billionaire Pablo Escobar, lorded it in a luxurious ranch and appeared sometimes on television. Abimael remained in hiding so mystifyingly complete as to fuel more speculation about his possible death. Gustavo suspected the party leader was still very much alive—and might give him an interview to prove it. He was half right. Abimael would soon make headlines by sitting down with a reporter for the first time, only not with Gustavo.

CHAPTER ELEVEN

The Party Congress

Abimael Guzmán sat at a table ceremoniously covered with a red table-cloth for the big meeting. The nineteen-member Central Committee and a few other party members circled around the living room. A red banner with the hammer-and-sickle symbol announced the occasion in hand-cut gold letters: "First Congress of the Communist Party of Peru." The *senderista* leaders had assembled in this suburban Lima house for the congress's opening session on January 24, 1988. It might have been a low-budget Chinese politburo meeting, down to the unattractive chandelier and the portraits of Marx, Lenin, and Mao on the wall. Augusta and Elena flanked Abimael as the two other Permanent Committee members. Both women had entered their forties, and, after almost a decade at war, they had become hardened rebel leaders.

Nobody there had known much about making war before going to battle. They were schoolteachers, lawyers, and professors by training, but had mounted a fierce insurgency. More than a thousand of their comrades had died in the secret army camps, street combat, and the prison massacres. Their own lives hung by a thread of careful security measures and revolutionary conviction. Three among those there that day—Elvia Zanabria, Deodato Juárez, and Yovanka Pardavé—would be gunned down by the police a few years later. Almost half the assembled rebel leaders were women, many recruited by Augusta and Elena. Most had short hair and all wore the same hand-sewn blue uniforms as the men. Everyone was supposed to be equal in their revolutionary vision.

No neighbor could have guessed at the doings in the house. Their hideout lay in the placid Monterrico subdivision. The unsuspecting owner had rented 459 2nd Street to a smiling, French horn–playing high school teacher. A former nun, Nelly Evans was secretly a rebel militant. The *senderistas* arrived spaced over the day to avoid attracting attention. Several commanders, like Óscar Ramírez, Comrade Feliciano, came down from the Andes. He was an army general's son and the hardnosed Ayacucho field director. "A pleasure to see you, Chairman Gonzalo," Ramírez said. "Long life to you directing the Party."

An embroidered portrait of Abimael hung near the party directorate's table. The middle-aged *senderista* leader looked in person nothing like the square-jawed Marxist Clark Kent of his official likeness. He was pasty-faced and somewhat chubby after so many years in hiding, although healthy enough for a man of fifty-four. His birthday had become a party holiday, and, in their leader's honor, the *senderistas* always marked the day by bombing down the power lines. "Long Live Chairman Gonzalo," came one birthday greeting from a local committee. "On this glorious day, we reaffirm our unconditional subjection to your magisterial command and personal leadership."

Everyone there felt growingly optimistic about their prospects. They had survived the military's savage counterinsurgency and jailhouse slaughter. Their recruitment efforts were aided now by the worsening poverty and mounting disenchantment with the foundering García government. Many new recruits joined the party in 1988 and 1989, although it was hard to give them adequate training in wartime. ("They lack ideological formation," Abimael complained.) The party had its own newspaper now, *El Diario*, which served as its mouthpiece much like Moscow's *Pravda*. No newsstand openly displayed it, but, if someone asked, the vendor pulled a copy from under the other papers. Their armed actions nationwide had grown from under 1,000 in 1982 to over 2,500 in 1986 and more than 2,800 in 1988. They imagined the possibility of seizing power sometime in the next decade.

Their improving outlook led Abimael to summon this first-ever party congress. The founding Peruvian Communist, José Carlos Mariátegui, apparently wanted to hold one, only to die young in 1930. Subsequent congresses held by assorted earlier Marxist parties did not count, according to the official *senderista* view. These were not true revolutionaries. Only thanks to Chairman Gonzalo had the Peruvian Communist Party been "reconstituted" to begin the people's war. Their congress would set the course to victory, they hoped.

The preparations took months. It had been Augusta and Elena's task to write discussion papers, each laying out the party line. Augusta took charge of her two favorite specialties, military strategy and international affairs. Her fifteen-page, single-spaced analysis of world affairs began with the Paris Commune, Russian Revolution, and mid-twentieth-century anti-colonial struggles before reviewing the "sinister" Chinese and Soviet betrayals of the Communist movement. Augusta retained her evangelical fervor about party dogma and its implacable optimism. They had nothing to fear, she wrote, because "the destruction of imperialism and the reactionaries led by Communist Parties—directing the proletariat and the people of the world—will become an incontrovertible reality."

Now Abimael rose to greet his fellow leaders. He opened by recalling their fallen comrades. Hadn't the greatest guide, Chairman Mao, warned that revolution demands its quota in blood and death? "We have indeed generously spilled our own blood," Abimael said. (He did not mention the thousands they had killed themselves.) This led into a grandiose Book of Revelation-meets-*The Communist Manifesto* soliloquy:

> The soul of the Party begins to burn even hotter, even louder, illu-minating the skies, and melting the earth . . . legions of iron will converge in a red sea, armed, rolling across the earth, shaking and upending it. . . . Tomorrow, comrades, our lives could end [but] we will have the glory, among other things, for having been Commu-nists because it is glorious to be a Communist, and the glory of being part of this First Congress.

A cassette recorder taped Abimael's speeches for transcription and clandes-tine distribution. They were intended to inspire fighters in the field—and to preserve the great leader's words for future generations. After all, as Abimael explained, "Never before have these lands seen blood as red as ours, of rev-olutionaries and Communists." Their war would go down as the "greatest epic in our people's history."

The *senderistas* never tried to conceal the revolution's cost. Every armed rebellion, of course, justifies killing and dying as necessary for the great cause, but Gonzalo Thought carried the creed of sacrifice to extremes. To destroy the "rotten old State," Abimael said, meant "destruction in our own ranks, of the Party, of those of the people's army, of the people." The culture of the *senderistas* tended to celebrate, glorify, and even poeticize bloodshed as the righteous path to Communism. "The blood of the people has a rich perfume / It smells like jasmine, geraniums, and daisies," went the lyrics to the unofficial *senderista* anthem, *La Flor de Retama*, or "The Broom Flower." Abimael never seemed to show any careworn Lincolnesque sadness about sending the young off to die. "Comrades, revolutionary war is so beautiful!" he concluded his opening speech.

Their congress was supposed to be a great party landmark. It was really no different from innumerable previous plenaries, conferences, and meetings, except for its length. They would hold three multiweek sessions over two years. Augusta had somewhat mysteriously missed some recent meetings. The others had been told that she was suffering from a "mental illness," with no more elaboration. There seemed no sign of any such distress this time, and Augusta expounded at length about their military situation. ("A great strategist," recalled Osmán Morote, a Central Committee member and the northern *senderista* commander.) Augusta's rank and natural authority commanded deference from even the most battle-hardened *senderista* leaders. "Yes, Comrade Norah, as you wish Comrade Norah," Morote said when Augusta suggested possible targets for attack.

As ever, though, Abimael monopolized the floor. His five congress speeches lasted more than twenty hours—and left over 100,000 words for party scribes to transcribe. ("That was his way," Elena smiled years later.) They included lengthy reviews of Peruvian Communist history and global developments with references to Cervantes, Chiang Kai-shek, Douglas MacArthur, Louis Althusser, Thomas Edison, Fidel Castro, the Nicaraguan Sandinistas, and the recent Palestinian intifada against Israeli occupation. "To command absolute truth," as philosopher Eric Hoffer observes in his classic *The True Believer*, "is to spread the net over all eternity." A shut-in life afforded the bookish Abimael more time than ever to read—newspapers, magazines, novels, philosophy texts, scholarly articles. He underlined whole pages like a college student. Sometimes Abimael read Marx in the original German from having learned the language for his philosophy degree.

By now the cult of the Shining Path leader had reached its fullest expression. Didn't the war's advance confirm Chairman Gonzalo's leadership and wisdom? Who else could claim to be the world's greatest living revolutionary? Abimael's contemporaries from the old Ayacucho days, the *históricos*, had mostly been killed, purged, or left the party. A ritualized obeisance became mandatory in party communications. "Dear Comrades," began one cadre's report to the Central Committee:

> I give you my greeting and my full and unconditional submission to the greatest Marxist-Leninist-Maoist on earth: our beloved and respected Chairman Gonzalo, chief and guide of the Peruvian revolution and the world proletarian revolution, teacher of Communism and party unifier. I give you my greeting and full and unconditional submission to the scientific ideology of the proletariat: Marxist-Leninist-Maoist and Gonzalo Thought, especially Gonzalo Thought, all-powerful and infallible ideology that illuminates our paths and arms our minds.

———

The congress ratified Abimael as "Secretary General of the Party, People's Guerrilla Army Commander, and Permanent Committee Head." A multiplying string of honorifics characterized the cults to Lenin, Castro, Hoxha, Mao, and Kim Il-sung, too. Those other Communists captained victorious revolutions and ruled their countries. It was a peculiarity of Shining Path to deify its leader before winning anything at all.

That bothered some. "Chairman Gonzalo?" one party member complained in an Ayacucho bar. "Is he a God or what? I was at the ILA, in the countryside, the prison. What am I? Nothing! Are they [Abimael and the Central Committee] going to be the ones fighting?" His comrades reported the man. He was expelled from the rebel ranks.

A midlevel Lima commander, Juan Fulano, found himself troubled, too. "They castrated your capacity for analysis," Fulano said. "You had to always 'incarnate Chairman Gonzalo.' If you didn't, they'd call you a conciliator, a saboteur, a rightist." Juan and a few other militants got up before dawn to proselytize entering workers at factory gates. Their propaganda

Abimael Guzmán, 1953, a student at
Arequipa's La Salle High.
Courtesy *Caretas*.

Augusta La Torre, ca. 1960. By Walter Alejos.
Courtesy Baldomero Alejos Archive.

Abimael Guzmán and Augusta La Torre, Wedding Day, February 3, 1964, with Augusta's parents
Delia and Carlos. By Walter Alejos. Courtesy Baldomero Alejos Archive.

Abimael Guzmán, top row center, with other UNSCH professors, ca. 1972. Courtesy *Caretas*.

Augusta La Torre (hand on head), family outing, 1967. Courtesy Walter Alejos.

Elena Iparraguirre, 1962, high school graduation, Lima. Courtesy *Caretas*.

Deng Xiaoping, hung in effigy, Lima, 1981. Courtesy *Caretas*.

Accused traitors, killed by Shining Path, 1981. "This is how exploiters and stool pigeons who are against the people die. Long Live the War of Guerrillas! Long Live the Peruvian Communist Party!" Courtesy *Caretas*.

Shining Path prisoners transported to El Frontón, 1982. By Óscar Medrano, *Caretas*.

Gustavo Gorriti and Óscar Medrano, Ayacucho airport, 1983. Courtesy *Caretas*.

Huaychao *varayoq*, or staff-holders, at the grave of lynched *senderistas*, 1983.
By Óscar Medrano, *Caretas*.

Villagers removing dead journalists, Uchuraccay, January 1983. Courtesy *Caretas*.

Mario Vargas Llosa in Uchuraccay, 1983. Courtesy *Caretas*.

Lucanamarcans show General Clemente Noel bloodstains in church. *Senderistas* massacred sixty-seven villagers there on April 3, 1983. By Óscar Medrano, *Caretas*.

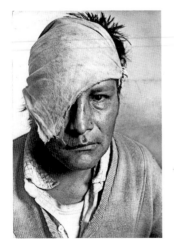

Eduardo Camana, a Lucanamarca survivor, photographed in Ayacucho hospital by Óscar Medrano, 1983, *Caretas*.

Peasant woman in Cochas, Ayacucho, grieving relatives murdered in Shining Path attack, 1986. By Alejandro Balaguer.

Mass grave at Pucayacu, outside Huanta, executed by government forces, 1984. Courtesy *La República*.

Abimael Guzmán addresses the First Military School, April 1980.
Note head placement relative to Marx, Lenin, Mao.

Abimael Guzmán, Chairman Gonzalo,
plants the flag in Ayacucho.

Prison mural of Chairman Gonzalo.

María Elena Moyano, ca.
1987. By Christina Hee
Pedersen.

María Elena Moyano, with children David and Gustavo, 1985. Courtesy Diana Miloslavich.

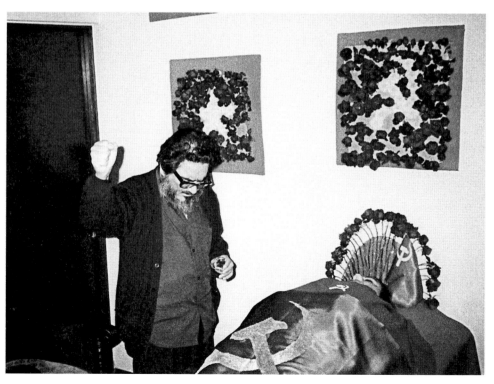

Abimael Guzmán, at wake for Augusta La Torre, 1988. Courtesy *Caretas*.

Alberto Fujimori, presidential campaign, 1990. Courtesy *Caretas*.

Mario Vargas Llosa, campaigning, 1990. Courtesy *Caretas*.

Osmán Morote denounces judge César Ruiz after his 1991 conviction.
A Shining Path hit squad killed Ruiz two days later. Courtesy *Caretas*.

Narciso Sulca (left), with fellow Huaychao *ronderos*, 1991.

Village *rondero* with homemade gun, 1991.

Village *ronda* flag-raising, Qaraccensa, near Huaychao, 1994. By Ponciano Del Pino.

Alberto Fujimori and spymaster Vladimiro Montesinos (second from left). By Óscar Medrano, *Caretas*.

Female *senderista* prisoners salute Chairman Gonzalo, 1991. By Óscar Medrano, *Caretas*.

María Elena Moyano, 1991. Emma Hilario, at left, survived a Shining Path assassination attempt two months later. Courtesy *Caretas*.

Villa El Salvador, funeral procession for María Elena Moyano, 1992.
By Óscar Medrano, *Caretas*.

Senderista car bomb kills twenty-five on Tarata Street in Miraflores, 1991. By Óscar Medrano, *Caretas*.

A caged Abimael Guzmán faces the press after his capture, 1992. By Óscar Medrano, *Caretas*.

A defiant Elena Iparraguirre, 1992. Courtesy *Caretas*.

The Special Intelligence Group, or GEIN, 2003. Benedicto Jiménez and Marco Miyashiro at right. Courtesy *Caretas*.

Narciso Sulca, with
Miguel La Serna, 2016.

Abimael Guzmán and
Elena Iparraguirre, in
court, 2017. Courtesy
Caretas.

Gustavo Gorriti, 2016.

work, graffiti-painting, and occasional armed actions did not end until after midnight. They survived on soda, cookies, and three hours' sleep. When Juan's girlfriend, also a fighter, took a bullet in a shoot-out with police, she died from blood loss in their apartment. Did Abimael care about low-ranking fighters, Juan wondered? He eventually became a police informant, although careful not to let that be known even decades later. "This Is How Stool Pigeons Die," warned placards pinned to the blindfolded dead bodies of those who betrayed the revolution.

A grumpy Abimael reminded the others at the Monterrico house about the reason for his sanctification. It was historical inevitability, not personal ambition, he said. "Objective reality always generates a leader or leaders to symbolize the revolution." Abimael gave other examples of men becoming metonyms for a movement—Dante and the Italian language; Newton and physics; Robespierre and the French Revolution. He would not stoop to "false, hypocritical modesty" to deny his own duty to command. Abimael had always believed the party needed a strong centralizing hand. So did Augusta and Elena, who knew, if not their names, about disaffected commanders like Juan Fulano. The Gonzalo cult performed, at least in theory, an agglutinating function by so literally demanding "full and unconditional submission." It betrayed the ruling triumvirate's unspoken anxiety about the precariousness of their great endeavor.

The congress gave Abimael an opportunity to review strategy. They had killed tourists in the Machu Picchu train bombing, and, more recently, shot a German traveler in the Huaylas Valley, the Peruvian Swiss Alps. Their purpose, Abimael explained, was weakening the government by scaring away visitors and their money. ("But we must be careful, we can't kill every tourist we see," he noted.) Agitation and propaganda. Sabotage. Guerrilla combat. Targeted assassination. They must continue employing these multiple tactics to hit the enemy nationwide.

It was telling that Abimael dwelled upon the targeted assassinations at particular length. So much *senderista* killing had alienated potentially sympathetic leftists in Peru and abroad. There had first been Benigno Medina in 1982 and, besides massacres like Lucanamarca, the rebels had gunned down more than three thousand mayors, policemen, judges, development workers, and supposed traitors. *Aniquilamiento selectivo*, "selective annihilation," they called it. ("The act of dying became a technical detail," as one critic observed about Stalin's Soviet Union, without "any intimate bodily feature.") Abimael wanted to make sure the others understood the justification, namely to destabilize the "reactionary democratic bourgeois system." The Viet Cong, Abimael said, assassinated 13,000 people, more than twice the number killed by Shining Path so far. His reasoning had not changed, despite the increasing butchery. Achieving Communism and its new society justified almost any blood price in the final reckoning.

Always, it was their ideology that mattered most, Abimael reiterated. A party document explained that their leader had succeeded in applying Marxism's "universal truth to the concrete conditions of the Peruvian revolution." All great Communist leaders built upon the teachings of their predecessors, and that made Gonzalo Thought the "highest human expression of the ideology of the proletariat—true, scientific, and invincible." Gonzalo Thought was both "a microscope and telescope," Abimael explained to his fellow revolutionaries at the Monterrico hideout, and a weapon more powerful than any gun or tank. Party propaganda often depicted Abimael with Marx, Lenin, and Mao as if to carve his place on the exclusive Mount Rushmore of Communist heroes.

It was preposterous to place the *senderista* leader in the company of such earlier giants. Among the most original and powerful thinkers of his age, Marx had revolutionized social theory by insisting upon the material foundations of human consciousness. His texts about capitalism's hurricane-like transformation of history and society read powerfully even today. ("All that is solid melts into air," Marx and Engels wrote in *The Communist Mani-*

festo. "All that is holy is profaned.") As pitiless as his tactics could be, Lenin led a revolution that shook the world, and besides that, was a serious intellectual who wrote influential books about imperialism and revolutionary theory. Mao innovatively sought to incorporate the peasantry and some traditional Confucian thought into a "sinified" Marxism suited to the world's most populous country. His *Little Red Book* became a cult classic for global leftists. He and Lenin stamped their personalities on the twentieth century, their authoritarian brutality notwithstanding.

Only a *senderista* loyalist could imagine that their leader ranked with these legendary Communist leaders in any real way. As a young man, Abimael showed some limited signs of a more original Marxist viewpoint. He had since steadily hardened back down into pedestrian "scientific socialist" orthodoxies. His "invincible" Gonzalo Thought made some small doctrinal innovations, like the assertion that a "liberated zone" could be established before the revolution's victory. As much as Abimael liked to show off his learning, he espoused a predictable Communist dogma of a very unimaginative kind. He showed his odd verbal tic of employing the adverb "principally" over and over again in his rambling and repetitive speeches at the congress. "We are doing the work of the prophets without their gifts," an ex-Communist laments in Arthur Koestler's 1941 *Darkness at Noon*. He could have been describing the *senderista* leader.

Abimael lacked even the abilities of his party's founder, José Carlos Mariátegui. This influential Peruvian journalist, intellectual, and philosopher grew up in the southern town of Moquegua, and later lived for a time in Rome and Buenos Aires. Mariátegui tried to adapt Marxism to Peruvian realities between modernist experimentalism, nationalist mythmaking, and *indigenismo*, the early-twentieth-century Indianist revitalization movement. Abimael frequently invoked Mariátegui's name, but appraised his writings as "not universal thought." Instead he quoted Marx, Lenin, and Mao at endless length while admonishing constantly against deviation from the correct line. "The greatest danger is revisionism," Abimael reminded the party leaders at Monterrico.

Few *senderistas* doubted the essential truth of Gonzalo Thought and their great cause. Any sect, Marxist or not, requires its members to suspend disbelief in exchange for righteous certainty. "We craved to become simple and simple-minded," a lapsed British Marxist explained the bargain. Who had time for graduate seminar hairsplitting anyway? They had a war to fight. And the army's village massacres, worsening poverty, and—Abimael had that right—capitalism's undeniable injustices did not invite rethinking either. "Nowhere is the power of a fistful of millionaires more grossly demonstrated," Abimael described the United States, with some reason. The spell of Gonzalo Thought's crude, ponderous, sometimes even truthful magic prevailed for the moment in the curtained Monterrico hideout.

The party leader remained a considerate man in person. When visiting commanders came down from the mountains, Abimael cooked their favorite dishes. He was as insistent about having the right ingredients as about party discipline. If the chicken, peppers, or potatoes did not suit his specifications, he sent undercover comrades to the market again. It satisfied him to see his battle-weary fighters eat well.

Some weeks into the congress, after discoursing for yet more hours, Abimael noticed some glassy-eyed faces. "Forgive me," he apologized. "But we must continue, Comrades. I know attention flags and we get tired, but that's why we have our ideology."

Everyone there was pleased about *El Diario* falling under party control. They'd had to mimeograph propaganda until then. (Their Department of Organizational Support operated from the Monterrico house where they were meeting.) To celebrate the "great victory" of their congress, Abimael gave his first-ever interview. He often read Gustavo Gorriti's stories in *Caretas*, and considered him among the best of journalists from the "bourgeois press." If he sat down with Gorriti, however, it would mean a tough grilling. To do the interview with *El Diario* would allow him to set the questions, edit the answers, and ensure a panegyric tone about his leadership. A trusted *senderista* brought the newspaper's editors, Luis Arce and Janet Talavera, to the Monterrico house during a break in the congress. Augusta and Elena were there to monitor the proceedings, both apparently hooded to conceal their identities. The *El Diario* editors later published a note about an all-day car ride to a mysterious Andean hideout. The shaggy-dog story was meant to divert attention from Abimael's actual Lima location right under the government's nose.

The interview caused a minor sensation upon its publication a week or so later. *El Diario* trumpeted it as the "Interview of the Century," and Abimael's surfacing headlined every Lima newspaper (though they all described him as a sadistic terrorist). To ensure the interview met specifications, Augusta and Elena reviewed the final text before publication. Their editing shortened Abimael's answer to a question about the prison massacres to party boilerplate about the "high expression of revolutionary heroism." "We don't want to seem too dramatic, to be the victims, to show too much," Augusta said. Elena agreed. After so many years at the revolution's helm together, the two dear friends saw almost everything alike.

Anyone expecting interesting revelations was disappointed. Chairman Gonzalo's friends? "I don't have any, only comrades," he replied. His interview added up to a series of tedious, abstract mini-speeches about bureaucratic capitalism and imperialist evil. Abimael name-dropped Shakespeare and Einstein, criticized Hitler, harangued Ronald Reagan, denounced Alan García as a fascist, and, of course, cited Lenin and Mao's unimpeachable authority at every turn. The "filthy" revisionists of Peru's moderate United

Left coalition, he said, had accepted "parliamentary cretinism" by running in elections. Sacrifice and difficulty awaited, but "the people will emerge victorious." "Peruvian Rebel Offers Grim Prophecy in Rare Interview," reported the *Washington Post*.

The party congress took up some practical matters in the first session's second month. What about weaponry, some wondered? The *senderistas* still had only captured guns and their homemade bombs, which included the *queso ruso*, a timed charge for ambushes, and the *camote*, or sweet potato, for blowing holes in buildings. Their jungle units extorted some money from drug traffickers, a "tax," the party called it, but it was not enough to buy much weaponry. Their victory would eventually demand obtaining bazookas, antiaircraft guns, and more rifles. They still had their ideology and superior conviction. "When we fight, we always do it with an eye to combatting and destroying the enemy completely and finally," Augusta wrote before the congress.

No party meeting could end without criticism and self-criticism. Every good Maoist knew that unmasking insufficiently militant views was an unending task. "We combat reconciliation because it suckles the right," a Shining Path document explained. So often did the *senderistas* employ the term *línea oportunista de derecha*, "the rightist opportunist line," that they shorthanded it as the "LOD" in party records. They could be victorious only through strict ideological faith and absolute obedience to party orders.

Abimael, the former lawyer, cross-examined suspected offenders once again. Only Augusta, Elena and, naturally, he himself could be considered above suspicion about deviationist tendencies. Police had recently raided an apartment occupied by Yovanka Pardavé, Comrade Sara, who headed *Socorro Popular*, the Shining Path Lima support organization. They seized potentially compromising party documents. This led Abimael into a long discourse about failings in party discipline, which included "feudal" lording by local commanders and "daring to impute pridefulness to Chairman

Gonzalo." Everyone must remember that "the Party ends and begins with the Central Directorate and its leaders," Abimael added. (He frequently referred to himself as the "Central Directorate.") Only "fatuous, superficial revolutionaries" could doubt his leadership.

It took some time for Abimael to finish with Pardavé. "What measures have been implemented, or are proposed, to remedy the problems?" he asked. Pardavé explained that several comrades had gone underground because their names appeared in the captured documents. She suggested suspending Comrade Eustacio for two months. He was the *Socorro Popular* sub-secretary and the chief culprit for the breached security. "Comrade Eustacio is hereby suspended from his duties as sub-secretary," Abimael said.

Two other Central Committee members also found themselves under scrutiny for supposed transgressions. Abimael accused Osmán Morote, Comrade Nicolás, the northern *senderista* commander, and the Ayacucho leader, Óscar Ramírez, Comrade Feliciano, with laxness in executing party orders. Morote had to undergo what the *senderistas* called an *acuchillamiento*, literally a "self-knifing," an extended exercise in apology and penitence. The lesser challenge of *tomando posición*, "taking a position," fell to Comrade Feliciano. He swore fealty once again to Chairman Gonzalo and Marxist-Leninist-Maoist-Gonzalo Thought. It took some time before Abimael was provisionally satisfied with the wayward comrades. "You have made progress insofar as you have tried to understand your situation."

───────

Their first congress session went on for three months with occasional recesses. When it ended on July 27, 1988, the *senderistas* raised a toast in the stuffy living room. The humiliating ablutions of self-criticism left Óscar Ramírez resentful towards Abimael and his two female lieutenants. "The Holy Trinity," a few disgruntled lower-ranking party members called them. Everyone else would remain loyal to their leader to the end.

The time had come to disband for now. Osmán Morote would return to his command in the northern La Libertad mountains. His militancy went back to Ayacucho and the early years. Morote had roamed the countryside on the war's eve like a Marxist monk in a poncho, woolen hat, and a poor farmer's sandals. ("Not for camouflage, but because of the hard cold," he explained the peasant garb.) The younger Osmán had several previous run-ins with Abimael besides this latest *acuchillamiento,* supposedly disagreeing about massacring villagers. He always admired the older man, however, and never left the fold. He dedicated a poem from his jail cell to "our Dear Teacher" many years later.

Augusta stopped Osmán before he left the house.

"Don't go yet," she smiled. "We want to cook for you."

Some Spanish Communists had been in Lima a few weeks before, Augusta explained. They belonged to a little global Maoist coalition, the Revolutionary Internationalist Movement, which held up Shining Path as a guiding light. The Spaniards met with the Permanent Committee, and, afterwards, cooked a paella to thank Abimael, Augusta, and Elena for their hospitality. It was not a very well-known dish in a Peru that had its own world-class culinary specialties.

"The comrades showed us how to prepare it," Augusta told Osmán. "We want to make one for you and the others." Their paella came out to steamy perfection. Osmán promised to make the dish for his northern fighters. Before parting, the *senderista* leaders hugged, wept, and declared their love for each other. The police would capture Osmán only a few weeks later—and that was not all. Augusta had less than a year to live, and some would charge Elena and Abimael with killing her.

CHAPTER TWELVE

The Death of Comrade Norah

One half of her eye was laughing while the other half wept. It had split in two, so that the woman could both laugh and cry at the same time, and with equal intensity.

—**Constantin Virgil Gheorghiu,**
The Twenty-Fifth Hour (1949)

Everyone gathered around the dead woman. A shiny flag covered everything but Augusta's face. "Honor and Glory to Comrade Norah!" read the banner affixed to the wall. Twenty-six red roses marked each year of Augusta's Communist Party membership. A hammer-and-sickle floral arrangement lay at the dead leader's feet. It was a Marxist state funeral in miniature, down to the customary blue uniforms worn by Augusta's grieving comrades. A dozen or so top party members had come to the hideaway for the ceremony.

Abimael looked devastated. Only forty-three, Augusta had died the day before, November 13, 1988. He wrote later to her parents, Delia and Carlos, exiles in Sweden, about their daughter's death. "Norah, my comrade and partner, is dead. My soul is wandering in the shadows." Augusta was eleven years Abimael's junior and, if he had died first, would have become the next party chairman. "We maintain the principle that the command is eternal," Augusta once wrote as if anticipating that possibility. Abimael did not doubt her capacities to take the torch. "You will replace me," he sometimes told Augusta. He had not expected her to leave first.

———

Nobody seems to have anticipated Augusta's death earlier in the year. She had been in glowing good spirits through the party congress's first session. A shaken, red-eyed Abimael had to summon Central Committee members back to Lima to inform them about Augusta's death. *A suicide*, he said. *Comrade Norah hung herself with a rope.* He sat alone by his dead wife's body before the final ceremony. His head was bowed, and, after some minutes, Abimael reached over gently to stroke and kiss Augusta's forehead as one would a child. His letter to Carlos and Delia gave no details about their daughter's death, perhaps to spare them from imagining her having killed herself. He described instead how Augusta had once lowered her "clear and unforgettable gaze" to say she would die before him. "I responded that children do not die so soon, that they must bury their parents," Abimael wrote. Elena did not find it strange that Abimael would speak to Augusta as if to a daughter. "He didn't have children," she said. "She was his daughter. Wife. Everything. He wanted to protect her. And love her."

Their ceremony was brief. "Comrade Norah lies before us, resting now," Abimael said. He affirmed their faith like a priest at the grave:

How powerful the power of the masses! How indispensable the Party! How great the ideology, Marxism-Leninism-Maoism!

Then he turned to Augusta's death, somewhat cryptically acknowledging her suicide:

> In her regrettable confusion, in her nervous illness, she did not see things clearly and preferred to destroy herself before striking the Party. . . . Today we can only say: Comrade Norah, your death sorrows us. . . . We have nothing to reproach you for. Great leader. We say to you: Heroine of the Revolution.

Abimael trailed off, for once at a loss for words. He raised a clenched fist and shot glass. The *senderistas* often played recorded music to conceal meetings from the neighbors. "Like violets, you will cry," sang the Italian pop singer Massimo Ranieri. The grieving leaders embraced under the suburban bedroom's dreary fluorescent light.

Augusta's death tore a hole in the party, not to mention leaving an awkward public relations problem. A good Communist did not take her own life. "My attitude to suicide," as Mao once wrote, "is to reject it" as a "physiological irregularity . . . [violating] the principles of life." Shining Path styled itself as invincible and glorious, and, if its beloved second-in-command had hung herself, that did not seem so much the case. If rank-and-file fighters learned about Augusta's death, it could be a demoralizing blow. Only six months later did a Central Committee resolution officially acknowledge her passing. Lower-ranking *senderistas* were told only that Comrade Norah died for the revolution. Abimael never provided Delia and Carlos with any more explanation either.

Instead the *senderistas* celebrated Augusta's life after their cultish fash-

ion. "Long Live Comrade Norah!" they intoned over her flag-draped body at
the wake. "The Greatest Heroine of the Party and Revolution." Augusta was
genuinely beloved by her comrades; even Óscar Ramírez, who increasingly
disliked Abimael, admired her spirited leadership. A necrophilic veneration
for dead leaders obeyed Communist tradition anyway. (Preserving Lenin's
body for Red Square exhibit required techniques "unprecedented in world
science," the supervising official boasted.) The *senderistas* sanctified Comrade Norah by praising her name in anthems and poetry:

> *Oh! Beautiful dove-eyed woman,*
> *Gentle intelligence total commitment*
> *You drank from the pure fountain of the Red Orient*
> *Great Marxist-Leninist-Maoist . . .*
> *Blessed one! You will never be forgotten*
> *Never erased nor rooted out*
> *You: the hope of fire that embraces the people.*

In 1989, at the congress's closing ceremony, the party awarded Augusta the
"Order of the Hammer and Sickle"—Joan of Arc meets Mao Zedong in its
hagiography. Her statue was to decorate a planned monument to the heroes
of the people after their revolution's triumph.

It became hard to know what tales about Augusta to believe. Their
fallen heroine personally directed the ILA, Initiation of the Armed Struggle, the party mythology claimed. That placed Augusta at the war's sacred
originary moment, but no eyewitness recalled her having been in Chuschi that night. And did Augusta really brave her way alone over snowy gla-
ciers to the next village? (That Ayacucho has no glacial peaks suggests at
least some exaggeration.) Her Ayacuchan friend Angélica Salas recounted a
more modest anecdote from before the war. One evening, Augusta arrived
to take Angélica to a party assembly. When Angélica's father objected to his

daughter being out at night, Augusta charmed him into allowing it with her irresistible smile—and a tall tale about a family party. Angélica later sold cosmetics for a time, before becoming a *senderista* and a trusted member of the inner circle. She ended up serving a life sentence for her guerrilla activities. Worsening dementia left Angélica forgetful and uncertain in her later years. About Augusta she admitted to no doubts: "Her physical beauty matched the beauty inside."

A few days after the wake, Abimael had Augusta's body moved to a house in Lima's Comas district. Her old companion Angélica and a few others saw to the task before dawn to avoid detection. The *senderistas* buried their comrade in the garden. They planted tulips and roses in the Communist red and yellow, as well as some black roses to symbolize death for the cause. Abimael and other top leaders came sometimes to mourn there, until a police raid in 1991. The detectives found only an empty grave that day, someone apparently tipping off the *senderistas*. They had taken Comrade Norah's body to some new secret resting spot until a permanent mausoleum could be built for her in the new People's Republic of Peru.

Some party leaders wondered about Augusta's death, and, if she hung herself, exactly why. Elvia Zanabria, Comrade Juana, suggested a formal investigation for the party record. She was a lawyer and headed the Department of Propaganda at the Monterrico house. Abimael refused to authorize an inquiry, which prompted the disillusioned Óscar Ramírez to question the suicide story in his own mind. Had Augusta been sick, perhaps dying from a fast-spreading cancer? Could she have been killed over some dispute about ideology and the revolution? Or because Elena and Abimael wanted Augusta out of the way to proceed with a covert love affair? It was typically self-serving, Ramírez thought, that Abimael professed his commitment to transparency and clarity, and yet rejected any party investigation into Augusta's death. "Whenever [party norms] did not serve his personal interests, he just ignored them or pushed them aside," Ramírez said years later.

A further development stoked suspicions about foul play. When the party congress, six months after Augusta's death, readjourned in mid-1989 for its third and final session, Elena and Abimael appeared as a couple. They maintained proprieties during formal meeting time, but held hands during breaks. Their romance encouraged speculation about a love triangle gone bad, and, later, the police promoted the theory that Elena and Abimael conspired to kill Augusta. "A crime of love and power," asserted Eduardo Barragán, a commander in the antiterrorism police's Lima division. The tale of a lustful murder plot made good tabloid fodder. It seemed a terrorist soap opera with two starring villains: Elena, a scheming black widow, and Abimael, the dissolute megalomaniac. Many Peruvians considered the *senderista* leaders to be murderous monsters altogether capable of such evil in real life.

Most of Augusta's girlhood friends subscribed to the murder theory. As a teenager, she was especially close to Teresa Carrasco, a vivacious and gifted Ayacuchan who went on to direct Peru's National Archive. They shared confidences and oven-fresh *chaplas*, the local rolls, in the plaza before school. Carrasco befriended Abimael as well, but thought he had lost his way in the war's madness. Elena poisoned Augusta, Teresa believed, Abimael doing nothing to stop it. Augusta's elementary school classmate, Sonia Meneses, accused Abimael of more actively conspiring with Elena to plan the deed. "They killed her," Sonia said flatly. Neither she nor Teresa had any contact with Augusta after she went underground, and yet they never accepted that she had become a pitiless *senderista* leader, authorizing atrocities. They preferred to remember the gentle girl of weekend expeditions to Iribamba. "We'd put secret messages in a bottle," Teresa recalled, "and float them away down the Cachi River."

the primary motive for Augusta's supposed murder. "We had ideological differences," Abimael acknowledged some years after her death. Only Augusta ever challenged him at party councils. She had spousal privilege and warrior credibility, not to mention the outspoken nature of a woman whose favorite song was "*A Mi Manera*," "My Way," the Argentine crooner Vicente Fernández's rendition of the Frank Sinatra standard. One disagreement was over relocating from Lima to direct the revolution from the countryside in true Maoist fashion. Any new hideaway would have to be at a lower elevation due to Abimael's polycythemia. (Several party members suggested the secluded Vizcatán jungle with its tropical canyons and secret caves.) Abimael claimed to support the move, but always delayed. The party chairman never decamped from his gated bedroom community comfort in the Lima suburbs.

But their disagreements do not seem to have led to any lasting acrimony. According to one later hypothesis, Augusta's opposition to the party's so-called "militarization" demonstrated her discomfort with the idea of a cruel war as the country's only solution. When readying for battle in 1979, Abimael had argued that they must "construct the Party around the gun . . . and the armed struggle to seize power." Augusta countered that both Mao and Lenin advocated a more equal weighting between the party's fighting units, front organizations, and consciousness-raising efforts. She strongly supported going to war, however, and dropped her opposition to the "militarization" proposal after the fighting began. Her fighters soon tortured Benigno Medina to death to set the standard for merciless atrocity. Augusta's last writings before the party congress did not suggest any hesitation about "selective liquidations" and village massacres. *The People's War is rooting out the entrails of the rotten old society, nothing will detain us, we are the future.* She remained a hardline Communist believer by all appearances.

It was also possible to explain away the limited circumstantial evidence for a murder. Although Abimael denied Elvia Zanabria's request for a party inquiry, that did not necessarily signify a cover-up. A lawyer with *senderista* ties and an unnamed Central Committee member did sign a death certificate for Augusta (though few people seem to have actually seen the document). Abimael may not have wanted any more open discussion to prevent the news of Augusta's suicide, if it was that, from leaking beyond the inner circle, or because he did not want to dwell any longer on such a painful matter. Eduardo Barragán, the police commander, insisted that Augusta's body had been spirited away to prevent an autopsy. "It will prove that she was poisoned when we find it," he claimed, an Agatha Christie mystery for future solving. The simpler explanation was that Comrade Norah's comrades did not want her body to fall into "reactionary" hands. They had good reason to expect disrespectful treatment of Augusta's remains should the police find them. The government returned the charred remains of the *senderista* prison massacre dead in filthy unlabeled cardboard boxes.

The best available indicators pointed to a suicide, just as Abimael said at the wake before clamming up about the matter. By more than one account, she sometimes struggled with nervous anxiety from early in life. Her absences from party meetings for supposed "mental illness" certainly hinted at the possibility of vulnerability to dark thoughts. Augusta took some sort of medication for depression, according to a relative with knowledge of the matter. Her namesake from *The Twenty-Fifth Hour* recognized life's frailty even for the brave: "Fate does not protect the bold forever."

Female *senderistas* bore a heavy stigma. They seemed to be a special breed of monster for rejecting social expectations about having children, polishing the silver, and keeping at a husband's beck and call. A police training manual on "subversive women" listed their "personality traits":

They are more determined and dangerous than men, they behave in absolutist fashion, and think themselves capable of carrying out any mission, they combine the dichotomy of weakness with hardness, they are indulgent, very severe . . . they exploit and manipulate the nearest to them, they are impulsive and take risks.

The posthumous perceptions about the most notorious female *senderista* of them all, Augusta, typically placed her at one end or the other of the archetypal sexist spectrum of deviant female excess. Was she the cruel Communist mastermind who urged a more timid husband to the bloodbath? Or the kind younger wife led astray? Her mysterious death permitted Peruvians to conjure mythical Augustas to suit the most fantastical sensibilities.

In all likelihood, Augusta cared little what the reactionaries said about her. Her responsibilities as a wartime commander did bring tremendous new pressures, which could also have played a part in her possible suicide. Her parents and siblings had left Peru, never to return. Fugitive confinement had always weighed especially heavily upon Augusta, perhaps partly explaining her insistence on the party command relocating to the Andes. As the second-most-wanted *senderista* after her husband, she could seldom leave the house, and then only briefly with a wig and fake ID card. "It was depressing, terrible, horrible for her to be shut in, just like Anne Frank." Elena said.

Only Augusta and Abimael likely knew the truth for certain. Unlike Anne Frank (a questionable analogy in the first place), Augusta apparently left no diary or personal papers. That leaves no way of knowing about her inner state of mind. Whatever their reasons in the final account, Elena and Abimael maintained their refusal to disclose any details despite knowing that left them as murder suspects in many minds. They would not even explain Abimael's puzzling eulogy reference to Augusta not wanting to "strike the Party." When asked in 2016 if Augusta had hung herself, a tear came to Elena's eye. It might be time to talk at last, she said, before regaining her composure to let the mystery be. "It's an interesting story," Elena closed off the interview that day.

––––––––

The party congress concluded on June 28, 1989, the end of the third and final session. New accords, slogans, and a "rectification" campaign to enforce party unity received the usual unanimous approval. After a five-minute silence in Augusta's memory and three minutes more for other fallen comrades, a resolution affirmed the "gratitude of the congress participants to President Gonzalo as the continuer of Marx, Lenin, and Chairman Mao Zedong." Abimael "received the resolution as the expression of deep and highly stimulating comradeship," according to the minutes.

The *senderistas* renewed vows in a landmark year, 1989, when the Berlin Wall fell and Communism entered its death throes. Almost overnight, the Soviet Union lost its Eastern European satellite states to plucky independence movements like Czechoslovakia's Velvet Revolution and Poland's Solidarity. Only three weeks before the Shining Path congress's final day, Communist China's leaders authorized the Red Army slaughter of pro-democracy student protestors in Tiananmen Square. A lone man tried to block a tank, and the first twenty-four-hour television news network, CNN, broadcast the video around the world. Whether of "tank man," as he became known, or exultant Germans on the crumbling wall, the images of 1989 conveyed the same message. The will to liberty and freedom seemed to have brought down Communist tyranny at last. In Estonia, Lithuania, and other breakaway Soviet republics, new governments would cart statues of Lenin and Stalin to the junkyard. Who wanted anything more to do with state socialism after the gulags, the five-year plans, and the Tiananmen massacre? Hadn't Communism proved only to be, as Susan Sontag put it, "fascism with a human face?" A little-known political philosopher and US State Department official, Francis Fukuyama, suggested that 1989 marked the "end of history" in a famous essay. The Marxist dream for a socialist future had died for good, he claimed. Only Western liberal democracy remained as a viable option for humanity's future.

The drama of 1989 did not discourage Abimael and his followers. It only appeared, quite the contrary, to confirm their orthodox convictions. The Tiananmen massacre? The fall of the Berlin Wall? Such developments had been expected. It was Deng Xiao Ping, after all, who ordered the tanks into Tiananmen, which demonstrated that the *senderistas* had been right to denounce him as a sinister "revisionist" traitor. That the rotten "social imperialist" Soviet Union was imploding did not surprise them either. "The restorations in China and the USSR," Abimael explained, only "underline the length and complexities of the process of the march toward Communism." *We thought it was absurd to say history had ended*, Elena said. Their latest slogan reaffirmed their dedication to "Serve the World Revolution Until Communism By Smashing the New Revisionist Counteroffensive." A true believer shows virtue by staying faithful through fickle fashions. That everyone else seemed to be jumping off the Marxist ship only added to the righteous moral satisfaction of party members. They left the Monterrico hideout more emboldened than ever to wreak havoc in Chairman Gonzalo's name.

Their mood was upbeat that last day. They had lost Augusta and so many others, but their "historic" congress had reaffirmed their dedication to moving forward. To celebrate the congress's last day, Abimael posed for a video with other party members. Someone uncorked a bottle and put on the foot-stomping theme from *Zorba the Greek*. (A standby in US baseball stadiums to rally the home team.) The song nodded to Augusta's memory. She and Abimael saw the 1964 Anthony Quinn movie together, and it remained among their favorites. "*Por Norita*—for our little Norah," cried the *senderista* leaders. Smiling women urged their party leader out to dance.

Abimael stood up, a little drunk. He mopped his brow with a hand towel.

"Let me see if I can remember how," he said. After adjusting his glasses, Abimael joined a beaming Elena on the floor. His unexpectedly nimble dance steps drew cheers. The party's new first couple circled close in the finger-snapping Greek wedding dance. Their love for each other and the great people's war waxed high that night—and they planned to raise the red flag even higher.

CHAPTER THIRTEEN

The Revolution Comes to Villa

María Elena Moyano looked out at Venice's azure lagoon from an outdoor café table. It was her first trip away from Peru, a fall day in 1989. She'd flown to Rome for an international development conference, then took the train to Venice for a few days. Her Italian friend from Villa El Salvador, Marina Rodinó, went along as the tour guide. Marina steered María Elena between the tourist hordes to the city's iconic sights—Piazza San Marco; the Doge's Palace; the Rialto Bridge. María Elena liked the succulent Italian peaches, not to mention Venice's flirty gondoliers, but she had no interest in staying. Her life lay back in gritty Villa. "She did say it would be nice to come back to Venice sometime," Marina recalled. "To show her boys."

The crisis of war and poverty back in Peru steadily deepened in the horrendous García government's last years. That had not kept María Elena from climbing to greater prominence in Villa. She'd been reelected in 1986 as the Women's Federation president. When Villa edged Corazon Aquino's Filipino People Power Movement to win Spain's 1987 Prince of Asturias Prize for social justice, María Elena flew in for the ceremony. The award honored Villa for its community spirit and innovative master plan. María Elena and Villa's mayor, Michel Azcueta, accepted congratulations from Spain's King Juan Carlos and Queen Sofia. "Come visit us in Villa, Your Highnesses," María Elena said. She chatted up the teenage Prince Philip, addressing him by the informal "tu." Her good energy brought some life to the stateroom.

María Elena retained her political ambitions. As the 1989 municipal elections neared, she was mentioned as a potential United Left candidate for Villa mayor. The male leftist kingmakers offered María Elena the vice-mayoral slot instead. Her popularity helped power another United Left win in Villa, making María Elena the district's vice mayor at thirty-one. When the latest American church activists or Canadian aid officials toured Villa, they left impressed by the charismatic young black woman. She was smart and confident, and she knew how to win people over. María Elena was becoming the best-known face of shantytown activism.

The achievements of Villa went only so far, however. Despite everything, the district remained another scrappy settlement at Lima's desert outskirts. When housewives hung out the wash, the clothes took forever to dry in the sticky air. Garments came off the line thinly coated with smoggy grime, like everything else in Villa. Few families had much money, even less with the Peruvian economy in tatters. María Elena walked safely down Venice's medieval alleys after dark, but Villa could be dangerous at any hour between drug-dealing, break-ins, and muggings at knife point. Some new settlers were Quechua-speaking villagers escaping the war. (Over six hundred thousand refugees would flee the Andes before it was over.) The poorest of Lima's poor, they put up their straw huts on the sandy hills. These new settlements resembled a starved migrant camp, complete with garbage piles, bony dogs, and circling buzzards.

María Elena and the early Villa settlers felt proud anyway. They sweated and suffered to make a home for themselves in the scorpion sands. Their district had become a teeming working-class neighborhood with its own factories and soccer leagues. What historian Antonio Zapata called a "culture of assembly" animated community meetings about everything from school fund-raising to a planned hospital. María Elena had a born orator's passion and clarity of expression. *Worse things are coming, compañeras,* she warned at a Women's Federation meeting one day. María Elena urged unity and strength in the good progressive way.

Her marriage to Gustavo had lasted for almost a decade. He remained the family breadwinner with his carpenter's earnings. (María Elena received only a token sum as vice mayor.) As María Elena and their two little boys slept, Gustavo left before daybreak for his furniture factory job. Gustavo's mother, who died young from cancer, had been a *morena clara*, a light-skinned black woman, but his father threatened to disown him if he married María Elena. A *negra* like her, a rung lower on the racialized caste ladder, would contaminate the family bloodlines. María Elena considered herself a shantytown mother first, black only second. (Although it pleased her when an elderly African leader at the Rome conference smilingly suggested that she looked like his daughter.) Black consciousness organizing had never taken hold in Peru by contrast to, say, the United States with its politicization of race and identity. Even so, María Elena was furious about Gustavo's father's objection to her skin color, which Gustavo ignored anyway. María Elena refused to have anything to do with her new father-in-law.

As her star rose, María Elena was increasingly away from the house. She made more trips to events abroad—Miami, Mexico City, a Canadian speaking tour arranged by Diana Bachand, her Quebecois friend from Villa. María Elena had her poor girl's broken teeth fixed. "It was very important to her," Bachand said. "That aesthetic detail had always bothered her. And she had to give speeches, presentations, interviews." In a brown country, Peru, white soap opera stars with sparkling smiles set the beauty standard.

Even when back in Villa, María Elena was always on the move. She went often up to Lima for speaking engagements and nights out with her feminist and foreign friends there. Her Spanish expatriate friend, Charo Torres, opened a hip nightclub called La Noche in an antique Barranco house all covered with vines. María Elena was often there, or, taking her boys, went with Diana Miloslavich, the Flora Tristán Center activist, for a day at El Silencio, a beach south of Lima. Its white sand and sapphire water provided the perfect escape from the moldy city. Gustavo never came. He drank beer, played soccer, and shot the breeze with his friends back in Villa.

A newspaper reporter came by to interview María Elena one day. She brought him into their little house, showing him to a chair. Gustavo walked in at one point.

"Yes, I'm married," María Elena smiled. "But he doesn't like to go out anywhere. So everyone thinks I'm single."

It was not easy for Gustavo. María Elena sometimes did not return until dawn, smelling of beer and cigarettes, or stayed overnight with Lima friends. Her mother, Eugenia, took Gustavo Jr. and David to school if María Elena did not show in time.

The tough-minded Eugenia offered Gustavo some unsolicited advice. "Why don't you kick her around some so she doesn't go out?"

"*If your woman gets too loud,*" an Andean *huayno* ballad counseled, "*apply hard wood.*"

Gustavo demurred. "I was never one to ask where did you go? Who were you with?" he explained. "Jealousy is for the insecure." His drinking buddies, including María Elena's brothers, ribbed him about being a *saco largo*, a girly dress wearer, the Peruvian term for a henpecked man. He ignored their taunts.

His wife, Gustavo realized, needed her freedom. "Gustavo knew how to partner this extraordinary woman," recalled Charo Torres, the Spaniard, many years later.

They fought sometimes. Gustavo threatened to leave more than once, tired of the late nights. An angry María Elena would shout back about Gustavo failing to appreciate her, but she refused to give up the marriage. "How could I leave him?" she told Cecilia Blondet, her sociologist friend. "He's a good man." There were really only three men in María Elena's life, Blondet believed, Gustavo and her two boys. She and Gustavo stayed together to the end.

Everything seemed to be falling apart in Lima by the late 1980s. Even in better times the Peruvian capital won no prizes for its welcoming charm. "In Lima beauty is a steel corset," the feminist poet Carmen Ollé wrote. The shortages and hopeless prospects of García's last years curdled the city's mood. Skinny children sang for a few pennies. Cruising thieves stripped tires from unwatched cars. A British journalist offered the standard visitor's lament. "I arrived in Lima, having forgotten what a vile city it is." Many people abandoned the country, if they could afford the plane ticket. They cared for Madrid's old people and cleaned houses in New Jersey.

The mood in Villa had soured, too. As its population reached a quarter million and growing, the district was losing its homesteading collectivist spirit. The municipality's leftist leaders brought a stabilizing continuity throughout the 1980s. Their influence waned amid the 1990 collapse of Peru's United Left coalition. The left's troubles and successive disastrous presidencies—Fernando Belaúnde and Alan García—bred cynical apathy. The biggest crooks are the *políticos,* the politicians, Villans said.

Hardly anyone reported crime to the police. It could mean being shaken down for a bribe, and, in some cases, the police were in cahoots with the thieves anyway. Gustavo kept a workshop on an especially sketchy Villa street. He installed a dead bolt, worried about someone stealing his tools. This was no longer the celebrated self-help shantytown where everyone looked out for each other. *You shouldn't go to the workshop at night*, a worried María Elena told Gustavo one day.

Growing Shining Path activity caused more concern. At the final season of the 1989 party congress, it had been agreed to expand operations in Lima. Until then, the Metropolitan Committee, which Elena Iparraguirre directed in the war's first years, had limited itself mostly to hit-and-run assaults. After surviving the military's bullish entry into the battle and the prison massacres, the *senderistas* wanted to go on the offensive in the capital. "Ayacucho is the cradle," Abimael liked to say, "But Lima is the catapult." Liberating the backwater countryside was all very well, although even that was becoming more unlikely because of the village militias. Shining Path needed Lima to win the war.

The city's decline provided the *senderistas* a perfect opening. They began to expand their organizing efforts in the mammoth *barriadas,* the poor districts, spreading out beyond the downtown. Their expectation was to win over the cart vendors, bus drivers, maids, ditch-diggers, factory workers, the unemployed, and the other downtrodden masses there. To ramp up their campaign in the shantytowns, the *senderistas* did more agitprop after the party congress. Student activists from Lima's San Marcos University organized night marches in Villa, melting away when the police appeared. Other militants infiltrated labor unions and neighborhood councils. The *senderistas* attacked the main district station in 1989, leaving two policemen dead. They burned buses to discourage voting in the municipal elections that same year. Their total actions in greater Lima multiplied almost fourfold, from 292 in 1984 to more than a thousand in 1989.

It was impossible not to notice in Villa. When María Elena walked the boys to school, she saw the latest big red Shining Path slogans painted on the street walls along the way. Gustavo Jr. and David went to Faith and Happiness, a big Catholic school. At least one teacher there, unbeknownst to María Elena or anyone else, happened to be a secret *senderista*—and a well-connected one at that. Nelly Evans was the former nun who rented the Monterrico hideaway for Abimael Guzmán, and saw him quite often. Her Villa reading club became a small recruitment center for the revolution.

Nobody knew who might be a *senderista*. "It could be your best friend," one Villan said, "or your brother." As they were in the Andes, schoolteachers like Nelly Evans were sometimes party organizers. The commander for the whole *cono sur*, the southern districts, taught school in Villa. "I lived a double life," José Vizcardo recalled, "teaching by day—organizing by night." María Elena knew some probable Villa *senderistas* and understood their mindset from having almost joined herself. She wondered if Doris Quispe, a longtime friend, might belong to the MRTA, the smaller Marxist rebel movement. That suspicion turned out to be true when the police arrested Quispe one day. María Elena went to visit her friend in prison.

The *senderistas* wanted control of the Villa Women's Federation and its 20,000 members. At least a handful of women there—no one could ever say how many—supported Shining Path. They began a whispering campaign to undermine María Elena and her presidency. *Why did she take so many overseas trips? Where did she get money to buy a house? Wasn't she just out for herself?* The *senderistas* wooed needy women with sacks of rice, noodles, and flour to feed their gaunt children. These overtures won the rebels considerable sympathy in the straw hillside encampments.

Their activities grew more open and poisonous late in 1989. A story in *El Diario*, the Shining Path mouthpiece, denounced María Elena as a "reactionary trafficking with the hunger of the people." This "pseudo-leftist" and friend to "bourgeois feminists" promoted "assistentialist programs" aimed at "suffocat(ing) the revolutionary struggle of the masses." *La Moyano* forced unwilling women to pay federation dues, according to *El Diario*. The newspaper often faked quotes and invented charges to tar the party's enemies. María Elena siphoned international donations, it claimed, to buy "four big houses" and a cheese factory. "She is a trafficker, manipulator, revisionist, and electoral stooge," the story quoted an unnamed Villa housewife.

The trouble boiled over at a federation meeting one night. A member of the leadership council, Pilar Anchita, was a *senderista* sympathizer. Some believed Anchita pilfered food from the federation warehouse for guerrilla outreach efforts. That did not keep her from rising to repeat the charges about María Elena stealing money. Some women looked away to avoid trouble, others shouted Anchita down. A sullen Anchita muttered a threat before taking her seat again.

"You *negra de mierda*—black piece of shit! Any day now I'll see you dead."

It took more than loose threats to scare the street fighter in María Elena. The *senderistas* had recently murdered Ayacucho's United Left mayor, Fermín Azparrent, for organizing a peace march, which they regarded as an affront to the people's war. María Elena did not yet fear for her own safety, at least in Villa. "I'm nervous sometimes in Lima," she told friends. "I always feel at home once back in Villa."

Little discouraged María Elena, an optimist by nature. Her friend Virginia Vargas, the Flora Tristán Center founder, would be heading to Europe on a visiting fellowship. María Elena organized the customary Peruvian good-bye party, a *despedida*, at the federation's offices. That meant drinking, dancing, and declarations of love and affection. When the beer ran out after midnight, María Elena went with Virginia and another Villa activist, Esperanza, to search for a store open that late. When they encountered a pack of stray dogs on an empty street, one of the animals lunged at Esperanza, gashing her calf. María Elena and Virginia helped their injured friend into the car. The bloodied Esperanza began to weep, and Virginia moaned at their misfortune. María Elena soon lost patience.

"Why the hell are two grown-up feminists crying about a dog bite?"

Virginia and Esperanza composed themselves.

A doctor stitched up the wounded leg.

The three friends brought the beer back to the party.

CHAPTER FOURTEEN

A Fish Out of Water

Mario Vargas Llosa raised his hands to salute the crowd. More than thirty thousand people filled a Lima soccer stadium to cheer the novelist-turned-presidential candidate. Vargas Llosa had never imagined a political career. His boyhood dream was to be a matador, dazzling aficionados with his red cape and gleaming blade. The surrealist Michel Leiris once claimed that writing and bullfighting had risk in common. A blank page could be a capricious frightening beast, Vargas Llosa concurred. He enjoyed the new challenge of trying to master campaign crowds through his oratory. The country would pick a new president on April 8, 1990, less than four months away. He led the opinion polls.

Vargas Llosa was fifty-three, still boyish and handsome. His last venture into public service had been the 1983 Uchuraccay investigation. That ended with Vargas Llosa falsely blamed for covering up the army's supposed killings of the journalists there. ("A useful idiot," a leftist editorialist said.) Although the indignant Vargas Llosa insisted, unconvincingly, that the criticism did not bother him, he retreated to his study. He churned out two novels, *Who Killed Salvador Palomino?* and *The Storyteller*; a play; three short stories; and collected essays. His opinion pieces championed the free market and denounced state socialism's brutality. (He continued to speak out against right-wing dictatorships, too.) Those views may have explained why the left-leaning Swedish Academy had not yet awarded Vargas Llosa the Nobel Prize. They had already denied the prize to another more center-right Latin American literary luminary. The great Jorge Luis Borges joked that he had lived so long that "the people in Stockholm thought they had already given me one."

It had become Vargas Llosa's new ambition to rescue Peru from itself. His native country always intrigued, maddened, and summoned him back. Now, the writer felt, it was reaching a point of no return. A discredited president and wrecked economy had led many Peruvians to lose faith in the system. If the *senderistas* won, they would yoke Peru into a troglodyte Communist dictatorship. Vargas Llosa regarded Latin America's twentieth-century romance with populist strongmen, nationalist drumbeating, and Marxist revolution as the outdated worship of false gods. (He had recently depicted a bumbling, ideology-obsessed Trotskyite's pathetic attempt at revolution in *The Real Life of Alejandro Mayta*.) That state socialism was falling to pieces, he felt, proved Western liberal democracy to be humanity's best answer. Only a free, well-educated, market-oriented Peru would find its way forward.

That would take the right president, Vargas Llosa believed. He detested Alan García for his grandstanding, corrupt, and manipulative ways. *Caballo loco*, "Crazy Horse," the president's critics called him. Although Vargas Llosa regarded the *senderistas* as murderous fanatics, he was one of relatively few prominent Peruvians to denounce the 1986 prison butchery. That mountain of bodies, Vargas Llosa explained in an open letter to García, betrayed a true democracy's obligation to human decency and the rule of law. The writer captained the opposition to García's attempt to nationalize Peru's banks a year later. His speech at a big nighttime rally in the Plaza San Martín painted nationalization as a tyrannical assault on freedom and liberty. García backed down from the bank takeover, but the fight made the young president and the famous writer mortal enemies. Why did Vargas Llosa care so much about rich white bankers? García taunted. The novelist began considering running for president.

His wife tried to talk him out of it.

It'll only give you more wrinkles, Mario, Patricia protested. *Just like Uchuraccay. You'll serve your country, then get stabbed in the back, then be sorry you ever did it.*

The couple had been married for twenty-five years. Like his first wife, the glamorous Aunt Julia, Patricia was Vargas Llosa's relative, a first cousin. Only women from his own family seemed to interest the renowned writer, his publisher joked. That was not quite true, since Vargas Llosa reportedly had multiple affairs. Sex, money, and religion should be private matters, he demurred when an interviewer inquired about his rumored infidelities. "I'm a difficult man. Patricia puts up with me."

The novelist managed to win his wife over to a presidential run. It was his moral duty to their drowning country, he said. That might be true, Patricia thought, but she knew her husband also wanted a new adventure. This would be his chance to be the protagonist in a real-life political novel. Vargas Llosa declared his candidacy in 1988, almost two years before the elections. He enjoyed strong support from Peru's wealthy white minority for his anti-populist, pro-business views. His challenge would be convincing the whole country.

It had been over a year since Augusta La Torre's death. Despite the risks of them both being captured in a single raid, Elena and Abimael began living together in the same hideaways. "We needed to be together," Elena explained. "We missed Augusta and were still grieving for her." They did not suspect the disaffection of Óscar Ramírez, the Ayacucho commander, and Abimael named him to replace Augusta as the third Permanent Committee member. But Ramírez was mostly away in the mountains, giving him little say in anything. The party's operations seemed to grow even more efficient, lethal, and numerous. At the 1988 Seoul Olympics, the Peruvian women's volleyball team improbably won the silver medal, an amazing feat for a penniless minor country. What two things still worked in Peru? The volleyball team and Shining Path, a joke had it.

The party had many romances besides its new leading couple. "We fell in love just like anyone else," one Central Committee member said about her affair with a comrade. As in everything, however, the struggle mattered most. "Love," said the Lima leader Laura Zambrano in an *El Diario* interview, "serves the function of the People's War." At the party congress, the *senderistas* formalized marriage procedures. They approved their own fill-in-the-names wedding ceremony script, complete with lengthy quotations from Marx and Mariátegui. "*In the name of the Communist Party that represents the new society and before witness Comrades . . . . and . . . . I declare you husband and wife so you may support, help, and assist each other so that you may serve the Revolution more and better.*"

It was effectively prohibited for any *senderista* to take up with an outsider. To do so risked betrayal if a romance went bad, not to mention a potential distraction from the all-consuming business of revolution. A teenager named Fabiola in young Lurgio Gavilán's little band made the mistake of falling for a policeman. She was a cheerful person who gladly took her turn cooking and washing clothes. When the leaders found a note from Fabiola's boyfriend in her pocket, they ordered Lurgio and some others to hang her from a tree. They buried the body afterwards, but found it later at the bottom of a nearby gorge. Fabiola had apparently regained consciousness to crawl out of the shallow grave, only to fall to her death. "Bad weeds never die," said the leaders.

Family obligations sometimes created complications. Although militants were supposed to cut ties, some *senderistas* kept their children with them. One boy's *senderista* parents hosted night meetings in their house. "They were soldiers without barracks," José Carlos Agüero would write in a memoir. "No grand or epic battles." His family lived in El Agustino's old tenements near downtown. The neighbors kept their secret, believing José Carlos's parents to be fighting for the poor. His father died in the 1986 prison massacres. When his mother received death threats, José Carlos begged her to leave. "Everybody could see that she was going to be killed." She would not give up the fight, even though party commanders criticized her for spending too much time with José Carlos and his brother. A passerby found her near the beach one night, executed by three bullets to the head. "[I] felt relief at her being gone, and then guilt at that relief," José Carlos wrote. At least he did not have to explain a *senderista* name. Later, José Carlos met a young man who bore the name Gonzalo after the great man himself.

The upcoming presidential elections occupied the real-life Gonzalo in late 1989. Both Abimael and Elena liked Vargas Llosa's novels. ("My countryman, a great writer," Abimael described his fellow Arequipan.) His politics were something else. "The arrogant preacher of individual success, individual liberty, and the market economy," Abimael wrote in a new tract. *Elections, No! People's War, Yes!* The American imperialists, he explained, aspired to cash their Cold War triumph over the Soviets into planetary hegemony. That meant imposing neoliberalism and its free market agenda everywhere across Latin America. Vargas Llosa would be their Peruvian stalking horse. Hadn't Margaret Thatcher blessed his campaign? The steely British prime minister had become the global left's bogeywoman for her union-busting, market-oriented policies. That she endorsed Vargas Llosa seemed proof enough of the writer's reactionary tendencies. Even more temperate Latin American leftists routinely dismissed Vargas Llosa as the conservative establishment's apologist.

Once again, Shining Path intended to fulfill its revolutionary duty by sabotaging the voting. According to party dogma, the Peruvian elections were always "a farce," but Abimael saw new significance in the impending presidential voting. Worried Peruvian reactionaries and American imperialists wanted, he wrote, to ratchet up the counterinsurgency under the cover of a new elected government. "The elections, therefore, are an instrument of counterrevolutionary war." The party would as usual murder candidates, paralyze transport, and threaten or persuade voters to boycott the elections. That would send a message about the revolution's brilliant advances.

A month before the voting, Vargas Llosa retained a commanding lead. Every new story about the García administration's corruption and wrongdoing outdid the next. (The agriculture minister, Remigio Morales, gained the nickname "Rotten Meat" after reported payoffs for certifying spoiled Argentine beef.) The country wanted a new face. Who better than its most famous son? He seemed to be an honest man. His worldly success indicated a capacity to guide Peru away from the brink.

The novelist promised a modernized country. He had long since renounced his socialist student leanings, taking inspiration from the new freedom-fighting, anti-Soviet leaders like Poland's Lech Wałęsa. (His campaign borrowed its logo from Wałęsa's Solidarity Movement.) Detractors branded Vargas Llosa as a "right-winger" or "neoliberal," but he preferred "liberal" in the more dignified European liberty-and-markets tradition. "The utopian collectivist idea is a decomposing body," he declared in a 1989 speech. Vargas Llosa saw Lima's street sellers and small businesses as testimony to an indomitable Peruvian spirit of entrepreneurship. He would end corruption and slash bureaucracy to empower business big and small. His plans pleased corporate interests like the powerful Romero group, who donated to his campaign. Vargas Llosa had made his way on his own to

Europe on a scholarship, and yet he descended from Spanish aristocrats and belonged to the privileged white minority. The writer had no brown faces in his inner circle.

Those donations enabled Vargas Llosa to hire a US political consulting firm, Sawyer Miller, a first in Peru. His son, Álvaro, a recent London School of Economics graduate, became his press secretary. Cousin Luis Llosa flew down from Hollywood to give media advice. A well-known filmmaker, he would later direct the kitsch Jennifer Lopez hit, *Anaconda*. The reluctant Patricia set aside her misgivings to stump for her husband.

An obvious obstacle for Vargas Llosa was his having lived abroad for so long. His critics called him an arriviste who had abandoned Peru for Europe's bright lights, only running for president out of crass ambition. To show himself a true Peruvian and man of the people, Vargas Llosa took his campaign to mountain villages, jungle settlements, and desert cities. His charter plane would touch down at a little airstrip, or sometimes on a soccer field or river bed. He caravanned into town to greet local dignitaries, give a speech, and be pulled out to dance a *huayno* or *marinera*. An earlier Peruvian literary luminary, José María Arguedas, described Peru as an "old country" for its part-Incan, part-Spanish affection for ceremony and protocol. Vargas Llosa had to suppress his own punctual instincts on his trips to towns like Jauja and Ica. You could not stick to a modern political campaign's fast-break timetable there.

The war was never far. One day, as he campaigned in Huancayo, a big city in the central highlands, Vargas Llosa heard bombs and shots some blocks away. The *senderista* attack killed two soldiers and wounded another. At the army commander's request, Vargas Llosa agreed to transport the injured survivor back to Lima in his small plane, leaving a bodyguard behind to make room. The novelist saw that the little soldier was only a boy, probably under the army's legal eighteen. He had been shot, and Vargas Llosa held the plasma bag over his head. "He stared blankly into space, with an astonished, wordless desperation, as though trying to understand what had happened to him." The doctors saved the boy's life at Lima's military hospital.

The *senderista* obstruction campaign picked up in the months before the elections. They managed to kill more than three hundred mayors, government officials, and candidates. (Several hundred more withdrew to avoid being targeted.) In March 1990, with the elections less than three weeks away, a guerrilla squad shot down a candidate on Vargas Llosa's Ayacucho slate. A tailor with five children, Julián Huamaní Yauli was well-liked in the town. At the funeral in the old cathedral, Vargas Llosa saw Huamani's bullet-pocked body in its coffin. He hugged a mourning peasant woman, who sobbed Quechua words he could not understand. His car back to the airport passed by San Cristóbal University where his fellow Arequipan Abimael Guzmán had hatched his revolution three decades before.

It proved an arduous campaign. Vargas Llosa was a personable and charming man with countless friends across the continents. (He attended Lima bullfights with the *Caretas* photographer Óscar Medrano, an old newspaper mate.) He disliked, though, the "semihysterical pushing and pulling, kissing, pinching and pawing" at campaign rallies. Nor did he embrace the good campaigner's duty to deliver the same stump speech over and over again. "Mario was a master at intellectually defining an issue and a policy," recalled Mark Malloch Brown, his chief consultant from the Sawyer Miller PR firm. "But he avoided repetition. He always moved on to the next thing." The Englishman tried fruitlessly to get the novelist to stay on message.

A *senderista* assassination attempt was always possible. ("Are you well-protected, Mario?" a motherly Margaret Thatcher had inquired on a Downing Street visit.) The campaign did not preannounce the candidate's travels to prevent ambushes. A spiteful Alan García tried to undermine Vargas Llosa at every turn as well, after their run-ins over the prison massacres and bank nationalizations. The notorious thugs from García's APRA party, the *búfalos,* beaned Patricia with an egg in the desert town of Casma. Vargas

Llosa had to go around Lima in an armor-plated Volvo, and a small army guarded his apartment. He missed his intellectual's privacy.

Patricia could not resist some payback one night. "Do you remember once upon a time when you were a writer?"

Vargas Llosa found some bedtime pleasure in his books. As an antidote to the campaign's dumbed-down world, he picked some challenging new texts, like philosopher Karl Popper's *Conjectures and Refutations.* (Vargas Llosa was too much the traditional humanist to approve of French poststructuralists like Jacques Derrida, Roland Barthes, and, a onetime Paris friend, Jean Baudrillard.) He also turned to old favorites, among them Malraux's *The Human Condition,* Melville's *Moby-Dick,* and Faulkner's *Light in August.* Sometimes the weary Vargas Llosa read only a poem, usually a sonnet by Luis de Góngora, a luminary of the seventeenth-century Spanish Golden Age. We short-lived beings inhabit a universe where "the sun warns every man that he is a comet," de Góngora wrote.

His campaign garnered global attention. A celebrated novelist going back to run for president in his war-torn native land made good copy. "Peru, in its darkest hour, may be close to dawn," the *Wall Street Journal* reported. Vargas Llosa maintained a healthy lead two weeks before the elections. His campaign advisors felt confident their man would soon don Peru's red-and-white presidential sash.

––––––

Not a few Peruvians had grown so sick of the endless campaigning and annoying political ads as to welcome election day. The tropical winter fog blanketed Lima once again, and, even before daybreak, tanks and armored vehicles rumbled out from the barracks. To keep the *senderistas* from attacking polling stations, the government mobilized more than 100,000 policemen and soldiers nationwide. The law required all Peruvians to vote, so banks and government offices closed for the day. Some Andean peasants did not vote for fear of Shining Path reprisal. *Senderista* fighters blocked several highways with stones and murdered an election clerk in one mountain province. The balloting went off smoothly enough besides that.

Vargas Llosa and his supporters took over the downtown Sheraton for their victory celebration. The party never had a chance to get started. Early exit polls showed a dark horse candidate, Alberto Fujimori, capturing almost a third of the vote. The final results showed the former university rector only five points behind the favored Vargas Llosa, both under 50 percent. That meant a runoff election. Both the socialist parties and Alan García's center-left APRA party regarded Vargas Llosa as a right-winger, even a "fascist" according to his most aggressive critics. They would support Fujimori. The math meant that Vargas Llosa would almost certainly lose the runoff election.

"This has gone to shit!" said young Álvaro, the son-turned-press-secretary. "Is it conceivable that a country is going to throw away its last chance to join the modern world?"

The result should not have been surprising. Early in the campaign, the Sawyer Miller man, Mark Malloch Brown, laid out the demographics of the electorate. You could divide Peruvian voters, he explained, into groups A, B, C, and D. The rich and the middle classes could be counted on for support, but they made up less than 10 percent of the population. Vargas Llosa needed to persuade enough Cs and Ds, the poor and the very poor, the biggest groups by far, the brown-skinned inhabitants of the country's vast interiors and the expanding shantytowns. Their tiny businesses, evangelical churches, and dance colosseums embodied an unwillingness to play the docile servant class any longer. *Cholo soy y no me compadezca*— "I'm a *cholo* but I don't want your pity," went the song. A patrician white novelist would have a tricky time winning the necessary peasant, migrant, and *cholo* votes.

A weak feel for the new Peru handicapped Vargas Llosa. When he left for Paris as a young man, Peru had still been a country of planta-tions, hat-doffing Indians, and scrawny houseboys. That the novelist sur-rounded himself with advisors from the manicured professional classes sent the wrong message in a brown majority country. So did his alliance with two smallish conservative parties, Popular Action and the Popular Christians, which had little support outside of Lima's country club set. His advisors cringed when Vargas Llosa once mentioned his honorary Prince-ton degree, as if that would be a big selling point with Lima slum dwell-ers. The fine-boned Patricia arrived at rallies in the latest Milan and Paris fashions. Too much about the campaign made Vargas Llosa look like the white elite's man.

His own attitudes created obstacles, too. "I don't believe all cultures are equal," Vargas Llosa once said. "Some cultures have gone much farther towards humanization, the human ideal of liberty and tolerance." Although the Incas and Peru's enduring indigenous traditions intrigued the novel-ist, he saw the modern West as the gold standard for human achievement. Peru should be more like Switzerland, the writer suggested in a campaign debate. Indignant critics attacked Vargas Llosa for denigrating the *patria*, the homeland, and only running to satiate his own personal ambitions. His awkward manner in a campaign commercial with peasant farmers rein-forced perceptions of a privileged outsider who did not know how to relate to everyday Peruvians.

These vulnerabilities set Vargas Llosa up for defeat by the right chal-lenger. Alberto Fujimori had been made to order for the part. A long-shot candidate at the start, this little-known agronomy professor and univer-sity administrator came from Japanese immigrant stock, the son of a flower shop owner and his wife. His ancestry made Fujimori a *chino*, the Peru-vian catchall for anyone of East Asian descent, and an outsider who did not belong to the white oligarchy. In contrast to Vargas Llosa's impecca-ble Castilian diction, Fujimori spoke a sometimes ungrammatical Spanish more like Andean villagers whose first language was Quechua. The upstart candidate campaigned hard in Lima's poorer districts. He drove around on a tractor, the "Fujimobile," or donned a poncho and Andean cap to dance with housewives. A *chino,* a *cholo,* and a *negro,* Fujimori happily described his polyglot ticket. (The Peruvian constitution prescribed a first and second vice president.) His campaign posters promised *A President Like You.*

Many voters considered Fujimori's Japanese ancestry as a positive. Although Vargas Llosa's talk about Europeanizing Peru rubbed many the wrong way, the average Peruvian would freely admit to the country's "ignorance" and "underdevelopment." *El Chino*'s supporters hoped he would bring some Toyotaesque efficiency, order, and prosperity to their shambolic land. "You never see a broke Japanese person," one woman told a journalist. Actually, Fujimori had never been to Japan and knew little about its culture. That did not keep him from putting on karate robes and the rising-sun headband to brandish a samurai sword for a photo shoot. "I have always been methodical and organized," Fujimori said. "I believe this is a cultural inheritance." The candidate hinted at a big Japanese aid package should he be elected.

Most voters wanted to be done with Peru's corrupt politics as usual. Fujimori had never held office, and, unlike Vargas Llosa, did not ally himself with any party. "I don't support heterodoxy, orthodoxy, liberalism, communism, or populism, just pragmatism," he declared. Fujimori began at a microscopic 0.6 percent only to have almost defeated the favored Vargas Llosa in the election's first round. His campaign made a pleasing underdog story.

Vargas Llosa went to see Fujimori a day after the election.

He offered to withdraw from the runoff for national unity.

"I don't accept your resignation," Fujimori said. "We can't decide the president ourselves."

The novelist's advisors believed he could defeat the agronomist.

"OK, you've persuaded me," Vargas Llosa said at last. "I'm not going to resign, and besides, that son of a bitch didn't accept it anyway."

The runoff turned ugly fast. Fujimori proclaimed independence, but enjoyed secret backing from the incumbent García and his APRA party. One day, an APRA-supporting radio announcer indignantly read erotic passages from Vargas Llosa's newest novel.

Your serpentine tongue and your sweet saliva have both served me and used me.

A pornographer, *El Chino* called his rival. Perhaps also a pedophile, he suggested.

An aggressive Fujimori also played to fears about Vargas Llosa's economic platform. The writer wanted to tame hyperinflation by ending subsidies and price controls, and by slashing government spending. That would be the first step to stabilizing the country, he explained reasonably enough. An APRA-financed attack ad employed horror footage from Pink Floyd's *The Wall* to show that this "shock" plan would turn Peruvians into bloodied zombies. Fujimori avoided specifics about his own proposals. His vague slogan promised only "Honesty, Technology, and Jobs." For a novice, he was proving a skilled politician.

A little religious war capped the runoff campaign. Because Fujimori wooed Peru's growing evangelical population, the Catholic archbishop of Lima endorsed Vargas Llosa. The writer was a self-described agnostic, but at least he wasn't a Protestant. He might yet discover the Lord, the bejeweled prelate indicated. The archbishop's backing only exacerbated perceptions about Vargas Llosa as the establishment candidate. No one paid much attention to his lovely closing speech about Peru being a beautiful, ancient book whose next pages had yet to be written. Polls on the eve of the runoff showed the novelist trailing Fujimori by a substantial margin.

The voting indeed gave *El Chino* a massive triumph, almost 60 percent of the vote. Fujimori crushed Vargas Llosa in working-class Lima as well as the Andes and jungles. "I always expected to win," the president-elect explained. "Three months is plenty to learn to be a politician." He had pulled off one of Latin America's biggest electoral upsets.

———————

No one knew what to expect from the new administration. Less than two weeks after Fujimori's July 28, 1990 inauguration, his economics minister came on television one evening. To combat hyperinflation and close the budget deficit, he announced the government was imposing drastic austerity measures, effective immediately. The news stunned Peruvians. Fujimori ran against Vargas Llosa's "shock" proposal, but now he was implementing almost exactly those same stark belt-tightening policies. What soon became known as the *fujishock* left the Peruvian inti to float free against the dollar, among other liberalizing changes. That would more than triple the price of food and everything else in a threadbare country where the minimum monthly wage was the equivalent of fifteen US dollars. "May God help us," the economics minister signed off that night.

Noisy Lima awoke eerily quiet. Stores shuttered fearing looters. Hungry slum dwellers sacked one food market anyway. "The price of chicken has just flown away," a housewife told a *New York Times* reporter. Bus drivers stayed home because gas had risen from 41,800 to 1,200,000 intis a gallon. A promised social aid fund to soften the pain of the fujishock was only in the planning stages. Even the few tourists still braving wartime Peru found themselves caught in the mess. Airlines retroactively raised tickets as much as sixfold. Fuming travelers milled around inside the dank Lima airport.

An unruffled Fujimori did not back down. He was not especially eloquent or charismatic, but he beamed self-confidence. The new president grew up in working-class districts, Barrios Altos and La Victoria, and learned there how to get by. His La Molina lectures were so boring, one student recalled, that "after class you just wanted to say, whew, thank God it's over."

But Fujimori graded easily to garner big enrollments. Then the bespectacled, methodical, and ambitious young mathematician outmaneuvered rivals to win election as the university's rector. "He was learning to aggressively grab what he could, without giving an inch to defeat and destroy his opponents," journalist Luis Jochamowitz noted. Fujimori saw that strict austerity measures offered the only way out for Peru. Betraying his campaign promise not to implement them did not bother him.

The new president also went on the offensive against Shining Path. Unlike his predecessors, he personally took the fight to their strongholds, among them Lima's San Marcos University. *Senderistas* sometimes openly carried guns there, and graffiti covered the walls. When Fujimori made an unannounced visit to San Marcos early in 1991, a shower of rocks welcomed him. A big security detail accompanied the president, and, quite calmly, *El Chino* ducked under one policeman's riot shield. He grasped a roller to paint over *senderista* graffiti for the television cameras. "No longer will the terrorists control the university," he told nervous students. "You will be able to study." An army detachment stayed behind to keep order, and troops were also stationed at three other universities. The soldiers marched away and probably executed three suspected *senderista* students at San Marcos, which seemed not to bother Fujimori at all. He wanted to show a hard hand against the expanding insurgency.

It would not be easy to make inroads. In a rare success, the police had managed to capture Osmán Morote in downtown Lima, shortly after the party congress's first session. When the northern *senderista* commander went to trial at last in 1991. Morote refused to answer the judge's questions during the month-long proceedings. Then, after being sentenced to twenty years in prison, he rose to denounce the judge, César Ruiz Trigoso, as corrupt, a servant of the oppressors. (Ruiz had ruled enough times against poor squatters to earn the nickname "Judge Eviction.") *This trial has been a political farce staged by the genocidal regime,* Morote shouted. He pointed a menacing finger back at the bench. And, sure enough, a guerrilla hit squad blocked the judge's car in Miraflores two days later. A woman and two men moved in with guns blazing. The unlucky Ruiz died in the hospital, a *God-father*-like revenge killing.

Such bloody actions only fortified Fujimori's resolve. He faced off increasingly with the congress for blocking judicial reforms, and, at one point, joked that "perhaps an Emperor would be good for Peru." Many Peruvians liked *El Chino*'s toughness, but rebel actions did not diminish in his presidency's first year. The best way to cripple and perhaps destroy the *senderistas* would be putting their beloved Chairman Gonzalo behind bars. Only Fujimori and a few government higher-ups realized that moment might not be so far away. A secret intelligence unit had been formed to hunt down Abimael—and was making unexpected progress.

CHAPTER FIFTEEN

Ghostbusters

Marco Miyashiro was at his desk in the police immigration office when his division chief walked in unannounced. "*Chino*, I just got off the phone with the Director. You're transferred effective immediately. Report to DINCOTE at 3 pm today."

The capable Miyashiro belonged to the National Investigative Police, or PIP, Peru's FBI. He had already risen to the rank of major at thirty-nine, and, at immigrations, supervised visa services at the downtown office with its clattering typewriters and long lines. Now Miyashiro was being reassigned to the PIP's counterinsurgency unit, the DINCOTE. The PIP and Peru's other three police branches rotated their men to new postings every so often. That way, the theory went, officers would not become entrenched anywhere, and thus would be less prone to corruption. This did not exactly pan out in practice since bribe-taking, graft, and extortion abounded everywhere. It could cost hefty fictitious "fines" to convince a PIP officer to fix your visa problem.

Miyashiro had worked in the big immigrations building for a year. There he watched his fellow officers discreetly tuck shakedown money into their wallets. The moralizing whistle-blower role was not for Miyashiro, who did not want to sabotage his career by earning the enmity of his colleagues. But he had never forgotten a conversation with his mother, Eugenia, many years before. Miyashiro had graduated first in his PIP academy class. It wasn't too late to pick another career, she said. He could go into business.

"Why?" the young Miyashiro asked.

"The only police I know are drunks, womanizers, or *sinvergüenzas* (shameless crooks)," his mother said. "I don't want you turning into one." Miyashiro had never taken a bribe as a PIP officer.

His new DINCOTE assignment would be his second stint with the counterterrorism division. In the late 1980s, he had supervised intelligence operations against the MRTA, the littler Marxist guerrilla group. (Oddly enough, that group's leader, Victor Polay, had been little Miyashiro's scoutmaster in the Callao Boy Scout troop 3.) Miyashiro expected reassignment to the MRTA, not realizing a different mission awaited. He packed his desk to head over to the DINCOTE headquarters a few downtown blocks away.

Fighting terrorists had not been in Miyashiro's career plan. Like the new president Alberto Fujimori, he descended from Japanese immigrants, making him a *chino* as well. His parents owned a bodega in the port district of Callao that sold candy, laundry soap, beer, and other sundry necessities. So many Asian-Peruvian families ran these neighborhood establishments that el *chino de la esquina*, "the corner store Chinaman," became a common slang term. As a boy, Miyashiro helped in the store, and, as the exacting Eugenia expected, brought home good grades. He learned judo at his uncle's *dojo* and his grandparents prepared sushi for special occasions, but, three generations removed from Japan, Miyashiro considered himself Peruvian. His mother's lasagna ranked among his favorite foods. (She learned to make pasta from an Italian neighbor.) The Boy Scouts occupied Miyashiro's weekends.

Scouting set the young Miyashiro on the path to the police. His troop volunteered at a decrepit youth detention center. As a decorated teenaged scout, Miyashiro led kids at the facility on nighttime beach walks. They sometimes built a bonfire. One by one, each boy threw in a twig to symbolically free himself from a trouble, bad habit, or fear. These spirited urchins could have come from Fagan's gang in *Oliver Twist*. Miyashiro liked scouting's quasi-military structure and its commitment to contributing to the social good. He began to think about a career in law enforcement.

At a neighbor's suggestion, Miyashiro attended high school at a Lima military boarding school, the Colegio Leoncio Prado. Its most famous graduate, Mario Vargas Llosa, set his best-selling first novel there. *The Time of the Hero* depicted a closed adolescent world of hazing, cheating, bullying, and jumping the wall for adventures in sex and rebellion. By comparison to his mother's demands, Miyashiro found the regimented academy schedule almost relaxed. If the other boys thought to pick on the little *chino*, they had it wrong. He had become a judo black belt at his uncle's dojo. (The young Gustavo Gorriti also trained there sometimes.) Once, Miyashiro crouched in a wrestler's stance, then challenged the other boys to push him over. They could never move their short yet strong schoolmate from his spot. He was popular with his classmates.

Just weeks after graduating, Miyashiro decided to join the PIP. It was a plainclothes investigative force and attracted livelier, better-educated young men than the other police branches, also paying a little more. Higher-ranking PIP officers cultivated a G-man cool: dark suits, manicured fingernails, gold watches. Miyashiro detested the cadet dress code at Leoncio Prado, and, in his view, not having to wear a uniform was one more reason for choosing the PIP. His first assignment after finishing academy training was to the security detail of then-president Francisco Morales Bermúdez, a more conservative general who replaced Velasco in 1975. After a year in the provincial town of Huánuco supervising local operations against Shining Path, Miyashiro moved in 1986 to DINCOTE headquarters, and the MRTA intelligence oversight assignment. The DINCOTE had its offices in El Sexto, a medieval-looking downtown compound where Abimael Guzmán had been briefly held in 1969 and then a notorious prison. (Thirteen hostages had been chopped to pieces in one macabre riot before its closure.) Everyone called the building *La Fortaleza*, the Fortress.

Miyashiro would be posted there again now. The DINCOTE chief indeed reassigned him to the MRTA, placing twenty officers under his command. Some days after arriving, Miyashiro ran across an old friend, Benedicto Jiménez, who had been in the DINCOTE for some years. As PIP academy students, they had produced their own radio show together— a detective drama loosely based on real cases. Benedicto went on to join the DINCOTE's Delta Force, a rapid response team to answer *senderista* attacks and detain suspected guerrillas. Its approach frustrated him, he explained to Miyashiro. When the Delta Force received a tip about a possible *senderista*, it rushed in to make arrests. Benedicto thought suspected operatives should be shadowed instead to track their connections to the party leadership. He went to the head of the PIP, General Fernando Reyes, to explain. The general decided to establish a new intelligence-gathering group, the *Grupo Especial de Inteligencia del Perú* (GEIN). He appointed Benedicto to head the new unit.

All this intrigued Miyashiro. Like Benedicto, he understood that the army had gotten nowhere with its village massacres and death camps. It would be almost impossible to defeat the *senderistas* as long as Abimael and other top leaders remained at large, and hunting them down would require patient investigation. After discovering their shared views, Benedicto asked Miyashiro to join him in the GEIN. The DINCOTE chief consented only if Miyashiro agreed to continue supervising the anti-MRTA unit as well.

Although Benedicto was also a major, Miyashiro had seniority, which automatically made him GEIN's commander under the PIP's military-style hierarchy. Miyashiro did not want Benedicto to feel subordinate in a unit that had been his idea in the first place. *You'll always have the last word*, he promised his friend.

The two men became effectively the GEIN's co-leaders, albeit with Benedicto running day-to-day operations. They made a Peruvian Starsky and Hutch in their contrasting styles. A pragmatist by nature, Miyashiro had a stern commander's authority, and yet made friends easily with his dry humor and crooked smile. A head taller than his partner, the more withdrawn Benedicto had a dreamer's big brown eyes. His mother, a Greek immigrant, took up with a black stevedore. Their brief affair gave *el negro*, as everyone called Benedicto, his copper-toned skin and handsome head of black curls. He could sound more like a professor than a policeman, and liked to read the Roman poets in Latin. That Miyashiro and Benedicto liked each other freed the GEIN from the jealousy, backbiting, and credit-claiming of other units.

The first glimpse of the GEIN's office shocked Miyashiro. Their unit had been given a single room on the third floor of a new office building across the street from the Fortress. They had one desk, a few chairs, and not even a telephone. Miyashiro was going to be in charge of their budget and staffing—and had always been good working the system. He would convince DINCOTE higher-ups to give them more space.

"Exactly how many men do we have?" he asked. Benedicto told him that they had four. Miyashiro promised to find two more.

The agents only had one field radio, Benedicto added.

"I'll get another one," Miyashiro said.

Benedicto wasn't finished. The GEIN's lone car had broken down, he explained. His agents had to shadow suspects on foot.

"I'll find a car, too."

Their mission would have been daunting, no matter the budget. Neither the DINCOTE nor the Army Intelligence Service had made much progress towards cracking *senderista* secrecy over a decade of war. They seldom shared much information or coordinated efforts due to institutional rivalries. When stationed in the jungle hills of Huánuco in the early 1980s, Miyashiro once sent men to take down a red *senderista* banner. Panicked soldiers mistook his plainclothes PIP officers for guerrillas, opening fire. Miyashiro lost a man in that senseless incident.

Much mystery still surrounded Shining Path and its leader. To better understand the *senderista* mindset, Benedicto and Miyashiro read Communist history, Guzmán's speeches, and text from captured documents. That task especially appealed to Benedicto's scholarly instincts despite the endless pages of tedious jargon. "Know the enemy. And know yourself," Benedicto wrote on the office blackboard. He liked to quote from Sun Tzu's *Art of War.*

Benedicto did have one concrete lead before Miyashiro's arrival. His Delta Unit had detained a suspected *senderista* in 1985. They eventually released the young university secretary, Judith Díaz, uncertain about her guilt. A few months later, the police received an anonymous letter from a distraught mother. Her son, the woman explained, had been recruited by Díaz into Shining Path. She wanted the police to know about Díaz, who lived with her father in the seedy La Victoria district. That letter had reached Benedicto. He kept it to himself for the moment. If he shared the information with his commanders, they would simply order him to raid Díaz's house. That would waste the opportunity to put a likely *senderista* organizer under surveillance—and perhaps identify a bigger guerrilla network. As soon as Benedicto had the GEIN, he tapped Díaz's phone and sent agents to watch her house. They connected her to a fugitive *senderista*, Alfredo Castillo, who reportedly organized a gruesome embassy bombing (the Indian one this time, in retaliation for New Delhi's friendliness with then-president Alan García). Tailing Castillo was leading now to other *senderistas*.

"This is really good stuff, *chino*." Benedicto said. "We just don't have the men to really work the case."

They would have to make do for now. As weeks passed, the GEIN drew gossip and even ridicule from other agents. One story had the unit fronting some drug trafficking operation. Benedicto reported directly to General Roca, the national PIP chief, which irritated the DINCOTE director and other higher-ups at the Fortress. At one big meeting in the courtyard, an angry colonel went on about loyalty and treachery. Everybody knew he meant Benedicto, Miyashiro, and the GEIN.

Another DINCOTE commander once interrupted Benedicto's explanations about Shining Path's Maoist principles.

"I don't care who Mao's grandma was!" he snapped. "I want arrests."

Even their friends jokingly baptized the GEIN the *Cazafantasmas* ("Ghostbusters," after the Hollywood hit). It was accurate enough insofar as nobody had sighted their ultimate quarry, Abimael Guzmán, for more than a decade. "We were essentially chasing a ghost," Miyashiro said later. "Who You Gonna Call?" went the *Ghostbusters* tagline. Not the GEIN: their office still didn't have a phone.

The GEIN kept Judith Díaz under surveillance for three months. Their clever tech specialist, Walter Cápac, made video recordings at stakeouts. He lugged around his cumbersome Betamax camcorder in a gym bag to conceal it from view. Although Cápac had to film from a distance and often in bad light, his videos established a baseline of names and faces. Miyashiro managed to procure both a car and a van, which they fitted with radio equipment and painted orange to look like a telephone company repair vehicle. A few more agents came on board, mostly street-smart young men, who used code names like Gypsy, Blackie, and Squirrel. A muscular ex-navy man sometimes drove for their team. He became Popeye, of course.

The CIA began to take some interest in the GEIN, too. In the early 1980s, the Americans had paid limited attention to Shining Path, preoccupied with combatting Communism in Central America. The Soviet empire must not gain a beachhead that close to the US border, warned then-president Ronald Reagan. His administration armed a murderous counterinsurgency battalion in El Salvador and a secret war against the leftist Nicaraguan Sandinistas. Increasingly, however, the Peruvian rebellion had attracted Washington's notice. A 1989 US State Department fact sheet described Shining Path as "an extremely dangerous and unpredictable terrorist and insurgency group." The Lima embassy secretly cabled Washington *Night of the Living Dead* horror stories. One report described how *senderistas* "cut off a (policeman's) lower jaw . . . slit open his stomach and chest, emptied it of its organs," and then, "one at a time, squatted over the man and defecated into his chest cavity." That story may have been exaggerated, but a *senderista* did carve the hammer and sickle into a Lucanamarcan's skull in the 1983 massacre. "Are these killers human?" an embassy analyst asked. Yes, he concluded. "The single most frightening aspect of Sendero Luminoso is that what these terrorists do, they apparently do for ideological reasons."

The top US South American priority remained cocaine trafficking. As the crack epidemic and its gang battles ripped America's big cities apart, the new president George H. W. Bush declared a war in 1989 on Colombia's drug lords. The DEA and CIA joined the hunt for cocaine king Pablo Escobar—and American money financed eradication efforts in the coca-growing jungles of Colombia, Bolivia, and Peru. In Colombia, some Marxist guerrillas began trafficking cocaine themselves, but not Shining Path. The *senderistas* made only a little money from "taxing" the trade, keeping their sights on revolution. A US congressional report still asserted, absurdly, that the "narcoterrorist" Abimael Guzmán and his followers earned as much as $100 million a year in cocaine cash.

The CIA station chief learned about the GEIN and its efforts to track down the *senderista* leadership. He began to provide about a thousand dollars a month. One CIA operative, who had a glass eye and went only by "Del," gave Benedicto and Miyashiro's men a training course. "We knew most of it already," a young GEIN agent, José Gil, said. Their unit did happily accept some high-tech listening devices from the Americans.

Then, halfway into 1990, the GEIN got its big break. They'd begun to decipher Judith Díaz's coded messages to other rebels. (She used words like "soap," "nails," and "brooms" to communicate the latest orders from above.) Her main contact was an unidentified woman whom the agents called "Cris." One day, as the tailing detectives watched from across the street, Cris met with another seeming rebel conspirator. This unsuspecting *senderista* was eventually tracked to a white house in the Mariscal Castilla subdivision of the quiet Monterrico neighborhood. The house had a comfortable suburban look, with the customary security wall around it. 459 2nd Street, the GEIN men noted down the address.

They had no clue yet about the house's importance. It headquartered Shining Path's Department of Organizational Support, or propaganda wing, and had hosted their congress the year before. Even now, Abimael and his new partner, Elena Iparraguirre, sometimes came to review new publications here. The *senderista* leader had a study in an upstairs bedroom packed with reports, minutes, plans, and correspondence.

A stakeout produced nothing interesting at first. A few unidentified people came and went without staying long. An old gardener shuffled around the sidewalk strip, planting and weeding a bit. (A later legend had it that the man was Abimael in disguise.)

"There goes that damn gardener again," the detectives radioed from their unmarked car. "You can bet nothing interesting's happening today."

Then, some days later, Cris led detectives to an apartment in another Lima suburb.

Surveillance there paid off almost immediately. On the morning of June 1, 1990, a half dozen *senderistas* gathered for a meeting at the apartment, including Cris. Benedicto, Miyashiro, and the younger officers hurriedly discussed options in their downtown office. They decided to raid the apartment and the Monterrico house simultaneously.

Benedicto enjoyed the moment's drama.

"Boys, unleash the storm," he radioed.

That became his customary code for launching operations. At the apartment, José Luis Gil and several other agents wanted to grab the *senderistas* as they left their meeting. When a pregnant *senderista* came out and went to the bus stop, the detectives handcuffed her before she could board a bus (which caused momentary outcry among other waiting passengers thinking the plainclothes officers rapists or thieves). Some time later, they wrestled down Cris and two more suspects, when they emerged from the apartment. Cris cried out to alert her comrades, and Gil, the team leader, feared that the last *senderistas* inside might have heard her.

"Come on, we've got to move in!" he shouted.

The agents rushed into the apartment, guns drawn. They found no one in the living room, only some empty chairs. Then Gil spied a woman scampering up a stairway. She flung a stick at him, but the agile detective grabbed her by the ankle. It was Sybila Arredondo, the widow of the celebrated writer José María Arguedas. The striking black-haired Sybila had been arrested once before. Many Lima feminists, writers, and academics knew her, and, assuming a mistake had been made, petitioned for her freedom. When the police released Sybila after the protests, she brought some *senderista* propaganda to the feminist activist Diana Miloslavich, María Elena Moyano's friend. *Oh, shit,* Diana thought. Her friend did belong to Shining Path.

One agent noticed a missing *senderista*.

"There's one more!" he yelled.

It took them some searching to find the last rebel. He had fled across the roof to a neighboring apartment. An agent spotted the toes of his shoes in a bedroom closet.

At the Monterrico house, the GEIN detectives waited for their chance. It seemed to be empty, and, for that reason, had been given a lower priority than the apartment. Only three agents had been stationed there—Juan Villanueva, whom everyone called "Felupdini" after a skinny soap opera character; Jorge Sánchez, a former Delta Force member; and the GEIN's only female detective, Elena Vadillo, who went by *La Morocha* ("the Moor"), for her dark complexion. Late in the afternoon, the three agents saw a woman come down the sidewalk. She unlocked the house's garage door to go inside, giving them their chance. They sprinted out from their car to duck in behind her. Juan Villanueva grabbed the escaping woman on the patio just beyond the garage. The other two detectives rushed through an open door into the house. Inside they found an almost bored man and a woman, who made no effort to get away.

"Who the hell are you?" the woman said. "Why are you here? Get lost!"

The detectives asked for IDs, which the couple indignantly produced. Elena Vadillo frisked them with no result. They appeared to have made a mistake.

"I think we fucked up," murmured Sánchez.

Then he noticed a whiteboard in the kitchen.

It held some scribbled red phrases.

GRCP [Great Proletarian Cultural Revolution]*! Long Live Maoism! Bureaucratic capitalism—process in the country!*

"Holy shit!" Sánchez said. "They're really terrorists, look!"

Now the detectives handcuffed the couple. The man turned out to be a lower-ranking *senderista*; however, his companion was Elvia Zanabria, Comrade Juana, the Central Committee member who unsuccessfully proposed an inquiry into Augusta's death. She directed the Department of Organizational Support from this suburban house.

Miyashiro and Benedicto soon arrived. They walked through the downstairs rooms to find embroidered hammer-and-sickle wall hangings; *retablos*, the traditional Ayacuchan carved boxes, these showing guerrilla actions; a commemorative red flag signed by attendees at a party meeting; and, of course, many admiring portraits of the great Chairman Gonzalo with that stern yet benevolent visage of a Communist warrior–philosopher king. An envelope held a handwritten note from the man himself together with some dried flowers from Augusta's mausoleum, which he apparently intended to send to a party loyalist. ("A memento of yesterday, today, and a better tomorrow.") *It's like a museum,* Miyashiro thought.

Their discoveries did not end there. They found the upstairs bedroom and its stacked files, packed bookcases, and faked identity cards ready for use. An agent discovered an address list atop a bookshelf, although it had no names. A trove of precious new material had fallen into their hands.

"Four tons of terrorism," Miyashiro later joked.

No longer did Abimael seem like a make-believe phantom. To accompany its so-called Interview of the Century in 1988, *El Diario* had published a photograph of the Shining Path leader, bent over signing some proclamation. The picture did not give a clear view of Abimael's face, but the desk and wall, Miyashiro noticed, matched the upstairs bedroom. Abimael had been in Lima all along, they realized for the first time. Their search also turned up some Tigason pills, a medication for psoriasis, from which the fugitive guerrilla chieftain was known to suffer. It seemed probable that their quarry was still somewhere in the city.

Only nine days remained until the runoff election between Fujimori and Vargas Llosa. When the lame duck Alan García learned about the Monterrico discovery, he conveyed his congratulations to the GEIN's leaders. The interior minister invited reporters to see the trophies and crow over this rare progress in the counterinsurgency. (He did not mention the GEIN by name, to protect its cover.) "As far as we know," *Caretas* reported, "it's the first time the police have practically stepped on Abimael Guzmán's talons."

————————

Abimael and Elena had no clue as to how the police had picked up their trail. They had been at a hideaway not far from the Monterrico house that afternoon. If it had been a different day, they might have been working there, and likely captured. Their security arrangements included armed lookouts, escape plans, and spies inside the police. Various comrades received an admonishment about maintaining greater vigilance next time. It always upset Abimael when party members did not pay attention to detail. "We oppose laxness," he said at the party congress. "Where does it lead? Defeat." But the police did not appear to have any more information about other party safe houses. Watchful *senderistas* detected no signs of surveillance there in the following weeks.

Everything else was breaking the revolution's way. "We hated losing the [Monterrico] house," Elena said, "but it was not a severe blow." Although Fujimori, after winning the runoff, promised to bring the terrorists to justice, that did not especially concern the *senderistas*. The new president was a novice, and his tough talk seemed little more than bluster. They had survived the whole Peruvian military's best efforts to crush their rebellion by blood and fear. That Fujimori was allying himself with the generals, Abimael wrote, showed "galloping state reactionariazation" to "intensify the repressive and bureaucratic system of the State and extends its barracks control over the population." Fear about the revolution's victory forced the ruling classes to this new "centralized absolutism."

So much bad government had left the country in shambles. Mountain roads became barely passable for their unfixed potholes. Parasite-infested, undersized shantytown children went even hungrier after the *fujishock* and its drastic fiscal measures. Along with the blackouts, the decrepit water system began to fail in Lima, especially during the day. Collecting water for the next morning's dishwashing and spit baths in plastic washtubs became a nightly ritual. That did not matter so much in neglected outlying settlements, which were so poor as to have no water service at all. Residents there spent their few pennies to fill buckets from water trucks that made undependable rounds through the neighborhoods.

The capital felt increasingly like a city under siege. Almost every night the *senderistas* bombed one or another government building downtown. When the latest US ambassador, Anthony Quainton, was batting the ball around at an exclusive tennis club one day, he heard a big explosion. *A bomb wrecked the wall to your residence*, an embassy staff member phoned soon afterwards. A favorite *senderista* sport had long been firing stray shots at the police guarding the Italianate mansion belonging to Yankee imperialism's highest representative in Peru. This time they had really been trying to kill the US ambassador, a secret CIA report concluded later. That could only be a guess, since American intelligence officers had limited contacts beyond their bunkered embassy.

A panicking country was just what Shining Path had always wanted. The power vacuum would allow the People's Guerrilla Army to smash into power at last. "My God," a tabloid headline wondered about the worsening situation, "Where Are We Headed?" That blood, hunger, and uncertainty smelled to the rebels like nearing victory.

Didn't Chairman Mao have it right again in one saying?

Everything under the sun is chaos; the situation is excellent.

PART III

CHAPTER SIXTEEN

The Clever Frog

Huaychao became a ghost village at night. The jungle fog billowed up to seal its stone huts in a witchy fastness. Those villagers assigned to patrol duty headed out at dusk into the mountains. Only a few bristly pigs rooting around in the creek broke the chilly still. Everyone else barred the door and went to bed to rise early for the next day's labors. Roosters began crowing an hour before dawn, and, in the darkness, farmhouses rustled slowly to life. Peasant women lit their little wood fires to warm water for sugared herb tea.

This evening, early in 1990, it was Narciso Sulca's weekly turn for patrolling. He and his family had only recently returned from Carhuahurán, where most Huaychainos had fled the *senderistas* in 1983. They suffered in exile there, a miserable band of refugees camped around the army post. After some years of back-and-forth fighting across the Iquichan heights, village *rondas* and army patrols had gained the upper hand by the late 1980s. It became safe enough for the Huaychainos to risk returning home.

Having just turned twenty, Narciso Sulca served as the Huaychao *ronda* committee secretary. He had grown little from his schoolboy days, barely five feet tall and weighing maybe a hundred pounds. Even so, Isidro Sulca's son could hike across mountains or turn earth for hours without tiring just like any other villager. Narciso talked constantly, too, this a deviation from the more reserved country way. Some Huaychainos enjoyed his endless stories, while others regarded him as a braggart. Narciso had been elected *ronda* committee secretary almost by default, because few other villagers could read or write. The secretary kept meeting minutes in a big bound notebook as expected by peasant protocol. As a leader, a *dirigente*, Narciso tried to set a good example, *poner un ejemplo*. He took his patrol turn as required of every able-bodied village man. It seemed a lifetime away from his boyhood stargazing with his younger brother Leandro before Iquicha had been engulfed by war.

Every Tuesday evening, Narciso and his *ronda* group assembled for their night patrol. They carried *huaracas*, the stone-throwing slings, and few homemade weapons like *tirachas*, one-shot guns and hand grenades concocted from evaporated-milk tins packed with dynamite and nails. If a man failed to show for duty, Narciso rousted him from his farmhouse. Then the patrollers tramped away to guard duty in their rubber sandals.

They came upon a llama one misty night.

"*Hui, hui, hui,*" the animal hissed.

It might be a *jarjacha*, a deceased villager who'd committed incest, an evil spirit condemned to wander the dark forever. Those ghosts seldom bothered the living anymore. Now the patrollers had to worry about the other nightwalkers, the *puriqkuna*, the devilish lice-infested remnants of Chairman Gonzalo's guerrilla army. Every man kept alert for a sliver of light, a muffled voice, an ambush around the next switchback.

At dawn, the patrollers dispersed to their farmhouses. Along the path home, Narciso wadded a few more minty coca leaves into his cheek. The mild buzz fortified him through days and nights. Even though he'd become an *evangélico,* a born-again Christian, Narciso hadn't given up his coca or his *copas,* cane liquor. Stricter villagers did not drink, dance, or *chacchar,* chew. As occurred in quite a few other places during the war, many Huaychainos had converted to the new Pentecostal faith that matched their apocalyptic wartime experience. Some nights the Quechua hymns about the fires of Judgment Day shook Huaychao's mud chapel.

Narciso sang his way back to his hut.

Señor Jesus chaskikuhuayku mañakamusqaykuta qayllayquipe quñuykanakuq kuya wauqillaikupaq. ("Lord Jesus, I pray that we will be reunited so I may also stand before you and my dear brothers.")

He slept for a few hours before heading to the fields.

It was only about two hundred miles by the condor's flight from Huaychao's heights to Lima and a blocky modern house on 265 Buenavista Street. There Abimael and Elena were regrouping after losing their party archives to the police raid at Monterrico. Abimael spent most days reading, writing, and plotting strategy, occasionally receiving visitors. To learn how to use a computer donated by some European supporters, Elena took a night class at a downtown Lima academy. The police still did not even know about her existence, which allowed her to go out with a few discreet party bodyguards. Elena's fellow students had no clue that their pleasant older classmate was a feared terrorist leader. A Liman from girlhood, Elena felt comfortable among the smoke-belching buses and sidewalk vendors. She and Abimael were increasingly focused on the battle for the capital and its outlying districts. The giant city would soon reach panic's edge under the intensifying *senderista* assault.

It was another matter altogether back up in the mountains. As Fujimori assumed the presidency in 1990, the *senderistas* found themselves in deep trouble there. Their founding Maoist mythology assumed that the peasantry would rally to the glorious Communist cause. Instead, disaffected villagers were rising up to chase the rebels from their originary Andean strongholds. The *rondas*, as most people called the peasant militias, had stalled in the mid-1980s, but were galvanizing now into a mass movement. More than three thousand villages across Ayacucho, Junín, Huancavelica, Andahuaylas, and Apurímac would form their own militia committees by 1991. The expanding patrols helped to drive Shining Path from many mountain areas altogether.

That Huaychao claimed the first *ronda* gave Narciso and other villagers considerable pride. The *senderista* call to revolution against hunger and oppression had seemed reasonable enough back in 1983, at least to Narciso. But then the *senderistas* tried to force their way into Huaychao, and shot recalcitrant village leaders, the *varayoq*. The retaliation killings at the rock of justice had marked Huaychao's declaration of war against Chairman Gonzalo's forces.

Elsewhere the discontent developed more slowly. At first welcoming the rebels, some villagers in regions like Junín and Huancavelica wearied of their authoritarian rule. "We had the hacienda owners," reasoned one peasant from a hamlet near Huaychao. "Why would we want new authorities?" The *senderista* people's trials on village greens could turn into ugly score-settling between feuding families. Sometimes, the rebels took away village children to make them into fighters. Nor had the essential Shining Path promise been fulfilled. A Communist paradise? Liberation for the poor? Instead the only result had been suffering, death, and a war with no seeming end.

The new Fujimori administration saw an opportunity. It encouraged the rising *rondas* as a centerpiece of its counterinsurgency strategy. The grinning, tireless *chino* personally captained the effort. He praised peasant patriotism and approved giving *ronderos*, the patrollers, guns for the first time. Fujimori helicoptered into one mountain town to bless the Model 1300 Winchester rifles for the holy war. "Fierce wolves which look like humans," he called the *senderistas*. His aid agencies prioritized road-building and handouts to consolidate peasant support for the government.

A functionary distributed sneakers in Iquicha.

"Who gave you these?" the man asked.

"FU-HEE-MOR-EE!" he led the chant.

Huaychao kids got grey sweat suits.

A savvier army joined the hearts-and-minds efforts, too. After so many years of massacres and cruelty, government forces had failed to wipe out the *senderistas*. Officers finally realized that a more populist, peasant-friendly style produced better results. They mingled at village fiestas to warn their "brother peasants" against the *terrucos*, the terrorists. The indiscriminate massacre of peasants ceased almost completely under the Fujimori presidency. (As late as 1988, an army patrol slaughtered about fifty villagers at Cayara down the mountains from Huaychao.) According to Mao's famous dictum, guerrilla fighters should move among the people as fish swim in the sea. Instead, the *senderistas* found themselves confined to the peaks, and the buzz-cut young soldiers, or *cachacos*, as everyone called them, played in peasant soccer tournaments. More villages wanted a protective army garrison than area commanders could spare troops to man.

The army even flipped some long-time red zones. In the settlements along the Huanta Valley's bottomlands, a little upstream from the now abandoned La Torre estate at Iribamba, the villagers had long given succor to the *senderistas*. A new colonel took valley command in 1990, a tall pale man nicknamed *El Bananazo*, the Big Banana. He jeeped down in a convoy to warn the peasants to begin *rondas*, or else. Almost overnight, they turned against the rebels as if some evil spell had been broken. When the *senderistas* killed a few people to scare the others back into line, the villagers built adobe brick guard towers, escape tunnels, and control gates to protect against more raiding. Their settlements had almost the look of fortified medieval towns like San Gimignano or Rocamadour.

Not every *ronda* was run by peasants. In the sweltering Apurímac Valley down from Ayacucho, a part-time denture maker, Pompeyo Rivera Torres, renamed himself Commander Huayhuaco to crusade against the *senderistas*. His patrollers were mostly poor coca-growing settlers. They wielded guns supplied by local drug traffickers. What narco wanted Marxist guerrillas interfering with business? The flamboyant Huayhuaco became a formidable warlord. He was eventually jailed for drug trafficking himself. Such cases remained the exception, at least in highland regions. Most villages elected their *ronda* leaders.

Nor did the party completely lose its provincial operating capacity. *Senderista* bands still waylaid buses to request "contributions" from the terrified passengers. They killed many village *ronda* leaders, and the occasional policeman. The guerrillas even boasted a new jungle stronghold in the Ene Valley. They confined the native Amazonian tribespeople there, the Asháninka, to starved encampments. When a group of Asháninka at an isolated Catholic mission refused to leave, the *senderistas* closed in to massacre them. The supervising Franciscan priest, Mariano Gagnon, an American, frantically arranged an evacuation. Army helicopters flew two hundred Asháninka away to a new encampment.

Shining Path tried to dismiss the *rondas* as contemptible puppets. *Las mesnadas*, "auxiliaries," *El Diario* invariably described them. The party mouthpiece promised that "the poorly armed *ronderos* defending an unjust cause will be the targets of a policy of counter-establishment by the New Power in the countryside." That meant punishing villages for forming *ronda* committees. *Senderistas* would descend upon some isolated hamlet before dawn. They clubbed down villagers with sticks and machetes, and then set thatched rooves aflame. A young American anthropologist hiked around the Ayacuchan countryside in 1991. "It was eerie," Raymond Starr recalled.

"Everywhere you saw the abandoned shells of adobe houses and whole hamlets burned down by the *senderistas*." One weeping peasant mother told Starr about her baby's death in a raid only the week before. They had smashed the child's head open on the rocks. Sometimes surviving villagers camped in their ruined houses rather than rebuild right away.

But terror tactics increasingly backfired now. As they did in the Huanta Valley, *senderista* assaults often hardened a desperate resolve, especially as peasants saw the possibility of the war's end. Many one-time rebel sympathizers switched sides to become patrol leaders. *Los arrepentidos*, the penitent ones, people called them. The balance of power in Peru's interiors changed dramatically during 1990 and 1991. Most places the *senderistas* found themselves in retreat as never before.

Several hundred *ronderos* traveled down to march in Lima's Independence Day parade on July 28, 1991. This patriotic procession always featured flag-waving schoolchildren, uniformed nurses, goose-stepping soldiers, and tanks and Humvees. The ponchoed Andean villagers—shouldering their new Winchesters—and some spear-carrying Amazonian warriors contributed some exotic color to the procession. Fujimori and his generals had arranged truck transport for the *ronderos* to stage this show of a Peru rising up against the evil Abimael Guzmán's terrorist wolves. The president saluted the marching militia men from the reviewing stand.

———

Most villagers recognized the unfairness of the *ronda* arrangement. "We're suffering and dying every night, doing the job for the army," a committee president in the Satipo jungle explained. He and others boasted about their accomplishments even so. "We're bringing peace back. Not the soldiers. Not the president. Not the congress." These Amazonian homesteaders, Andean peasants, and valley farmers saw themselves as the nation's unsung heroes. They'd taken up arms against an invading menace. Some journalists compared the *ronderos* to the mountain fighters, the *montoneros*, who battled the Chilean occupiers in the War of the Pacific a century before.

Only a peasant like Narciso knew how hard the fight had really been. When he was a boy, his father recounted an Andean fairy tale. A fox catches a frog. "Listen, *zorro*, before you eat me let's have a race to the mountaintop," the frog says. Then he slyly stations his frog friends along the trail. Every time the fox races off, he hears more croaking up ahead. He puffs faster up the hill to get in front. At the peak, the fox finds a frog already there. He collapses dead from exhaustion in the story's unsentimental ending.

The Huaychainos had needed a similar ingenuity to beat back the *senderistas*. When they resettled their village in the late 1980s, the rebels still posed a threat. Narciso sometimes instructed his fellow *ronderos* to cinch up their ponchos. "We'll look like soldiers that way," he said. Across the centuries, villagers bowed and scraped before the steel-wielding Spanish conquerors, plantation owners, and government officials. Taking on the *senderistas* restored some manly pride. Narciso liked the Special Forces–sounding name, *commandos*, sometimes used for patrol leaders. His own war name, Falcon, could have come from the Rambo movies he'd watched in town.

Huaychao's patrollers had misadventures. Once they flogged a few supposed *senderista* sympathizers only to discover they had nothing to do with the rebels. Some other village *ronderos* strangled a Huaychaino, falsely suspecting him of belonging to the nightwalkers. The war's rage left mercy and more reasoned investigation in short supply.

Narciso loved recounting patrol stories, even about the mishaps.

"*Soy ronde-raaasso*," he would laugh. "I'm a bad-ass patroller."

Many women joined the fight too. Their skirts, black braids, and flower-adorned hats gave Huaychao *mamitas* the postcard Andean Indian look (in contrast to the somewhat more Westernized profile of men like Narciso, who wore a T-shirt and warm-up jacket under his poncho). Everywhere in the Andes, as anthropologist Marisol de la Cadena noted, village women presented a more Indian appearance than their men. This greater "Indianness" included speaking less Spanish, the conqueror's tongue, since peasants often did not send girls to school. The legend of the man-eating Inca warrior queen, Mama Huaco, attributed a stereotypical Indian savagery to women. At Uchuraccay in 1983, village *señoras* had certainly exhibited some ferocious toughness in the fear and panic at *senderista* assaults. Enraged *mamitas* led the way in stoning the weeping journalists.

A visiting army patrol organized a women's *ronda* committee in Huaychao. Its commander picked Narciso's aunt, Juana, for its first president. A single mother who'd always fended for herself, she accepted the job. Now, when they pastured their flocks on the moors, Huaychainas kept lookout for any stranger's approach. Sometimes the army drilled the women around the village. They were to form Huaychao's last defense with their rocks and kitchen-knife-tipped wooden spears. Juana wondered about her unit's fighting capacity. "Only God knows my fate," she sighed.

The war exacted a heavy cost from every villager. Sometimes, when recalling his patrol exploits in later years, Narciso fell uncharacteristically silent. He and other Huaychainos had always suffered through unset broken bones, abscessed teeth, and the occasional outbreak of deadly diseases like bubonic plague and typhoid fever. Peasant women gave birth in their farmhouses a day's walk from the nearest clinic. In the war years, however, a whole new lexicon for sorrow, suffering, and mistrust developed—*iquyasqa*, a bone-penetrating exhaustion; *iskay uyukuna*, two-faced people; *sasachukuy*, the universe gone bad. *Llakiwan kachkani*, Narciso's mother Francisca would say. *I am in pain.* Her ailment responded to neither the sorcerer's guinea pig divining nor the town pharmacy's pill.

Huaychao held its own little celebration that 1991 Independence Day. It might have surprised Mario Vargas Llosa to see the red-and-white

Peruvian flag run up a splintery flagpole. His primitivizing 1983 *New York Times* Uchuraccay report claimed that the concept of Peru remained an "incomprehensible abstraction" to Andean villagers like the Huaychainos. The novelist could not see that these country people considered themselves to be every bit Peruvian, or *piruanos* as their Quechua-accented Spanish had it. They wanted recognition as full citizens after so long a struggle as the country's most downtrodden class. Most peasants were more insistent about claiming their Peruvianness, in fact, than the cosmopolitan Vargas Llosa (who once called nationalism a "pernicious" obstacle to the "dissolution of frontiers, integration, common denominators"). Some Huaychainos drew a stick-figure *rondero* on the national flag, as if to underscore that peasant efforts were rescuing a sinking Peru from the terrorists. The banner hung limply on its pole for the morning ceremony in the village green.

Even in wartime the Huaychainos managed to find moments of reprieve. They might gather in someone's farmhouse for a fiesta to celebrate a baptism or saint's day. Isidro, Narciso's father, played the *arpa*, a harp, and the violin. His teenaged niece might join to sing in the high-pitched Andean way. They still kept an ear out for shouted warning about *senderista* attack.

The dead rebels tested Narciso's Christian forgiveness. He regarded them still as *supaypa wachasqan,* the devil's children, the wild Marxist animals. They would not escape the Lord's wrath at Judgement Day.

He expected their spirits to burn for eternity.

Shining Path remnants still threatened some in 1991. Vigilant *ronderos* reported any guerrilla movement along to other villages, almost like the *chasquis*, messengers, on the Inca Trail centuries before. When Raymond Starr, the American anthropologist, visited one Iquichan hamlet, the schoolteachers told him that *senderistas* had raided a few days before. They garroted the *ronda* president in the village square. If the chapel bells rang during the night, the American should run, one teacher counseled. He could join them in a hole they had dug for a hiding place down the canyon. Then she looked again at the tall gringo. "You won't fit. Just keep on running." The anthropologist slept that night with his tennis shoes on.

One day, Narciso received a request from Chaca, a hamlet down the canyon. The *ronderos* there wanted help guarding a new Chinese tractor from the *senderistas*. In its continuing efforts to woo the peasantry, the Fujimori government had donated the machines to mountain communities. They were a welcome novelty for villagers who had only foot plows and oxen to prepare their fields. The Chacans had been given two tractors, but the *senderistas* had already torched one. Narciso brought some men over to guard the surviving machine. He carried a Winchester, one of three rifles the army had provided to the Huaychainos. As soon as the sun went down, some rebels began shooting from somewhere in the dark. Narciso took cover behind the tractor.

Pan! Pan! Pan! the bullets glanced off it.

The attackers withdrew before long. When Narciso looked down at his leg, he found he had been struck by a ricocheting bullet. "My blood was pouring out. It soaked two blankets," he remembered. Only after many hours did the others find a truck to bring the wounded Narciso down to Huanta's Red Cross. "I almost bled to death on the way down, *carajo.*"

Only reluctantly did Narciso ever recount this war story. It was too painful to recall that night, and a little embarrassing, too. He, the "bad-ass patroller" who once took on bullies twice his size, had been shot in the groin, the bullet narrowly missing his private parts. After some weeks in Huanta, Narciso returned to Huaychao with a limp and some unremoved shrapnel. He went back to patrolling every Tuesday night. Writer José María Arguedas, the imprisoned Sybila's dead husband, once summed up peasant hardiness in a Quechua poem's last line. *Kachkaniraqmi. We still exist.*

It had grown harder for the *senderistas* to deny the *ronda* threat. The village militias must be "confronted with great clarity and resolution," Abimael acknowledged in 1990. He claimed they grew only because the military coerced villagers at gunpoint. "Imperialism and the reaction use the masses as cannon fodder in their eagerness to annihilate the People's War." Their moth-eaten Maoist orthodoxy had always blinded the *senderistas* to rural complexities. A man who had not set foot in the Andes for more than a decade, Abimael could not accept that peasants might make their own calculations. "Objectively, the *rondas* do not represent the people," Abimael said. "We do." The solution? Burning tractors, terrorizing villagers, killing patrol leaders. "Mistaken ideas always end in bloodshed," Albert Camus wrote. "But it is always someone else's blood." The *senderistas* gave their own blood as well, but peasants did most of the dying in a war supposedly waged to liberate them. Between Shining Path and the military, an estimated two-thirds of the dead would be Andean villagers by the end.

These setbacks in the Andes pointed to a crippling *senderista* flaw, namely their inflexibility. Both Lenin and Mao displayed a considerable willingness to compromise in order to achieve revolutionary victory. Despite his diatribes against concessions and the incorrect line, the Bolshevik leader accepted the German kaiser's help against the tsar. Mao allied with Chiang Kai-shek's Nationalists to fight the Japanese before seizing China for himself by driving them to Taiwan. In Nepal, a poor mountain country like Peru, a man named Pushpa Kamal Dahal, Prachanda to his followers, would soon mount his own Maoist rebellion. He called his insurgency the Prachanda Path in tribute to Abimael, but later allied with center-left and regional parties to be elected Nepal's prime minister. By contrast, the *senderistas* maintained their absolute contempt for elections and any negotiations with the government. They never developed any strategy for dealing with disaffected villagers besides trying to bludgeon them into submission. That brutality was self-defeating by now.

The *senderistas* still claimed to enjoy the peasantry's whole-hearted support. A new prison mural depicted Chairman Gonzalo's gigantic approving visage over a massed peasant army. (The individual village fighters were tiny, almost indistinguishable, since their leader was history's real giant.) In truth, Abimael had never been very interested in village traditions or in the Quechua language, much less in spending time in the countryside. He did like waxing poetically about the Andes, especially his Ayacucho years. "The incomparable clearness of its mountain sky on May nights with its sparkling stars," he wrote. "The faithful, burning furnace of the revolution." His rebellion had bloomed, fitfully, in the Ayacuchan mountains for a few years, but it was dying there now. The big *ronda* rebellion had ended the party's hope for victory in the countryside.

A larger question lay in how much the rural Andes mattered any longer. When Mao led his Communists to victory, it had been in an overwhelmingly agrarian country. To encircle the cities from the countryside had been Shining Path's copycat plan for the Peruvian revolution. By the 1980s, however, the great village migrations were turning Peru into an increasingly urbanized nation. Highland dirt farmers no longer mattered much to the national economy or, really, in any essential way at all. An Indian Maoist guerrilla group, the Naxalites in Chhattisgarh, controlled some large jungle areas for decades, but the captured regions were so poor and remote that the government had little to fear. An urbanizing planet made cities into the necessary prizes for a rebellion. It would be in Lima that Shining Path won the war—or lost it.

Some militants doubted that their top leaders ever cared about the countryside. As Juan Fulano, the Lima fighter, saw it, Abimael and Elena preferred their comfortable Lima hideaways. Only Augusta, Fulano thought, ever objected to massacring peasants (which did not quite square with her backing for Lucanamarca and other hardline actions). The party had betrayed Chairman Mao's plan for peasant revolution, he complained. "Everything became the city, Lima." The war was indeed shrinking down to the battle for the capital, and headed for a surprise ending there.

CHAPTER SEVENTEEN

The Birthday Party

The GEIN earned new credibility with government higher-ups after its Monterrico raid. Marco Miyashiro and Benedicto Jiménez's unit could no longer be dismissed as *Cazafantasmas*, "Ghostbusters." "All that work just for some terrorist scrap paper!" a few PIP officials downtown still sometimes joked. The GEIN's detectives ignored the teasing and captured a high-ranking Central Committee member, Deodato Juárez. President Fujimori sent a congratulatory letter on the first anniversary of the unit's establishment. The agents had demonstrated "utmost professionalism, full-time commitment, and daily risk of their lives," he wrote. The unit expanded to occupy its building's entire third floor, employing about eighty detectives and office staff in total—and had more than a few telephones. Only top government officials still knew as yet about its existence.

Those new GEIN members had plenty to stay occupied. Their expanded surveillance led them to a propaganda printing operation where Juárez and several other Central Committee members fell captive. Despite his lower rank, Benedicto still directed operations, as Miyashiro insisted from the start. Benedicto liked to go on about the campaigns of Julius Caesar, the Bolsheviks, and the GEIN's own latest plans. He was also a good listener, though, and encouraged dissenting opinions. A difficult childhood, speculated one agent, gave Benedicto his introspective, almost vulnerable side. (He was very close to his Greek mother, whom his father beat before abandoning.) He preferred guilt and persuasion over shouting to enforce discipline. On learning that a young detective skipped duty to go off with his girlfriend, Benedicto called the man into the office. "We're here to work," he said. "I know it's not fun. Why don't you take a six-month vacation? Collect your salary. Take a car too." The shamed officer promised not to fail again. Benedicto was almost uniformly admired, even adored, by his men.

The detectives liked Miyashiro, too. His big eyebrows, silent stare, and fireplug build conveyed confidence in their mission. When Miyashiro wanted a report, he'd take a drag on his cigarette, leaning back in his chair like a hard-boiled TV detective. But he also liked to joke around, a complement to the contemplative Benedicto. *Los miyashiros,* the agents called the sneakers that Miyashiro obtained for them at the Japanese embassy. His ancestry gave Miyashiro an in there—and also with the Fujimori government. He had never met the new president himself, but he knew an influential minister, Jaime Yoshiyama, through Lima's Peruvian-Japanese Cultural Association. Yoshiyama invited Miyashiro and Benedicto to dinner one night with Santiago Fujimori, the president's younger brother and confidante. "Come to me for anything you need," Santiago told the GEIN's co-commanders.

Most GEIN agents got along well with each other. One detective, Jorge Sánchez, the officer who spotted the tell-tale Maoist scribblings in the Monterrico raid, sometimes invited everyone over for lunch and a few beers. He would prepare a neighborhood specialty, cat, which he simmered in vinegar, cumin, pepper, and ground *ají,* yellow peppers. *It was quite delicious,* everyone admitted between the joking. They nicknamed Sánchez *Comegato*, "Cat-Eater." Elena Vadillo, the first female GEIN officer, had been joined on the force by Cecilia Garzón and Lita Fernández, and they also came to these gatherings. Vadillo's husband complained about her being away so much, since Benedicto demanded long hours, even on weekends. "That's when the enemy most often meets."

The GEIN and the *rondas* gave the Fujimori government two promising instruments for its counterinsurgency efforts. On the advice of his shadowy intelligence chief, Vladimiro Montesinos, the new president also approved the Grupo Colina, a secret army death squad. Its plainclothes military men cruised Lima's streets in their SUVs like blue-jeaned black riders. They pulled on dark balaclavas to storm a weekend barbecue in the scruffy Barrios Altos district, supposedly organized by *senderista* sympathizers. Gunfire left fifteen dead partygoers, among them an eight-year-old boy. An army major named Martín Rivas led the Grupo Colina. He had attended the US Army's School of the Americas some years earlier. That training program rewarded anti-Communist Latin American military officers with a free trip to the Georgia academy for counterinsurgency training, not to mention the opportunity to visit Washington and Disneyworld. Many School of the Americas graduates directed death squads, village massacres, and secret torture centers in their home countries. "The School of the Assassins," critics called it.

Vladimiro Montesinos became Fujimori's most influential advisor. This former army intelligence officer also went to the School of the Americas. His unsavory past included jail time in the late 1960s for selling state secrets to the CIA. Montesinos later had a law practice, and, the rumor had it, assisted cocaine lords with money laundering and evading prison. A tall, balding, unctuous Arequipan, the forty-five-year-old spy chief maneuvered himself into Fujimori's inner circle. He used army spies to keep tabs on political opponents and soon effectively controlled the military-run National Intelligence Service, while placing allies in top government positions. Montesinos held no official title. He did not like to be photographed. Few Peruvians yet realized his clout in the new administration.

Every few weeks, Miyashiro and Benedicto reported to Montesinos. Along with receiving their updates, the spymaster kept tabs on the GEIN by sending his own men to its offices. One happened to be Martín Rivas, the Grupo Colina leader, whom Benedicto once met in Ayacucho early in the war. No one knew yet about the Grupo Colina's existence, but Benedicto had never liked Rivas and wanted no meddling in their investigation. He gave Montesinos's envoys a stack of boring *senderista* manifestos in pretend cooperation. "I knew they wouldn't read them," he said. "We kept the good documents away from them." Nor did the GEIN commanders reveal addresses of possible *senderista* hideaways or their plans for upcoming raids.

Their latest target was 265 Buenavista Street. The spacious modern house lay in a pricey development, Chacarilla del Estanque, favored by business executives and military officers. To give cover for loitering around on the street, the GEIN's agents chose working disguises: garbage man, gardener, street sweeper. These young officers came mostly from provincial origins and possessed the necessary brown skin to pass for menial laborers. Perhaps the most obsessive among them, Carlos Iglesias, earned the nickname *El Loco*—the crazy guy—in tribute to his apparent enthusiasm for the garbageman role. At the Buenavista house, he donned his stinky jumpsuit to pick up trash left outside every morning. Iglesias became skilled at sorting through stakeout refuse, but found nothing suspicious. His GEIN colleagues liked to joke about his various close encounters with snarling guard dogs. Many Lima families kept a mastiff for protection against increasing crime.

Three women came and went at 265 Buenavista Street, each of them well-coiffed enough to pass for a bank president's wife. As the watching agents had no clue to their identities, they nicknamed them *Paloma Uno, Paloma Dos,* and *Paloma Tres*—the three doves. On December 2, 1990, Dove Three pulled out from the garage. An unmarked GEIN car followed the woman to a department store. There the agents got their first good look at Dove Three.

About forty-five years old. Light-brown skin. Short hair. Elegantly dressed, driving a gray Toyota.

The unsuspecting Dove Three purchased men's cologne. A clerk gift-wrapped the box for her. Then she drove back to 265 Buenavista and the big garage door closed behind the Toyota again. A GEIN team parked down the street to resume surveillance. The two detectives munched baloney sandwiches inside their parked car. No one else left the house that day.

———————

The police had no clue that Abimael was holed up inside. That elegant Dove Three had been Elena Iparraguirre. It was the day before Abimael's birthday, and, as was their custom, the *senderistas* planned to bomb down some electrical towers to honor their Chairman Gonzalo. Elena arranged a more traditional celebration inside the Buenavista hideaway. She invited Angélica Salas, Augusta's Ayacuchan friend, and Nelly Evans, the former nun who sometimes rented their houses. (They were the police's mystery Doves One and Two.) Other trusted Central Committee members came as well, among them María Pantoja, an accountant's daughter who had commanded the party's southern military operations. The rebel leaders drank boxed Chilean wine, ate cake, and sang "Happy Birthday" to Abimael in the cigarette smoke–filled living room.

No one realized that the GEIN was closing in again. After the Monterrico raid six months before, the *senderistas* kept closer watch than ever, and Elena hoped that the police might have lost their scent. Back in the 1980s, she sometimes drove Abimael down the Pan-American Highway to meetings in Cañete and Chincha. His beard and a civil engineer's fake identification gave cover enough. They no longer risked such forays. When moving between their Lima hideouts, Abimael crouched under a blanket in the

Toyota's backseat. Other precautions included keeping no current photographs of Abimael, Elena, or Central Committee members, in case of police raids. But they also relied on the counterintuitive choice to live in exclusive Chacarilla del Estanque, an even more improbable spot than their previous suburban hideouts. The Buenavista house lay just a few blocks from Peru's giant military command center, *El Pentagonito*, the Little Pentagon. The *senderista* command was hiding in plain sight.

Their ideological convictions left them oblivious to bigger realities once again. Only three weeks after Abimael's birthday, the Soviet Union collapsed at last, and the Russian Federation flag replaced the hammer and sickle over the Kremlin. The only surviving Communist power, China, remained so in name only, on its way to becoming a land of Nike sweatshops and glassy skyscrapers. State socialism shrank to Fidel Castro and the flip card propaganda shows in Communist North Korea's Pyongyang Stadium. Young leftists worldwide poured their energy into new causes like gay rights, feminism, and the environmental movement. Even the protestors in Seattle and Genoa against the new US-led world order's injustices marched under the Marxism-lite banner of anti-globalization activism. Hardly anybody wanted to be a Communist anymore.

The very idea of violent revolt had also lost favor. Gentler crusaders like the Dalai Lama, Vaclav Havel, and Nelson Mandela (a one-time Communist firebrand aged into a saintly peacemaker) became the great post–Cold War icons. Most other Latin American Marxist insurgencies had been crushed, disbanded, or, in the case of Colombia's FARC, reduced to financing their operations with kidnapping ransoms and drug money. The FMLN rebels in El Salvador laid down their arms in 1992 to stand in new elections. Military juntas gave way to elected governments everywhere across the region. It seemed only Serb death squads and bearded Afghani jihadists saw the gun as the way to power. Few leftists spoiled for a street fight any longer besides the stray anarchist skinhead.

The planet's new zeitgeist made the *senderistas* more anachronistic by the day. They upheld a dying ideology, Communism, and a discredited tool, the gun. *We base ourselves firmly in Marxist-Leninist-Maoist Gonzalo Thought; certain and convinced about the triumph of the world proletarian revolution and the unstoppable march of humanity towards Communism.* Except for that modest addition of Gonzalo Thought, the aging Abimael's guiding principles remained stubbornly unchanged from his youthful Ayacuchan days. "The word of the Party had never been proved false by reality," he said. His faith in world proletarian revolution increasingly recalled the certainty of those early-twentieth-century champions of the horse and buggy who expected the automobile fad to pass before too long. The *senderistas* could not see that the gulags and the lying party officials had discredited the old Communist brand for good. Abimael still praised Stalin in 1992 as "a great Marxist-Leninist, a great man." Many historians would say instead that the fearsome Soviet strongman had been among the twentieth century's biggest mass murderers (and some also placed Lenin and Mao in that number as well).

Their expanding Lima activities gave the *senderistas* hope. They might have lost Andean ground to the *rondas* and the army, but they were on the attack in the capital. An emboldened Abimael would soon declare that the people's war had achieved "strategic equilibrium." That was the step before the final offensive in Mao's theory of protracted war. They would now begin their "3rd Campaign of the Great Plan to Develop Bases in Function of Seizing Power in the Country." (Every plan still had to be numbered and titled, in the hoary Communist tradition.) *The 1990s will be ours*, Elena thought.

A daring confidence showed in more open shantytown organizing. The *senderistas* made a little liberated zone of Raucana, a squatter settlement under the mountains in Lima's outer orbit. They instructed residents to put up their straw huts in a good socialist grid. A communal vegetable garden was planted, while the *senderistas* organized indoctrination sessions and people's trials to punish petty criminals. The hammer and sickle flew openly over the sandy streets there. "As long as there is hunger and misery," a resident told a *Los Angeles Times* correspondent, "Sendero will grow."

The government would not allow a *senderista* shantytown. An army battalion occupied Raucana. In keeping with the more hearts-and-minds flavor of Fujimori's new counterinsurgency, the troops provided free haircuts, medical checkups, and food handouts along with barked lectures about patriotism and the terrorist criminals. This time the rebels did not retreat as they might have in earlier years. Their sit-down strike closed the Central Highway over honking horns and cursing truck drivers. A guerrilla hit squad followed a top Raucana army commander near a Miraflores beach to assassinate him there. The settlement remained a Shining Path stronghold even after party activists slipped away to other postings.

One day, a GEIN agent shadowed a suspected rebel into another shantytown. The detective had not bothered with a disguise. A mob of squatters, probably urged on by *senderista* activists, almost lynched him with clubs and stones. He fired a panicked warning shot before sprinting for his life. The hazards of the job led one agent to abandon the GEIN to become a professional salsa dancer.

The *senderistas* never aimed to win popularity contests, at least at the start. Their strategy was to lead the doubting masses towards the revolution's red dawn in stages (or "to rivet ideas into [their] minds," as Abimael less picturesquely put it). Nevertheless, an opinion poll showed 15 percent of Peruvians viewed Shining Path favorably. "Sendero will never win," remarked political scientist Fernando Rospigliosi. "But they can tear the country to pieces."

The GEIN began watching 265 Buenavista only a few days before Abimael's birthday party. On the morning of the party, an agent, Guillermo Bonilla, got out of his car to find some breakfast. A few moments later, his partner's voice crackled over the radio. Dove One was leaving the house, he warned.

She was headed towards a newspaper kiosk down the street. As a boy in sun-scorched Lambayeque in northern Peru, Bonilla watched *The Streets of San Francisco* and *Hawaii Five-O*. His GEIN gumshoeing gave the lanky young northerner the chance to be in a real-life thriller. He sidled up to the newsstand behind Dove One, Angélica Salas, the old Ayacucho friend of Augusta's who turned from cosmetologist to Communist leader. That day's headlines reported new terrorist assaults to celebrate Abimael's birthday. The vendor politely handed Angélica the main newspapers, but she paid without replying. Bonilla watched her walk back to the house.

Only women had been spotted at Buenavista so far. The GEIN's unidentified Doves—Angélica, Nelly, and Elena—seemed in charge there. By now, even the slowest-witted policeman knew that a *terruca*, a female terrorist, might be the one to shoot him dead on the street. The police also finally began to realize how many women occupied the party's higher ranks. They comprised the Central Committee's majority or close to it, among them stalwarts like María Pantoja and Laura Zambrano. "The terrorist men are *sacos largos*," the GEIN detectives sometimes joked. They still mistakenly believed a man, Deodato Juárez, to be Abimael's likely successor, at least before Juárez's arrest. The real second-in-command was Elena. She would become the new party chairman if Abimael fell captive to the police.

That Elena and the others could pass for rich *señoras* bespoke their own comfortable city upbringings. The *senderistas* greatly admired the Cultural Revolution, but Mao's Red Guard had ridiculed "bourgeois" intellectuals during that period, shipping them off to break rocks in the countryside. To get around the awkwardness of their improper class background, Abimael and his main lieutenants had developed a justifying explanation. You decontaminated yourself by giving yourself to the revolution, perhaps dying for it. Proletarianization, the *senderistas* called it. Elena had some Indian blood, but not too much. Her correct Spanish and stylish handbag made it easy even for her to disguise herself as garden club lady.

Their life at the Buenavista house had its routines. To try getting in better health, Abimael cut his cigarettes to three or four a day. Elena made him fresh orange, grapefruit, and papaya juice. The former pharmacist's assistant insisted that he take a Tigason pill daily to keep down the rashing from his psoriasis. Angélica or Nelly often did the cooking, and sometimes prepared Abimael's favorite dishes like *mondongo* (yellow stewed tripe) or *ceviche negro de pescado* (raw fish blackened with squid ink). Abimael still liked to work late into the nights. He would stay up past the others with a book or to finish some new report.

Patriarchy's conventions might have appeared to hold sway in the hideout. A circle of women cooked, washed, and typed for an older male leader. A journalist later derided Elena as Abimael's "concubine," while others dismissed the *senderista* women as his harem. Others compared the arrangement to the pope and his nuns, with Elena as the Mother Superior. Nelly Evans had been a sister earlier in her life. Elena and Angélica left their children behind to take their guerrilla vows. When asked why Augusta had been so well-read, Angélica sounded like an adoring novice. "She had the best school in the world—Dr. Guzmán." Chairman Gonzalo was Marxism's highest emissary, the one who held the keys to Communism's earthly paradise much like the pope held Saint Peter's keys to the heavenly kingdom.

Any assumptions about Abimael's manly authority held true only by degrees. When asked years later if she had been the party leader's kept woman, Elena snorted. "Absurd. I had plenty of power." Her pragmatism counterbalanced Abimael's sometimes airy philosophizing, and he increasingly relied on her schoolteacher's efficiency to run the party. Abimael had always taken the opinions of high-ranking female *senderistas* seriously, at least as much as he did anybody's but his own. "Other leftist groups just saw us as secretaries," María Pantoja told an interviewer. "We were equals in the party." She smiled that women made better guerrillas anyway: "men are too crude, careless, not so precise." Their party had many rank-and-file female members just as it did back in the 1970s. That women occupied top leadership positions made Shining Path even more unusual among so many male-dominated Latin American insurgencies. A cigar-smoking boy's club, some critics described Fidel Castro and his Cuban revolutionaries.

The death of Augusta left Elena as Abimael's main advisor as well as his new lover. He quoted *Macbeth* to warn against treachery in one party speech. *(Where we are / There's daggers in men's smiles.)* His relationship with Elena gave him a companion with a Lady Macbeth's steely will, but devoted to him and their cause without reservation. They planned together a massive 1989 assault in the jungle town of Uchiza. Several hundred *senderistas* overran the big police station to seize its weapons, then looted local stores for supplies. The guerrillas held a "popular" trial of three surrendered policemen before forcing them to their knees to be shot.

The watching GEIN agents detected new movement at Buenavista on the evening of Abimael's birthday. They had dubbed Elena's Toyota, "the Rat," and Angélica's lemon-yellow VW Bug, "the Cockroach." At least three times, the two cars left the garage, returned, and then went out again. Could the women be picking up other *senderistas* to bring them to the house? The agents could not tell for sure in the twilight. *Something's happening in the house,* the men radioed back to the GEIN office. Benedicto and Miyashiro agreed that raiding would be premature given the uncertainty about just who might be inside. The order went back to the other agents at the stakeout just to keep watch for the moment.

That some special occasion had been celebrated became clear the next morning. When Carlos Iglesias picked up the trash, he found empty red wine cartons and cigarette butts in abundance. A wiretap intercepted a *senderista* phone call in which Nelly Evans said that the "children's party" had been great. It appeared that the guerrilla leaders might have been gathered inside Buenavista, and perhaps some were still there.

What now, Benedicto and Miyashiro wondered?

Miyashiro wanted to raid.

The more deliberate Benedicto disagreed. *We've only watched the house for a week,* he said. Hadn't the police's big mistake always been to rush in too quickly rather than gathering as much intelligence as possible before making arrests? *Ok, negro,* Miyashiro said. They would wait.

That proved to be a dreadful mistake. The GEIN had Abimael and Elena there for the taking at the birthday party. Their capture would have enfeebled and maybe destroyed Shining Path, averting many deaths. Instead, the party's governing couple remained at large to oversee the war's gruesome end game.

A week or so after the birthday party, the *senderistas* realized their danger. When Angélica Salas drove back to the house after a trip to the market, she noticed a blue pickup parked down the street. It had followed her, Angélica realized. She sounded the alarm to the others. Óscar Ramírez, Comrade Feliciano, happened to be in the house then. He got into the VW with Angélica, while Abimael ducked into the Toyota's back seat under a blanket. Angélica pulled out first. She hoped that the agents would pursue her, and, if anyone fell captive, it would not be Abimael. He must be protected above all else.

Two GEIN cars trailed Angélica's VW, one driven by Guillermo Bonilla, the *Streets of San Francisco* aficionado. The police dispatcher soon radioed that the Rat, Elena's Toyota, was also leaving the house. Bonilla peeled away to follow. At first, Elena drove unhurriedly, as if unaware she was being tailed. Then, suddenly, she made a U-turn onto Caminos del Inca Avenue, leaving Bonilla stuck in traffic. The other GEIN car followed Angélica's car to a little plaza. It was getting dark by then, but the agents saw a tall man, Óscar Ramírez, get out there. He flagged a taxi, which disappeared into the night. Angélica drove off, too, and soon lost her pursuers with a few eva-sive maneuvers. "A feeling of sadness and impotence," a frustrated Bonilla described that day years later.

The GEIN kept Buenavista under watch, on the unlikely chance the *senderistas* might return. A new stakeout held more promise, an apartment in the La Victoria district. In late January, agents spotted their Buenavista Dove Two, Nelly Evans, and an unidentified man arriving there. They unloaded some cardboard boxes, making several trips to bring more. The two *senderistas* struck the agents as jumpy and nervous. They wondered whether the boxes had special importance.

Benedicto did not hesitate this time.

Boys, unleash the storm, he radioed.

One team broke into Buenavista, empty by then. As the agents looked around, they saw signs from the hasty flight a month before. Various telltale clues showed that Abimael had been hiding there: some leftover Tigason pills, the butts from his preferred Winston Light cigarettes, and still more empty wine boxes from the birthday party. Benedicto's delay had cost them capturing the *senderista* chieftain, although his loyal agents always defended the decision. "We were young, just getting started. We didn't have full surveillance set up," said José Luis Gil, the Trujillo native who had captured Sybila Arredondo the year before. He and Guillermo Bonilla were Benedicto's top lieutenants.

The apartment produced a big consolation prize. A team under Miyashi-ro's command grabbed Nelly Evans, Dove Two, when she answered the door, and found the Buenavista boxes stacked in the living room. They were mostly papers, but an agent found some VHS tapes in a plastic bag. He had everything brought to the downtown office.

Nobody expected much from the tapes.

"Probably porn," an agent smiled.

The unit's tech specialist, Walter Cápac, connected his camcorder to a television just to be sure.

At first the agents did not know what to make of the tapes. They showed a heavyset bearded man who might have been a janitor or somebody's crazy uncle in his dark jumpsuit. One by one, various men and women walked up to pose with him beneath portraits of Marx, Lenin, and Mao. The man joined a woman to dance to *Zorba the Greek*. His partner smiled radiantly in his company.

Guzmán, Miyashiro and Benedicto realized after some moments.

The *senderistas* had videoed their congress's last day.

"This is pure gold," said Walter Cápac.

The tapes gave the GEIN new advantages. Now, at last, they had good pictures of Abimael. A wanted poster and TV ads would soon circulate the chunky, bearded leader's face everywhere. Almost as importantly, the GEIN also had a complete photograph album of top *senderistas*. "It was a big mistake to film," Elena acknowledged later. "We were so happy about the congress ending that we let down our guard." The video appalled the disaffected rebel commander, Juan Fulano. "It was Abimael's arrogance, wanting to keep the film for history."

One cassette showed Augusta's wake. For the first time, almost three years after the fact, the police realized that she had died. It appeared from the lustful Zorba dance that Abimael had found a new lover, but nobody recognized Elena at first. The agents soon matched names to pictures to discover Elena's name and everyone else's at the party congress.

Benedicto and Miyashiro screened the video for the interior minister.

"Who's the bearded man?" he asked.

"Gonzalo and his court," Benedicto said.

The government released an edited clip, only the most unflattering bits. They made Abimael look like an unkempt drunk partying with younger women. The revolution's Caligula, it seemed, swilled wine while Peru burned. News announcers crowed that the myth of Gonzalo's invincibility had been shattered. Surely Peru's Public Enemy Number One would be brought to justice soon.

That turned out not to be the case. After the early 1991 raid, Abimael vanished once again. His fighters further ratcheted up their Lima offensive. For the first time, the capital's wealthy seaside neighborhoods would feel the war's full weight. Their residents cowered behind *guachimanes,* watchmen, electric fences, and wrought-iron gates. Millions in Lima's outer districts enjoyed no such protection from the revolution's bloodlust. The vice mayor of Villa El Salvador, María Elena Moyano, had seen enough. She decided to fight back against the *senderistas*, intending to rally the district behind her.

CHAPTER EIGHTEEN

A Death Foretold

"My God," María Elena wrote in her journal, "how I've lived. Thank you for giving me so much! Love, the opportunity to give everything of myself. Everything."

Her life had been careening forward so fast in recent months. It was already early 1992 by now, and, wanting some family time, she took Gustavo Jr., David, and their cousin Jorge to the beach. They headed afterwards to a *pollada*, a chicken barbecue fundraiser, in the plaza of Villa's Sector One. María Elena had arranged for a pickup truck to bring over a sound system from the municipality. After seeing to its installation, she got plates of the roast chicken for herself and the boys. She drank a beer while mingling with the crowd with the *chicha* music already thumping away. The sun colored the tropical dusk a hazy rust.

Then someone yelled a warning. Gunshots. Screams. Running. A man and a woman appeared across the cement patio. They had pistols, heading for María Elena. She shouted to her friend Bertha to get the boys away.

"Run, *carajo*," María Elena said, "they've come for me."

———————

The war had grown even uglier and more terrifying in the *barriadas* lately. María Elena had not long before been at the funeral of Andrés Sosa, a reputed MRTA leader from Villa. He had been killed in score-settling between rival factions in the group. A few months before that, late in 1991, the *senderistas* left a bullet on the doorstep of Juana López, a shantytown activist in Callao. When López ignored their warning to resign as coordinator of the free breakfast program there, a guerrilla hit squad shot her down. María Elena went to that funeral too. Only a week later, the rebels dynamited the warehouse of the Villa Women's Federation, in which María Elena had remained active after entering politics. The building stored powdered milk, noodles, and rice for the federation's ninety-four affiliated *comedores populares*, or soup kitchens. The blast wrecked the front wall and a delivery truck parked outside.

The rebels meant to send a message. As part of winning Lima's poor districts, they wanted no other organizations in the way. Breakfast programs and soup kitchens run by shantytown housewives had grown to feed more than 500,000 hungry people a day. Some committees had been started by Lima's then-leftist mayor in the early 1980s, and others had ties to the APRA or to the Catholic Church. They had together become a backbone of shantytown life and, exactly for that reason, an inconvenience for Shining Path. Soup kitchen "assistentialism" supposedly dulled revolutionary appetites, and the groups were even more suspect for receiving aid from "imperialist" donors like USAID and the European Community. Forcing their closure would make for chaos, hunger, and a clearer path to *senderista* rule. The Juana López assassination and Villa bombing warned the *barriada* food program leaders to stand down. The rebels would gun down these brown-skinned activist women just as well as peasant *ronderos* to advance the world proletarian revolution.

At one time, María Elena laughed away the *senderistas*. When a hit squad in 1990 murdered her friend Enrique Castilla, a labor leader, she had admitted the danger for the first time. Then there had been Juana López and many others. Assassination had become the Shining Path way of life, María Elena thought. They would not hesitate to destroy anybody in their way.

———

That the *senderistas* would come after María Elena seemed inevitable. She already had her run-ins with the rebels back in 1980, and now she was Villa's United Left vice mayor. The rebels still reviled the "revisionist" socialist coalition for participating in the "electoral farce." As a government official, a member of the United Left, and a leader of the "assistentialist" soup kitchens, María Elena found herself in triple jeopardy with the circling revolution. The Villa Women's Federation bombing brought the threat closer to home than ever before.

Then, a few days after the attack, someone showed María Elena a Shining Path flyer. To her astonishment, it accused her of planting the bomb. The "treacherous, imperialist" Moyano had dynamited the building to cover up some unspecified embezzlement scheme. The *senderistas* had long wanted to force the influential María Elena to stand down from the Women's Federation presidency, perhaps take it over themselves. With their earlier fake charges about cheese factories and this new bombing claim, the rebels hoped to destroy her reputation. Their whispering campaign showed new results in an increasingly gloomy, apathetic, and fearful Villa. Some people believed the ludicrous story about María Elena sneaking over at night to lay the dynamite charges at her own federation's warehouse.

The *senderistas* were facing their own difficulties by 1991. They might be advancing in the shantytowns, but remained on the retreat in the Andes. The GEIN's pursuit had Abimael and Elena on the run—two hideaways discovered; their faces everywhere; key party activists like Deodato Juárez and Nelly Evans jailed. Although many disaffected, mostly young Peruvians still wanted to join the revolution, training them adequately was hard. In Lima's outer districts, Popular Aid, the front organization, increasingly staged its own attacks, sometimes not well coordinated with the party's regular fighters. Fraying communication frustrated Abimael's ability to maintain oversight over everything. "We lost touch," Elena recalled. "We were getting cut off from the base." *El Diario* bragged about the party's latest "demolishing," "crushing," and "decisive" actions. "Initiative in the Hands of the Communist Party of Peru," one headline claimed. The actual hope for victory had been reduced to seizing Lima before the police captured the rebellion's leaders.

The bombing accusation enraged María Elena. Until then, she had avoided confronting Shining Path, but now her reputation hung in the balance. She dashed off a rebuttal letter to the newspapers. Embezzling aid money? Destroying the warehouse? Apparently, María Elena taunted her *senderista* accusers, their supposed thousand eyes and ears did not work so well. "My custom is to build," she wrote. She catalogued her community involvement—tree-planting with her mother; volunteering as a preschool teacher; supporting soup kitchens; and much more. "Radical discourse and calumny can't change that."

María Elena concluded the letter by rebuking the rebels.

"Revolution is not death, nor imposition, nor submission, nor fanaticism. Revolution is new life—the belief and struggle for a just and dignified society. . . . *Viva la vida*—Long Live Life."

She planned a Villa rally to repudiate Shining Path. Only about fifty demonstrators showed up to wave little white peace flags. Most locals were afraid to come, fearing *senderista* reprisal. María Elena took a reporter and his photographer afterwards to a soup kitchen. She peeled potatoes with the other women for the camera to show the bombing had not dimmed spirits. Her interview for the story pulled no punches.

"We want them [Shining Path] to show their faces," María Elena said. "We're shutting down the barbarism by feeding our people."

No Lima leader had openly defied, much less derided, the rebels. Unlike so many Andean villages banded into their *rondas*, the sullen capital left the fight to the police and army. María Elena was putting herself on the front line against the *senderista* killing machine. She still did not think the rebels would dare to harm her, at least in her hometown Villa.

Everyone knows me, María Elena told Diana Bachand, her Canadian aid worker friend.

I'll be safe here.

———

Even María Elena had to wonder about these grim new times. The sensation of a country in crisis had only worsened a year into Fujimori's presidency. His austerity plan, the *fujishock*, halted hyperinflation, but the economy remained in tatters. A cholera epidemic infected the country by way of that favorite Peruvian dish, ceviche, after ocean sewage infected fish used to make the raw seafood salad. More than 150,000 people fell sick, and 1,100 died. To reassure the panicking citizenry, a smiling Fujimori spooned down a ceviche for the cameras at a market stall. The president vanished for several days afterwards. Some said *El Chino* had contracted cholera in his show of bravado—and been hooked to intravenous salts. The country had been brought low by blackouts, massacres, garbage, traffic, water shortages, drug trafficking, and corruption. That a medieval plague should be the latest calamity seemed miserably appropriate by now.

"At what precise moment," asks a character in Mario Vargas Llosa's *Conversation in the Cathedral*, "did Peru fuck itself up?"

Several thousand shantytown women assembled for a downtown Lima protest march against hunger and terror in late September 1991. They had endured poverty, war, and the hardships of a *barriada* life, and only days before, the *senderistas* had killed Juana López, the Callao breakfast program leader. Assorted leftist politicians, middle-class feminist activists, progressive priests, and university students joined too. They shouted slogans demanding an end to the war and more emergency aid to mitigate the *fujishock*'s punishing austerity cutbacks. The march ended in the Plaza San Martín and various speakers took the bullhorn to address the crowd from the steps under the bronze equestrian monument to the hero of the Independence wars. María Elena delivered an impassioned speech with a raised fist.

A television news show invited her on that Sunday. María Elena joined a panel with a well-known politician and a retired general. One conservative newspaper, *Expreso,* singled out her performance the next day. "The person who made the greatest impression was Ms. Moyano." María Elena was becoming a wartime celebrity.

The besieged capital certainly needed a heroine. Especially to prosperous Peruvians in the upscale oceanside districts, it was comforting to see a shantytown woman of color confronting the *senderistas.* The white minority's worst nightmare, after all, had always been the downtrodden brown masses rising to slit their throats some day (a fear that had come partly true during Túpac Amaru's eighteenth-century anti-colonial rebellion). Those latent anxieties had been updated for the late twentieth century to imagine every Ayacuchan gardener as a possible bomb-throwing terrorist. Admiring stories about María Elena began to appear in establishment newspapers like *Expreso* and *El Comercio* as well as leftist ones. "Exemplary reaction," a new magazine, *Sí,* praised the young Villa leader's boldness.

María Elena had the star quality to play the brave heroine. Having just turned thirty-two, strong and sure of herself, she bore a resemblance to the most famous living black Peruvian—the volleyball star, Cecilia Tait, the "golden southpaw" who led Peru to its improbable silver medal in the 1988 Olympics. That María Elena came from poverty made for a package of intelligence, charisma, and authenticity unlike anybody else.

What admiring coverage failed to say was that many Villans doubted María Elena and her intentions. "She inspired strong emotions," as political scientist Jo-Marie Burt later explained. "Some people loved her. Others hated her." One new rumor attributed María Elena's outspokenness to her political ambitions. That story had some truth. María Elena always dreamed big. (Few Peruvians faulted striving male leaders by the misogynistic double standard.) She would soon contact the former UN secretary general Javier Pérez de Cuéllar. He planned to challenge Fujimori in the next presidential election. This reserved older white man had lived abroad for decades. He might find María Elena just the person to balance the ticket.

But her opposition to the *senderistas* had more to do with genuine conviction than calculating ambition. María Elena remained a socialist in broad strokes—a daughter of liberation theology, teacher strikes, and brave talk about "the people." Unlike many hidebound leftists, she understood that the new post–Cold War world demanded a pragmatic progressive agenda. Frustration about partisan politicking, María Elena knew, led Villans to vote overwhelmingly for an unknown independent in Alberto Fujimori. "People have felt deceived, disillusioned, and haven't found other options," she explained in an interview with journalist Mariella Balbi.

It distressed María Elena that no leftist party publicly denounced the warehouse bombing or other Villa attacks. Yes, she replied, when Balbi asked whether the established left had tolerated the rebels for too long. She did not spare the police and military, either.

"Let them do justice for the dead and disappeared," she said. "Only then might we have any faith."

María Elena showed a clear-sighted, almost sociological, grasp of the *senderistas*. Hunger and disillusionment, she explained, opened their path to rebellion. They did best in Lima's most forsaken settlements like Raucana and her own Villa's hillside straw-and-cardboard encampments, where some saw the guerrillas as "something mythical, fighting for justice." Then, too, María Elena noted the revolution's attraction to students and the new generation. "Young people are rebellious, impulsive, vehement." She hoped dialogue and open conversation might still be possible with the rebels.

She remained blunt about Abimael Guzmán's followers.

"They're not revolutionaries, but terrorists."

————————

The rebels had to stop this one-woman assault. María Elena's example was dangerous. "Big, rapid zig-zags," as Lenin warned, characterize "the course of revolutionary movements." The war had turned against the rebels with avalanche speed in the Andes. They could not allow Villa's vice mayor to set a Lima counterrevolution in motion.

That Fujimori and his generals wanted to organize urban *rondas* especially worried the rebels. At Huaycán, where the GEIN agent had almost been lynched, the army directed the locals to form a *Comité de Autodefensa,* a Self-Defense Committee. It would be a model for anti–Shining Path patrols across Lima's outer districts, the government hoped. But the *senderistas* killed two Huaycán leaders who supported the *rondas*. Patrols never took hold there.

"I don't agree with the army coming in," María Elena told Balbi in their interview, "arming people, and directing the committees."

She did want Villa's neighborhood watch committees to keep out *senderistas*. Should they carry guns, Balbi asked? "I've resisted that up to now," María Elena said. "That would depend anyway on the people deciding and doing it on their own." Even mentioning armed resistance became one more black mark against María Elena in the lengthening Shining Path score sheet.

One day María Elena's husband, Gustavo, found a note under their door.

We will kill you. Bitch. Thief. Traitor to the people.

Gustavo was growingly worried. "They're serious, *negra*. They'll put a bullet through your head."

María Elena could no longer minimize the threat.

Her friend Diana Miloslavich, the Flora Tristán Center activist, suggested leaving Peru for a while. María Elena stayed for six weeks with Diana's sister in Mexico, but did not like being away.

"What good am I here?" she asked Diana over the phone.

She returned to Peru a few days later.

———

It would still have been possible for María Elena to escape danger on her return. Her predicament was not quite like that of Santiago Nasar, the murder victim in Gabriel García Marquez's *Chronicle of a Death Foretold*. "There's no way out of this," one character says about Nasar's death. "It is as if it already happened." Had María Elena called off her anti–Shining Path crusade, she could probably have avoided further trouble. The Episcopal Social Action Commission, a leading human rights organization, offered refuge at a convent in the sunny Chaclacayo suburb. The rebels would not have found her there.

Backing down was almost unthinkable. No one had ever bullied María Elena into silence, except perhaps her mother. Her clippings also hemmed her in. If María Elena gave up the fight, her new reputation as a courageous freedom fighter would suffer. Then, too, she saw her country's future at stake. Somebody had to save Peru from Shining Path.

"She couldn't *defraudar*—disappoint," her friend Cecilia Blondet said. "It was impossible."

Upon returning from Mexico late in 1991, María Elena plunged back into the fray. The biggest Peruvian business group invited her to keynote its annual conference in a sleek wood-paneled auditorium. A black activist addressing white executives—the novelty indicated María Elena's new standing. Although most big businessmen backed Vargas Llosa in the 1990 election, they had become bullish on Fujimori and his free-market funda-mentalism. María Elena called for a kinder, more just Peru.

"We cannot combat terror if we do not also combat the people's hunger," she said.

The leading leftist newspaper, *La República*, named María Elena its 1991 Person of the Year.

That same December week, a rebel squad burst into the small house of yet another Lima soup kitchen leader. Emma Hilario tried to ward off her would-be assassins. A bullet shattered her arm, but the hospital doctors saved her life. She fled to Holland and then Costa Rica.

María Elena knew that she might be next on the hit list.

She wrote a half-despairing, half-defiant letter to Hilario.

"There is no name for what they have done. I do not tell you to be careful because many people tell us that, and, in the end, nobody takes care of us or supports us. All that remains, Emma, is the strength that comes from the hearts of our oppressed people."

María Elena received new telephone threats from the rebels.

Traitor. Imperialist. You will die.

Somebody followed her when she walked the boys to school one morn-ing. María Elena's biggest fear was something happening to them.

Gustavo lost his patience.

"This isn't a game," he said, threatening to leave. "What will happen to the kids, to me, if you are gone? If you don't stop this, you can do it alone."

María Elena consented to police protection. Her young bodyguard did not have a car. He came to Villa by bus.

Her mood swung between denial and fear. She still could not quite believe the rebels would kill her. They'd known her for years, the local *sen-deristas* at least, among them her nemesis Pilar Anchita at the Women's Fed-eration. Surely, even now, they could talk. The other part of María Elena knew it was too late for that. The *senderistas* hated her too much. They did not believe in dialogue and compromise anyway.

"She'd cry," a Villa friend, Rocío Paz, recalled. "What will happen to my children? To Villa?"

Staying in Villa had become too dangerous. After the New Year, María Elena slept at the houses of Lima friends, mostly the two Dianas—Miloslavich in Lince and Bachand in Miraflores. Those more affluent districts offered only limited protection. "It wasn't so safe at my house either," Miloslavich said. The *senderistas* might have already tracked María Elena there.

"A lot of people were scared to put María Elena up," Miloslavich said. "She didn't have many places to go."

An acquaintance saw María Elena once at a conference. "She looked like a dead woman walking," said Enrique Bossio, a pioneering Lima gay activist. María Elena drew tensely at cigarettes during breaks. She'd begun smoking more.

Her friends pleaded with María Elena to leave the country again. She went to the Chaclacayo convent, but only for a few days. The director of the Episcopal Social Action Committee, José Burneo, had arranged for other threatened Peruvians—some hunted by Shining Path, others by the army—to take refuge in Chile. It was only a bus ride away down the desert. "She said she would," Burneo later said, "but then wouldn't."

It being María Elena, she had some fun even on the run.

"We'd bought some wigs as a disguise, ugly blonde ones," remembered Diana Bachand. "We'd joke about looking like hookers."

Nor could María Elena stay away from Villa for long.

One night she showed up at a *techado*, a roof-raising party, at her friend Rocío Paz's invitation. This folk custom dated back to the Incas and even before, albeit customized to modern times by bottled beer and boom-box dancing. Friends and family gathered to put a roof's last bricks in place, say a prayer, and then, of course, to party. "The *techado* was for my parents' new house," Paz said. "María Elena had always said she wanted to meet them." María Elena dismissed her police bodyguard, and, at one point, pulled Paz aside to complain about being abandoned by both her old party, the United Mariateguistas, and new one, the Socialist Action Movement. "Those gutless assholes have left me out in the cold," María Elena said. She stayed past midnight—dancing, drinking, and charming Paz's parents. It felt like an old-time Villa gathering.

María Elena wrote more in her journal, trying to keep up hope. "I felt death nearer, nearer than before," she noted after the funeral of Andres Sosa, the MRTA leader. "I understood how difficult sacrifice is. I thought about my children, my life, my history. . . . And I felt life rise up within me again."

The rebels declared a *paro armado*, an armed strike, for Thursday, February 14th. That meant bus burnings and warnings to shopkeepers against opening that day. Guerrilla fighters bombed the government tax office—and, that perennial favorite target, the US embassy. There were slogans new and old for the occasion.

Against hunger, misery, and unemployment!
For the People's Rights and the People's War!
Long live President Gonzalo!

María Elena organized a counterdemonstration for the same day as the Shining Path *paro armado*, a Villa peace march. That seemed risky, almost crazy, to her friend Diana Bachand. "I tried to persuade her not to do it. I thought it was too much of a provocation." Bachand oversaw a Canadian development group's programs in Peru. She had to close down operations when the guerrillas murdered one of her local employees near Lake Titicaca. All outside aid programs "give crumbs to the people to keep them from joining the people's war," a leaflet charged. Most groups had withdrawn by now.

At dawn on the day of their armed strike, the rebels detonated a big bomb outside the house of Michel Azcueta, the former Villa mayor. The current one, Johnny Rodríguez, had been threatened too. Azcueta wanted to join the peace march, but had to flee instead. Shock waves from the explosion boomed over Villa's cinder-block houses.

Only a few people appeared for María Elena's peace march.

María Elena was not too disappointed. She had decided, or so she told her friends, to heed everyone's wishes—and leave for Spain. The Spanish embassy would give her political asylum and a plane ticket. Her family could come afterwards.

She headed after the Villa march to meet Diana Miloslavich at her office. Diana had planned to attend a reception, but it happened to be Valentine's Day and María Elena talked her out of it.

"Two beautiful women alone on Valentine's Day," María Elena joked. "That's wrong. Let's go out."

They headed to Charo Torre's nightclub. María Elena had adopted the mafia don's habit of always seating herself with a view of the door. That way she could spot an entering assassin. More friends trickled in to drink and talk over the live band. María Elena and some others strolled later to Juanito, the bohemian watering hole on Barranco's plaza. They stayed until two in the morning—laughing, arguing, and tipsily pontificating. Countless María Elena friends would later recall being at that last supper with beer and ceviche. Nobody wanted to admit having missed it.

María Elena stayed that Saturday night at Diana Miloslavich's house. If everything went according to plan, she would fly to Madrid early the next week. She wanted to say goodbye to Gustavo and her boys before leaving.

"I'm taking the boys to the beach today," María Elena told Diana.

"Why don't you just go to the Spanish embassy now?" Miloslavich asked.

"Don't worry," María Elena said, "I'll be back in the afternoon. You can help me pack and we'll go."

She had lunch in Villa. María Elena's friend Bertha joined her and the boys for a trip to a well-used beach, the Oasis, across the Pan-American Highway from Villa. Gustavo stayed to finish an order in his workshop.

María Elena had bought tickets for that evening's Sector One *pollada* some weeks before. That advance purchase was a mistake, a gift to the *senderistas*. Someone alerted the local cell, probably a woman at the federation. This could be their chance, the rebels knew. They made preparations.

A lookout watched for María Elena's arrival at the *pollada*. According to later testimony, it was a nine-year-old girl, probably a *senderista's* daughter. María Elena had already been at the party for almost two hours before the full hit team arrived at last. If not such a social animal, she would have already been back in Lima—and soon on the plane to Spain. Being at the *pollada* took María Elena back to her Villa roots.

"She was relaxed," a friend recalled, "just talking and drinking."

The hit squad numbered more than ten, big for an urban attack. They first took out María Elena's police bodyguard, who was waiting for her by some parked cars. A *senderista* shot him in the stomach. The policeman crawled away bleeding behind a car. Then the rebels came for María Elena.

She had prepared David and Gustavo Jr. for this moment. *If anyone tries to hurt me, get away from me.* They ran now to Bertha at her command. The patio had cleared. María Elena faced her assassins alone.

The *senderistas* shot her down. According to newspaper accounts, the shooter was "an Andean-featured woman with short hair." María Elena fell, still alive. Her killers wanted to send a fearsome message. They tied a big dynamite charge to the wounded María Elena, then backed away.

A thunderous explosion rocked the square. It lifted David and Gustavo Jr. off their feet. Jorge, María Elena's nephew, had not kept far enough away. He caught shrapnel in his neck and shoulder.

Black smoke plumed into the sky.

María Elena had vanished.

"*Mami escapó,*" cried Gustavo Jr.

She had not escaped.

The bomb blew her to pieces.

––––––––––

Gustavo had been at his carpenter's workshop a few blocks away. He did not hear the explosion over a band saw. "It was strange," he said. "The machine stopped right when María Elena was killed." A neighbor pounded on the door some minutes later.

"On television it says they killed María Elena," she said.

Gustavo ran to the square. Soldiers had blocked it off, letting Gustavo through only after some shaken explanation.

He found other friends and family there.

That they saw no body created some confusion. "I thought maybe María Elena had survived, that she might be hiding in a house somewhere," remembered her friend Rocío Paz, who rushed over after a radio report.

Several people searched the vicinity, among them María Elena's younger sister Martha. They soon found proof that María Elena was dead—a shred of flesh, a blood-stained wall, a finger on a rooftop. It took hours to collect the pieces.

A panicking Gustavo could not find his children at first. It turned out that María Elena had made contingency plans. She'd instructed Bertha to take the boys if anything happened to her. They arrived at Diana Bachand's front door that night. Gustavo Jr. and David were still spattered with their mother's dried blood. (Jorge eventually had to be operated on to remove shrapnel.) Gustavo came over shortly afterwards.

María Elena's murder prompted outrage, finger-pointing, and soul-searching in the following days. "An odious crime," read a joint statement from leading Peruvian artists and intellectuals, including Mario Vargas

Llosa. It denounced "the totalitarian ideology of Sendero . . . [and its] not just archaic, but unrealizable and suicidal goal of destroying society and the State to found a New Order."

The great Peruvian theologian, Gustavo Gutiérrez, the founder of liberation theology, offered a prayer.

"Thank you, Lord, for having taught us by her [María Elena's] example the path to ending the murderous hunger and assassin's bullets; solidarity with the people; sacrifice; and hope and happiness."

"We killed her," another editorialist wrote, blaming an indifferent society.

Everyone rushed to acclaim María Elena's sacrifice. It had always been the Peruvian way to demand a gory martyrdom for a place in the pantheon of national heroes. The Spaniards tried to rip the neo-Inca rebel Túpac Amaru apart with horses in Cuzco's square before beheading him; Alfonso Ugarte, an army officer, rode his horse over a cliff to prevent the enemy Chileans from capturing the sacred Peruvian flag; the Lima airport namesake, Jorge Chávez, fatally crashed while attempting the first Alpine crossing. "Defeat in whatever cause they have embraced is inevitable," journalist Robin Kirk explains. "The gesture is what counts." The Fujimori government later officially declared María Elena a national hero—and a bronze statue of her, as she had joked about with her friends, went up in Villa. The government proclamation ignored that María Elena was a socialist and strongly opposed the military's war crimes too. She had been abandoned in life only to be sanctified after her death.

It became a commonplace to describe María Elena as *Madre Coraje*, Mother Courage. A *Caretas* journalist apparently took the name from the heroine of Bertolt Brecht's great play. Such a lugubrious, matronly designation hardly fit the fun-loving and complex young woman María Elena had been. But the Mother Courage of Brecht's play is actually no cardboard saint either. A war profiteer of sorts, she peddles necessities to soldiers during the

Thirty Years' War, even though her children perish along the way. "Once you're in [a war] you're hooked like a gambler," a sergeant in *Mother Courage* declares, "you can't afford to walk away from the crapshoot once you're deep in it." That had been exactly what María Elena had discovered.

No one wanted to believe that she had died for nothing. Isn't the sacrificial victim's function to make society's renewal possible? One newspaper unsubtly invoked Christ's death in a headline about María Elena's murder. "She Died So That Peru Might Live."

Her funeral did seem, momentarily, to turn the war. A cortège of over ten thousand people crossed the sand hills to Villa's cemetery behind the white coffin. Many mourners carried the fallen activist's picture, and their grief, shock, and outrage against Shining Path was palpable. Government officials and politicians drove in with their bodyguards. They included the minister of the interior; senators and congressmen; and the former president Fernando Belaúnde and his wife, Violeta (whom María Elena had befriended over shared interests in women's health). Few tarried, for nervous fear about the *senderistas*.

Gustavo and Eugenia bowed over the coffin at the cemetery. Shouting mourners pressed in around them. The boys stood stunned by it all. David turned nine that day; María Elena had promised him a bicycle for his birthday. *Will I still get it?* he'd asked his father that morning.

The war's biggest previous funeral march had been for a fallen *senderista*. Back in 1982, when Shining Path had been a brave new adventure in Ayacucho, the city turned out for the dead young *senderista* Edith Lagos. A red Communist flag covered her coffin. By contrast, the color at María Elena's funeral was white for peace—the banners some carried, the one over the coffin, the coffin itself. "Guzmán's Great Mistake," a *La República* editorial said. Some pundits predicted that the María Elena killing would unite Peruvians against the terrorists at last. "Closing Ranks Against Sendero," one headline read.

That proved wishful thinking. Once the mourners left the cemetery,

Lima reverted to fear and apathy. Shining Path showed no contrition. "Long Live the Just Punishment of the Imperialist Agent M. E. Moyano!" a leaflet from Villa's Classist Revolutionary Movement declared. "If anyone has a problem with the Party, they will receive a just and exemplary punishment. We will find you no matter how long you try to hide from us."

The rebels shot down another shantytown activist at the very hour of María Elena's funeral.

A grieving Rocío Paz invited others to paint a wall mural for María Elena a few days later. No one showed up except Rocío's boyfriend. People feared angering the *senderistas*.

Exactly who gave the final order for María Elena's murder would be disputed later. "I didn't have anything to do with that situation," Abimael maintained in 2002. (The lawyer in him would never admit directly to any killing at all.) It may possibly be true that the Shining Path leader did not issue any direct command, especially amid so much hasty flight from the GEIN. Even so, the party had been threatening María Elena for many months. The murder itself had been planned at least a week in advance and, even if Abimael did not give the order, he did nothing to stop it. Besides, he believed the treacherous María Elena deserved to die. "About Mrs. Moyano, I had information," Abimael claimed without providing any evidence. "An agent of the Armed Forces." He objected only to blowing up the body. "A useless excess."

It had become so dangerous that Gustavo decided to flee Peru with his boys. María Elena's friends helped them to gain asylum in Spain and bought the plane tickets for Madrid. Before leaving, Gustavo arranged for his wife's coffin to be removed from its niche in the Villa cemetery and had the bits and pieces of her destroyed body cremated at a funeral parlor. "*Papito*," she had once instructed him. "I want you to leave my ashes in my favorite places." Eugenia and María Elena's siblings accompanied Gustavo to spread the ashes. They scattered some at the Women's Federation, the municipality, and the beach.

Guido Sattin, the Venetian doctor, heard about María Elena's death back in Italy. He wrote a short story set years afterwards. Rain never falls in Villa, but in Sattin's story a miracle occurs. A thunderstorm booms down from the heavens, and red flowers blossom across the desert, exactly at the February hour of María Elena's murder.

The heart of María Elena, her friends say.

CHAPTER NINETEEN

The Wolf and the Whale

Gustavo Gorriti devoted a *Caretas* column to María Elena's murder. He'd met María Elena only briefly, but her death was another dismal development. Perhaps, Gustavo wrote, others would now "come forward, people who by their brave, intelligent action will mean fewer María Elenas to weep for in the future." He did not expect any groundswell against Shining Path despite the peace flags and brave sloganeering at the funeral march. His column avowed that neither Marx, Hayek, nor Tocqueville described the situation any longer. Only Hobbes's "war of all against all" sufficed for the savagery, dread, and loneliness by this point.

At least María Elena's death attracted notice. More than fifty thousand Peruvians had perished almost anonymously in the fighting in the Andean highlands. Forensic anthropologists were still finding mass graves years later. Others would probably never be discovered. If an archaeologist's dream in pre-Columbian treasures lay beneath Peru's surface, these newest subterranean deposits held yellowed teeth, a bit of tennis shoe, a skull cracked by a bullet hole. They detailed a modern war's history.

Few Limans cared much about the mountain carnage. Peruvians loved their ancient Incas. Even the national soft drink, Inca Kola, bore the name of Cuzco's Indian lords. But their modern peasant descendants carried no such romance in most city eyes. They could be posed for the tourist postcard in exotic native costume with the inevitable llamas, but their lives counted for little in Peru. It took a big village massacre to make headlines. Few paid attention to other deaths in the Andes unless the victim happened to be a tourist, foreign aid worker, or journalist.

Escalating Lima attacks made Shining Path much harder to ignore. In July 1991, a guerrilla hit squad gunned down Manuel Inamine Shimbak-uru, a native of Okinawa and well-known sensei. After Alberto Fujimori's victory, anyone of Japanese descent became a new Shining Path target. The new president was wooing Tokyo's aid and investment—and the *senderistas* wanted to keep the Japanese away. They killed Inamine, and also two Japanese engineers working north of Lima. A rebel bomb went off in Hiraoka, a big-box electronics store, even though it was owned by second-generation immigrants. Inamine had been Gustavo's first instructor and set the boy on the path to his five national championships. Gustavo published a furious, loving obituary for his murdered sensei.

Gustavo was covering Fujimori's presidency with mounting unease. He'd been favorably disposed to *El Chino* after his underdog victory, especially since judo gave him a soft spot for anything remotely Japanese. Increasingly, however, he had become concerned about Vladimiro Montesinos's expanding power. A contact in the US embassy first warned Gustavo about the lawyer and cashiered intelligence officer. When Gustavo dug around for more information, he discovered the Arequipan's hand everywhere. Even generals feared *El Doctor*, as Montesinos liked to be called, who was replacing top military officers with his own loyalists. Gustavo wondered if Montesinos had effectively become the novice president's Rasputin. It would come out later that *El Doctor* funneled millions into his private bank accounts.

Gustavo had become the country's most prominent journalist. He still wrote for *Caretas*, but also contributed frequently to *El Pais*, Spain's largest newspaper. When a New York foundation awarded him a year-long writing fellowship, Gustavo returned to Cambridge, at last finding time to finish his book about Shining Path's first years. It became a surprise Peruvian bestseller and led to speaking invitations at various military seminars. The army perpetually claimed to be about to wipe out the *delincuentes subversivos*, subversive delinquents, once and for all. When Gustavo chatted with officers after his presentations, he heard private doubt, almost helplessness, especially about the battle for Lima. "We don't know how to stop them," one officer told him.

The government had built the new Canto Grande penitentiary to hold captive *senderistas* following the bloody prison mutiny in 1986. On visiting days, rebel prisoners in the women's cellblock allowed in journalists to watch a well-rehearsed Cultural Revolution-style propaganda show, among them a BBC film crew. The *senderista* women wore Mao caps and red blouses—and carried imitation machine guns, real lighted torches, and red banners. To drumming and applause from family members, they goose-stepped around the prison yard. Their Maoist anthems rang out in both Spanish and the original Mandarin. (The ethnomusicologically minded Osmán Morote had recorded these hymns on a trip to China.) For a climax, the *senderistas* produced a big portrait of Abimael and smaller ones of Mao, Lenin, and Marx. They paraded around their Chairman Gonzalo like the molasses-wood Jesus statue at Lima's Lord of the Miracles procession. Prison authorities were afraid to intervene, the television newscasters reported. Their stories reinforced the impression of a bizarre yet menacing rebellion.

These appearances concealed the revolution's shaky realities. Abimael and Elena had been forced into an itinerant existence for over a year now. A few times, after losing the Buenavista hideout, they slept roadside in a car to evade GEIN. If the Grupo Colina, the army death squad, found them, the two *senderista* leaders would almost certainly be shot on the spot. Sometimes, when camping in an empty apartment, they kept the lights off to avoid attracting attention. They dined on canned food some nights. Elena missed the ocean most in their shuttered confinement.

Their rebellion had meanwhile become even more anomalous. As the Cold War's victor and the only remaining superpower, the United States sent troops in 1991 to drive invading Iraqis from Kuwait. Their victory made the little emirate safe again for its billionaire sheiks and multinational oil companies. That torchbearer for American culinary values, McDonald's, planned a new franchise for Moscow's Red Square, and, when Poles elected the Solidarity leader Lech Wałęsa as their president, it drove another nail into Communism's coffin. A few assorted Marxist groups soldiered on in the world's far corners: India's Naxalites, the Kurdish Worker's Party in Turkey. (The Nepali Maoists laid down arms in 2006 when their leader, Prachanda, became prime minister.) Only Shining Path declared full-fledged planetary ambitions any longer. *Chairman Gonzalo, magisterial director of the brilliant world revolution*, the Canto Grande prisoners chanted. They could not see that Communism had proved to be twentieth-century history's biggest dead end. Abimael was captaining the last revolution of its kind.

At least to a degree, the party leaders recognized the changing planetary realities. The United States had provided a reminder of its Latin American clout by invading Panama in 1989 to remove the drug-trafficking Gen. Manuel Noriega from power. Even if the *senderistas* bombed their way into power, their People's Republic of Peru would be a pariah, the only Communist South American country. Elena tried to put aside any doubts. "We knew a stage of world communism had ended. But what could we do? Give up?" Their convictions allowed no compromise even now. "Let Strategic Equilibrium Shake the Country!" Abimael titled a new document as if victory neared. They had reached "the highest point of the People's War so far."

A new living arrangement gave some greater security. Early in 1992, Elena and Abimael moved in with a young professional couple. Although they were not party members, Maritza Garrido and Carlos Incháustegui sympathized with Shining Path. A slender coal-eyed beauty, Maritza came from a wealthy Callao family. She'd gone to the Lima white elite's favored finishing school, the Catholic University, also studying ballet (once posing in her leotard for a *Caretas* spread). There, the aspiring dancer became a convinced Marxist and learned more about Shining Path through her aunt, Nelly Evans. Maritza's partner, the handsome Carlos, worked at an architecture firm and had pro-*senderista* friends in his bohemian Liman circles. When a friend asked the couple to hide two fugitive party leaders, they agreed. Some days later, nervous party bodyguards escorted their new houseguests through the door.

"I was shocked when it was Abimael and Elena," Carlos said.

The young professionals provided the perfect cover for the hemisphere's most wanted terrorists. Their rented house in the Surquillo neighborhood crowded against a bodega, but had the necessary wall and metal gate for privacy. Maritza cleared the downstairs living room to offer children's modern dance lessons. Though they were only lovers and not married, Maritza gave Carlos a wifely peck for show on his way out to work every morning. The neighbors never noticed anything unusual about the couple or the house.

The second floor became the party's new command center. Abimael and Elena occupied one bedroom and used the other for an office with bookshelves and a desk. A third room held a television and couch for overnight visitors. María Pantoja, Óscar Ramírez, and a few others sometimes came for strategy sessions. Little girls in leotards relevéd below. Their mothers would never have imagined that mad Marxists lived in the attic.

It took some time for Carlos and Maritza to feel comfortable in Abimael's company. "He had been a mythic creature to me," Carlos said. "When my friends and I were stoned, we wondered if Chairman Gonzalo was just a hologram."

The iconoclastic Carlos had long been drawn to radicalism and experimentation. When he was a boy, his father carried him on his shoulders to see the fiery President Velasco speak. Carlos embarked on a hippie backpacking trip across South America after finishing his degree. To support himself, the young Peruvian sold jewelry on a Rio de Janeiro sidewalk. He had been drawn back in Lima to the small hardcore punk scene. The *sutes*, or undergrounders, spoke to Carlos's subversive spirit. He used his considerable artistic talents to help organize a collective punk installation.

Some *sutes* had Shining Path sympathies, and Carlos drifted towards the rebels. On learning one day in the late 1980s that the police had killed a *senderista* friend, he decided to become more actively involved. The bickering legal leftist parties had lost credibility. Only Shining Path seemed to be acting upon its revolutionary convictions.

The one-time punk rocker found the mythical Chairman Gonzalo to be good company.

"He was serious, the reserved Arequipan, but he was curious and considerate," Carlos said. Abimael gave him some money for a younger brother who had gotten into trouble.

Carlos sometimes cooked for everyone. When the cholera epidemic struck Lima, he bought market fish for almost nothing, washing it in water with a little chlorine to kill the bacteria. Carlos took the further precaution of not fixing raw fish dishes like ceviche or *tiradito*. Abimael and Elena would come downstairs for *pescado encebollado,* fish steamed in tomatoes and onions. Sometimes they stayed for hours to chat with their young hosts.

Once Abimael paused to listen to Carlos's rock music. "He plays a beautiful guitar. Who is it?"

"Carlos Santana," Carlos said.

He could not convince Abimael about punk's revolutionary qualities, though.

"I'd prefer more action, less shouting," Abimael said.

———

Journalists and ill-informed CIA analysts continued to speculate about Shining Path's supposed drug-trafficking fortune. The actual main source of the quite limited rebel operating budget was the César Vallejo Institute in downtown Lima. The *senderistas* secretly controlled this university preparatory academy, which took in about $20,000 a month. That cash paid for the rent and living expenses at Abimael and Elena's hideouts.

A bespectacled younger man named Luis Arana directed the institute. Unbeknownst to students at the academy, he belonged to Shining Path's Central Committee. Arana received word early in 1992 that Abimael wanted to see him. He was brought to the hideout by an almost comically complicated route. A coded meeting place. Secret hand signals. Fancy car maneuvers. Switched drivers. Then, finally, a beautiful young woman, Maritza. She draped a towel over Arana's head to keep him from seeing the hideout's location. It was better to take precautions with all but the most trusted inner circle.

Arana had not seen Abimael for several years.

He looked the same, maybe a little heavier.

Abimael greeted Arana warmly. He asked after his family, while Maritza brought snacks and wine, before getting to the point. "There's a special police group hunting us now," Abimael warned. They had deduced the GEIN's existence by this time. "You need to be especially careful not to be followed." Arana would have a new go-between for money handovers, Abimael said. They chatted for another hour or so before Maritza had Arana drape the towel back over his head to drive him away.

One night, April 5, 1992, Abimael and Elena switched on the television. President Fujimori came on to make an emergency announcement. He was shutting down congress and the judiciary. "*Dis-ol-ver*, diss-olv-ing*," he enunciated for effect. His clipped, nasal accent carried grim authority. Army tanks rolled into the streets even before the president had finished speaking.

The announcement seemed puzzling at first. This was not precisely the regulation Latin American military coup, since *El Chino* had been democratically elected. He was using the army's muscle, however, to shut down the government's other two branches, giving himself quasi-dictatorial powers. An *autogolpe*, or self-coup, critics labeled Fujimori's actions.

A palace drama preceded the *autogolpe*. A week before, the first lady, Susana Higuchi, held an unexpected press conference. She charged her husband's younger brother and trusted advisor, Santiago, with profiteering from Japanese clothes donations for the poor. The peeved president eventually divorced Susana, after, by her account, locking her in a mental asylum. Their daughter, Keiko, replaced her mother as the new first lady. She accompanied her father on state visits.

Almost certainly, Fujimori planned the *autogolpe* even before his wife's news conference. The congress had turned mostly against the president in reaction to his harsh anti-inflationary package, the *fujishock*, and leftist groups allied with the populist APRA party to block new legislation. Fujimori had become frustrated by the courts, too. Corruption ruled there, and, whether from incompetence or fear, judges released several *senderista* leaders. One high-ranking Central Committee member, Laura Zambrano, was arrested and then freed twice. His new administration would mark "the starting point for a search for an authentic transformation," Fujimori concluded the televised announcement.

Abimael and Elena turned off the set. This latest development only momentarily surprised them. "The genocidal traitor," Abimael had described Fujimori in a party document, and the *autogolpe* only confirmed him to be a lackey of the imperialists and the oppressor classes. Their task remained to blast forward the revolution to victory.

Gustavo stayed up late the night of the *autogolpe*, finishing a story about it. When the doorbell rang at 4 a.m., he looked up from his keyboard. Any visitor at this hour must have urgent business.

"Who's there?" Gustavo asked.

"Police," a voice said. "We just want to ask a few questions."

Gustavo had been expecting trouble. His latest reporting exposed Vladimiro Montesinos's corrupting clout at the presidential palace, earning him a spot on the shady spymaster's enemy list. President Fujimori doubtless hated Gustavo for making him look weak and manipulated. Gustavo suspected, rightly, that Fujimori had relied upon Montesinos to orchestrate the *autogolpe*. The president and his powerful advisor had free rein now to silence their critics. It seemed possible that Montesinos had sent the men at his door.

Gustavo did not want to give them a pretext for shooting him. He put away his pistol and locked up the family dogs, Cerberus and Simba. As the mastiffs growled furiously from the kitchen, Gustavo hurried to his office to phone a well-connected friend. He needed to sound the alarm before perhaps disappearing into an army prison's black hole. The impatient men outside pounded at the door.

From the window, Gustavo saw two armed men jump the garden wall. A third covered their advance, as if entering a lone journalist's house

demanded a military-style commando raid. These plainclothes commandos, Gustavo saw, were not policemen at all. They likely belonged to the
army intelligence service under Vladimiro Montesinos's command. He had
no choice but to open the front door. "Why don't we talk?" he asked the
group's apparent leader.

"No, we're bringing you in," the officer said.

His men took Gustavo's Mac and detachable hard drive. They let him
give Esther and their two sleeping girls a kiss, then escorted him outside to
a waiting Jeep Cherokee. Some fifty soldiers cordoned off the block.

That SUV confirmed Gustavo's suspicions. All the plainclothes army
units under Montesinos's command, among them the Grupo Colina death
squad, drove Jeep Cherokees, which the United States donated to the Peruvian government to fight drug trafficking. The street's cordoning suggested
a secret operation, too. Montesinos and his men did not want anyone to
witness Gustavo's detention.

The Cherokee took Gustavo to the Little Pentagon, the army command
compound. It entered by the back gate, polarized windows rolled up, so even
the sentry could not see inside. Would he become the newest *desaparecido*,
Gustavo wondered? His captors locked him in a grubby room.

Gustavo was tough, an experienced fighter. When two interrogators
appeared, they demanded his computer password. Gustavo refused, and,
before the men left, one threatened torture on their return. *We have other
methods*, he said. Electric shocks applied with a car battery. Hanging for
hours by the arms. Head pushed into a toilet bowl to simulate drowning.
Gustavo knew about these army interrogation techniques from his war
reporting. Hope left a prisoner more vulnerable to his captors, he believed.
Banishing positive thoughts, he paced his cell to stay alert.

Back at their house, Esther had gone into action. She phoned Gustavo's
daughter Edith in New York, and they began calling Gustavo's many friends

in Peru and abroad. News spread quickly about the prominent journalist's disappearance into army custody.

The Spanish ambassador demanded Gustavo's release.

So did the US assistant secretary of state, Bernard Aronson, then in Lima for a meeting. Aronson refused to leave until Gustavo was freed. Other diplomats and organizations protested to the Fujimori government as well.

Gustavo had no idea about the outcry. After twenty-four hours locked in the room, he heard boots outside. Had they come to begin torturing him? Instead he was driven downtown in a Nissan 4×4. There the army intelligence men turned Gustavo over to the police, though keeping his computer and hard drive. The police let him go a few hours later.

Everyone wanted to hear Gustavo's story. Without bothering to change his sweaty shirt, he held a news conference, connecting his kidnapping to the *autogolpe*. Fujimori wanted to become Peru's dictator, Gustavo said, and to shut down the free press. (Several other journalists had also been rounded up that night.) He would not back down from *El Chino* and his crooked intelligence chief.

Everything seemed up for grabs after the *autogolpe*.

President George H. W. Bush and most Latin American leaders urged Fujimori to reopen congress and the courts. "We are very concerned by [your] abandonment of democracy," Bush told *El Chino* in a phone call. If the United States had once backed military dictatorships to stop Communism's spread, it had made democracy and free markets its new mantra for post–Cold War times. The aging Fidel Castro's socialist Cuba was left as Latin America's only dictatorship.

An appalled Mario Vargas Llosa heard about the *autogolpe* on a trip to Berlin. He called for sanctions against his former rival's new regime, and, back in Lima, the Peruvian vice president broke with Fujimori. He tried to set up an interim constitutional government, with little result.

The hard-nosed Fujimori refused to back down. Had Peru been a real democracy, *El Chino* asked? According to his description, the dissolved congress was "a large, heavy, thick-skinned pachyderm," and judges no better for selling themselves to the highest bidder. *"Coimacracia*—a bribocracy," Fujimori called the old system. He would take on terrorism and poverty—and efficiently engineer a better Peru. There would be elections for a new congress, eventually.

Gustavo found the spectacle disturbing, albeit predictable enough. With its spies, tanks, and death squads the new Fujimori regime had become a version of Hobbes's Leviathan, which the great British philosopher saw as the only way to ensure order. It would not be bothered by democratic niceties any longer.

Government officials moved immediately to crack down on Shining Path. A few weeks after the *autogolpe*, they announced plans to close down the women's cellblock at Canto Grande. The women would be transferred to a new jail in Chorrillos. There would be no more *The East Is Red* musicals there.

The *senderistas* decided to mutiny against the cellblock closure. They believed the shutdown to be part of the government's "genocidal plan," as party propaganda called it, to exterminate them for good. In anticipation of a battle, Shining Path teams had built defensive walls inside the prison, smuggling in cement, bricks, and sand for the fortifications. They launched their uprising by jumping two guards, killing the men and taking their guns. Two captured rifles, some homemade clubs, and their revolutionary resolve would have to do for weapons. The *senderistas* were prepared for a fight to the death like the so-called Day of Heroism six years before.

Fujimori and his generals wasted no time. Two thousand soldiers and policemen massed around Canto Grande. Helicopter gunships chopped overhead and tanks blocked the entrance to its desert canyon. Assault forces smashed through the wall on the siege's third day. They did not slaughter every prisoner this time, but they did have a kill list. The commanding officers wanted to eliminate the main *senderista* leaders.

"There's *la negra*," a policeman yelled. He'd spotted Janet Talavera, the deputy editor of *El Diario*, between the dust, shouts, and explosions.

A sniper shot her down.

The assault team executed more surrendered prisoners later, among them several Central Committee members.

Television news showed a stone-faced Fujimori contemptuously walking between the humbled survivors.

Only a week later the *senderistas* staged their customary kabuki theater of revenge. A guerrilla band occupied a small town near Lima, then shot a Canto Grande prison guard who lived there. They left his body to the dogs and vultures. "This Is How Traitors Die," the standard placard read.

The government soon built a new prison called Yanamayo. Like a penal colony on Neptune, it sat on Lake Titicaca's desert, an unheated concrete jail at an oxygen-deprived 12,700 feet. Inmates had no running water, lights, or windows to block the wind. An American charged with belonging to the MRTA, Lori Berenson, served time at Yanamayo too.

No longer did accused *senderistas* have any real legal rights. Instead, Fujimori established special anti-terrorism tribunals, which summarily handed down long sentences on scant evidence. Like medieval executioners, the judges wore black hoods so they could not be identified. These so-called faceless judges convicted more than a thousand people, among them many innocents. A *senderista* flyer promised to track them down to face "the people's justice" sooner or later.

Gustavo resorted in *Caretas* to a mixed zoological metaphor.

"We're between the hour of the wolf and the whale."

Gustavo went back to work after his detention. He uncovered new evidence for Vladimiro Montesinos's ties to cocaine lords, and, early in May, testified in Washington at a congressional hearing about the *autogolpe*. A criminal dictatorship ruled Peru now, Gustavo insisted. He would soon learn that a general, Jaime Salinas, was secretly plotting a countercoup, promising new elections afterward. That might be the only way to restore democracy.

Back in Peru, Gustavo felt isolated. Many Peruvians did not share his outrage about the *autogolpe*. Who mourned the squabbling congressmen, the pompous bosses, and the greasy judges? Perhaps *El Chino* could clean up the mess. Fujimori had initially been elected to office, the overwhelming pick of the brown majorities. That gave him a certain mandate, at least more than a run-of-the-mill dictator. So much crime, chaos, and duplicity also fortified a certain generalized longing for a hard hand. Some peasants approvingly recalled the "respect" once imposed by the old-time hacienda owners with their stocks and whippings. Fujimori would always be popular in mountain villages across the hinterlands.

Let *El Chino* have his way, most people seemed to think. How could things get any worse, anyway? A poll showed that as many as 70 percent of Peruvians approved the *autogolpe*. Compliant media outlets supplied favorable coverage.

Watching other journalists become sycophants appalled Gustavo. He had Enrique Zileri's backing for investigating the murky machinations in the presidential palace. The aging *Caretas* publisher still took pride in publishing the truth, no matter the consequences.

Gustavo found other editors turning cold. They feared angering the Fujimori government by publishing its fiercest opponent. *Gorriti has lost touch*, he knew some whispered. *He's gotten obsessed with Montesinos.* Gustavo suspected that the spymaster himself planted the rumors.

It had indeed become personal for Gustavo, to a degree. Montesinos had him kidnapped, after all, terrorizing his family. His mother had been the teenage anti-fascist resistance fighter—and her family died in Hitler's ovens. He would not be scared into silence any more than María Elena.

Gustavo saw Peru's future at stake. If Fujimori and his bagmen had their way, it would destroy real hope for a free society. There'd be trappings of openness with promised new elections and no direct press censorship. Generals, drug traffickers, and Montesinos would control the country from behind the scenes. It rankled Gustavo to find himself labeled as too partisan, too bitter, and too negative about the Fujimori government.

Even the big international papers seemed to wonder about Gustavo's reporting. He wrote for the *Los Angeles Times*, *New Republic*, and *New York Times*, and, his main outlet, *El Pais*, having become their Peru correspondent. The editors at the Madrid-based *El Pais* worried about their paper losing access to the government, and also for Gustavo's safety. Their South American bureau chief took Gustavo to lunch one day. The man, an old friend, recalled a brave Jesuit activist from his time covering El Salvador's war. He had been murdered by the army for documenting its atrocities. Gustavo was on the same suicidal course, his friend suggested. He should pull back.

Gustavo received his first death threat in late May. He had not only testified before the US Congress earlier that month, but also given interviews and think-tank talks about Fujimori's despotic designs. His outspokenness abroad likely angered the new regime.

You're going to die, you fucker, the voice on the phone said.

Gustavo was becoming the new María Elena. Although a white journalist and a black activist, they were both crusaders. One took up the fight against the wolf, and the other was challenging the whale. Both found the country largely indifferent to their message.

Esther encouraged Gustavo to stay the course. Her father, an APRA militant, had been jailed in the party's glory days when it fought dictatorship. Ever since they'd married after growing up on neighboring farms, Esther had assumed a conventional housewife's role. She raised the girls and ran the house. (They did have a maid, like every middle-class Peruvian family.) She and Gustavo shared the same strong spirit for all that. They set up escape routes from the house. Esther's mother hid Gustavo's most sensitive files in her house.

Gustavo cleaned his pistol and hired two off-duty Marines to protect Esther and the girls. He planned to fight rather than be taken prisoner again.

Then in early June, a bomb exploded at Channel 2. The *senderistas* wanted to shut down this big television station for its pro-Fujimori stance.

Gustavo was interviewed live outside the destroyed building. He took advantage of the giant television audience to decry Fujimori's authoritarian ways. Only an honest, democratic government, Gustavo said, could beat Shining Path, preventing more tragedies like this one. He expected the producer to shut off his microphone. Instead, the man winked and let him go on for some time.

Exactly then, the maid answered the phone at Gustavo's house. *Turn on the TV, you fucking bitch*, the woman said. *That motherfucker Gorriti won't make it home. We'll fucking kill him, then his bitch wife and daughters.* When the shaking maid told Esther about the call, she tried unsuccessfully to contact Gustavo. A few hours later, when he returned home, he found reporters at the house and Esther, for the first time, in tears. She thought the anonymous caller had made good on her threat to kill Gustavo.

Things seemed to be spinning out of control. Two weeks after the Channel Two bombing, a *senderista* car bomb detonated on Tarata Street in the heart of Miraflores. It contained approximately 900 pounds of ammonium nitrate mixed with fuel oil. The blast killed 25 people, wounded 155, and left a city block in smoking ruins. That well-heeled Miraflores had been attacked sent Lima into full panic.

Two days later the Grupo Colina stepped from its SUVs at La Cantuta University. The school had long been a *senderista* stronghold; Abimael briefly taught there before the war.

The army death squad sought retaliation for the Tarata bombing. It kidnapped ten students and a professor, ditching their corpses in the dunes. Gustavo knew that he and Esther could be next.

It was becoming impossible for them to carry on. Editors stopped calling Gustavo. Old acquaintances, sometimes friends, crossed the street to avoid being seen with him. He and Esther had exhausted their savings. The Carnegie Endowment for International Peace in Washington offered Gustavo a full-time salaried fellowship for the fall. He could carry on opposition there. The girls would be safe, too.

Gustavo decided to leave. He flew to Washington late in July, soon joined by Esther and the girls. In those same days, the *senderistas* set off thirty-six more bombs, apparently unintimidated by the Grupo Colina or anything else. As much as the exiled Gustavo detested Fujimori, he feared a Shining Path victory and a retrograde Communist dictatorship even more. Gustavo followed the news from back home with growing apprehension. The war seemed to be heading towards a climax, and perhaps the *senderistas* might succeed in establishing their People's Republic of Peru after all.

CHAPTER TWENTY

Fat Cheeks, Affirmative!

Marco Miyashiro stared at the unidentified woman in a grainy surveillance photograph. "Lola," the GEIN agents called her. "I've seen this woman," Miyashiro mumbled to himself. He swiveled, pulling a metal box from under his desk. The box held pictures and documents from Miyashiro's previous assignment hunting the MRTA guerrillas. The detective's black eyebrows furrowed over a 1987 photograph: a woman chatting with a young man on a red Honda motorcycle. The woman appeared only coincidentally in the shot. Miyashiro's men had been shadowing the man, her boyfriend, an MRTA leader.

Yes, Lola, younger, longer hair.

"Look, *negro!*" Miyashiro said, showing Benedicto Jiménez. "Lola is Maritza Garrido."

The GEIN's co-commanders had been zeroing in on Maritza's house on 459 Varsova Street in Surquillo. It was the one that the dancer shared with her partner, Carlos Incháustegui, whose name the detectives had only learned a few weeks before. Miyashiro and Benedicto had begun to suspect that the couple might be hiding Abimael himself there. (They called the fugitive rebel chieftain *El Cachetón*, Fat Cheeks, after his jowly 1979 mug shot.) Their agents could now run a background check on Maritza knowing her real name. She turned out to be the niece of Dove Two, Nelly Evans, the Villa schoolteacher and inner-circle member captured by the GEIN a year before. Those family connections suggested that the dancer might be entrusted with harboring the Shining Path leader.

The detectives had been watching 459 Varsova Street for over two months. It was an unremarkable mustard yellow house with an unfinished terrace on the rooftop. By chance, a police colonel lived across the street; he allowed the GEIN to film comings and goings from his third floor. Other agents loitered around the block, one disguised as an ice cream vendor with his cart. Most mornings Carlos went to the bakery, but "Lolo," as the detectives called him, bought more rolls than needed for two people. That had been the first inkling that he and Maritza might not be the only residents in the house.

The evidence began accumulating after that. Maritza left the trash daily at the gate, and, after nothing interesting the first few weeks, the agents discovered some Winston butts, Abimael's brand. They also found an empty Swedish liqueur bottle, hypothesizing that the exiled La Torres might have sent it from Stockholm. "Garbage speaks an eloquent language," Benedicto liked to quote Umberto Eco's *The Name of the Rose*. Maritza's purchase of a large-size pair of men's underwear also seemed suggestive. That she had been identified as a possible *senderista* gave yet more justification for their suspicions about the party leader being concealed at 459 Varsova Street.

Their chief garbage interpreter remained Carlos Iglesias, *El Loco*, an expert by now. Three days after Miyashiro figured out Maritza's name, Iglesias excitedly brought a soggy piece of scrap paper to GEIN headquarters. *Meeting of P.B.* [Politburo]. *III Plenary of C.C.* [Central Committee]. A police graphologist matched the handwriting to a Buenavista document in Elena Iparraguirre's hand. "They're fucked," Miyashiro told Benedicto. He leaned back in his chair, blowing a satisfied puff of cigarette smoke above his head. "This is going to cost them badly." They began preparing plans for storming the house.

The war had been escalating in those last days of August. Only a few weeks before, the giant Shining Path bomb had laid waste to Tarata Street, and the Grupo Colina had gone on its retaliatory La Cantuta murder spree. New *senderista* car bombs destroyed eight more buildings and left twenty more people dead. A correspondent for the *The Guardian* claimed that the remaining foreigners in Peru had grown so fearful of Shining Path and street thieves that they "dyed their blond hair dark." Concerned American officials warned about a rebel victory. "If Sendero were to take power, we would see this century's third genocide," assistant secretary of state Bernard Aronson testified before the US Congress. Aronson predicted a bloodbath like the Nazi Holocaust or the Khmer Rouge's Cambodian killing fields. Some observers drew parallels between Abimael and the psychotic Khmer Rouge leader, Pol Pot, both Communists heading murderous armies. That comparison irritated Abimael, who derided Pol Pot as a "pseudo-Marxist" and promised that only multimillionaires would suffer in the coming People's Republic. Few Peruvians trusted the word of a man who was overseeing a bombing campaign that scattered severed limbs across the streets.

The poll numbers showed Fujimori's popularity trending downward. When seizing emergency powers earlier in the year, he had promised results, and sounded steely in a televised address after the Tarata attack: "Those who are bleeding Peru to death, killing our children, will be eliminated." Various new measures included trying *senderistas* as "traitors" before military courts. They could be executed by firing squads that way, the president indicated. This did little to satisfy Fujimori's critics, who blamed him for rising rebel power. His *autogolpe* had "created a political vacuum which Sendero is ready to fill," said Hernando de Soto, a well-known economist. A big bomb had cratered de Soto's US-funded Institute for Liberty and Democracy a few weeks after Tarata. *El Chino* needed to crush Shining Path before Peruvians lost faith in his leadership.

These exigencies lent new urgency to the GEIN's hunt for Abimael. They had identified 459 Varsova Street as Abimael's possible hideout by flipping a Central Committee member, Luis Arana, the college prep academy director. After finding Arana's address at Buenavista, detectives had placed him under watch. Their surveillance revealed his active role in the party. He rendezvoused frequently with other rebels, many coming downtown to the academy. The agents nicknamed Arana *Cholo Sotil* after a star midfielder from Peru's 1978 World Cup team. Like *Cholo Sotil*, Miyashiro explained later, Arana "distributed the ball," sometimes handing off a mysterious bag to a *senderista* contact. The GEIN brought him in for questioning.

It had long been common for the police to utilize torture in its interrogations. Even before the war, an officer might use *el submarino*, a simulated drowning, or *el periquito*, hanging by the arms, to try to break a thief. Both the police and the army employed these methods with captured *senderistas* as well as many others. As Benedicto and Miyashiro knew, however, the *senderistas* seldom broke under any physical pressure. When one agent interrogated a fighter accused of a policeman's recent murder, the man didn't blink. "The death of a mangy reactionary dog is part of the people's war strategy." GEIN agents tried to seduce, cajole, tire, deceive, and win confidence even in hardcore cases. They would get nowhere with shocks and waterboarding.

Benedicto and Miyashiro's men had arrested Arana's wife, too, and the couple had a baby. Eventually, Arana agreed to talk. He would cooperate in exchange for his wife's release and her being allowed to keep a few thousand dollars confiscated from the academy. His own sentence would be reduced to a few years.

"The last time I saw Chairman Gonzalo was on April 4th," the academy director said.

"Where?" Benedicto asked.

Arana didn't know. That was when Maritza drove him to the hideout. She'd put the precautionary towel over his head. Arana did not know Maritza's name, either, describing her only as a *pituca miraflorina*, a Miraflores rich girl. He did remember the parking lot where Maritza had picked him up. And her car's make—a purple Hyundai.

An agent went to the parking lot, eventually tracing the car and its owner: the one-time hippie and punk rocker, Carlos Incháustegui. That information led, after more gumshoeing, to 459 Varsova Street, which the GEIN immediately put under watch. The agents called the house *El Castillo*, the Castle, in hopes that Abimael might be concealed behind its gated walls.

The first days had shown no evidence for anyone hiding there. Only dance pupils and their mothers came to the house. *Just women and children*, Benedicto began to think. That the neighborhood was scruffier than Abimael's earlier hideouts led him to doubt, too. He ordered the team to end the watch only a few weeks after it had begun.

His two lieutenants believed Benedicto's decision to be premature. The easygoing Guillermo Bonilla, who had a hipster's look in his flowered shirts, might have obeyed anyway. His diminutive yet brash partner, José Gil, convinced him that they should keep watching *El Castillo*. They faked expense receipts for Benedicto, while persuading Carlos Iglesias and some other agents to help maintain surveillance of the house. After finding the Winstons and Swedish liquor in the trash, they had gone to Benedicto. He forgave their disobedience with a bear hug.

"You're my tiger," he told Bonilla, recognizing his mistake.

Then Iglesias found Elena's note.

The only remaining cause for hesitation was having seen no sign of anyone besides Carlos and Maritza inside the house. They had been watching closely for more than two months with only the considerable circumstantial evidence for Abimael being there. But then, a few days after the note's discovery, a *senderista* bomb blacked out the neighborhood. The watching agent radioed in from the crow's nest in the police colonel's house down the block.

"Right now, Lola is on the patio," he reported. "Lola" remained their code name for Maritza. "Lolo is behind her," the agent added. The couple seemed to be out for a look at the darkened sky.

Moments later, the agent suddenly said, "Boss, boss! There's something on the second floor."

A candle flickered. A bearded man's chunky silhouette appeared behind the shades.

"Ok, calm down," Miyashiro radioed back. "Keep watching and keep us posted."

He looked at Benedicto for confirmation.

"Yes," his partner said, "we've got to strike."

The GEIN co-leaders spent several more days finalizing the plan. Together with Luis Valencia, the unit's third-ranking officer, they decided on two simultaneous raids. One team headed by Bonilla and Gil would capture Zénon Cárdenas, Comrade Arturo, who was Abimael's go-between to Luis Arana, the academy director. Miyashiro would direct agents at 459 Varsova Street, hoping to seize Guzmán there. "Operation Victory," they called the plan. They agreed to stage the operation on National Police Day, September 15, less than two weeks away. That would be an appropriately symbolic date to bring the Shining Path leader to justice, Benedicto and Miyashiro agreed. They shared the Peruvian affection for dates and ceremony.

Three days before the planned raid, Miyashiro could see that Benedicto was growing impatient. "What's up, Chemist? Any news?" he radioed Miyashiro even before his co-commander had arrived at the office. (Miyashiro was "Chemist," Benedicto "Physicist," and Valencia "Engineer" to confuse any eavesdropper from Shining Path or Montesinos's army intelligence service.) When Miyashiro arrived, Benedicto proposed launching Operation Victory that night, September 12. He worried the *senderistas* could get wind of their plan if they delayed any longer, giving Abimael a chance to escape once more as he had from the Buenavista house. They could not fail this time.

Miyashiro looked over at Valencia.

"*El negro* is a wizard when it comes to these things," he said. "If he says today's the day, then today's the day."

Valencia nodded, putting out his half-smoked cigarette and lighting another.

In the end, the GEIN commanders had no say in the matter. While they readied operations at headquarters, Gil and Bonilla forced the issue. At a bus stop on Mexico Avenue, they handcuffed Zénon Cárdenas, Comrade Arturo—the Fox, as the GEIN called him. *We have the Fox,* Gil radioed Benedicto. This meant, he knew, that the Castle raid had to take place that night, since Cárdenas's arrest would alert Abimael to his peril. "We had been anxious and worried," Gil said. "We couldn't let Guzmán get away again."

They returned to headquarters with Cárdenas in custody.

Benedicto stared at his wayward agents.

"Why?"

"Because Fat Cheeks is there," Gil said. "If he isn't, I'll resign tomorrow. But we have to move now. Before he does." They had already decided to raid that night, Benedicto said, and he did not reproach his agents. He and Miyashiro did have to deal with the DINCOTE director, Ketín Vidal, who summoned them to his office a few hours later. They found Vidal upset at having been informed about the planned raid only after the fact. "I've already made the call, sir," Benedicto offered. "I'll take responsibility, but right now we need to focus on the operation."

"Someone's head will roll if it goes badly," the director frowned. "And it won't be mine."

Benedicto and Miyashiro went back to the GEIN office.

Just before dusk the agents received their order.

Boys, unleash the storm.

Miyashiro and his team drove to the Castle. A few agents would be posted secretly nearby. Several more would hang around the street posing as celebrating fans returning from the Universitario–Alianza Lima game, a big soccer rivalry. The last two, Julio Becerra and Cecilia Garzón, would pretend to be lovers dallying at the bodega next door to the house. The agents wanted to storm in with maximum surprise.

They did not have to wait long before a VW pulled up. A middle-aged couple stepped out. Carlos and Maritza had invited Maritza's uncle and his girlfriend for dinner that night. Miyashiro radioed a command from his post down the block. *Move when the door opens and the people come out*, he said. If Abimael had armed bodyguards, the agents might find themselves in a firefight. Miyashiro had instructed them to be ready for that.

The dinner dragged on for several hours inside. "We were talking about Quyllurit'i," Carlos remembered. He had gone several times on this well-known pilgrimage to a Cuzcan glacier in his hippie days. As the table conversed about the festival and Andean customs, Miyashiro walked down to the bodega. He found Becerra and Garzón in character, holding hands and gossiping about imaginary friends. Miyashiro bought a cigarette, glancing at the house's outer wall. It did not look that high, at least to a former judoka like him. He made a hopeful motion to suggest that Becerra might hop over it, which his agent ignored. The only thing left was to wait.

Just before nine the metal gate ground open.

Carlos, Maritza, and their guests came out for goodbyes.

"This is it," Becerra whispered. He and Garzón drew their guns and rushed over to the gate.

"Freeze, dammit! Don't move, dammit!" he barked. "Police, you're under arrest!"

Maritza played the indignant *pituca*.

"What's going on?" she asked. "Is this a robbery? What do you want?"

Carlos lunged for Becerra's gun.

The agent pulled it away, firing a warning shot. Miyashiro and his men sprinted down the street. As one detective helped Becerra wrestle Carlos to the ground, the others charged into the house. Miyashiro lowered his shoulder to break the door to the second floor. He rushed in with Becerra and more agents behind.

Abimael sat calmly in a leather chair.

A panicked Elena shielded him. "Easy, dammit! You're under arrest. I'm a cop!" said Becerra. "One move and I'll kill you."

"Easy, son," Abimael said. "Calm down. You win."

"Bingo," Miyashiro radioed Benedicto. "Do you copy, Physicist?"

"Copy, Chemist," Benedicto replied.

"That's an affirmative on Fat Cheeks," Miyashiro said.

Elena tried to regain her composure. "I was terrified inside. My only thought was protecting Abimael." The intruders wore street clothes. If they belonged to the Grupo Colina, she and Abimael would probably be shot or maybe worse right there. "Don't kill him!" Elena said. "Who are you? Who's in charge?"

Miyashiro stepped forward. "We're DINCOTE."

The agents rummaged around for weapons.

One ordered Abimael to empty his pockets.

"No one touches him," Elena said. Her eyes shone with what Benedicto afterwards colorfully described as "fanaticism and lovesick devotion."

Abimael removed a handkerchief from his back pocket. That was all he had, he said, folding it carefully before putting it back.

A short while later, Benedicto arrived with Ketín Vidal. Vidal introduced himself to Abimael. "I'm General Ketín Vidal. Director of the DINCOTE."

Abimael extended his hand. "Ruben Manuel Abimael Guzmán Reinoso."

The bespectacled Vidal looked more like a business professor than a policeman. "Well," he said to Abimael, "I'm here to inform you that you are officially under arrest. You must know that in life you win some, and you lose some. And this time, sir, you've lost."

His little speech seemed scripted. The ambitious DINCOTE chief had ordered Walter Cápac, the GEIN videographer, to film the arrest. Although he had questioned the raid only hours before, Vidal recognized the opportunity. He would claim credit for bringing the country's most hated man to justice at last. He'd be a hero.

"We're going to immortalize ourselves," Vidal told Benedicto.

Vidal offered Benedicto a chance to appear on camera, too. Benedicto declined. Of course, he also wanted the glory, and yet thought it wiser to remain anonymous for now. That way, he could more easily track down remaining *senderista* leaders. He later wrote two lengthy books about the capture. The Pacifier, Benedicto sometimes called himself.

Elena hovered around Abimael. The *senderista* leader kept a little hammer and sickle on his desk like a party functionary in the old Soviet days. As Cápac recorded the whole capture sequence, Elena grabbed the small flag, awkwardly holding it up for the camera in the background. Their arrest could not be allowed to halt humanity's march towards Communism.

A courteous Vidal gestured for the couple to have a seat on the sofa. "*Tranquilos*—calm," he said. "We couldn't be calmer," Abimael replied. They talked for a while, and, seldom at a loss for words, Abimael expounded a bit on Marxism, world history, and their revolution. He showed Vidal a medal of Mao. The DINCOTE chief examined it before handing it back.

After fifteen minutes or so, Vidal had heard enough. Then, the camera switched off, the DINCOTE chief had his prize captives driven downtown to the Fortress, the anti-terrorism police headquarters. The unmarked black car carrying Abimael and Elena sped down the dark Lima streets between armed escorts. Flashing police lights gave the appearance of a visiting dignitary's motorcade. A second car conveyed María Pantoja and Laura Zambrano, also captured in the raid. They formed the shrunken politburo that had been planning for that Third Central Committee Plenary. The fifth member, Óscar Rámirez, only escaped arrest because he had been delayed in Ayacucho.

No GEIN agent had expected such an easy capture. "We thought there'd be blood or that he'd get away somehow," said Miyashiro. The single most wanted Latin American fugitive, Pablo Escobar, would soon be gunned down fleeing the police. Across the border in Bolivia way back in 1908, it had required a long shootout to bring down the legendary Butch Cassidy and the Sundance Kid. Not a drop of blood had been shed here at 459 Varsova Street. The war's outsized saga of love, madness, and revolution culminated anticlimactically with a middle-aged couple on their study couch. An unperturbed Abimael had been wearing a gray sports jacket and black slacks. He might have been expecting Miyashiro and his men.

"You can kill a man," Abimael told Vidal, touching his finger to his temple. "But you can never kill this."

Marxist-Leninist-Maoist-Gonzalo Thought.

Who could question that?

CHAPTER TWENTY-ONE

The Silence of the Lambs

Every television station interrupted programming for the stunning bulletin. *Abimael Guzmán, caught at his Lima hideout.* A video clip showed the DINCOTE chief Ketín Vidal conversing with the terrorist mastermind and his fanatical-looking wife. Most reporters guessed that the captives had been transported to DINCOTE headquarters, the Fortress, although the government would not yet confirm it. In the next few days, a rumor spread that Guzmán had not been captured at all. Perhaps the Shining Path mastermind had performed a vanishing trick to escape once again, or if not, the police had already dumped his body in the ocean with a bullet in his head. The capture video might have been faked with a double. Most Peruvians had learned not to trust the official story.

Finally, eleven days after the raid, journalists received a government press release summoning them downtown. Although the "criminal subversive," as the DINCOTE described Abimael, was indeed being held in the Fortress, he would be displayed on a newer office building's rooftop. More than a hundred Peruvian and foreign reporters eagerly crowded up the elevators to find that a big zoo-like cage had been set up there. Police snipers manned the rooftop's edges and army tanks hulked on the street four stories below. A rope line kept the journalists some fifty feet from the cage, curtained to conceal its contents. An Oscar-winning movie about a devious mass murderer, *The Silence of the Lambs*, was playing in Lima theaters just then. Now the world would see Peru's own Hannibal Lecter for the first time. Unsmiling DINCOTE agents in their G-man suits and Ray-Bans lowered the blue curtain slowly for dramatic effect. The journalists strained forward for their first glimpse of the fabled Abimael Guzmán. They aimed microphones, cameras, and video recorders at the cage.

There stood the bearded *senderista* chieftain, surprised by the reporters at first. He wore a black-and-white striped pajama suit like a cartoon convict. Fujimori claimed later this had been his idea, a way to humiliate the fearsome Chairman Gonzalo. Abimael's uniform bore the number 1509, September 15, the National Police Day (Benedicto and Miyashiro's original target date for the raid). The costume had been especially sewn for the caged man, since prisoners in Peru's dismal jails wore street clothes and had no numbers. His oversized dark glasses gave Abimael more the look of an aging mobster than a revolutionary leader. "The last stage of Communism is surrealism," the Romanian poet Andrei Codrescu has suggested.

It had taken some fuss to dress Abimael back at the Fortress. The police had convict costumes made for Elena and the other Varsova Street captives, too. *They want to display us like animals,* a distraught Elena realized. The tough-minded Laura Zambrano momentarily escaped down the hallway to avoid putting on her uniform. Abimael tried to calm down Elena. "We know who we are," he said. "The habit doesn't make the monk." He would show no weakness before the gloating reactionaries.

Journalists expecting a cowed apology soon realized their mistake. Abimael began lecturing from the cage. "This is only a setback. That's all."

His frustration left him increasingly agitated, as if their revolution's defeat had dawned on him only then. "Enough of imperialism!" he shouted at the media pack.

A Channel Two crew was there. *Idiot. Murderer. Clown*, the cameraman yelled back at Abimael. The *senderistas* had bombed his station only months before, killing a reporter and two security guards. Other Peruvian reporters abandoned any show of objectivity. They joined in screaming insults at the caged man.

Abimael raised his fist to sing the opening lines of "The Internationale": *Stand up all victims of oppression, for tyrants fear your might.* The press corps almost immediately launched into Peru's national anthem to drown him out. Abimael fell uncharacteristically silent—and the agents pulled the curtain back up. The reporters raced off to file stories. No one knew how much longer the rebel chieftain even had to live. Fujimori was said to be considering making good on his threat to put top *senderistas* before the firing squad.

––––––––––

At his press conference later that day, a grinning Fujimori expounded upon this great victory in the war on terrorism. "This capture means that we have beheaded the brains of this organization." *El chino de suerte,* "the lucky Chinaman," some called the president. He had not been informed in advance about the raid, but raced back from an Amazonian fishing expedition to claim credit. The capture justified his *autogolpe*, the power grab, earlier in the year, or so Fujimori wanted everyone to think. He could claim to have presided over the deadly Shining Path's defeat.

Ketín Vidal, the DINCOTE chief, benefitted too. He apparently leaked the video clip of his conversation with Abimael and Elena just after the raid. Many observers in Peru and abroad, exactly as Vidal had expected, praised him as a master policeman for tracking down the fugitive Shining Path leader. Hollywood's *The Dancer Upstairs* made Vidal the model for its detective protagonist, played by the Spanish star Javier Bardem. Fujimori's opponents especially celebrated Vidal. He seemed the antidote to Montesinos and his spies, death squads, and dirty tricks. Some hoped the DINCOTE director would run against *El Chino* in some future election.

Few realized that Vidal played little part in the capture. He had been named to head the DINCOTE less than a year before—and Benedicto and Miyashiro seldom consulted him about anything. If anybody could claim to be the heroes, it was the GEIN co-commanders and their detectives. Nor did anyone yet know much about Vidal's own checkered past. He had been forced to resign from the police in 1986 on a money-laundering charge. According to a later investigation by journalist Carlos Paredes, Vidal went to none other than Vladimiro Montesinos for help. That was when Montesinos had been a lawyer for cocaine lords. He reportedly arranged for Vidal's full reinstatement, with back pay. The spymaster supported, perhaps suggested, his former client's appointment as DINCOTE chief in late 1991. Vidal was hardly the white knight of his clippings.

An irritated Fujimori wanted the spotlight for himself. When the president asked Vidal about the leaked video clip, the DINCOTE director suggested the guilty parties might be Miyashiro and Walter Cápac, the GEIN videographer. At a ceremony to award bonuses for the capture, Miyashiro stood up to deny the charges. "Mr. President, this is unjust . . . if you don't trust me, investigate me," Miyashiro said. The media-savvy Vidal earned more praise by promising to donate his share of the bonus money to Ayacucho war orphans. (Whether he really did would be disputed later.) Back at the office, the GEIN members agreed to split their bonuses with Miyashiro and Cápac, who had received nothing after being blamed for the video leak. Vidal exiled Miyashiro to run operations against the MRTA in northern Peru.

A friend phoned Gustavo Gorriti to report Abimael and Elena's arrest. He and Esther had rented an apartment in Washington after fleeing Peru for their lives. That the *senderista* chiefs had been captured was great news,

Gustavo knew. The party could likely not survive the jailing of its leaders and the shattered myth of Chairman Gonzalo's invincibility. Their arrest seemed as unexpected and miraculous as the divine gilded sunburst in the altarpiece of Ayacucho's seventeenth-century cathedral. A ghastly war would wind down at last.

The capture was bittersweet for Gustavo.

He turned to Esther after putting down the phone.

"We won't be going home for a long time."

Until then, they had hoped that Fujimori and his cronies might be forced from power. Only a few weeks before the capture, Gustavo had joined Mario Vargas Llosa and other prominent Peruvian exiles for a secret Washington meeting, where they received an update about the planned countercoup to restore democracy. Peru's best journalist, Gustavo, and its finest novelist, Vargas Llosa, had always been wary of each other. (Gustavo had written a quite critical *New Republic* piece about Vargas Llosa and his failed campaign.) Both men shared a repugnance for Fujimori, however, and wanted him removed from office by any means necessary. Surely Peruvians would finally see the folly of ceding their country to Fujimori, Montesinos, and their regime.

Instead, the capture cemented Fujimori's popularity for the time being. Late in 1992, the coup plotters were arrested on tips from loyalist officers. Gustavo took a job as editor of Panama's biggest newspaper, *La Prensa*. The Panamanian president tried, unsuccessfully, to expel the meddling Peruvian after he dug up ties between government officials and Cali's cocaine cartel. At the same time, Gustavo kept abreast of the latest developments back in Peru, among them how Montesinos bribed and blackmailed opposition politicians to keep them in line. He sent a vitriolic op-ed to the *Washington Post* about Fujimori and his government's corrupt tactics. The *Post* declined. *We want journalism, not propaganda*, Gustavo was told. He hated to see Fujimori gaining acceptance abroad.

A discouraged Vargas Llosa abandoned further political aspirations. "Peru is a problem, but also a possibility," the mid-twentieth-century historian Jorge Basadre once said. With Fujimori's new power, Vargas Llosa saw no redemption for his native country. He became a Spanish citizen in 1993, although retaining Peruvian nationality and professing his love for both countries. The citizenship change, Fujimori taunted, showed that his globe-trotting former rival had never been a real Peruvian in the first place. Vargas Llosa tried to ignore the barbs, and, over the next years, wrote a memoir and more novels, among them the best-selling *The Feast of the Goat*. In 2010 the Swedish Academy awarded Vargas Llosa his overdue Nobel Prize for Literature. His acceptance speech was an ode to reading and writing. "The fictions of literature have multiplied human experiences, preventing us from succumbing to lethargy, self-absorption, and resignation," Vargas Llosa declared.

The DINCOTE kept Abimael and Elena in basement cells at the Fortress.

Nobody tortured the prize prisoners. It was their good fortune to be captive twentieth-century rebel leaders, not eighteenth-century ones. Before putting Túpac Amaru to his own hideously agonizing death in 1781, the Spaniards forced him to watch his wife and co-conspirator, Micaela Bastidas, have her tongue ripped out and then be garroted. Abimael's jailers addressed him as *Doctor* and Elena as *Señora*. They gave Abimael his Winston cigarettes, and a *lomo saltado* one day for lunch. No common *cholo* Shining Path fighter enjoyed such courtesies. That Abimael was a white *doctor* and a celebrity prisoner afforded him more consideration.

A GEIN officer wanted a picture with Abimael and Elena. They obliged, even raising their fists for the shot.

Still, the police did not go too easy on their captives. Upon arrival at headquarters after the arrest, they demanded that Abimael take off his shirt for a mug shot. He did so wordlessly. His captors distributed the demeaning pictures of the saggy, potbellied fifty-seven-year-old to the newspapers.

Guillermo Bonilla and José Luis Gil handled the interrogation. The young GEIN agents had proven themselves as quality detectives in the hunt for Abimael and had become experts at browbeating and cajoling information from suspected *senderistas*. They strode into Abimael's cell on Monday morning some thirty-six hours after he'd been taken prisoner.

"About time," Abimael said sarcastically.

The questioning lasted ten days. Abimael went on about Ayacucho and party history, but parried questions about details. "Shining Path is the people," he replied when asked his group's exact numbers.

Abimael did say his capture had been like a "baseball bat to the head."

"Who killed Augusta?" Gil asked.

Abimael looked disdainful and refused to answer. "You think I know everything," he said. "But I don't." He would only say that any suggestion that he or Elena murdered Augusta amounted to "slander" and "mud-throwing" by those "politically and ideologically incapable of combatting the revolution." Where was Augusta buried? Gil asked. "I don't remember," Abimael said.

At one point, Gil and Bonilla mentioned the GEIN's trophy collection of captured *senderista* artifacts. Abimael asked to see it. Five officers escorted him to a room upstairs. It held banners, wall hangings, signed proclamations, unexploded bombs, the usual Chairman Gonzalo portraits, and other exotica like a bottle of Abimael's Tigason pills. The exhibit shone in the red and yellow of the party's beloved Communist colors.

One case contained a few of Augusta's possessions, including her reading glasses.

Abimael stopped, seemingly lost in memory.

"Come on, *Doctor*," one officer said, "time to go."

Benedicto Jiménez questioned Elena in the meantime. He played the good cop, almost flirtatiously. Elena revealed nothing, although she and the good-looking detective had their lighter moments.

"Listen, *Señora,* Doctor Guzmán is a little old. Can he still get it up?"

Elena chuckled.

"Commander, you don't understand love in Communism. It's not necessarily something physical."

Anyone who saw Abimael and Elena together, Benedicto wrote, "could see they loved each other deeply."

He compared Elena to the Emperor Justinian's wife Theodora, a powerful Byzantine empress. Abimael "was like a child by her side such that he did nothing without asking her opinion." Elena was the real force behind Shining Path, in Benedicto's view.

The interrogations finally ended, followed by the rooftop circus. In his signed affidavit, Abimael complained that the cage exhibit and shirtless mug shot violated "all laws, customary norms . . . and fundamental human rights" as well as the presumption of innocence. Abimael and Elena would repeatedly demand the law's fullest protections over the next years. They had never shown any such concern about due process for María Elena, the Lucanamarcans, or the other victims of their party's red terror. Their lawyers often cited the Geneva Conventions, even though the *senderistas* had gruesomely violated every humanitarian stricture.

It had been decided to transfer Abimael to military custody. He would be the only prisoner in a makeshift barbed-wire camp on the navy's San Lorenzo Island. Elena worried that he'd be killed, wondering if she'd ever see him again. "It was awful," she said later. "I didn't know what to say to him." They said their goodbyes before the guards, Abimael quietly allowing himself to be shackled afterwards. "He thought you just went forward," Elena said.

The *senderista* leader would never give up the fight. His persistence recalled the lost Japanese World War II infantryman said to have soldiered on for years in the jungle without being informed about the emperor's surrender. Abimael could not see that the battle for a world Communist revolution captained by heroic Marxist strongmen and their vanguard parties had already ended in a crushing defeat. When a last Latin American insurgency, the Zapatistas, arose in southern Mexico little more than a year after Abimael's arrest, it drove home how discredited the old Leninist model had become. Their leader, Subcomandante Marcos, mixed socialist libertarianism, indigenous Mayan philosophy, and a nose for a good photo op. He encouraged no personality cult—a kind of anti–Chairman Gonzalo—and the Zapatistas avoided bloodshed when possible to become the global left's new darlings. Only Abimael, his remaining faithful, and a few other far-flung rebel groups held up the old Communist torch any longer.

The victory of the Bolshevik Revolution nonetheless changed the course of twentieth-century history. When Lenin's men occupied the Winter Palace on October 25, 1917, they inspired many more Marxist insurrections worldwide, victorious and not. Over half the earth's then two billion people, as the history books remind us, lived under at least putatively socialist regimes at Communism's high-water mark in the late 1980s. When did the so-called Red Century end for good? It might have been on September 24, 1992, when the caged Abimael attempted to sing "The Internationale." The song sounded almost as archaic and exotic as a vanishing tribe's last incantations, before being drowned out by the Peruvian anthem-singing reporters. Any new hope for a planet still awash in poverty and hatred would have to take new forms in the aftermath of the Lucanamarcas, the reeducation camps, and the failure to deliver on socialism's promises. Even the Berkeley Internationalist bookstore took down its display about the glorious Peruvian People's War some years later.

The *senderistas* tried to put a brave face on their leader's arrest. "The reactionaries dream that this fact will annihilate the revolution," a statement warned. "They don't realize that their end is near no matter how much blood they shed." Urban *senderistas* managed to kill a few last policemen before Lima attacks virtually ended. The war shrank down to occasional skirmishes between small guerrilla bands and government forces in the intersecting jungle valleys of the Apurímac, Ene, and Mantaro rivers.

Many *senderistas* ended up behind bars, among them Maritza Garrido and Carlos Incháustegui. The young caretakers of Abimael and Elena each served more than twenty years for harboring terrorists. When a folklore group gave a prison show one day, a laughing Maritza grabbed another woman to show off her old steps. (She dismissed the film about her, *The Dancer Upstairs*, as trash.) Carlos taught art to his fellow prisoners and made sculptures from twisted iron bars. María Pantoja and Laura Zambrano, the two other rebel leaders captured in the raid, received life sentences from Fujimori's military tribunals. These various jailed *senderistas* had no regrets about joining the revolution. They remained loyal to Abimael.

His captors made him don the striped suit again for the transfer to San Lorenzo, which lay a few miles out to sea near the wrecked El Frontón prison. The navy fitted a speedboat with another metal cage, albeit with the odd courtesy of an overstuffed easy chair for Abimael. As AK-47-wielding commandos locked in the prisoner and the boat pulled out into the Pacific, photojournalists snapped away. The most reviled man in the land of the Incas stared out at the receding city coast from behind his dark glasses.

———

It was Karl Marx who noted how tragedy can devolve to farce.

Treeless San Lorenzo Island had once been a vacation spot for navy officers. To house their notorious prisoner, Abimael's jailers wrapped razor wire around an abandoned cabana like Christmas tree tinsel. The military guards stationed outside wore black ski masks, fearful enough still to hide their identities. A few days after the transfer, they unlocked the gate to allow in Vladimiro Montesinos, who wore his usual business suit and carried a briefcase. The spy chief greeted Abimael politely before sitting down at the table.

Had Abimael been well treated? Did he need anything?

Abimael began complaining, especially about his Hollywood convict uniform. His jailers made him wear it for his meeting with Montesinos.

Montesinos nodded sympathetically. He and Abimael might be on opposing sides, and yet, he said, they were lawyers and Arequipans, *paisanos*, too. He proposed "academic conversations" about Peru and its future.

He'd inquire about the offending uniform. If he couldn't do anything about that, he'd wear one himself next time. That way they could talk as equals. Montesinos brought his own striped uniform a week later as if to keep his word. (It bore the number 2 to suggest rank below only the president.) He wasn't actually about to put it on, only intending to come across as his *paisano's* friend. Montesinos pretended to receive a phone call just then. "Good news, *Doctor*," he said. "You won't have to put on the suit anymore." He pulled out a box of chocolates from Arequipa's famous La Ibérica candy store. *Here, paisano,* the spymaster offered, *have one.* The terrorist chieftain accepted a chocolate.

That candy launched a strange courtship. Rather than shooting Abimael, and possibly martyring him, Fujimori and his chief advisor wanted to persuade the rebel leader to sign a peace agreement. Montesinos and Abimael conversed for hours about their childhoods, politics, and the world. Elena had also been brought to the island. Montesinos arranged conjugal visits. He furnished a radio, newspapers, even a birthday cake for Elena, and reportedly escorted the couple on a boat excursion. He wired the island to listen in on everything.

The wackiest episode occurred late in the courtship. Montesinos had Abimael and Elena brought to a conference room. He pumped Abimael's hand like a used-car salesman welcoming customers to the lot. Abimael looked healthier, having lost his potbelly in captivity, although he now sported an

unfortunate Hitler moustache. Elena had also been paraded before reporters in her own striped uniform after their arrest, defiantly shouting slogans.
Here at the island, several months later, she wore a somewhat peculiar doll-
collared blouse and a more cheerful expression. *Good day, Doctor*, Elena
greeted Montesinos. He courteously waved the couple to a seat.

It had been Montesinos's strategy to woo the couple and yet keep them
off balance. Now, he said, he had a surprise, switching on a video player.
Frank Sinatra belted "My Way" at full volume. *Regrets, I've had a few,
but then again, too few to mention.* Montesinos had learned that this was
Augusta La Torre's favorite song—and he liked Sinatra too. (He did not
realize that the dead leader preferred Vicente Fernández's Spanish version.) He wanted to upset Elena by playing it, a reminder that she was
only a latecomer to Abimael's affection. That way she could more easily
be manipulated, or so hoped Montesinos, who prided himself as the con-
summate counterinsurgency operative. He wanted to convince Elena and
Abimael to sign a peace agreement unconditionally surrendering to the
government.

His new friends smiled uncomfortably. Elena squeezed Abimael's hand,
and, secretly, wondered at Montesinos's making them listen to the dead
Augusta's anthem. *What an idiot*, she thought. Watching a grainy videocas-
sette of "My Way" changed nothing at all.

No agreement would ever be reached. Eventually, after some negotia-
tion, Abimael did read a televised statement, a declaration of his willingness to negotiate for the remaining *senderistas* to lay down their arms. The
statement acknowledged that the "objective reality of class struggle requires
fighting for a peace agreement," even calling their preliminary talks a "matter of transcendental importance." Other captured Central Committee
members also signed the statement, but it was a holding action. The *senderista* leader had no interest in an actual accord unless it entailed their release.
His supporters repeatedly called for reconciliation and a general amnesty

over the next decades. A grieving, unforgiving Peru did not want any Shining Path commanders freed under any circumstances.

That their great guide had mentioned peace created consternation among his remaining followers. Some suggested that Abimael might have been drugged or tortured, or that the video was faked. The top *senderista* still at large, Óscar Ramírez, broke away from the party, declaring Abimael no longer its leader. Ramírez had never forgotten that humiliating self-criticism session back at the party congress. His "black" Shining Path faction retreated, like the last Inca emperors, to the jungle. Army troops captured Rámirez in 1999. The captain of the pro-Abimael "red" loyalists, Florindo Eleuterio, Comrade Artemio, managed to evade government forces for more than a decade. In 2012 he was wounded and arrested by police commandos. Comrade Artemio had appeared in the infamous *Zorba the Greek* video. His capture meant that every Central Committee member had been imprisoned or killed.

A smug Montesinos took credit for the war's conclusion. As a memento from the battle against the villainous terrorists, he kept a book of Mao's writing autographed by Abimael. His unfulfilled hope, bizarrely, was to coauthor a book with the Shining Path leader. Abimael would write about the war in the first part, then Montesinos would describe how he had cleverly manipulated the *senderistas* into peace talks. The spymaster commissioned a documentary, too. *Avalanche in the Andes* spliced footage of the fall of the Berlin Wall, the Tarata bombing, and Montesinos's conversations with Abimael over a soundtrack that included, unaccountably, another Frank Sinatra song, "New York, New York." He gave copies to visiting dignitaries at his fortified luxury villa.

The reign of *El Chino* and Montesinos lasted a decade. Fujimori easily won reelection in 1995, and then, despite fraud accusations, a third term five years later. His government crushed the smaller MRTA rebellion as well. When those rebels took hostages at the Japanese embassy in 1996, Fujimori supervised the commando raid to free them (a hostage crisis fictionalized in Ann Patchett's *Bel Canto*). He reportedly gave the order to shoot surrendered MRTA leaders afterwards. His approval ratings received a big boost from the dramatic televised spectacle.

But Fujimori's presidency crumbled almost overnight in 2000. A television station released the so-called Vladivideos, secretly recorded tapes of *El Chino*'s manipulator-in-chief bribing everyone from media moguls to politicians and military commanders. "We all need to work together," Montesinos told Alberto Kouri, an opposition congressman, before handing him $15,000 in cash to join Fujimori's ruling party. The videos scandalized even cynical Peruvians. After various soap opera twists, the disgraced Montesinos fled Lima by night in a sailboat. He was extradited from Venezuela (despite having undergone plastic surgery to avoid being identified), then jailed for racketeering, murder, and drug trafficking. The president's right-hand man would eventually be convicted of ordering Gustavo Gorriti's 1992 kidnapping, among other charges.

Then it became Fujimori's turn to flee the country. After the scandalous revelations in the Vladivideos, public outcry forced the president to seek refuge in Japan. New investigations showed that *El Chino* had come away with $600 million in graft money with Montesinos's help. (According to Transparency International, Fujimori ranked as the world's seventh-most-corrupt head of state during his time in office.) Prosecutors investigated charges of forced sterilizations of Andean women under his administration. The former president was extradited from Chile to face trial in 2005, and, after a complex trial, given a twenty-five-year sentence for authorizing the Grupo Colina's Barrios Altos massacre and various other crimes. A corrupt dictator, many said, who should die in prison. His boosters, the *fujimoristas*, credited their man with ending terrorism, and, after the *fujishock*, the economy's improvement under his government. A controversial Christmas 2017 pardon freed the cancer-stricken Fujimori, an old man by then. The *fujimoristas* under his daughter Keiko's command remained a force to be reckoned with in national politics.

Many people had doubted Gustavo Gorriti's reporting about the Fujimori regime and its machinations. A sinister spymaster? An antipolitician turned embezzling despot? It had seemed like melodramatic conspiracy theory at the time. Vindicated, Gustavo moved back to Peru after Fujimori's flight. He turned down an offer to become defense minister, and, eventually founded an investigative journalism center mentoring a new generation of journalists. His reporting on the massive *Lava Jato*, or Car Wash, scandal helped lead in 2018 to the resignation of the latest corrupt Peruvian president, Pedro Pablo Kuczynski.

The GEIN and its co-commanders would eventually receive fuller credit at last. After returning from his posting in Chiclayo, Miyashiro climbed the ranks to become Peru's national police chief and later a congressman. An honest policeman could have a real career after all. Things did not go so well for Miyashiro's partner, Benedicto. After a failed run for Lima mayor as the APRA party's candidate, he was arrested in a money laundering scandal. He had seemingly become the corrupt cop of Miyashiro's mother's fears. Benedicto and his old police academy buddy Miyashiro remained friends. When journalists came to his jail cell, Benedicto recounted with gusto the tale about the hunt for Abimael. His two lieutenants, Bonilla and Gil, always spoke warmly about their former boss. They gave their own interviews turning themselves into protagonists. *Success has a thousand fathers*, as Benedicto liked to say. *And failure is an orphan.*

A military tribunal of Fujimori's hooded judges gave Abimael a life sentence in 1992 without a real trial. After *El Chino* fled to Japan, the new president, Alejandro Toledo, ordered Abimael, Elena, and other *senderista* leaders to be retried. The aging rebels enraged the president by raising fists and shouting slogans in the courtroom. "We have not forgotten the bombs, the killings, and the burials of the terrorists' victims," Toledo said the next day. "There will be no more birthday cakes [for terrorists]." Abimael was soon given multiple life terms for terrorism and murder. The judge took six hours to read the verdict.

The *senderista* leader would serve his sentence in a new maximum-security navy prison. His fellow inmates there included, ironically enough, Vladimiro Montesinos as well as the MRTA leader Víctor Polay and the dissident Óscar Ramírez. One story circulated about the rebel chief and the fallen spymaster sometimes playing chess together. It was not true, Elena said. "Abimael never liked to play games." She had been transferred to a new high-security facility, Piedras Gordas Penitentiary, an hour up the coast. "Like my skin being torn away," Elena described her separation from Abimael. They formally married in 2010 to claim annual visitation rights.

Abimael grew old in his cell. He did not especially like watching television, an old-school believer in the written word. His first two volumes of party history came out online. They amounted to a tedious compendium of plenaries, plans, and positions. (Chapter titles included "General Political Line and Reconstruction," "Internal Struggles and the VI National Conference," and "Defending the Life of the Party.") Only a final volume about the war years remained yet to be written. The greatest Peruvian poet, César Vallejo, might have wondered whether there was anything left to say:

Y si después de tantas palabras / no sobrevive la palabra.

And what if after so many words / the word does not survive.

Epilogue

A low-slung concrete building wedges into the crumbling bluffs above Lima's oceanfront. The Memory Place for Tolerance and Social Inclusion, its awkward official name, opened in 2015, a museum about the war years. With artifacts and high-definition video, it covers main events from Uchuraccay to the Grupo Colina and the Tarata bombing. The bare grey lines of the building's architecture follow the mournful anti–Arc de Triomphe tradition of Maya Lin's Vietnam Veterans Memorial and the later United States Holocaust Memorial Museum. War has no winners, these bleak postmodern memorials tell us. The Memory Place wants every Peruvian to know something about the María Elenas, the slaughtered peasants, and the atrocities of Shining Path and the military. We must learn from the past's mistakes to avoid repeating them, as the modern mantra has it.

Attendance at the museum has somewhat disappointed its organizers. Only some school groups, random Limans, and the occasional foreign tourist wander through on many days. An early-twentieth-century French sociologist, Robert Hertz, noted how the "unquiet souls" of the war dead can haunt the living. But most Peruvians do not seem very interested in the Shining Path years. Many are too young to remember the conflict or were not even born yet. In a fleeting moment of optimism and openness after the fall of Fujimori's quasi-dictatorial rule, the new government established a Truth and Reconciliation Commission to provide a public accounting of the war's fuller history. Both the *senderistas* and the Peruvian military hated its nine-volume report for documenting their brutality. That the commission was largely composed of white Lima professionals did not help its credibility with Andean villagers. Some peasants dismissively derided the *Cumisión Llullamanta,* or "Lie Commission," refusing to be interviewed. They wanted monetary reparations for lost loved ones, and some eventually received small payments.

A few fine war memoirs appeared. Lurgio Gavilán's *When Rains Became Floods* documented the peasant boy's odyssey from *senderista* combatant to army sergeant, Franciscan priest, and then anthropology professor. One day, a surprised Gavilán received a lunch invitation from Mario Vargas Llosa. The novelist had made peace with Peru, again returning most summers to Barranco. *We want to make a movie based on your book,* the Nobel Prize winner said. Vargas Llosa would write the screenplay himself.

———

It can sometimes seem as if nothing has changed in Peru. "A beggar on a throne of gold," the nineteenth-century critic Manuel González Prado once described the country. As back in Viceroy Toledo's day, the mining industry powers the growing Peruvian economy, and yet the shacks of impoverished migrants still cling to hills at Lima's outer edges. The city has a population of over ten million, an immense tangle of traffic-choked roads bulldozed through crumbling Chimú pyramids. Thieving politicians remain a constant. "I'm going to drown five hundred congressmen and some sewer rats," one man says to another. "Why the rats?" comes the joke's reply.

The country has reinvented itself in other ways. Back in the war's darkest hours, no one could have imagined the five-star Lima restaurants or the crowded shopping malls. Even the former ground zero for Shining Path, Ayacucho, brims downtown with small businesses and street life nowadays. Limited progress has been made nationwide towards reducing rural poverty, and, in the cities, upwardly mobile *cholos* have browned the growing middle classes as well. The intrepid village-born photographer, Óscar Medrano, built a big house for his family in the comfortable Surco district. He and millions more Peruvians continue to speak Quechua and many lesser-known indigenous languages. A well-known rock group, Uchpa, performs in the Incan tongue, and a young Amazonian rapper, Gaviota Tello, has a viral video in her native Kukama. "Tradition is alive and mobile," José Carlos Mariátegui recognized long ago. "Quite the opposite from what the traditionalists want to think."

It remains a hard life in the Andean countryside. Back in the heights of Huaychao, unmarried peasant girls continue to brim their hats with flowers, only plastic ones nowadays. A health clinic operated briefly before shuttering, and, when the teachers do not come up from the city, the village school also closes. Most young Huaychainos must leave to find their fortune, or, more likely, a menial job like wheelbarrowing cement at a construction site in Ayacucho or Lima. A new guerrilla insurgency might find some takers in the neglected backcountry even now.

The biggest attraction of Peru for foreigners is still the great stone ruin of Machu Picchu. Its splendid heights seldom disappoint, even though the swarming crowds can make the ancient Incan citadel feel more like Grand Central Station. All three top Shining Path leaders had connections to the Lost City of the Incas—the smiling Elena Iparraguirre guiding American tourists there in the early 1960s; Abimael Guzmán and Augusta La Torre making a honeymoon stop there before returning to Ayacucho to plan their war. What visitor to Machu Picchu knows that now—or would care? Nor do many people realize that the *senderistas* bombed the tourist train back in 1986.

But the war's aging protagonists forget nothing. The bloody 1980s marked their lives forever, and, no matter their role, they have stories to tell about Peru's own Tolstoian epic of war and peace. Abimael's navy jailers allow no visitors besides his lawyer, and, once a year, Elena. "Our work, yours and mine, is over," he wrote to her a few years after the war's end. The party, they claim, no longer exists. Some question that, and, in any event, a Shining Path–allied organization, MOVADEF, holds occasional street rallies and stirs up trouble now and then. Abimael was brought to a military courtroom in 2017 to be retried for the Tarata bombing, along with a few other *senderista* leaders. The stooped, almost toothless octogenarian warmly hugged his aging terrorist comrades. He flashed his old form to deliver a caustic speech about the trial's "farce" and get himself expelled from the courtroom. "You don't know who you're dealing with!" Abimael warned before the bailiffs led him away. He was no King Lear or Oedipus, able to recognize the madness of his illusions at the end of it all.

The Piedras Gordas maximum-security penitentiary lies in the desert at Lima's far northern limits. Elena's cellblock holds twenty or so aging *senderista* ladies, mostly former party leaders. Older Peruvians recall her from TV news footage as a severe woman, like a Marxist Frau Farbissina from the Austin Powers movies. The real Elena is pleasant, attractive, and forceful at almost seventy. She writes poetry and paints well. (A self-portrait recalling her solitary confinements owes debts to Picasso's *Guernica* and Munch's *The Scream*.) The graying matrons at Piedras Gordas no longer goose-step with lighted torches and fake machine guns as in the old Shining Path days. Their collectivist spirit still shows in the cellblock's tidy common area, group meals, and language and art classes. Elena teaches French. Her rank makes her the cellblock's queen bee, the first among equals. In another life, she might have been a capable corporate executive.

A more tempered Elena no longer displays quite the same arrogant Maoist certainty. "We committed many errors," she admits. "Things got out of control." That admission does not extend to any real remorse, however, and Elena does not dwell for long upon the war's human costs. The armed struggle for a Communist country, she claims, had a productive outcome despite the more than 70,000 deaths. "Oppressed people know their rights now!" It would be unthinkable for Elena to acknowledge that their revolution actually left little trace besides the mutilated bodies and a wrecked country. "I'd do it again, only do it better," Elena says. She complains about being held when imprisoned armed rebels in Colombia and Northern Ireland have received amnesty by now.

A good revolutionary keeps her spirits. "I'm hopeful about the future because with computers young people can inform themselves about everything," she says. When a visitor explains about pornography, video games, and other online time wasters, Elena looks only momentarily disappointed. She will likely not set foot beyond the razor wire again. Others will determine the planet's fate.

Across the Atlantic, Gustavo Pineki, María Elena's widower, does not especially like sharing his stories. "It's too soon to talk," Gustavo excused himself to a reporter after her murder. "The boys are the main thing now." He fled to Madrid in 1992 to raise Gustavo Jr., David, and their cousin Jorge in a working-class Madrid neighborhood among other exiles, migrants, and refugees. They kept a shrine to María Elena in their apartment's living room for many years: pictures, some keepsakes, a crucifixion. The boys grew up to marry Spanish women, and, eventually, Gustavo packed away the shrine after remarrying himself. He tells little María Elena, Gustavo Jr.'s girl, stories about her famous grandmother, and yet still tries to avoid the occasional interview request. The retired cabinetmaker feels no need to explain, justify, and lathe history's loose boards to his own specifications.

Many villagers do not like discussing the war either. "My father will not come alive again," one Ayacuchan peasant explained refusing to testify before the Truth and Reconciliation Commission. "It would be for nothing." Country people like him, this man believed, already knew what had happened in that age of death and sadness anyway. Only the *ciudadrunakuna,* city dwellers, might not. Nor do former peasant supporters of the *senderistas* especially want to admit their original enthusiasms. *We were deceived,* many will say.

The voluble Narciso Sulca has never been reticent about his wartime adventures. At almost fifty, he remains a pixiesh man, by turns thoughtful, boastful, and sad. His Huaychao had risen up against the *senderistas* only for Narciso to be left as poor as ever with shrapnel in his leg. He and his wife, Asunción, now live in a canyon a few miles above Huanta. They make a slim living herding a wealthier peasant's cows up into the *jalca,* the mountaintop pastures, and then back down to their makeshift corral in the evening. Their little boy brings up water for cooking and washing from the creek, and, when they have enough milk, Asunción makes salty cheeses to sell at the market. Their farmhouse in the eroded gully is a long walk from the nearest neighbors. Narciso wants a house in town, without much expectation that it will ever happen.

Nothing is ever certain, that much Narciso knows. He remembers how the young *senderistas* descended from the hill to their deaths at the judgment rock three decades before. They sang a sad ballad:

Adiós pueblo de Ayacucho / Goodbye, land of Ayacucho,
paqarinmi ripuchkani perlaschayay / Tomorrow I'll return
kawsaspaycha kutimusaq / I'll return if I live
wañuspayqa manañacha / Not if I die

The *senderistas* had joined the wandering dead spirits in the lonely night. It could just as easily have been Narciso to writhe helplessly against the strangling rope that day, the peasant boy who had thought about joining the *cumpas* himself. "It's only thanks to God I'm alive," he nods.

Every evening Narciso rounds up the cattle from the moors.

His whistle drives the animals down the darkening canyon.

SOURCES AND ACKNOWLEDGMENTS

We have followed the story of Shining Path for more than five decades between us. When Orin Starn was a young anthropologist back in the 1980s, he cowered under a table during a rebel surprise attack in the Andes. Miguel La Serna, still a child, happily sang "Happy Birthday" when his *abuelita* lit the candles after the latest guerrilla-induced blackout. Both of us wrote about the war, too. Speaking with top Shining Path commanders was almost impossible back then, however, and many Peruvians were not ready to come forward to tell their stories. The smoke and fear complicated the best efforts to make sense of wartime experiences in their full complexity.

It has been long enough to know much more about those dramatic years. In writing *The Shining Path*, we have drawn on much fine scholarship about the rebels. Foundational writings by Carlos Iván Degregori and Gustavo Gorriti set the standard for studying the *senderistas*. Other researchers helped to establish "Senderology" as its own little field, including valuable anthologies edited by David Scott Palmer and Steve J. Stern. More recent work sheds new light on topics like the rebel command structure and the politics of postwar memory. We are indebted to studies by journalists Umberto Jara, Carlos Tipe, and Ricardo Uceda; historians Ponciano Del Pino, Jaymie Heilman, Lewis Taylor, and Antonio Zapata; anthropologists Olga González, Kimberly Theidon, and Caroline Yezer. Memoirs by José Carlos Agüero and Lurgio Gavilán, with his extraordinary *When Rains Became Floods*, give us views from inside the insurgency. We invite readers to consult our endnotes for ideas about further reading.

The Shining Path draws extensively on our own archival research. We gained access to a thirty-eight-volume set of unpublished Shining Path documents held by Peru's Anti-Terrorism Directorate (DINCOTE). The trial records of the so-called *megajuicio*, the "megatrial," of Shining Path leaders, provided another voluminous source. In addition to nine published volumes, the Peruvian Truth and Reconciliation Commission kept recordings of many interviews. We also gathered stray documents—village record books; army propaganda pamphlets; Shining Path flyers; presidential letters; CIA and State Department cables. The war left a massive paper trail with much still to tell future researchers.

We interviewed over two hundred people for the book. They included key wartime figures like Gustavo Gorriti and Elena Iparraguirre, both over multiple sessions, and many lesser-known ones—old friends and family of María Elena Moyano; village witnesses to Shining Path assaults; GEIN agents and military officers. We returned to Ayacucho, Huanta, and Huaychao, which Starn first visited in 1991 and La Serna wrote a book mostly about. Our research also took us for the first time to Ayzarca, Villa El Salvador, and other places that appear in these pages. Our interviewing spanned Peru, the United States, Canada, Spain, Italy, and Sweden. Some people had never fully shared their war memories with researchers, among them Augusta La Torre's mother, Delia Carrasco, and Shining Path Central Committee member Osmán Morote.

Perhaps the biggest novelty for us was speaking with *senderista* leaders. We had only previously interviewed deserters and lower-level imprisoned fighters. Through his lawyer, Abimael Guzmán expressed his willingness to talk with us, but his military jailers prevented that. We did spend considerable time with Elena Iparraguirre, María Pantoja, Angélica Salas, and other imprisoned leaders at the Piedras Gordas penitentiary as well as with Osmán Morote after his 2018 release to house arrest. In addition, Carlos Incháustegui warmly assisted us, sharing stories about hiding Guzmán and Iparraguirre before their capture. We also met Incháustegui's former partner, Maritza Garrido, in prison. She was freed in 2017 after serving her twenty-five-year sentence.

Getting to know prominent *senderistas* had its peculiar moments.

"You know, *Señora*," Starn half-joked to Iparraguirre one day, "your people almost killed me a few times."

"Oh, no, *Doctor*, we always distinguished between the individual and imperialist countries."

Actually, the *senderistas* killed a number of random American, French, German, and Japanese tourists and aid workers. It was part of their master plan for isolating Peru in preparation for the final assault, a strategy which Iparraguirre had earlier explained to us herself (though acknowledging regret for the slaying of a few stray backpackers). But now, thirty years later, it seemed better just to let that be and go on with the interview. In the first of our six all-day conversations, we explained to Iparraguirre that our book would not be flattering, that we intended to write the history as we saw it. All Iparraguirre asked, fairly enough, was for her views to be accurately presented. We have tried our best to do that for everyone who appears in these pages.

Our research forced us to think anew about the *senderistas*. We learned more about the crucial role of two women, Iparraguirre and Augusta La Torre, in captaining the war. Many *senderistas*, Iparraguirre among them, proved more well-traveled, better-educated, and cosmopolitan than we had expected. The rebels could indeed be stone-cold killers, and their aging jailed leader was as dogmatic as ever in his Callao jail cell. The tragedy was that their motivating desire to end poverty and injustice was so admirable, at least in the abstract. History smiles, deservedly so, on María Elena Moyano, Marco Miyashiro, Benedicto Jiménez (whatever or not his later sins), Gustavo Gorriti, Narciso Sulca, and others who fought to save Peru from a backward Communist dictatorship. All of our book's characters proved to be complex and sometimes contradictory in the inevitable human way. Our aim has been to chronicle rather than to pass judgment, without imagining it is ever entirely possible to do one without the other.

We chose to write *The Shining Path* as a conventional third-person historical narrative, albeit a would-be readable one. The task of reconstructing events as they occurred in the moment presented many challenges, not least being just what and whom to believe. Written documents speak only partial truths, for that matter. Doing our best to ensure accuracy required crosschecking, verifying, and exercising our informed judgements about reliability. *The Shining Path* contains much dialogue, trying where possible to convey the inner thoughts of its characters. Our wish has been to do justice to the human drama of their stories.

It was both rewarding and necessary for us to work together. Neither of us could have written this book alone. The story's epic sweep demanded our pooled experience and research efforts. An anthropologist and a historian, we brought complementary skills and perspectives, and our own different histories of engagement in Peru. We conducted some interviews together, some separately, and exchanged chapter drafts on the way to the final manuscript.

We owe many people thanks for their help along the way. Our agent, Gail Ross, provided her customary indefatigable guidance. Gail's associate, Dara Kaye, gave savvy feedback to set the project on its way. It proved our marvelous good fortune to have W. W. Norton's Tom Mayer for an editor. Only thanks to his spectacular editing and enabling enthusiasm did we manage to get the book to the end. Emma Hitchcock and Nneoma Amadi-obi gave indispensable guidance too.

For kind assistance beyond duty's call, *mil gracias* to: Walter Alejos, Carlos Aguirre, Renzo Aroní, Roberto Ayala, Michel Azcueta, Diana Bachand, Michelle Berger, Lori Berenson, Ruth Borja, Fitz Brundage, José Burneo, Kathryn Burns, Jo-Marie Burt, Roberto Bustamante, Andrea Cabel, Leigh Campoamor, Miguel Canales, Pedro Cárdenas, Sebastián Carassai, Ricardo Caro, Rosario Casquero, John Chasteen, Sebastián Chávez Wurm, Fredy Cisneros, Mariana Dantas, Cathy Davidson, Paulo Drinot, Kathleen DuVal, Josefin Ekermann, Manuel Fajardo, "Juan Fulano," Joe Glatthaar, Zenaida Gógora, Gisela Fosado, Shane Greene, Michael Hardt, Leandro Huamán, Rebecca Karl, Richard Kernagahan, Gabi Kuenzli, Luis Lumbreras, Cathy Lutz, Alberto Morote, Katia Morote, Osmán Morote, Diane Nelson, Angel Paez, David Scott Palmer, Tony Palomino, María Pantoja, José Luis Rénique, Rocío Paz, Nelson Pereyra, Lou Pérez, Gustavo Pineki Jr., Neal Prose, Cynthia Radding, John Rick, Angélica Salas, Tatiana Seijas, Alpa Shah, Irene Silverblatt, Francisco Soberón, Patrick Stawski, Rebecca Stein, William Sturkey, Brendan Thornton, Charo Torres, Joshua Tucker, George Vickers, Caroline Yezer, Coletta Youngers, Victor Vich, Chuck Walker, Ben Waterhouse, Brett Whalen, Luise White, Mikael Wikstrom, Ken Wissoker, Shellen Wu, Alexei Yurchak, Laura Zambrano, Antonio Zapata, and Marco Zileri.

We gratefully acknowledge fellowship support from the National Humanities Center (via the Andrew W. Mellon Foundation's John E. Sawyer Fellowship) and the American Council of Learned Societies. Brooke Andrade and her phenomenal team at the NHC tracked down elusive sources. At Duke University, we had key help from Tracy Carhart, Natalie

Hartman, the Duke Center for Latin American and Caribbean Studies, and the Trent Foundation. At the University of North Carolina at Chapel Hill, Adam Kent, Joyce Loftin, Jennifer Parker, Beatriz Riefkhol, the Institute for the Study of the Americas, the Institute for the Arts and Humanities, and the Department of History, offered unwavering support. The Duke and UNC-Chapel Hill librarians, Holly Ackerman and Teresa Chapa, provided remarkable assistance as always.

Very special thanks to: Nancy and Betty Angéles, Mats Dannetun, Óscar Arriola, Julián Berrocal, Cecilia Blondet, Alejandro "Chan" Coronado, José Coronel, Marisol de la Cadena, Esther Delgado, Karina Fernández, Marcelita Gutiérrez, Leandro Huamán, Walter Huamaní, Carlos Incháustegui, Ralph Litzinger, Óscar Medrano, Wilder Méndez, Diana Miloslavich, William Mitchell, Marina Rodinó, Mario Rossi, Guido Sattin, and Vladimir Uñapillco. Jaymie Heilman provided tremendously smart feedback on draft chapters. So, too, did Julia Lovell and, that master of Peruvian agrarian studies, Lewis Taylor. A departed friend, Carlos Iván Degregori, spoke to us from across the divide.

Several key people gave especially crucial help with the book. We are grateful to Lurgio Gavilán, Elena Iparraguirre, Benedicto Jiménez, Marco Miyashiro, and Miguel's *compadre*, Narciso Sulca. Martha Moyano and Gustavo Pineki shared memories about María Elena Moyano; Humberto La Torre and Delia Carrasco did so for Augusta La Torre. Alfredo Crespo provided indispensable assistance at many points.

Thank you Gustavo Gorriti and Ponciano Del Pino—for your remarkable insight, generous support, and unstinting friendship.

Our families make everything possible for us. Orin: to beloved friends who count as family by now in Anne Allison and Charlie Piot; Enrique Bossio and Lucien Chauvin, the Córdova-Paz clan; to my children, Frances, Ray, Lucien; and, of course, to my best friend, wisest counselor, and true love, Katya Wesolowski. Miguel: to my Peruvian family who helped at every step, and in loving memory of *tío* Ricardo La Serna; to my sister and brother, Korah and Matías; to my children and inspiration, Mateo Gael and Micaela Renee; and to Jillian Joy, always.

We dedicate this book to our beloved parents, Randy and Frances, Sabad and Susan.

Qawkalla kawsakusun.

NOTES

Prologue

11 **"Good evening, Guzmán"**: Frecuencia Latina. *Punto Final* [video file], May 24, 2014. Retrieved from www.youtube.com/watch?v=4-uKF6et2a0. All translations are by the authors, unless otherwise noted. Thanks to Julián Berrocal and Ponciano Del Pino for checking the Quechua ones.

12 *Make this traitor Communist piece of shit*: "Abimael Guzmán declaran imprescriptible," *El Comercio*, February 16, 2016, www.elcomercio.pe/politica/justicia /abimael-guzman-declaran-imprescriptible-caso-arata-noticia-1974139; "Abimael Guzmán presentaría un cuadro de deshidratación severa," *Correo*, February 6, 2016, www.diariocorreo.pe/politica/abimael-guzman-presentaria-un-cuadro -de-deshidratacion-severa-727654/.

12 **"Miriam, my only one"**: Abimael Guzmán Reinoso, *De puño y letra* (Los Olivos, Peru: Manoalzada, 2009), 351.

13 **"an almost built-in optimism"**: Comité Central Partido Comunista del Perú (CCPCP), "Entrevista al Presidente Gonzalo," 1988, www.solrojo.org/pcp_doc /pcp_0688.htm.

Chapter One: The Train to Machu Picchu

17 **Susan had just split up**: Phone interview with Susan Bradshaw, June 19, 2015.

17 **Buz ran his own travel company:** Phone interview with Buz Donahoo, April 17, 2015.

18 **"they have no love of foreign tourists":** John Brooks, ed., *The 1986 South American Handbook* (Bath, UK: Trade and Travel Publications, 1986), 754.

19 **"Mother of stone / condor's foam":** Pablo Neruda, *Canto General: Song of the Americas*, trans. Mariela Griffor (North Adams, MA: Tupelo Press, 2015), 29.

19 **Guevara described the citadel:** Ernesto Guevara, "Machu-Picchu, Enigma de piedra en América," December 12, 1953, http://cheguevaralibros.com/web/es /articulo/show/Machu-Picchu,-enigma-de-piedra-en-Am%C3%A9rica/32. The best biography of Guevara remains Jon Lee Anderson's *Che: A Revolutionary Life* (New York: Grove, 2010).

20 **"bloody, indiscriminate terrorist aggression":** *Caretas*, "La Mochila Roja," June 30, 1986, 18.

20 **"Violence is a universal law":** CCPCP, "Entrevista al Presidente Gonzalo." Guzmán was quoting Mao here.

20 **studied philosophy at Jerusalem's Hebrew University:** Interview with Gustavo Gorriti, Lima, June 18, 2015.

21 **"I don't publish your excuses":** Interview with Óscar Medrano, Lima, May 29, 2015.

22 **"A master of disguise":** Simon Strong, *Shining Path: The World's Deadliest Revolutionary Force* (London: HarperCollins, 1992), 46.

22 **"It was sheer luck":** Interview with Gustavo Gorriti, Lima, August 4, 2016.

23 **"Reading is traveling":** The phrase is widely attributed to Salgari, though never sourced.

23 **not just to "understand society but to change it":** Karl Marx, "Theses on Feuerbach," 1845, www.marxists.org/archive/marx/works/1845/theses/theses.htm.

24 *"Allinllachu taytay"*: Interview with Óscar Medrano, Lima, May 29, 2015.

25 **"Peru owes its misfortune":** Alejandro Deustua, *La cultura nacional* (Lima: Author, 1937), 68.

26 **"It turned scary quiet":** Interview with Raymond Starr (a pseudonym), Durham, NC, February 20, 2018.

26 **"Journalists are liars":** Gustavo Gorriti, *The Shining Path: A History of the Millenarian War in Peru*, trans. Robin Kirk (Chapel Hill: University of North Carolina Press, 1999), 149–150.

26 **"from a well of sadness":** Ibid.,150.

26 **An older officer noticed:** Interview with Óscar Medrano, Lima, August 24, 2016.

27 **Gorriti wrote a story:** Gorriti, "La búsqueda del Sendero," *Caretas*, October 26, 1981, 22–25, 80.

27 **"People killing each other":** The song, "Mamacha de las Mercedes," was written and sung by Martina Portocarrero.

27 **Nearly 70,000 Peruvians would perish:** The best available statistics can be found in the final report of Peru's 2003 Truth and Reconciliation Commission. The full Spanish version was published as Comisión de la Verdad y Reconciliación (CVR), *Informe Final* (Lima: Universidad Nacional Mayor de San Marcos/

Pontificia Universidad Católica del Perú, 2004). The report is partially available on-line in English translation at www.cverdad.org.pe/ingles/. Both the military and Shining Path have challenged the commission's findings, each claiming lesser responsibility. For more about the politics of postwar memory, see Ponciano del Pino and Caroline Yezer, eds., *Las formas del recuerdo: Etnografías de la violencia política en el Perú* (Lima: Instituto de Estudios Peruanos, 1983); Olga González, *Unveiling the Secrets of War in the Peruvian Andes* (Chicago: University of Chicago Press, 2011); Kimberly Theidon, *Intimate Enemies: Violence and Reconciliation in Peru* (Philadelphia: University of Pennsylvania Press, 2014).

28 **"untranscendable philosophy"**: Jean-Paul Sartre, *Critique of Practical Reason: Theory of Practical Ensembles*, trans. Alan Sheridan-Smith (New York: Verso, 1991), 822.

29 **"The future lies in guns and cannons"**: Comité Central Ampliado Partido Comunista del Perú (CCAPCP), "Somos los Iniciadores," 1980, www.solrojo.org /pcp_doc/pcp_240880.htm.

29 **"the ruthless extermination"**: V. I. Lenin, "Lessons of the Commune," 1908, https://www.marxists.org/archive/lenin/works/1908/mar/23.htm.

29 *Forgiveness did not exist in the party*: Lurgio Gavilán, *When Rains Became Floods: A Child Soldier's Story*, trans. Margaret Randall (Durham: Duke University Press, 2015), 19.

29 **A "dwarf star"**: Carlos Iván Degregori, "A Dwarf Star," NACLA: *Report on the Americas*, 1990, Vol. 24, No. 2, 10–38.

30 **the United States employed its own brutal means:** Greg Grandin gives a compelling history of ugly US Cold War tactics in Latin America—and their later application in the post-9/11 "war on terror"—in *Empire's Workshop: Latin America, the United States, and the Rise of the New Imperialism* (New York: Holt, 2007).

31 **"She sacrificed everything"**: Personal communication, Humberto La Torre, October 5, 2015.

31 **"An Ayacucho afternoon in April"**: Guzmán, *De puño*, 347.

Chapter Two: A Tree Can Be a Weapon

32 **It was raining early in 1962:** Abimael Guzmán and Elena Yparraguirre, *Memorias desde Nemesis* (Author: 2015), 32.

33 **"He was polite"**: Interview with Delia Carrasco, Stockholm, Sweden, August 22, 2016.

33 **ambitions to become a top university:** Carlos Iván Degregori, *El Surgimiento de Sendero Liminoso. Ayacucho: 1969–1979* (Lima: Instituto de Estudios Peruanos, 1990), 42, 56–58.

33 **"We thought we were geniuses"**: Interview with Luis Lumbreras, Lima, August 12, 2016.

34 **no novelty . . . to arrive a stranger in a new place:** For more on Guzmán's childhood, see Guzmán, *De puño*; Guzmán and Yparraguirre, *Memorias*; Santiago

Roncagliolo, *La Cuarta Espada: La historia de Abimael Guzmán y Sendero Luminoso* (Barcelona: Random House, 1997); Simon Strong, *Shining Path* (London: HarperCollins, 1992); LUM. *La vida segreta de Abimael Guzmán Reynoso, Parte 1* [video file], February 18, 2016. Retrieved from www.youtube.com/watch?v=0c1XC3KRV1s.

34 **"Something of the Andes surely stayed":** Guzmán, *De puño*, 28.

34 **"My son, take care":** Ibid.

34 **Leaving children with relatives was quite common:** See Jessaca Leinaweaver, *The Circulation of Children: Kinship, Adoption, and Morality in Andean Peru* (Durham: Duke University Press, 2008).

35 **Arequipa's most exclusive high school:** Guzmán, *De puño*, 31–33; CVR, Entrevista a Abimael Guzmán Reynoso y Elena Iparraguirre, May 28, 2002.

35 **A half sister of Abimael's described:** Susana Guzmán, *En Mi Noche de Fortuna* (Madrid: Montesinos, 1999).

35 **kept a Parker fountain pen she gave him:** Interview with Elena Iparraguirre, Piedras Gordas, August 20, 2017.

35 **"He was introverted . . . but he had a great sense of friendship":** This college friend of Abimael was interviewed in *La vida segreta de Abimael Guzmán Reynoso*.

36 **"Copy that . . . Lieutenant, Sir":** Montesinos, *Sin Sendero*, Vol. 1, 257–258. Although not generally a reliable source, Montesinos interviewed Guzmán extensively; this anecdote about military training class comes from those taped conversations.

37 **"lyrical affirmations":** Abimael Guzmán Reinoso, "El estado democrático-burgués," (B.A. Thesis, Universidad Nacional de Arequipa, Facultad de Letras, 1961), 187.

37 **"space has a material reality":** Abimael Guzmán Reinoso, "Acerca de la teoría kantiana del espacio," (B.A. Thesis, Universidad Nacional de Arequipa, Facultad de Letras, 1961), 165.

38 **"At the head of each group":** Strong, *Shining Path*, 23.

38 **a "dedicated Communist":** Guzmán, *De puño*, 56.

38 *You can't understand Peru unless you go:* Armando Barrera, interviewed in LUM, *La Vida Segreta de Abimael Guzmán Reynoso*.

38 **Efraín Morote, greeted his newest hire:** Jara, *Abimael*, 59.

39 **"Their families made big sacrifices":** Interview with Alberto Morote, Lima, August 6, 2016.

39 **Does God exist?:** Interview with Juana López (a pseudonym), Lima, June 7, 2015.

39 **"He was serious":** Quoted in Strong, *Shining Path*, 31.

40 **"the single passion for revolution":** Sergei Nachayev, "The Revolutionary Catechism," 1869, www.marxists.org/subject/anarchism/nechayev/catechism.htm.

40 **the revolution's priestly elect:** See Kenneth Jowitt, *New World Order: The Leninist Extinction* (Berkeley: University of California Press, 1992).

40 **"Without a Communist Party . . . nothing will be done":** Archivo de la Dirección Contra el Terrorismo (ADINCOTE). *Documentación de la Organización Terrorista 'Sendero Luminoso,' Tomo XXIX*, 22. These thirty-eight volumes are

held by the Peruvian Anti-Terrorism Directorate and were curated by Abimael Guzmán and Elena Iparraguirre after their capture.

42 **"the bonds of hunger, ignorance, and poverty"**: John F. Kennedy, "Special Message to the Congress on the Peace Corps," March 1, 1961, www.presidency.ucsb .edu/ws/index.php?pid=8515.

42 **"monster of the north"**: José Martí, *Inside the Monster: Writings on the United States and American Imperialism*, trans. Philip Foner (New York: Monthly Review Press, 1975).

42 **a foreigner could be a *pishtaco***: See Gonzalo Portocarrero, *Sacaojos y Pishtacos: Crisis Social y Fantasmas Coloniales* (Lima: TAREA, 1991) and Mary Weismantel, *Cholas and Pishtacos: Race and Sex in the Andes* (Chicago, University of Chicago Press, 1991).

43 **"And then they'd destroy us"**: Phone interview with David Scott Palmer, November 3, 2015.

43 **volunteers noticed these "foreboding signs"**: David Scott Palmer, "Expulsion from a Peruvian University," in Robert Textor, ed., *Cultural Frontiers of the Peace Corps* (Cambridge, MA: MIT Press, 1966), 255.

43 **"a big fish in a small pond"**: Phone interview with David Scott Palmer, November 3, 2015.

43 **trouble keeping her students' attention**: Phone interview with Jane Wilson (a pseudonym), November 15, 2015.

44 **charging Wilson with insulting**: Palmer, "Expulsion from a Peruvian University," 256.

44 **"misnamed Peace Corps"**: Guzmán and Yparraguirre, *Memorias*, 59.

44 **"defeat a powerful enemy"**: "'Exclusive' Comments by Abimael Guzmán," *World Affairs*, Vol. 1, No. 156 (Summer 1983), 54.

44 **"[We] felt strong"**: Ibid.

45 **"That was just politics"**: Phone interview with David Scott Palmer, November 5, 2015.

45 **The Chinese hosted more than three thousand visitors**: Matthew Rothwell, *Transpacific Revolutionaries: The Chinese Revolution in Latin America*, Ph.D. dissertation, Department of History, University of Illinois–Chicago Circle, 2009.

45 **He had hoped to visit Lenin's tomb**: Guzmán and Yparraguirre, *Memorias*, 83.

45 **killed as many as eighteen million people**: Dennis Tao Yang, "China's Agricultural Crisis and Famine of 1959–1961: A Survey and Comparison to Soviet Famines," *Comparative Economic Studies* 50 (2008), 1–29.

46 **"A tree is a weapon"**: Quoted in Roncagliolo, *La Cuarta Espada*, 70.

46 **"A humble weapon of the people"**: Ibid., 71.

46 **"like having no soul"**: Mao Zedong, "On the Correct Handling of Contradictions Among the People," February 27, 1957, www.marxists.org/reference/archive/mao /works/red-book/ch12.htm.

46 **"masterful courses"**: Guzmán and Yparraguirre, *Memorias*, 83.

47 **"It's not hard to start a revolution"**: José Sotomayor Pérez, *¿Leninismo o maoísmo?* (Lima: Editorial Universo, 1979), 24.

Chapter Three: Comrade Norah

48 **"My life is my own"**: C. Virgil Gheorghiu, *The Twenty-Fifth Hour* (New York: Knopf, 1950), 256.

48 **"Don't take it too hard"**: Ibid., 391.

49 **"ready to surrender my life"**: Ibid., 256.

49 **Augusta and her friends played** *zampay*: For this and more about Iribamba, see director Mikael Wikstrom's fine 2015 documentary *Storm in the Andes*.

49 **the La Torres kept black house servants**: Interview with Pedro Cárdenas, Ayacucho, February 13, 2017.

49 **belonged to the Communist Party**: See Jaymie Patricia Heliman, "Family Ties: The Political Genealogy of Shining Path's Comrade Norah," *Bulletin of Latin American Studies* Vol. 29, No. 22 (2010), 155–165.

49 **"Don't touch what's mine!"**: The quote comes from an unnamed family friend interviewed in *Storm in the Andes*.

50 **serving dishes being solid silver**: Interview with Elsa Coronado (a pseudonym), Huanta, June 4, 2015.

50 **"Oh, nothing. My shoe just split"**: Interview with Delia La Torre, Stockholm, August 22, 2016.

50 **"too high for a respectable lady"**: Osmán Morote Barrionuevo, "La falda descosida" in *Norah Presente: 70° aniversario, 1945–2015* (no editor or publisher given, 2015), 28–41.

51 **She stumbled around**: Interview with Gisela Huamán (a pseudonym), Huanta, June 4, 2015.

51 **"Hey, Alberto"**: Interview with Alberto Morote, Lima, June 11, 2015. See also Alberto Morote Sánchez, *Tormenta Genocida: Sucesos ignorados que precedieron al Inicio de la Lucha Armada* (Lima: Tarea Asociación Gráfica Educativa, 2016), 98.

52 **"enemies of god"**: George Politzer, *L'Esprit* (Paris: Éditions Rieder & Cie, 1926), 48.

54 **"What are you doing, Augustita?"**: Interview with Gisela Huamán, Huanta, June 15, 2015.

54 **"Woman is the most beautiful creature"**: Guzmán and Yparraguirre, *Memorias*, 14.

54 **"An extraordinarily lucid man"**: Quoted in *Perú, los senderos posibles*, Hernando Calvo Espina and Katlijn Declerq, eds. (Tafalla, Spain: Editorial Txalaparta, 1994), 130.

55 **"Augusta suffered"**: Interview with Delia Carrasco, Stockholm, August 22, 2016.

55 **Augusta's smile giving way to tears**: Interview with Sonia Meneses, Huanta, Peru, August 10, 2016.

55 **"She was a beautiful woman"**: Interview with Luis Lumbreras, Lima, August 12, 2016.

55 **They wed on February 3, 1964**: Photographer Walter Alejos Calderón, recalls

that day in *¿Casualidad o Propósito? De rockero a congresista* (Lima: Author, 2015).

56 **honeymooned at Machu Picchu:** Guzmán, *De puño,* 347.

57 **"more active involvement":** Lowell Dittmer, *China's Continuous Revolution: The Post-Liberation Epoch,* 1949–1981 (Berkeley: University of California Press, 1987), 104–5.

57 **"greatest political movement":** Quoted in Jara, *Abimael,* 141.

57 **the presents his older sister brought:** Personal communication, Humberto La Torre, Stockholm, October 5, 2015.

57 **"The Ayacuchan can't be bought":** From "Ofrenda" by the Ayacuchan musician Carlos Falconí, www.youtube.com/watch?v=HZbKR5pK1mA.

57 **"drown[ed] in exploitation":** Guzmán and Yparraguirre, *Memorias,* 37.

58 **"He was energized":** Interview with José Coronel, Ayacucho, August 12, 2016.

58 **attract more recruits:** Roncagliolo, *La Cuarta Espada,* 234.

58 **"Burning books?":** Interview with José Coronel, Ayacucho, August 12, 2016.

59 **"She looked anxious":** Interview with José Coronel, Ayacucho, Peru, June 4, 2015.

59 **"From your first timid steps":** Quoted in Calvo Ospina and Declerq, eds., *Peru,* 134.

59 **"Very intelligent":** Interview with Luis Lumbreras, Lima, August 2, 2016.

60 **"Hey there, *mamita*":** Interview with Gisela Huamán, Huanta, June 4, 2015.

60 **"We'll be there!":** Ibid.

60 **"Let's go skinny-dipping":** "Vamos Carnaval," by the Duo Ayacucho, www .musica.com/letras.asp?letra=2037478.

61 **"the Master will no longer feed":** Juan Velasco Alvarado, "'The Master Will No Longer Feed Off Your Poverty'," in *The Peru Reader,* Starn et al., eds., 279. For more on the agrarian reform, Enrique Mayer, *Ugly Stories of the Peruvian Agrarian Reform* (Durham: Duke University Press, 2009). Many older peasants still gratefully remember Velasco as their emancipator from the haciendas.

62 **schools as the "black box":** Carlos Iván Degregori, *Del Mito de Inkarri al Mito del Progreso: Migración y Cambios Culturales, Obras Escogidas III* (Lima: Instituto de Estudios Peruanos, 2013).

62 **"The largest rally ever":** Guzmán and Iparraguirre, *Memorias,* 232.

63 **"the pro-Peking agitator":** "Director del Diario 'El Paladín' denuncia complot subversivo," *El Comercio,* June 24, 1969, 4.

63 **"I doubt it":** Interview with José Coronel, Ayacucho, February 13, 2017.

64 **killing more than fourteen people:** Carlos Iván Degregori, *El surgimiento,* 61–64.

64 **"The blood of the people":** The song was composed by Ricardo Dolorier in 1970s, though about the Huanta student protests and not Shining Path.

64 **boy bleeding in the street:** Interview with Zenaida Gógora, Miraflores, December 28, 2016.

64 **"provocateur" and "Communist agitator":** *Documenting the Peruvian Insurrection* (DPI) [microfilm]. Nota de información 467, Reel Nine, Box Two.

65 **"The masses headed by Norah":** Guzmán and Yparraguirre, *Memorias*, 233.

65 **"eyes, a nose, a mouth":** Gheorghiu, *The Twenty-Fifth Hour*, 108.

Chapter Four: The Great Rupture

66 *Socorro Rojo*, **Red Aid:** This was the original name for *Socorro Popular*, a Shining Path support group.

67 **the two women headed into the city:** Interview with Elena Iparraguirre, Piedras Gordas, June 7, 2015.

67 **Elena replaced her as Abimael's wife:** For more on Iparraguirre, Antonio Zapata, *Habla el Enemigo: La Guerra Senderista* (Lima: Taurus, 2017).

67 **"It's the only way":** Interview with Elena Iparraguirre, Piedras Gordas, June 7, 2015.

68 **"Disunited States of the South":** Víctor Raúl Haya de la Torre, "El Imperialismo," 1955, www.marxists.org/espanol/haya/1950s/1955-impe.htm.

69 **overcoming her squeamishness:** See the recollections of Iparraguirre's mother, Blanca Revoredo, 2005, www.pagina-libre.org/asociacion-peru/Textos/Documentacion/08_05_Prisioneras_Elena.html.

69 **most students professed to being Maoists:** See Nicolás Lynch, *Los jóvenes rojos de San Marcos: el radicalismo universitario en los años 70* (Lima: Zorro de abajo, 1990).

69 **"narcissism of minor differences":** Sigmund Freud, *Civilization and Its Discontents* (Penguin: London, 2002), 305.

71 **"Socialist in words":** Quoted in Max Elbaum, *Revolution in the Air: Sixties Radicals Turn to Lenin, Mao, and Che* (Verso: London, 2002), 99.

71 *"Serás mujercita":* Interview with Elena Iparraguirre, Piedras Gordas, December 18, 2016.

71 **they asked no questions:** See Richard Wolin, *The Wind from the East: French Intellectuals, the Cultural Revolution, and the Legacy of the 1960s* (Princeton: Princeton University Press, 2010).

72 **"rightist liquidationist":** Guzmán and Iparrraguirre, *Memorias*, 157.

72 **only about fifty members:** Antonio Zapata, *La Guerra Senderista*, 64.

73 **"why hasn't it taken up arms yet?":** Interview with Elena Iparraguirre, Piedras Gordas, June 7, 2015.

73 **"Now we do":** Zapata, *La Guerra Senderista*, 26.

73 **"He is Professor Guzmán":** Interview with Elena Iparraguirre, Piedras Gordas, June 7, 2015.

74 **"hair austerely tied up in a bun":** Gilberto Hume, "Augusta La Torre: 1973," *Debate*, November–December 1998, 45.

75 **"How old are you?":** Interview with Elena Iparraguirre, Piedras Gordas, June 7, 2105.

75 **"The struggle of Peruvian women":** Movimiento Femenino Popular, "Declaración de Principios," 1973, www.marxists.org/espanol/adrianzen/mmmf/04.htm.

76 **recruitment efforts had been paying off:** See Robin Kirk, *The Monkey's Paw: New Chronicles from Peru* (Amherst: University of Massachusetts Press, 1997), 62–110.

76 **Women's Popular Movement agreed to expand:** CCPCP, "El Marxismo, Mariátegui y el Movimiento Femenino," 1975, www.solrojo.org/pcp_doc/pcp_0475.htm.

76 **"I don't have time for kids":** Interview with Elena Iparraguirre, Piedras Gordas, June 7, 2015.

76 **"The political work couldn't wait":** Abimael Guzmán and Elena Yparraguirre, Interview by CVR, November 6, 2002.

78 **"the time of the gun":** Vijay Prasad, "Communism and the Lost Time of the Gun." Paper delivered at "The Cultural Revolution and Beyond" conference, Duke University, October 28, 2016.

78 **"constitutionalist illusions":** Guzmán and Yparraguirre, *Memorias*, 143.

78 **"The oppressed are allowed":** V. I. Lenin, *The State and Revolution: The Economic Basis of the Withering Away of the State,* 1917, www.marxists.org/archive/lenin/works/1917/staterev/ch05.htm.

78 **"rightist opportunists":** Guzmán and Iparraguirre, *Memorias*, 509.

78 **"immediately and swiftly":** Ibid., 506.

79 **"I accept the call":** Interview with Elena Iparraguirre, Piedras Gordas, June 7, 2015.

80 **"a sack of potatoes":** Karl Marx, *The Eighteenth Brumaire of Louis Napoleon,* 1869, www.marxists.org/archive/marx/works/subject/hist-mat/18-brum/ch07.htm.

80 **"Countryside as center":** Abimael Guzmán and Elena Iparraguirre, Interview by CVR, October 21, 2002.

80 **"Lima had the military garrisons":** Interview with Elena Iparraguirre, Piedras Gordas, February 20, 2017.

80 **a "chorus girl":** Quoted in Strong, *Shining Path*, 33.

80 **"battle will be cruel":** Guzmán, "We Are the Initiators," 313–314.

81 **"Light that melted earth":** Abimael Guzmán, "Forjar en los hechos," in *Guerra Popular en el Perú: El pensamiento Gonzalo,* Luis Arce Borja, ed. (Brussels: Author, 1989), 148.

81 **"enlightened by a more intense light":** Ibid.

81 **"we are on the inevitable path":** Ibid., 149.

81 **"millenarian sect":** Yuri Slezkine, *The House of Government: A Saga of the Russian Revolution* (Princeton: Princeton University Press, 2017).

81 **"it will be nothing at all":** Guzmán and Yparraguirre, *Memorias*, 169.

81 **"we all die of something":** Quoted in Calvo and Declerq, *Perú*, 132.

82 **Fifty-one party members gathered:** Victor Tipe Sánchez, *Abimael: La Captura* (Lima: Author, 2007), 15.

82 **the room fell silent:** Interview with Elena Iparraguirre, Piedras Gordas, June 7, 2015; See also Montesinos, *Sin Sendero,* 305.

82 **"we are entering the great rupture":** Abimael Guzmán, "ILA 80—Discurso del Presidente Gonzalo," 1980, www.nuevademocraciapanama.blogspot.com/2011/05/ila-80-discurso-del-presidente-gonzalo.html.

82 **"beautiful political poem of war":** CCPCP, "Entrevista al Presidente Gonzalo."

83 **"let yourself go":** Ibid.

83 **"I couldn't really say":** Ibid.

83 **"Constructing the future with our blood":** Quoted in Gavilán, *When Rains*, 22.

83 **Everyone lifted their glass:** Interview with Elena Iparraguirre, Piedras Gordas, June 7, 2015.

Chapter Five: First Blood

84 **a gas-powered mill:** Interview with Mario Anyoza Gamboa, Pujas, August 6, 2016.

85 **"Men and women carried homemade spears":** "Orgía de terror y sangre de 'Sendero Luminoso, Expreso, December 27, 1980, 10. For more on the Ayzarca attack, Umberto Jara, *Abimael* (Lima: Planeta, 2017), 207–214.

85 **killed a farmhand:** Comuneros en Ayacucho Dan Muerte a Hacendado," *La Prensa*, December 27, 1980, 2.

85 **the first to die:** One unverified source has Shining Path killing a mine administrator two months earlier than Medina, in late October 1980. DESCO, *Violencia Política en el Perú, Tomo 2* (Lima: DESCO, 1989), 65.

87 **She was "green-eyed":** Archivo Regional de Ayacucho, CSJ-JP, Leg. 188, Exp. 28480 (1980), Denuncia de Carlos Parodi Donayri (July 18, 1980); Preventiva del agraviado Carlos Parodi Donayri (fol. 546); Preventiva de la agraviada Flora Gutiérrez (fol. 557); Preventiva de la agraviada Sofía Sosa Ruíz, (fol. 561); Resumen de las manifestaciones del interrogado del detenido Mauro Antonio Castilla García (fol. 426); Manifestación de Maurio Antonio Castillo García (December 1, 1980). Thanks to Jaymie Patricia Heilman for furnishing us with this document. For more on the situation in the region, see Heilman's *Now Peru Is Mine: The Life and Times of a Campesino Activist* (Durham: Duke University Press, 2016).

88 **the *sinchis* interrogated Giorgina Gamboa:** "Testimonio de Señora Giorgina Gamboa García," CVR, April 8, 2002, www.cverdad.org.pe/apublicas/audiencias /trans_huamanga02e.php.

88 **"So many had raped me":** Ibid.

89 **reported a *Los Angeles Times* story:** "Shining Path Leads to Death," *Los Angeles Times*, July 8, 1983, A6.

89 **"Shining Path tells the Indians":** "The Shining Path to Death," *The Observer*, October 24, 1982, 2.

89 **1,520 dynamite cartridges:** DESCO, *Violencia Política en el Perú, Tomo 1*, 65.

90 **"Our people were long gone":** Interview with Elena Iparraguirre, Piedras Gordas, July 31, 2016.

90 **"sabotage the electricity":** CCPCP, *¡Elecciones, No! ¡Guerra Popular, Si!*, 1990, www.solrojo.org/pcp_doc/pcp_0590.htm. Abimael wrote this document, which was intended for wide distribution.

91 **capture "was imminent":** DESCO, *Violencia Política, Tomo 1*, 377.

92 "repeated oppression of the people": CVR, *Informe Final*, Vol. 5, 46.

92 "sacrifice 300 million Chinese": Quoted in Jung Chang and Jon Halliday, *Mao: The Untold Story* (Knopf: New York, 2005), 439.

92 "unless we resort to terrorism": V.I. Lenin, "Meeting of the Presidium of the Petrograd Soviet with Delegates from Food Supply Organizations," 1908, https://www.marxists.org/archive/lenin/works/1918/jan/14.htm.

92 "hatred and love coincided": This comes from Ignazio Silone's contribution to *The God That Failed*, Richard Crossman, ed. (New York: Bantam, 1950), 86.

93 "Augusta was the key person": Quoted in Jara, *Sendero*, 154.

94 "better than white": Robin Kirk, "The Deadly Women of Shining Path," *San Francisco Examiner* "Image" insert, March 22, 1992, 3.

94 "just for the sake": Quoted in Carlos Iván Degregori, *How Difficult It Is to Be God: Shining Path's Politics of War in Peru, 1980–1999* (Madison: University of Wisconsin Press, 2012), 116.

94 "the rich will disappear": Quoted in José Coronel, "Violencia política y respuestas campesinas en Huanta," in Carlos Ivan Degregori, José Coronel, Ponciano del Pino, and Orin Starn, *Las Rondas Campesinas y la Derrota de Sendero Luminoso* (Lima: Instituto de Estudios Peruanos, 1996), 70.

94 as historian Jaymie Heilman notes: Jaymie Patricia Heilman, *Before Shining Path: Politics in Rural Ayacucho, 1895–1980* (Stanford: Stanford University Press, 2010).

95 "furious mob": Terroristas Torturan y Matan Salvajamente a 5 Campesinos," *Extra*, December 27, 1982, 14.

95 "the Prussian junker road": Antonio Díaz Martínez, *Ayacucho: Hambre y Esperanza* (Lima, Mosca Azul, 1969), 37.

95 *senderistas* descended upon the farm: See Michael Smith's *Rural Development in the Crossfire: The Role of Grassroots Support Organizations in Situations of Political Violence in Peru* (Ottawa: International Development Research Centre, 1991), 33–43.

95 "We killed as many as we could": "Nicario," "Memories of a Cadre," in *The Peru Reader*, Starn et al., eds., 347.

95 "Why kill them that way?": Ibid.

95 "about eighty": Ibid.

95 "mad, stampeding": Mario Vargas Llosa, *Death in the Andes*, trans. Edith Grossman (New York: Picador, 2007), 48.

95 1,800 actions: DESCO, *Violencia Política, Tomo 1*, 23.

96 "all animals are equal": George Orwell, *Animal Farm* (New York: Harcourt, Brace and Company, 1946), 63.

96 "We will become brothers": Gustavo Gorriti Collection (GGC), Group A, Box 2, Folder 2, "PCP-SL," Segunda Conferencia Nacional del Partido Comunista Peruano (SL).

97 Comrade César: His real name was Óscar Vera.

97 At whatever price: Ricardo Uceda, *Muerte en el Pentagonito: Los cementerios secretos del Ejército Peruano* (Lima: Planeta, 2004), 36.

97 ripping out his IV: Gorriti, *Shining Path*, 169–170.

97 **"a knight in shining armor":** GGC, Group A, Box 2, Folder 2, "PCP-SL," Segunda Conferencia Nacional del Partido Comunista Peruano (SL). All the quotations here come from that meeting come from these documents, unless otherwise noted.

99 **"I criticize my comrades":** Interview with Elena Iparraguirre, Piedras Gordas, July 21, 2016.

99 **"Abimael wasn't more intelligent":** Ibid.

100 **Augusta apparently coined the phrase:** Jara, *Abimael,* 168.

100 **"Marxism is an ideology":** CCPCP, "Entrevista al Presidente Gonzalo."

101 **A growing "New Left":** For more about the new turn of the Latin American left, Jorge Castañeda, *Utopia Unarmed: The Latin American Left After the Cold War* (Vintage: New York, 2004).

101 **sea lion mistakenly waddled:** No author, *Testimonios de Heroicidad* (Lima: Ediciones Memoria, 2016), 37.

102 **"we are the vanguard":** Gorriti, "Sendero en El Frontón," 65.

102 **"to underestimate them":** Ibid.

Chapter Six: The Lynching

103 **She won a scholarship:** The full name of the university is now Lomonosov Moscow State University—and it ranks among the world's best today.

103 **"a bunch of corrupt old men":** Interview with Gustavo Gorriti, Durham, NC, March 3, 2016.

105 **"The armed people will win!":** Nicholas Shakespeare, "In Pursuit of Guzmán," *Granta,* No. 23, 1981, 181.

105 **"An Ayacuchan can't be bought":** The song, "Ofrenda," is by the well-known Ayacuchan musician Carlos Falconí.

105 *Yes sir, here we are!:* Lurgio Gavilán, *When Rains Became Floods,* 41.

106 **"I was just a poor boy":** Interview with Óscar Medrano, Lima, June 2, 2015.

107 **"The gringo can go":** Ibid.

108 *"Wisslla,"* **he said:** Interview with Leandro Sulca, Huamanguilla, June 5, 2015. We use pseudonyms for all the Sulcas—Leandro, Narciso, and Isidro.

108 **"Five hundred distinct varieties":** José María Arguedas, "Huk doctorkunam qayway/Llamado a algunos doctores" in John V. Murra and Mércedes Lopez, *Las Cartas de Arguedas* (Lima: Pontificia Universidad Católica del Perú, 1996), 253.

109 **"destroy the government":** Archivo de la Defensoría del Pueblo(ADP), Testimonio 201700. The subsequent description of Shining Path's arrival to the market is based primarily on this interview with Narciso Sulca.

110 **best to keep his distance:** Interview with Narciso Sulca, Huaychao, February 8, 2006.

110 **"cleansing the countryside":** See Lewis Taylor, "Sendero Luminoso in the New Millennium: Comrades, Counter-insurgency, and Narco-Trafficking on the Peruvian Frontier, *Journal of Agrarian Change,* Vol. 17 No. 1 (January 2017), 106–121, 107.

110 **"only Stones and sticks":** Quoted in Méndez, *The Plebeian Republic: The Huanta*

Rebellion and the Making of the Peruvian State, 1820–1850 (Durham: Duke University Press, 2005), 34.

111 **"ignorant about everything"**: Quoted in Uceda, *Muerte en el Pentagonito*, 70.

111 **"Nothing good will come of this"**: Our account of the confrontation between the Huaychainos and *senderistas* draws from Miguel La Serna, *The Corner of the Living: Ayacucho on the Eve of the Shining Path Insurgency* (Chapel Hill: University of North Carolina Press, 2012), 131–134, 175–190, as well as our interview with Narciso Sulca, September 5, 2016.

113 **"the army didn't care"**: Interview with Narciso Sulca, Huanta, Peru, June 9, 2016.

113 **"Let me cry through this rain"**: This ballad, "Pukuypukuysito," is from Canchis province in Cuzco appears in Rodrigo Montoya, Luis Montoya, and Edwin Montoya eds., *La Sangre de Los Cerros* (Lima: CEPES, 1987), 401–402.

114 **Their only hope lay in banding together:** La Serna, *The Corner*, 179–181.

114 **"Sir Subprifecture"**: Quoted in Ponciano del Pino, *En nombre del gobierno: El Perú y Uchuraccay: un siglo de política campesina* (Lima: La Siniestra Ensayos, 2017), 65. We have translated to capture the flavor of the original: "Senors Subprifectura de la Probincia de Huanta . . . emos acuerdado en Asamblía General y todos los comuneros emos levantagdo para no comprínderlo a los tirroristas."

115 **still echoed in the rocks:** Del Pino, *En nombre del gobierno*, 250–255.

115 **It detonated so loudly:** La Serna, *The Corner,* 180.

115 **"Get down, boy!"**: Interview with Narciso Sulca, Huanta, Peru, June 9, 2016. The subsequent description of that confrontation also comes from this interview.

116 **"the way to defend yourselves"**: La Serna, *The Corner*, 181.

116 **village patrollers captured six teenage boys:** Ibid., 188–190.

117 **"signs of extreme poverty"**: Gustavo Gorriti, "Trágicos linchamientos," *Caretas*, January 31, 1983, 23.

117 **"terribly bruised"**: Ibid., 24.

118 **"Something had changed"**: Interview with Gustavo Gorriti, Durham, NC, March 3, 2016. This interview is the basis for our subsequent description of the helicopter's eventual departure from Huaychao.

119 **"Men sharpen spears"**: Ranulfo Fuentes, "Carnaval 2000" in Chalena Vásquez Rodríguez and Abilio Vergara Figueroa, *¡Chayraq!: Carnaval Ayacuchano* (Ayacucho, Peru: CECAP, 1988), 282.

Chapter Seven: Inquest in the Andes

123 **"Lend me the new boy!"**: Quoted in Juan Gargurevich, *Mario Vargas Llosa Reportero a los 15 años* (Lima: Planeta, 2015), 34.

123 **"seeing a naked woman"**: Mario Vargas Llosa, *A Fish in the Water*, trans. Helen Lane (New York, Farrar Straus Giroux, 2011), 189.

124 **"stained her brown body"**: Quoted in Gargurevich, *Mario Vargas Llosa*, 36.

124 **"a long way from Peru"**: Vargas Llosa, *A Fish*, 43.

125 **"like fish in dirty water"**: Mario Vargas Llosa, *Aunt Julia and the Scriptwriter*, trans. Helen Lane (New York: Picador, 2007), 75.

125 **"a modern man and Marxist"**: Quoted in Daniel Jergin and Joseph Stanislaw, *The Commanding Heights: The Battle for the World Economy* (Simon and Schuster: New York, 2002), 367.

126 **fabricating the whole story**: See Juan Cristóbal, ed., *Uchuraccay o el Rostro de la Barbarie* (Lima: Editorial San Marcos, 2003).

126 **"serve my country best"**: Princeton Firestone Library (PFL), Mario Vargas Llosa Papers (MVLlP), Series 3: Correspondence, Box 77, Box 4, Folder 8, Letter to Fernando Belaúnde Terry, July 2, 1981.

126 **"this notebook and pencil"**: Mario Vargas Llosa, *Contra viento y marea (1962–1982)* (Barcelona: Seix Barral, 1983), 51.

127 **"Literature is fire"**: Ibid., 134–5.

127 **threatened Peru's fragile democracy**: Mario Vargas Llosa, *Contra viento y marea, III (1964–1988)* (Lima: PEISA), 129.

127 **"superficial, touristic" fashion**: "Conversación Sobre Uchuraccay," *Caretas*, March 7, 1983, 34.

127 **"colonial army"**: Alberto Flores Galindo, *Buscando un Inca: Identidad y utopía en los andes* (Lima: Editorial Horizonte, 1988), 398.

128 **"Where could she be?"**: Ranulfo Fuentes, "Huamanguino," in Orin Starn, Carlos Iván Degregori, and Robin Kirk, eds., *The Peru Reader*, 386.

128 **"It is sad"**: PFL, MVLlP, Notebooks, Box 8, Folder 2, J-11. Notebook entry, February 9, 1983.

129 **"Let's ring the chapel bell"**: Interview with Juan Ossio, Lima, August 10, 2016.

129 **"scarred cheeks"**: Mario Vargas Llosa, "Inquest in the Andes," *New York Times Sunday Magazine*, July 31, 1983, 51.

130 **"Será su costumbre"**: Quoted in del Pino, *En nombre del gobierno*, 50.

130 **"Comuneros of Uchuraccay"**: LUM. *Reunión de la Comisión Vargas Llosa con los comuneros de Uchuraccay* [video file], January 12, 2016. Retrieved from www.lum.cultura.pe/visita360.

131 **"I had many doubts"**: "Vargas Llosa: Donde Están las Pruebas," *Caretas*, December 3, 1984, 23.

131 **bruised tears**: Vargas Llosa, *A Fish*, 53.

131 **punched out . . . Gabriel García Márquez**: Gerald Martin, *Gabriel García Márquez: A Life* (New York: Alfred A. Knopf, 2009), 375.

132 **we killed the journalists**: Vargas Llosa, "Inquest in the Andes," 49.

132 **"Honorable Mr. Government"**: Ibid. See also Víctor Tipe Sánchez and Jaime Tipe Sánchez, *Uchuraccay: El pueblo donde morían los que llegaban a pie* (Lima: G7 Consultores SAC, 2015).

132 **"Change the subject, Mario"**: Interview with Juan Ossio, Lima, August 10, 2016.

133 **blackening their mood**: Tipé and Tipé, *Uchuraccay*, 131.

133 **"Among our combatants"**: Del Pino, *En nombre del gobierno*, 62.

134 **beat him to death**: Tipe and Tipe, *Uchuraccay*, 142–145.

134 **"abandonment"**: Comisión Investigadora de los Sucesos de Uchuraccay, *Informe*, March 3, 1983 at: http://www.verdadyreconciliacionperu.com/admin/files/articulos/612_digitalizacion.pdf, 21.

134 *"Futu, futu"*: Del Pino, *En nombre del gobierno*, 60.

135 **"stark clarities"**: John King, "Foreword," in John King, ed., *Mario Vargas Llosa, Making Waves* (New York: Farrar, Straus, Giroux, 2011), xx.

135 **more restrained critics**: See Enrique Mayer, "Peru in Deep Trouble: Mario Vargas Llosa's Inquest in the Andes Reexamined," *Cultural Anthropology*, Vol. 6, No. 4 (November 1991), 466–504.

135 **an "ancient, archaic" lifeway**: Vargas Llosa, "Inquest in the Andes," 51.

135 **an "almost absolute" isolation**: Ibid., 23.

135 **a land of "untouched" villages**: On the problem of what can be called "Andeanism," Orin Starn, "Missing the Revolution: Anthropologists and the War in Peru," *Cultural Anthropology* Vol. 6, No. 1, (February 1991), 63–91.

135 **"barbarism and civilization"**: Interview with Juan Ossio, Lima, August 10, 2016.

135 **"vertical archipelago"**: See Mary Van Buren, "Rethinking the Vertical Archipelago: Ethnicity, Exchange, and History in the South Central Andes," *American Anthropologist*, Vol. 98, No. 2 (June 1996), 338–351.

136 **others claimed**: For a sampling, Cristóbal, ed., *Uchuraccay*.

136 **"making money over the dead bodies"**: Ibid., 327.

136 **Later investigations would vindicate Vargas Llosa**: See Del Pino, *En nombre del gobierno* and Tipe and Tipe, *Uchuraccay*.

136 **"the basics right"**: Ponciano Del Pino, email communication, January 20, 2018.

136 **"context of abnormality"**: *Comisión Investigadora*, 21.

136 **"incurable romanticism"**: *El Comercio*, November 29, 1984, A6.

136 **"the worst offense"**: Mario Vargas Llosa, *Contra Viento y Marea*, III, 174–5.

137 **"I am not a hedonist"**: La Tremenda Corte," *Caretas*, December 2, 1984, 70.

137 **"shit savages"**: Quoted in Ponciano del Pino, "Family, Culture, and "Revolution": Everyday Life with Sendero Luminoso" in Steve J. Stern, ed., *Shining and Other Paths: War and Society in Peru, 1980-1995* (Durham: Duke University Press, 1998), 163.

137 **"Our suffering in those years"**: Ponciano Del Pino, "Looking to the Government: Community, Politics and the Making of Memory and Silences in 20th Century Peru, Ayacucho." Ph.D. Dissertation, Department of History, University of Wisconsin–Madison, 64.

Chapter Eight: Shouting in the Rocks

138 **camped in high spots**: We base these details on Gavilán's superb memoir, *When Rains Became Floods*, beautifully translated by Margaret Randall, as well as our multiple conversations with Gavilán.

139 *Gonzalo brought the light*: Ibid., 26.

139 **an old man**: Ibid., 12.

139 **"My little dove"**: *Literatura Quechua*, Edmundo Bendezú Aybar (Ayacucho, Peru: Biblioteca Ayacucho, 1989), 258.

139 *There are always reasons to keep on living*: Gavilán, *When Rains*, 13.

140 **"the miserable bastards"**: Ibid.

140 **a war machine:** Degregori, *El surgimiento*, 190.

140 **"We continued to believe":** Gavilán, *When Rains*, 33.

140 **where Chairman Gonzalo might be:** Interview with Lurgio Gavilán, Durham, NC, October 6, 2016.

140 **"remained invisible":** Gavilán, *When Rains*, 33.

141 **Others speculated:** See Nicholas Shakespeare, "In Pursuit of Guzmán," *Granta* 23, 1983, 151–195.

141 **he had died:** Alexander Watson, email communication, March 2, 2015.

142 *the whole block*: Interview with Elena Iparraguirre, Piedras Gordas, December 18, 2016.

142 **a police intelligence report:** DPI, Nota de información, 467.

142 **"Don't tell anyone":** Interview with Gisela Huamán, Huanta, June 4, 2016.

142 **no one would come to the dying man's aid:** Interview with Alejandro Coronado, Huanta, August 10, 2016.

142 **"Another of Augusta's childhood friends . . . had a policeman boyfriend":** Interview with Sonia Meneses, Huanta, August 10, 2016.

142 **she visited her cousin Adriana:** Gorriti, *Shining Path*, 256–258.

143 **"the first we'll burn":** Gustavo Gorriti, *Sendero: La historia de la guerra milenaria en el Perú* (Lima: Apoyo, 1990), 383.

143 **"I don't like it":** Interview with Elena Iparraguirre, Piedras Gordas, December 18, 2016.

144 **Humberto realized . . . they could not keep them:** Personal communication, Humberto La Torre, Stockholm, October 5, 2015.

144 **likeable, forthright Clara:** For more on Clara, Julio Roldán, "De estudiante a guerrillera: la llamaban Elvira. Se auto-llamaba Ana," *Pacarina del Sur,* www .pacarinadelsur.com/home/figuras-e-ideas/1082-de-estudiante-a-guerrillera-la -llamaban-elvira-se-auto-llamaba-ana.

144 **"I open the Retransmission":** Quoted in Uceda, *Muerte*, 41. Our account of the meeting is based on Uceda's *Muerte*, 36–52.

145 **could never be bad luck:** Uceda, *Muerte*, 51.

145 **"Dust will accumulate":** Mao Zedong, 1945, www.marxists.org/reference/archive /mao/works/red-book/ch27.htm.

146 **cried Carlotta Tello:** Ricardo Caro Cárdenas discusses the mythologization of Carlotta Tello and other young senderista women in "Ser mujer, joven y senderista: memorias de género y pánico moral en las percepciones del senderismo," *Allpanchis*, No. 67 (2006), 122–152.

146 **"they will die":** Gavilán, *When Rains*, 19.

146 **"We pulled roughly":** Ibid., 20

147 **"How could they send a child?":** Ibid., 25.

147 **"you fucker":** Uceda, *Muerte*, 110.

147 **"These militias are tough":** Gavilán, *When Rains*, 15.

147 **"We were human":** Ibid., 36.

148 **Mao's theory of protracted war:** See John W. Woodmansee, "Mao's Protracted War: Theory vs. Practice," *Parameters* Vol. 3, No. 1 (1973), 30–45.

148 A "river of blood": Quoted in Degregori, *How Difficult*, 87.

148 "democratic centralist": Guzmán and Yparraguirre, *Memorias*, 451.

148 "reddest of them all": Guzmán, *De puño*, 346.

149 "not the right move": Interview with Elena Iparraguirre, Piedras Gordas, July 31, 2016.

149 A "feudal-fatalist mentality": Quoted in Coronel, "Violencia política y respuesta campesina en Huanta," 46.

149 "'they're atheists'": Quoted in Uceda, *Muerte*, 71.

150 lit him on fire: CVR, *Informe Final*, Vol. 5, 82–84.

150 "revolutionary terror": Karl Marx and Friedrich Engels, "Sieg der Kontrerevolution in Wien" [The Victory of the Counter-revolution in Vienna], November 1848, www .mlwerke.de/me/me05/me05_455.htm. Thanks to Can Evren for his translation.

150 "a brief period of terror": CCPCP, *¡Elecciones, No! ¡Guerra Popular, Si!*.

151 the new mestizos: Degregori, *How Difficult*, 137–8.

151 "Sacsamarca will be ashes!": Gustavo Gorriti and Benito Portocarrero, "La matanza de Lucanamarca," *Caretas*, April 11, 1983, 17. See also Zapata, *La Guerra Senderista*, 135–140 and Mark R. Cox, *La verdad y la memoria; controversias en la imagen de Hildebrando Pérez Huaranca* (Lima: Editorial Pascalle, 2012).

151 "Give me back half": Poder Judicial (PJ), Juicio contra Abimael Guzmán y otros, Acta de la Trigésima Séptima Sesión. Testimonio de Marcelino Casavilca, March 30, 2006.

152 "The army's coming": Ibid., Acta de la Trigésima Séptima Sesión, Testimonio de Teófanes Allcahuamán Vílchez, April 3, 2006.

152 set buildings on fire: CVR, *Informe Final*, Vol. 5, 84–87.

152 "The poor were exterminated": The song appears in Carlos Cárdenas and Hector Gálvez's 2008 documentary *Lucanamarca*.

152 "militarist excess": CVR, Interview with Abimael Guzmán Reinoso and Elena Iparraguirre, April 30, 2002.

152 "a tough bone to gnaw": CCPCP, "Entrevista al Presidente Gonzalo."

152 "we must stop at nothing": V. I. Lenin, "Speech Delivered to the Third All-Russia Congress of Textile," April 19, 1920, www.marxists.org/archive/lenin/works /1920/apr/19.htm.

152 "To serve them": CCPCP, "Entrevista al Presidente Gonzalo." Here Guzmán refers generally to the purpose of actions like Lucanamarca designed to "teach the masses with convincing facts."

152 "army auxiliaries": Interview with Elena Iparraguirre, Piedras Gordas, February 20, 2017.

153 *I'm bringing lunch*: Interview with Óscar Medrano, Lima, August 24, 2017.

153 "*Urquy kay vendaje*": Ibid.

154 At least 2,255 people: CVR, *Anexo Estadístico* (Lima: CVR, 2003), 22. We subtract deaths attributed to the MRTA insurgents from our calculations here.

154 "caused by the reaction": Gorriti, *Shining Path*, 105.

154 bore responsibility for 46 percent: CVR, *Informe Final*, Vol. 8, 355, 358; ibid., Vol. 1, 71.

154 **established secret prisons:** See Uceda, *Muerte*, 78–148

154 **"came like a hurricane":** Interview with Elena Iparraguirre, Piedras Gordas, August 20, 2017.

154 **"novitiates to veterans":** Ibid.

155 **"We'd better go":** Quoted in Uceda, *Muerte*, 117.

155 **over one thousand reports of disappearances:** Amnesty International, *Report (1985)* (London: Amnesty International Publications, 1985), 182–183.

155 **Their interrogator focused on Carlotta:** We draw for details of the interrogation and killing on Uceda, *Muerte*, 117–120.

155 **raping them by one account:** Roldán, "De estudiante a guerrillera."

156 **"It is not serious":** Gavilán, *When Rains*, 38.

156 **"Stop, don't shoot!":** Ibid., 39.

156 **"a bit of intestine":** Ibid., 46.

Chapter Nine: The Queen of Villa

157 **Her three boys . . . brought in a few more coins:** On the complexities of child labor in Lima, see Leigh Campoamor, "Who Are You Calling Exploitative?": Defensive Motherhood, Child Labor, and Urban Poverty in Lima, Peru," *Journal of Latin American and Caribbean Anthropology*, Vol. 21, Issue 1 (March 2016), 151–172.

157 **moving that morning:** Interview with Martha Moyano, Villa El Salvador, July 5, 2016. See also Diana Miloslavich, ed., *The Autobiography of María Elena Moyano: The Life and Death of a Peruvian Activist*, trans. Patricia Taylor (Gainesville: University of Florida Press, 2000), 75–76.

158 **"tearless" sky:** Quoted in Carlos Aguirre and Charles Walker, eds., *The Lima Reader: History, Culture, Politics* (Durham: Duke University Press, 2017), 84.

158 **"Here's my room!":** Interview with Martha Moyano, Villa El Salvador, Peru, July 5, 2016.

158 **Eugenia shared:** Interview with Martha Moyano, Villa El Salvador, August 20, 2017.

159 **latest unexpected chapter:** A fine introduction to Lima is Aguirre and Walker's *The Lima Reader*.

159 **abandoned the Andes:** For more on the great migration to Lima, see José Matos Mar, *Las barriadas de Lima* (Lima: Instituto de Estudios Peruanos, 1977); Jürgen Golte and Norma Adams, *Los caballos de troya: Estrategias campesinas en la conquista de Gran Lima* (Lima: Instituto de Estudios Peruanos, 1987).

159 **"On the way to Arabia":** El cholo Juan, "That Sickly Applause," in Aguirre and Walker, eds., *The Lima Reader*, 236.

159 **"I recognize in the dark":** Quoted in *The Lima Reader*, Aguirre and Walker, eds., ix.

160 **a somewhat special history:** For more on Villa, Cecilia Blondet, *Las Mujeres y el Poder: Una historia de Villa El Salvador* (Lima: Instituto de Estudios Peruanos,

1991) and Antonio Zapata Velasco, *Sociedad y Poder Local: La Comunidad de Villa El Salvador* (DESCO: Lima, 1976).

160 **"Up, everybody!":** Interview with Martha Moyano, Lima, July 5, 2016.

161 **A cabinetmaker by trade:** Interview with Gustavo Pineki, Madrid, November 7, 2015.

162 **"liberation theology":** Gustavo Gutiérrez, *A Theology of Liberation: History, Politics, and Salvation* (Maryknoll, NY: Orbis, 1973).

162 **Abimael Guzmán, sometimes came to Villa:** Interview with Tony Palomino, Villa El Salvador, Peru, June 4, 2015.

162 **"I'm going to the mountains":** Interview with Gustavo Pineki, Madrid, November 7, 2015. Our account of the rest of this conversation is also based on this interview.

164 **An expatriate Spanish schoolteacher, Michel Azcueta:** Interview with Michel Azcueta, Villa El Salvador, Peru, June 5, 2015. For more about Azcueta, Zapata, *Sociedad y Poder Local.*

164 **apartheid South Africa:** Carlos Iván Degregori, personal communication, June 3, 1992.

165 **"Neither black nor Indian":** Rodrigo Montoya, "Homenaje a María Elena Moyano," *La República,* February 2, 1992, 8.

165 **"Am I really black?":** Interview with Gustavo Pineki, Madrid, November 7, 2018.

166 **"always caring for people":** Interview with Marina Rodinó and Guido Sattin, Venice, September 15, 2015.

166 *sacaojo* **tales captured anxiety:** See Portocarrero, *Sacaojos y Pishtacos.*

166 **"Who saw a *sacaojo*?":** Interview with Charo Torres, Lima, June 8, 2015.

167 **"gender complementarity":** Irene Silverblatt, *Moon, Sun, Witches: Gender Ideologies and Class in Inca and Colonial Peru* (Princeton: Princeton University Press, 1987).

167 **more manly powers:** See Blondet, *Las Mujeres y el Poder* and Susan Lobo's *A House of their Own: Social Organization in the Squatter Settlements of Lima, Peru* (Tucson: University of Arizona Press, 1981).

167 **"Women should not be serfs":** Elblogdebinario. *El Asesinato de María Elena Moyano* [video file], February 12, 2012. Retrieved from www.youtube.com/watch?v=S3Bzl291s9Q.

168 **The event did entertain the unwashed urchins:** Interview with Rocio Paz, Villa El Salvador, Peru, June 5, 2015.

168 **"I love your car!":** Interview with Cecilia Blondet, Lima, August 9, 2016.

168 **"I look thinner":** Skype interview with Diane Bachand, April 5, 2016.

169 **"She was exactly the same":** Interview with Cecilia Blondet, Lima, June 1, 2015. Blondet also related the anecdote about her mother's white suit in that interview.

169 **the *senderistas* operated covertly:** See Jo-Marie Burt, "Shining Path and the 'Decisive Battle' in Lima's *Barriadas*," in *Shining and Other Paths*, Stern, ed., 267–306.

170 *If He did:* Miloslavich, ed., *The Autobiography,* 78.

170 **"an extraordinary young woman"**: Interview with Marina Rodinó and Guido Sattin, September 15, 2015.

170 **"You'll be famous"**: Interview with Diana Miloslavich, June 2, 2015.

Chapter Ten: The Shining Trench

171 **"Indian hillbilly"**: Interview with Narciso Sulca, Huanta, August 11, 2016.

172 ***"entre prójimos"***: This is the title of Kimberly Theidon's important 2011 book.

173 **people of bad faith**: Theidon, *Intimate Enemies*, 215.

173 ***burrobomba***: DESCO, *Violencia Política, Tomo 1*, 133.

173 **four guerrillas opened fire**: Ibid., 131.

174 **"Here in Peru"**: John Rick, "A Terrorist Incident in Atocsaico," July 25, 1986, unpublished manuscript.

175 **"A little"**: Interview with Gustavo Gorriti, Durham, NC, March 3, 2016. We base our description of Gorriti's encounter with Macgregor on this interview.

176 **"barbarism with barbarism"**: DESCO, *Violencia Política, Tomo 1*, 131.

176 **"he may be the answer"**: Interview with Gustavo Gorriti, Lima, August 4, 2016.

176 **In Accomarca**: On this massacre and its aftermath, Jo-Marie Burt and M. Rodríguez, "Justicia, verdad y memoria: El proceso penal para el caso de la masacre de Accomarca," in *Políticas en justicia transicional: Miradas comparativas sobre el legado de la CVR*, Ludwig Huber and Ponciano del Pino, eds. (Lima: Instituto de Estudios Peruanos, 2015), 135–168; Renzo Aroni Sulca, "Choreography of a Massacre: Memory and Performance in the Ayacucho Carnival," *Latin American Perspectives* Issue 211, Vol. 43, No. 6 (2015), 41–53.

177 **no inquiry until decades later**: For more on the secret graveyard, known as La Hoyada, see Uceda, *Muerte*, and CVR, *Informe final*, Vol. 7, 71–73. General Mori and nine others received prison sentences in 2016 for the Accomarca massacre; two other officers were also eventually convicted for killings at Los Cabitos and the so-called Pink House detention center.

177 **synchronized mutiny**: See Carlos Aguirre, "Punishment and Extermination: The Massacre of Political Prisoners in Lima, Peru, June 1986," *Bulletin of Latin American Studies*, Vol 32, No. 1 (2015), 194–215.

177 **"nefarious policy"**: "Pliego Único Demandas Los Prisioneros de Guerra de las Luminosas Trincheras de Combate del Frontón, Lurigancho y Callao," June 18, 1986, http://www.pagina-libre.org/MPP-A/Textos/Presos/Pliego86.html.

177 **"on the day of his arrest"**: Quoted in José Luis Rénique, *La voluntad encarcelada: Las "Luminosas Trincheras de Combate" de Sendero Luminoso del Perú* (Lima: Instituto de Estudios Peruanos, 2003), 64.

178 **"black reactionary dungeons"**: Ibid.

178 **About thirty prisoners died**: DESCO, *Violencia Política, Tomo 1*, 133.

178 **"how scoundrels die"**: "Asesinato de alcalde rememora aniquilamiento de Castro," *La República*, January 9, 2010, www.larepublica.pe/politica/442431-asesinato-de-alcaide-rememora-aniquilamiento-de-castro-castro.

178 The *senderistas* had planned the action to coincide: Aguirre, "Punishment and Extermination," 201.

178 "drown the revolution in blood": CCPCP, "Entrevista al Presidente Gonzalo."

179 The order was apparently transmitted: In describing the prison massacre, we draw on Uceda, *Muerte*; Agustín Haya de la Torre, *El retorno de la barbarie: la matanza en los penales de Lima en 1986* (Lima: Bahia Ediciones, 1987); Aguirre, "Punishment and Extermination"; CVR, *Informe final,* vol. 7, 234–263.

179 "awoken a lion": CVR, *Informe final,* vol. 7, 237.

179 "authority has been imposed": Haya de la Torre, *El retorno de la barbarie,* 49.

179 "Long Live the People's War": Uceda, *Muerte,* 167.

180 "Eliminate them": Aguirre, "Punishment and Extermination," 206. Some reports said that army troops also participated in the massacre.

180 "just used their knives": Uceda, *Muerte,* 175.

180 They had good evidence: Interview with Gustavo Gorriti, Lima, August 4, 2016.

180 no matter the consequences: Interview with Marco Zileri, Lima, August 24, 2017.

180 ran in the next issue: Laura Puertas, Carlos Noriega, Gustavo Gorriti, Miguel González del Rio, "Lurigancho Después del Exterminio," *Caretas,* June 23, 1986.

180 "the deliberate atrocity": "Editorial," *Caretas,* June 23, 1986, 11.

180 "the ones who violated the law": Quoted in Aguirre, "Punishment and Extermination," 209.

181 "Either they leave": Ibid., 210.

181 "By sacrificing their lives": "Gran Marcha Hacia el Communismo," June 24, 2015, https://granmarchahaciaelcomunismo.wordpress.com/category/dia-de-la-heroicidad/.

182 compared writing and farming: Seamus Heaney, *New Selected Poems: 1966–1987* (London: Faber and Faber, 1990), 1.

182 "arms, munitions, homemade grenades": Gustavo Gorriti, "Lo que se quiso ocultar," *Caretas,* November 24, 1986, 16.

182 Twenty reporters had already been slain: The figures come from the Committee to Protect Journalists, www.washingtonpost.com/archive/opinions/1991/09/01/perus-war-against-magno-sosa/dba7b923-1a4c-46c8-b91a-168abf71abb5/?utm_term=.e3347a58e30c.

183 Bug bumped into Vilcashuamán: Interview with Gustavo Gorriti, Lima, August 4, 2016.

183 "here to see some friends": Interview with Óscar Medrano, Lima, August 25, 2016.

184 Fear and anger could spur them: For more about the military's wartime role, Jorge Ortiz Sotelo, *Acción y Valor: Historia de la Infantería de Marina del Perú* (Lima: Securitas, 2010) and Comisión Permanente de Historia del Ejército del Perú, *En Honor a la Verdad* (Lima: Comisión Permanente de Historia del Ejército del Perú). These official histories minimize military atrocities, but show the real difficulties facing the counterinsurgency. Navy infantrymen, for example, were trained mostly for coastal operations.

184 **Some generals realized:** See Renato Cisneros's *La distancia que nos separa* (Lima: Planeta, 2015) on his father, General Luis Cisneros, a complex man who helped to shape early counterinsurgency policy.

184 **Huamán was dismissed:** Lewis Taylor, "Counter-insurgency strategy, the PCP-Sendero Luminoso and the civil war in Peru, 1980–1996," *Bulletin of Latin American Research*, Vol. 17 (1998), No. 1, 45.

184 **"I'm leaving":** Interview with Gustavo Gorriti, Lima, October 4, 2016.

185 **"give a declaration for the three of us":** Interview with Óscar Medrano, Lima, May 29.

Chapter Eleven: The Party Congress

188 **Three among those there . . . would be gunned down:** All three died in the 1992 government storming of the Canto Grande prison.

188 **The unsuspecting owner:** Benedicto Jiménez, *La Captura del 'Presidente Gonzalo'* (Lima: Ediciones Rivadeyneyra, 2013), 131.

188 **"Long life to you directing the Party":** This was the standard party greeting.

188 **"Long Live Chairman Gonzalo":** These undated greetings were inscribed on a banner from the Lurigancho prison committee, in the Lima museum of the Anti-Terrorism Police Directorate (DIRCOTE).

189 **"They lack ideological formation":** Interview with Elena Iparraguirre, Piedras Gordas, February 20, 2017.

189 **The party had its own newspaper:** For more on *El Diario*, Juan Gargurevich, "Janet, La última periodista de Sendero," July 31, 2017, www.tiojuan .wordpress.com/2017/07/31/janet-la-ultima-periodista-de-sendero/. Guzmán claimed not to have editorial control over *El Diario*, but it published the party line. See CVR, Interview with Abimael Guzmán and Elena Iparraguirre, October 21, 2002.

189 **armed actions nationwide had grown:** DESCO, *Violencia Política, Tomo 1*, 23.

189 **"the destruction of imperialism":** Partido Comunista del Perú (PCP), "Bases de discusión de la línea política general," 1988. Augusta was the primary author of "Línea militar" and "Línea internacional," the first two parts of this five-party document, while Elena was the lead writer of the other three.

189 **"We have indeed generously spilled our own blood":** ADINCOTE, *Documentación, Tomo XXIX*, 23.

190 **"The soul of the Party":** Ibid., 23–25.

190 **"Never before":** Ibid., 20.

190 **"greatest epic":** Ibid., 25.

190 **"destruction in our own ranks":** Ibid., 26.

190 **"revolutionary war is so beautiful":** Ibid.

191 **"mental illness":** Óscar Ramírez Durand, *El Megajuicio de Sendero* (Lima: Author, 2006), 56.

191 **"A great strategist":** Interview with Osmán Morote, Chaclacayo, June 15, 2018.

191 **"Yes, Comrade Norah":** Ibid. See also Montesinos, *Sin Sendero*, 314.

191 "That was his way": Interview with Elena Iparraguirre, Piedras Gordas, February 20, 2017.

191 "To command absolute truth": Eric Hoffer, *The True Believer: Thoughts on the Nature of Mass Movements* (New York: Harper Perennial Modern Classics, 2002), 77.

192 "Dear Comrades": "Oath of Loyalty," Anonymous in *The Peru Reader*, Starn et al., eds., 350.

192 deify its leader before winning: Carlos Iván Degregori, personal communication, October 5, 1990.

192 "Is he a God or what?": Tipe Sánchez, *Abimael*, 61.

192 "They castrated your capacity": The authors conducted this interview in Lima on August 15, 2016. Juan Fulano is a pseudonym.

193 historical inevitability, not personal ambition: ADINCOTE, *Documentación, Tomo XXIX*, 270.

193 "Objective reality always generates": Ibid., 149.

193 "false, hypocritical modesty": Ibid., 270.

193 "we can't kill every tourist": ADINCOTE, *Documentación, Tomo XXXV*, 126.

194 "The act of dying became a technical detail": Arthur Koestler, *Darkness at Noon* (New York: Macmillan, 1941), 138.

194 "reactionary democratic bourgeois system": ADINCOTE, *Documentación, Tomo XXXIII*, 126.

194 The Viet Cong . . . assassinated 13,000 people: Ibid.

194 "universal truth": CCCP, *¡Elecciones, No! ¡Guerra popular, Si!.*

194 "highest human expression": PCP, "Bases de discusión."

194 "a microscope and telescope": ADINCOTE, *Documentación, Tomo XXXI*, 155.

194 "All that is solid": Karl Marx and Friedrich Engels, *Manifesto of the Communist Party*, 1848, www.marxists.org/archive/marx/works/1848/communist-manifesto/.

195 "sinified" Marxism: See Nick Knight, *Rethinking Mao: Explorations in Mao Zedong's Thought* (Plymouth: Lexington, 2007).

195 "We are doing the work of the prophets": Arthur Koestler, *Darkness at Noon* (New York: Macmillan, 1941), 135.

195 Mariátegui tried to adapt Marxism to Peruvian realities: Alberto Flores Galindo, *La agonía de Mariátegui: La polémica con Komintern* (DESCO: Lima, 1982), 12.

195 "not universal thought": ADINCOTE, *Documentación, Tomo XXIX*, 157.

196 "The greatest danger is revisionism": ADINCOTE, *Documentación, Tomo XXXI*, 31.

196 "We craved to become simple and simple-minded": Arthur Koestler, "The Initiates," in Richard Crossman, ed., *The God That Failed*, 43. The Hungarian-born novelist belonged to the German Communist Party in the early 1930s, later becoming a British citizen.

196 "a fistful of millionaires": CCPCP, *¡Que el equilibrio estratégico remezca más el país!*, 1991, www.solrojo.org/pcp_doc/pcp_1191.htm. This document was compiled from transcribed Abimael speeches.

196 **he sent undercover comrades to the market again:** Interview with Elena Iparraguirre, Piedras Negras, February 20, 2017.

196 **"Forgive me":** ADINCOTE, *Documentación, Tomo XXIX*, 229.

196 **"great victory":** CCPCP, "Entrevista al Presidente Gonzalo."

197 **A trusted *senderista* brought the newspaper's editors:** Luis Arce Borja, "Presidente Gonzalo rompe el silencio," *El Diario*, July 24, 1988, 2. For the real story of the interview see Juan Gargurevich, "Janet, La última periodista de Sendero."

197 **"We don't want to seem too dramatic":** Interview with Elena Iparraguirre, Piedras Gordas, February 20, 2017.

197 **"I don't have any, only comrades":** Quoted in Luis Arce Borja, "Presidente Gonzalo," *El Diario*, 47.

198 **reported the *Washington Post*:** "Peruvian Rebel Offers Grim Prophecy," *Washington Post*, August 19, 1988, A10.

198 **a "tax":** ADINCOTE, *Documentación, Tomo XXIX*, 476.

198 **not enough to buy much weaponry:** For more on their weaponry, see Carlos Tapia, *Las Fuerzas Armadas y Sendero Luminoso: Dos Estrategias y Un Final* (Lima: Instituto de Estudios Peruanos, 1997), 117.

198 **"When we fight":** PCP, "Bases de discusión."

198 **"reconciliation . . . suckles the right":** Ibid.

198 **Comrade Sara, who headed *Socorro Popular*:** Benedicto Jiménez, Inicio, Desarollo y Ocaso del Terrorismo en el Perú, Vol. 1 (Lima: INDECOPI, n.d.), 555–556.

198 **"daring to impute pridefulness to Chairman Gonzalo":** ADINCOTE, *Documentación, Tomo XXIX*, 15.

199 **"the Party ends and begins":** ADINCOTE, *Documentación, Tomo XXIX*, 346.

199 **"fatuous, superficial revolutionaries":** ADINCOTE, *Documentación, Tomo XXXI*, 15.

199 **"What measures . . . to remedy the problems?":** ADINCOTE, *Documentación, Tomo XXIX*, 367.

199 **"Comrade Eustacio is hereby suspended":** Ibid.

199 **the northern *senderista* commander:** For more on Shining Path in northern Peru, see Lewis Taylor, *Guerrilla Warfare in Peru's Northern Highlands, 1980–1997* (Liverpool, UK: Liverpool University Press, 2006).

199 **a "self-knifing":** Ibid., 47. Pardavé also performed an *acuchillamiento*.

199 **"taking a position":** Ibid.

199 **"You have made progress":** Ibid., 52.

199 **"The Holy Trinity":** Interview with Juan Fulano, August 15, Lima, 2016.

200 **"Not for camouflage":** Personal communication, Osmán Morote, January 6, 2018.

200 **"our Dear Teacher":** Osmán Morote Barrionuevo, *Ya No Soy, Simplemente Somos* (Lima: Mano Alzado, 2011), 28.

200 **"Don't go yet":** Morote, "La falda descosida," 28–29.

Chapter Twelve: The Death of Comrade Norah

202 **"Norah, my comrade"**: "La Muerte de Augusta," *Caretas*, July 1, 1991, 40.

202 **"We maintain the principle"**: PCP, *Bases de discusión*.

202 **"You will replace me"**: Interview with Elena Iparraguirre, August 20, 2017.

202 *A suicide*: Rámirez, *El Megajuicio*, 54.

202 **"I responded"**: A section of the letter appears in "La Muerte de Augusta," *Caretas*, July 1, 1991, 40.

202 **"He didn't have children"**: Interview with Elena Iparraguirre, Piedras Gordas, August 20, 2017.

202 **"Comrade Norah lies before us"**: His eulogy is transcribed in the anonymously authored "Augusta La Torre: La leyenda continua," www.imagenesytextosselectos .blogspot.com/2011/04/augusta-la-torre-la-leyenda-continua_03.html.

203 **"My attitude to suicide"**: Mao Zedong, "The Suicide of Miss Zhao," 1919, https:// www.marxists.org/reference/archive/mao/works/1919/miss-chao.htm.

203 **Only six months later**: ADINCOTE, *Documentación, Tomo XXXIII*, 10.

204 **"unprecedented in world science"**: Quoted in Slezkine, *The House of Government*, 217.

204 **"*Oh! Beautiful dove-eyed woman*"**: Laura Zambrano Padilla, "Perdura Tu Ejemplo," *Norah Presente*, 26–27.

204 **the "Order of the Hammer and Sickle"**: ADINCOTE, *Documentación, Tomo XXXIII*, 10.

204 **a more modest anecdote**: Interview with Angélica Salas, Piedras Gordas, March 11, 2018.

205 **only an empty grave**: Interview with Benedicto Jiménez, Lima, March 16, 2018.

205 **It was typically**: Ramírez, *El Megajuicio*, 58.

206 **"A crime of love"**: Interview with Eduardo Barragán, a pseudonym, Lima, June 23, 2015.

206 **"They killed her"**: Interview with Sonia Meneses, August 12, 2016.

206 **"We'd put secret messages"**: Interview with Teresa Carrasco, Lima, August 9, 2016.

207 **"We cried a lot"**: Ospina and Declercq, *Peru*, 135.

207 **"I miss him"**: See www.cierredenemesis.blogspot.com/2016/07/palabras-de-la-companera-delia-carrasco.html.

207 **she went public**: Interview with Delia Carrasco, Stockholm, August 16, 2016.

208 **"Whatever way we actually die"**: Interview with Elena Iparraguirre, Piedras Gordas, July 31, 2016.

208 **"We subject ourselves"**: PCP, "Bases de discusión."

208 **"We were both devastated"**: Interview with Elena Iparraguirre, Piedras Gordas, July 31, 2016.

209 **"We had ideological differences"**: Guzmán, "'Exclusive' Comments," 57.

209 **the outspoken nature**: CVR, Testimonio 100054.

209 **One disagreement**: Interview with Juan Fulano, Lima, August 15, 2016.

209 **claimed to support the move**: According to Elena Iparraguirre, a resolution

passed to support moving party command to the countryside, although no record apparently exists of it.

209 **discomfort with . . . cruel war:** Sociologist Anouk Guiné asserts that Augusta may have been killed for challenging party orthodoxy in "Peruvian Women at the Crossroads: Augusta La Torre and the Women's Popular Movement," *Millars*, Vol. XLI, No. 2 (2016), 97–128.

209 **When readying for battle:** CVR, Interview with Abimael Guzmán Reinoso and Elena Iparraguirre, April 30, 2002.

209 **Augusta's last writings:** PCP, *Bases de Discusión*, 23.

210 **medication for depression:** This family member preferred to remain anonymous.

210 **"Fate does not protect":** Gheorghiu, *The Twenty-Fifth Hour*, 154.

211 **"They are more determined":** Kirk, *The Monkey's Paw*, 65–66.

212 **"It was depressing":** Interview with Elena Iparraguirre, Piedras Gordas, August 20, 2017.

212 **a tear came to Elena's eye:** This occurred during our December 18, 2016 interview with Iparraguirre at Piedras Gordas. During a final interview for this book on June 17, 2018, Iparraguirre said she was ready to relate the story of Augusta's death, but that Guzmán was "reluctant." Just before *The Shining Path* went to press, she sent a message asking us to include for the record the following note from Guzmán to Delia Carrasco, Augusta's mother: Dear and respected Doña Delia: Allow me again to reiterate: NOBODY KILLED YOUR BELOVED DAUGHTER! AND OUR COMRADE AND ONE HEROINE! NEVER WOULD ANYONE HAVE COMMITTED SUCH A MONSTROSITY! PLEASE: DON'T AGAIN ACCUSE US OF THINGS THAT NEVER OCCURRED! AS ALWAYS OUR AFFECTION AND RESPECT TO YOU AND YOUR FAMILY. Abimael, CEREC [Prison], Callao, September 4, 2018.

212 **"gratitude of the congress":** ADINCOTE, *Documentación, Tomo XXXIII*, 395.

212 **"received the resolution":** Ibid.

212 **"fascism with a human face":** Susan Sontag et al., "Communism and the Left," January 2, 1998, www.thenation.com/article/communism-and-left/.

213 **"The restorations in China":** Abimael Guzmán, "In Celebration of the Fortieth Anniversary of the Chinese Revolution," *A World to Win* 15 (1990), 53.

213 ***"Por Norita":*** Cannabicus Prime. *Abimael Guzmán (Vídeo de Zorba el Griego) Completo* [video file], September 22, 2008. Retrieved from www.youtube.com /watch?v=FEzwDx-QAqs.

214 **"Let me see":** Quoted in Jiménez, *La Captura*, 171.

Chapter Thirteen: The Revolution Comes to Villa

215 **"She did say it":** Interview with Marina Rodinó, Venice, November 6, 2015.

216 **"Come visit us":** Interview with Cecilia Blondet, Lima, June 1, 2015.

216 **Over six hundred thousand:** Robin Kirk, *The Decade of Chaqwa: Peru's Internal Refugees* (Washington, DC: US Committee for Refugees, 1991), 3.

217 **"culture of assembly"**: Antonio Zapata, *Sociedad y Poder Local*, 125.

217 *Worse things are coming*: ADP, Audio Sala Yuyanpaq, Discurso de María Elena Moyano [audio], ca. 1991.

217 **threatened to disown him**: Interview with Gustavo Pineki, Madrid, November 7, 2015.

217 **refused to have anything to do**: Guido Sattin, email communication, March 5, 2017.

217 **"It was very important"**: Diana Bachand, email communication, February 15, 2017.

218 **"Yes, I'm married"**: Archives of the Centro de la Mujer Flora Tristán (ACMFT), "Malena Madre," *La República*, 1992 (no month, day, or page number).

218 **"Why don't you kick her"**: Interview with Gustavo Pineki, November 7, 2015.

218 *"If your woman gets too loud"*: Quoted in Orin Starn, *Nightwatch: The Politics of Protest in the Andes* (Durham: Duke University Press, 1999), 175. The song was written by the legendary mid-century Andean folk singer, Ernesto Sánchez Fajardo, the "Goldfinch of Huascarán."

219 **"this extraordinary woman"**: Interview with Charo Torres, Lima, June 7, 2015.

219 **"He's a good man"**: Interview with Cecilia Blondet, Lima, June 1, 2015.

219 **"In Lima"**: Carmen Ollé, "Adrenaline Nights," in *The Peru Reader*, Starn et al., eds., 508.

219 **"I arrived in Lima"**: Shakespeare, "In Pursuit of Guzmán," 51.

220 **"Ayacucho is the cradle"**: CVR, "Entrevista a Abimael Guzmán Reinoso y Elena Iparraguirre," 27.

220 **They began to expand**: Jo-Marie Burt, "Shining Path and the 'Decisive Battle' in Lima's *Barriadas*," 267–306.

220 **Their total actions**: We base our estimate on DESCO, *Violencia Política, Tomo 1*, 28.

221 **"It could be your best friend"**: Interview with Tony Palomino Quispé, Villa El Salvador, Peru, June 4, 2015.

221 **"I lived a double life"**: CVR, Testimonio 70047.

221 **"reactionary trafficking"**: ACMFT, "Chantajean a Mujeres de Villa El Salvador," *El Diario*, 15, 1989. No day or month.

222 **Some believed Anchita pilfered**: CVR, *Informe Final*, Anexo 01, "Testimonio Brindado Ante la Comisión de la Verdad y Reconciliación."

222 **"You *negra de mierda*"**: Interview with Rocio Paz, Villa El Salvador, Peru, June 5, 2015.

222 **"I'm nervous sometimes"**: Interview with Diana Miloslavich, Lima, June 2, 2015.

223 **"Why the hell"**: Virginia Vargas recounts this story in Miloslavich, ed., *The Autobiography*, 92.

Chapter Fourteen: A Fish Out of Water

224 **thirty thousand people**: Vargas Llosa, *A Fish*, 169.

224 **"A useful idiot"**: Cristóbal, ed., *Uchuraccay*, 325.

224 **Vargas Llosa insisted**: Vargas Llosa responded to critics in *Contra Viento y Marea, III*, 79–200.

225 **"the people in Stockholm"**: "Too Good for the Nobel Prize," *New York Times*, April 7, 1991, www.nytimes.com/1991/04/07/opinion/too-good-for-the-nobel -prize.html.

225 **a true democracy's obligation:** Mario Vargas Llosa, "Carta abierta a Alan García," www.scribd.com/document/165690980/Carta-abierta-de-Mario-Vargas-Llosa -a-Alan-Garci-a-en-junio-de-1986.

226 *It'll only give you more wrinkles:* Jeff Daeschner, *La Guerra del Fin de la Democracia: Mario Vargas Llosa vs. Alberto Fujimori* (Lima: Peru Reporting, 1993), 73. Daeschner's entertaining account of the campaign appears in English as *The War of the End of Democracy: Mario Vargas Llosa vs. Alberto Fujimori*, trans. Mirko Lauer (Lima: Peru Reporting, 1993). We take our citations from the original Spanish, more detailed in places.

226 **Only women:** Marcelo Armas, *Vargas Llosa: El vicio de escribir* (Santiago: Editorial Norma, 1991), 81.

226 **"I'm a difficult man"**: Quoted in Jorge Coaguila ed., *Mario Vargas Llosa. 80 años. Entrevistas Escogidas* (Lima: Revuelta Editores, 2016), 59.

226 **"We needed to be together"**: Interview with Elena Iparraguirre, Piedras Gordas, August 20, 2017.

227 **"We fell in love"**: Interview with Silvia Rodríguez, Piedras Gordas, August 20, 2017.

227 **"Love . . . serves the function"**: Quoted in Kirk, *The Monkey's Paw*, 94.

227 ***"In the name of the Communist Party"***: ADINCOTE, *Documentación, Tomo XXXV*, 156.

227 **"Bad weeds never die"**: Gavilán, *When Rains*, 21.

228 **"They were soldiers"**: José Carlos Agüero, *Los Rendidos: Sobre el don de perdonar* (Lima: Instituto de Estudios Peruanos, 2015), 32.

228 **"Everybody could see"**: Ibid., 52.

228 **"[I] felt relief"**: Ibid., 43.

228 **"My countryman"**: CVR, Interview with Abimael Guzmán and Elena Iparraguirre, January 27, 2003.

228 **"The arrogant preacher"**: CCPCP, *¡Elecciones, No! ¡Guerra Popular, Si!*.

229 **"The elections"**: Ibid.

229 **"Rotten Meat"**: "Gobierno de Alan García, 1985-1990," Actualidad, www .connuestroperu.com/actualidad/45208-gobierno-de-alan-garcia-1985-90, June 27, 2105. Historian Alfonso Quiroz insightfully examines government corruption in *Corrupt Circles: A History of Unbound Graft in Peru* (Baltimore: Johns Hopkins University Press, Washington, DC, 2008).

229 **"The utopian collectivist"**: Quoted in Daeschner, *La Guerra*, 164.

229 **an indomitable Peruvian spirit:** An influential book about the so-called informal economy was Hernando de Soto's *The Other Path: The Economic Answer to Terrorism* (New York: Basic, 2002).

230 **"old country"**: Quoted in Vargas Llosa, *A Fish*, 178.

230 **"He stared blankly"**: Vargas Llosa, *A Fish*, 220.

231 **hugged a mourning peasant woman:** Ibid.

231 "semihysterical pushing": Ibid., 486

231 "master at intellectually defining": Mark Malloch Brown, "The Consultant," Granta 36 (1991), 92.

231 "Are you well-protected, Mario?": Quoted in Álvaro Vargas Llosa, "The Press Officer," Granta 36 (1991), 80.

232 "Do you remember . . . when you were a writer?": Vargas Llosa, "A Fish," 179.

232 "the sun warns every man": Luis de Góngora y Argote, "Selected Sonnets," trans. A. S. Kline, http://www.poetryintranslation.com/PITBR/Spanish/Gongora .php.

232 "in its darkest hour": David Gallagher, "Peru, in Its Darkest Hour, May Be Close to Dawn," Wall Street Journal, February 23, 1990, A11.

233 "This has gone to shit!": Quoted in Daeschner, La guerra, 225.

234 "I don't believe all cultures are equal": Quoted in Coaguila ed., Vargas Llosa, 258–259.

235 "never see a broke Japanese person": Daeschner, La guerra, 217.

235 "I have always been methodical": Quoted in Daeschner, La guerra, 154.

235 "I don't support heterodoxy . . . only pragmatism": Quoted in Luis Jochamowitz, Ciudadano Fujimori: La construcción de un político (Lima: Peisa, 1994), 256.

235 "We can't decide the president ourselves": Daeschner, La guerra, 227.

236 Your serpentine tongue: Mario Vargas Llosa, In Praise of the Stepmother: A Novel, trans. Helen Lane (New York: Picador, 2002), 120.

237 "I always expected to win": Quoted in Jochamowitz, Ciudadano Fujimori, 209.

237 "price of chicken has just flown away": James Brooke, "Peru's Poor Feel Hardship of 'Fuji Shock' Austerity," August 12, 1990, www.nytimes.com/1990/08/12/world /peru-s-poor-feel-hardship-of-fuji-shock-austerity.html.

237 "thank God": Quoted in Daeschner, La guerra, 163.

238 "destroy his opponents": Jochamowitz, Ciudadano Fujimori, 219.

238 "No longer will the terrorists control": "Cuando el Ejército entró a San Marcos y La Cantuta hace 25 años," El Comercio, accessed February 28, 2018, https:// elcomercio.pe/huellas-digitales/archivo/ejercito-entro-san-marcos-cantuta-25 -anos-207690.

238 a political farce: Strong, Shining Path, 215.

239 "perhaps an Emperor would be good": Quoted in Bowen, The Fujimori File, 101.

Chapter Fifteen: Ghostbusters

240 "Chino, I just got off the phone": Marco Miyashiro, "Reflexiones sobre el MRTA y Sendero Luminoso," unpublished manuscript, 2000.

240 the PIP's counterinsurgency unit: It was known then as the DIRCOTE, renamed the DINCOTE in the late 1980s.

241 "The only police": Interview with Marco Miyashiro, Lima, May 30, 2015.

242 crouched in a wrestler's stance: Group interview with former Leoncio Prado classmates, Lima, August 8, 2014.

242 **His first assignment:** Marco Miyashiro, "Hoja de vida," 2012, unpublished manuscript.

243 **their own radio show:** Interview with Marco Miyashiro, Lima, May 30, 2015.

244 *You'll always have the last word:* Ibid.

244 **"Exactly how many":** CVR, Interview 68 (Marco Miyashiro), 2002; Idealterna Perú, 1509: *Operación Victoria* [Video file], July 12, 2011. Retrieved from www .youtube.com/watch?v=a0dnD5Hpuf8.

245 **Miyashiro once sent:** Interview with Marco Miyashiro, May 30, 2015.

245 **"Know the enemy":** Interview with José Luis Gil, Lima, August 22, 2017. For more on Jiménez and his leadership style, see Guillermo Bonilla Arévalo, *Golpe Mortal: La verdadera historia de la Pacificación Nacional* (Lima: Author, 2015).

245 **one concrete lead:** Interview with José Luis Gil, Lima, August 22, 2017. Benedicto Jiménez, *Inicio, Desarrollo, y Ocaso del Terrorismo en el Perú*, Vol. 2, (Lima: INDECOPI, n.d.), 706–707.

246 **"This is really good stuff":** Jiménez, *Inicio*, Vol. 2, 712; Interview with Benedicto Jiménez, Lima, August 23, 2017.

246 **"who Mao's grandma was":** Miyashiro, "Reflexiones," 36–37.

246 **"chasing a ghost":** Miyashiro, "Reflexiones," 37.

247 **"an extremely dangerous":** "Fact Sheet on the Terrorist Group, Sendero Luminoso," October 4, 1989, www.wikileaks.org/plusd/cables/89STATE319082_a.html.

247 **"Are these killers":** US Embassy (Lima) Cable, "The Mind of the Beast: Sendero Luminoso Brutality," August 7, 1991, www.nsarchive2.gwu.edu/NSAEBB/NSAEBB64/.

248 **the "narcoterrorist" Abimael:** "Peru and the Capture of Abimael Guzmán," *Congressional Record*, October 2, 1991, S16332.

248 **"We knew most of it":** Interview with José Luis Gil, Lima, June 10, 2015.

248 **They'd begun to decipher:** Tipe, *Abimael*, 50.

248 **"that damn gardener":** "Secretos del Cuartél," *Caretas*, June 12, 1990, 36.

249 **"unleash the storm":** Quoted in Tipe, *Abimael*, 49.

249 **"we've got to move in":** Ibid., 52.

249 *Oh, shit:* Interview with Diana Miloslavich, Lima, June 2, 2015.

250 **"There's one more!":** Quoted in Tipe, *Abimael*, 53.

250 **Jorge Sánchez:** This is a pseudonym, since this detective did not want to be identified.

250 **"Who the hell":** Quoted in Tipe, *Abimael*, Ibid., 54–55.

250 **Elvia Zanabria:** Jiménez, *La Captura*, 136.

251 *like a museum:* Miyashiro, "Reflexiones," 40.

251 **"Four tons of terrorism":** Interview with Marco Miyashiro, Lima, August 20, 2017.

252 **"As far as we know":** "El cuartel de Guzmán," *Caretas*, June 5, 1990, 19.

252 **"We oppose laxness":** ADINCOTE, *Documentación, Tomo XXIX*, 348.

252 **"We hated losing":** Interview with Elena Iparraguirre, Piedras Gordas, August 20, 2017.

252 **"state reactionariazation":** CCPC, *¡Que el equilibrio!*.

253 **a big explosion:** Personal communication, Anthony Quainton, Chapel Hill, April 14, 2015.

253 **"My God":** "¿A dónde iremos a parar?," *La República*, August 9, 1990, 6.

Chapter Sixteen: The Clever Frog

257 **Narciso Sulca's weekly turn:** Interview with Narciso Sulca, July 21, 2007.

259 **Huaychainos had converted:** Ponciano del Pino, "Tiempos de guerra y de dioses: Ronderos, evangélicos y senderistas en el valle del rio Apurímac" in *Las rondas campesinas y la derrota de Sendero Luminoso*, Carlos Iván Degregori et al., eds. (Lima: Instituto de Estudios Peruanos, 1996).

259 **"Lord Jesus":** Interview with Narciso Sulca, Huanta, June 9, 2016.

259 **took a night class:** Interview with Elena Iparraguirre, Piedras Gordas, June 7, 2015.

260 **three thousand villages:** Orin Starn, ed., *Hablan los ronderos: La búsqueda por la paz en los andes* (Lima: Instituto de Estudios Peruanos, 1993).

260 **"We had the hacienda owners":** Interview with Adrian Ñawpa, Purus, December 18, 1992.

261 **"Fierce wolves":** Quoted in Bowen, *The Fujimori File*, 91.

261 **"Who gave you these?":** Orin Starn, field notes, Chaca, December 10, 1992.

261 **Big Banana:** Orin Starn, Field Notes, Cangari Viru-Viru, December 12, 1992.

262 *Senderista* **bands:** See Richard Kernaghan's *Coca Is Gone: Of Might and Right in the Huallaga Post-Boom* (Stanford, CA: Stanford University Press, 2009).

262 **arranged an evacuation:** Mariano Gagnon, *Warriors in Eden* (New York: William Morrow, 1993).

262 **"the poorly armed *ronderos*":** Quoted in Starn, ed., *Hablan los ronderos*, 5.

262 **"It was eerie":** Interview with Raymond Starr, Durham, NC, November 16, 2017.

263 **the penitent ones:** See Kimberly Theidon, "La micropolítica de la reconciliación: Práctica de la justicia en comunidades rurales ayacuchanas," *Alpanchis* 60 (2002), 113–141. The Fujimori government issued a so-called *Ley de Arrepentimiento*, Repentance Law, which allowed low-level *senderistas* to escape major punishment if they gave themselves up.

263 **"We're suffering":** Interview with Humberto Orozco, Lima, May 25, 2018.

264 **battled the Chilean occupiers:** For more on the *montoneros*, Florencia Mallon, *The Defense of Community in Peru's Central Highlands: Peasant Struggle and Capitalist Transition, 1860–1940* (Princeton: Princeton University Press, 1983); Nelson Manrique, *Campesinado y Nación: Las guerrillas indígenas en la Guerra con Chile* (Lima: Centro de Investigación y Capacitación, 1981).

264 **Andean fairy tale:** Interview with Narciso Sulca, Huaychao, Peru, July 21, 2007.

264 **"We'll look like soldiers":** Interview with Narciso Sulca, Huanta, Peru, June 9, 2016.

265 **a more Indian appearance:** Marisol de la Cadena, "Women are More Indian: Ethnicity and Gender in a Community Near Cuzco," in Brooke Larson et al., eds., *Ethnicity, Markets, and Migration in the Andes: At the Crossroads of History and Anthropology*, 329–348.

265 **"Only God knows":** Quoted in La Serna, *The Corner*, 206.

265 **lexicon for sorrow:** Theidon, *Intimate Enemies*, 15, 47.

266 **"incomprehensible abstraction":** Vargas Llosa, "Inquest in the Andes," 56.

266 **as full citizens:** Del Pino, *En nombre*; Jaymie Patricia Heilman, *Before the Shining Path*; Méndez, *The Plebeian Republic*.

266 **a "pernicious" obstacle:** Quoted in Mario Vargas Llosa, "Nationalism has produced the most brutal and cruel wars in history," *The Herald*, June 8, 2012, www .heraldscotland.com/arts_ents/13061036._Nationalism_has_produced_the _most_brutal_and_cruel_wars_in_history_/.

266 **stick-figure *rondero*:** Orin Starn, field notes, Huaychao, December 4, 1991.

267 **received a request:** Interview with Narciso Sulca, Huanta, Peru, June 9, 2016.

267 *We still exist*: José María Arguedas, *Kachkaniraqmi, ¡Sigo siendo! Textos esenciales*, Carmen María Pinilla, ed. (Lima: Fondo Editorial del Congreso del Perú, 2004), 463.

268 **"with great clarity":** CCPCP, *¡Que el equilibrio!*.

268 **"Mistaken ideas":** Quoted in Tony Judt, *Past Imperfect: French intellectuals, 1944–1956* (Berkeley: University of California Press, 2002), v.

269 **"incomparable clearness":** Abimael Guzmán, *De puño*, 212.

269 **"burning furnace":** CCPCP, *¡Elecciones, No! ¡Guerra Popular, Si!*.

269 **Maoist guerrilla group:** Alpa Shah, *Nightmarch: A Portrait of India's Revolutionary Movement* (London: Hurst, 2018).

270 **The party had betrayed:** Interview with Juan Fulano, Lima, August 15, 2016.

Chapter Seventeen: The Birthday Party

271 **"terrorist scrap paper":** Miyashiro, "Reflexiones," 39–40.

271 **"utmost professionalism":** "Mensaje del Señor Presidente de la República con motivo del aniversario de la creación del GEIN, de la Dircote," Lima, March 5, 1991.

272 **"We're here to work":** Interview with José Luis Gil, Lima, August 22, 2017.

272 *Los miyashiros*: Idealterna Perú, 1509: *Operación Victoria*.

273 **Grupo Colina:** Umberto Jara, *Ojo por Ojo: La verdadera historia del Grupo Colina* (Lima: Carvajal, 2003).

273 **most influential advisor:** See Sally Bowen and Jane Holligan, *The Imperfect Spy: The Many Lives of Vladimiro Montesinos* (Lima: Peisa, 2003).

274 **boring *senderista* manifestos:** Interview with Benedicto Jiménez, Lima, August 23, 2017.

274 **snarling guard dogs:** Tipe, *Abimael*, 76.

274 **Dove Three:** Jiménez, *La Captura*, 168. According to GEIN agent Guillermo Bonilla's *Golpe Mortal*, 107, Dove Numbers One and Two also went to the store.

275 *forty-five years old*: Benedicto Jiménez, "Despejando la niebla," 2008, http:// elpacificador2008.blogspot.com/2008/01/despejando-la-niebla-en-el-caso.html.

275 **Pan-American Highway:** Interview with Elena Iparraguirre, Piedras Gordas, August 20, 2017.

277 *unstoppable march*: CCCP, *¡Que el equilibrio!*.

277 **"proved false by reality":** Ibid.

277 "a great man": Guzmán, "'Exclusive' Comments," 52.

277 twentieth century's biggest mass murderers: Anne Applebaum provides a chilling look at Stalin's murderous policies in the Ukraine in *Red Famine: Stalin's War on Ukraine* (New York: Doubleday, 2017). For a controversial yet not unfounded list of crimes against humanity committed by Lenin, Mao, and other Communist leaders, see Stéphane Courtois et al., *The Black Book of Communism: Crimes, Terror, Repression* (Cambridge: Harvard University Press, 1999). It should be noted that some serious observers charge the former US president, George W. Bush, with war crimes for torture and civilian deaths in the post-9/11 war on terror.

278 "Sendero will grow": "Peru Guerrillas Take Aim at Lima," *Los Angeles Times*, October 13, 1991, http://articles.latimes.com/1991-10-13/news/mn-1064_1_path-guerrillas.

278 panicked warning shot: Tipe, *Abimael*, 95.

278 "to rivet ideas": CCPCP, "Entrevista al Presidente Gonzalo."

278 viewed Shining Path favorably: "Peru Guerrillas Take Aim at Lima."

278 "tear the country to pieces": Ibid.

278 partner's voice crackled: Bonilla, *Golpe Mortal*, 108.

279 "*sacos largos*": Jiménez, *Inicio*, Vol. 1, 26.

280 life at the Buenavista house: Jiménez, *La Captura*, 155.

280 Abimael's "concubine": Carlos Paredes, *La Caída del Héroe: La Verdadera Historia de Ketín Vidal* (Lima: Planeta, 2006), 16.

280 "best school in the world": Interview with Angélica Salas, Lima, July 31, 2016.

280 "I had plenty of power": Interview with Elena Iparraguirre, Piedras Gordas, July 31, 2016.

280 "saw us as secretaries": Interview with María Pantoja, Piedras Gordas, July 31, 2016.

281 quoted *Macbeth*: Gorriti, *Shining Path*, 21.

281 assault in the jungle town of Uchiza: CVR, *Informe final*, Vol. 7, 329–347.

281 new movement at Buenavista: Gustavo Gorriti, "El Caso Buena Vista," *Caretas*, January 13, 2008.

282 They would wait: Some controversy exists over how the decision not to raid was made. In "El Caso Buena Vista," Gustavo Gorriti writes that Vladimiro Montesinos, Fujimori's intelligence chief, gave the order to wait. He speculates that Fujimori and Montesinos did not want Abimael Guzmán captured—to justify Fujimori's coming seizure of emergency powers. This may be true, but our own interviews with Benedicto Jiménez, Marco Miyashiro, and several key GEIN agents indicate that Jiménez advocated delay on his own. An agent watching the Buenavista house, Guillermo Bonilla, suggests as much in his *Golpe Mortal*, 111.

283 "sadness and impotence": Bonilla, *Golpe Mortal*, 111.

283 *unleash the storm*: Jiménez, *La Captura*, 243.

283 "just getting started": Interview with José Luis Gil, Lima, August 22, 2017.

283 some VHS tapes: Jiménez, *La Captura*, 172–173.

283 "Probably porn": Quoted in Tipe, *Abimael*, 77.

283 connected his camcorder: Interview with Benedicto Jiménez, March 21, 2018.

284 **"let down our guard"**: Interview with Elena Iparraguirre, Piedras Gordas, August 20, 2017.

284 **"Abimael's arrogance"**: Interview with Juan Fulano, Lima, August 10, 2016.

284 **"Gonzalo and his court"**: Quoted in Tipe, *Abimael*, 89.

Chapter Eighteen: A Death Foretold

286 **"how I've lived"**: Miloslavich, ed., *The Autobiography*, 89.

287 **"they've come for me"**: We base this account on interviews with Martha Moyano, Tony Palomino, Rocio Paz, and Gustavo Pineki. See also CVR, *Informe Final*, Vol. 8, 611–622; CVR, Anexo 01, "Testimonio Brindado Ante la Comisión de la Verdad y Reconciliación;" "La Muerte Más Anunciada," *Caretas*, February 17, 1992, 29–30; "Le dispararon a la cabeza y dinamitaron su cadáver, *La República*, 2–4; and various newspaper clippings from the ACMFT.

288 **a Shining Path flyer**: Interview with Diana Miloslavich, Lima, April 5, 2016.

289 **"We lost touch"**: Interview with Elena Iparraguirre, Piedras Gordas, August 20, 2017.

289 **"Hands of the Communist Party"**: "Chantajean a mujeres de Villa El Salvador," *El Diario*, April 22, 1991, 15.

289 **"My custom is to build"**: Miloslavich, ed., *The Autobiography*, 65.

290 **"shutting down the barbarism"**: "Sendero no da la cara," *Expreso*, September 12, 1991, 1.

290 *Everyone knows me*: Phone interview with Diana Bachand, April 5, 2016.

290 **"what precise moment"**: Mario Vargas Llosa, *A Conversation in the Cathedral*, trans. Gregory Rabassa (New York: Harper and Row, 1974), 3.

291 **"the greatest impression"**: Quoted in Jo-Marie Burt, "Accounting for Murder: The Contested Narratives of the Life and Death of María Elena Moyano" in *Accounting for Violence: Marketing Memory in Latin America*, Ksenija Bilbija and Leigh Payne, eds. (Durham: Duke University Press, 2011), 74.

291 **anti-colonial rebellion**: For more about the great neo-Incan revolt see Charles Walker, *The Tupac Amaru Rebellion* (Cambridge: Belknap, 2014).

291 **"Exemplary reaction"**: CMFT, "Terror . . . y Respuesta," *Sí*, undated, 30.

292 **"inspired strong emotions"**: Jo-Marie Burt, personal communication, May 25, 2015.

292 **former UN secretary**: Interview with Diana Miloslavich, Lima, June 2, 2015.

292 **"People have felt deceived"**: "Sendero será derrotado," *La República*, September 22, 1991, 9.

292 **"justice for the dead"**: Ibid., 10

293 **"Big, rapid zig-zags"**: V. I. Lenin, *Collected Works, Volume 27* (Moscow: Progress Publishers, 1972), 19.

293 **almost been lynched**: CVR, *Informe Final*, Vol. 5, 410–431.

293 **Gustavo was growingly worried**: Interview with Gustavo Pineki, Madrid, November 7, 2015.

294 **"What good am I here?"**: Interview with Diana Miloslavich, Lima, June 2, 2015.

294 **"as if it already happened"**: Gabriel García Márquez, *Chronicle of a Death Foretold*, trans. Gregory Rabassa (New York: Vintage, 2003), 61.

294 **refuge at a convent**: Interview with José Burneo, Lima, June 22, 2015.

294 **"She couldn't *defraudar*"**: Interview with Cecilia Blondet, Lima August 9, 2016.

295 **"the people's hunger"**: Quoted in Burt, "Accounting for Murder," 75.

295 **"hearts of our oppressed people"**: Miloslavich, ed., *The Autobiography*, 69.

295 **telephone threats**: Interview with Gustavo Pineki, Madrid, November 5, 2015.

296 **"What will happen to my children?"**: Interview with Rocio Paz, Villa El Salvador, Peru, June 2, 2015.

296 **"It wasn't so safe"**: Interview with Diana Miloslavich, Lima, June 2, 2016.

296 **"dead woman walking"**: Interview with Enrique Bossio, Lima, June 5, 2015.

296 **take refuge in Chile**: Interview with José Burneo, Lima, June 10, 2015.

296 **"ugly blonde ones"**: Interview with Diane Bachand, April 5, 2016.

296 **roof-raising party**: Interview with Rocio Paz, Lima, June 2, 2015.

297 **"I felt death nearer"**: Miloslavich, ed., *The Autobiography*, 89.

297 **"I tried to persuade her"**: Interview with Diana Bachand, April 5, 2016.

297 **"crumbs to the people"**: Quoted in Starn, *Nightwatch*, 199.

298 **join the peace march**: Interview with Michel Azcueta, Villa El Salvador, June 9, 2015.

298 **"Two beautiful women alone"**: Interview with Diana Miloslavich, Lima, June 2, 2015.

299 **A lookout watched**: ADINCOTE, *Atestado Nro. 031—D4-DINCOTE*. This document is the DIRCOTE's investigation into the killing.

299 **"just talking and drinking"**: CVR, Anexo 01, 007.

299 **"Andean-featured woman"**: "Sendero asesinó a dirigenta María Elena Moyano," *Expreso*, February 16, 1992, A2.

300 **"*Mami escapó*"**: Interview with Gustavo Pineki, November 7, 2015.

300 **"The machine stopped"**: Interview with Gustavo Pineki, Madrid, November 7, 2016.

300 **"maybe María Elena had survived"**: Interview with Rocío Paz, Villa El Salvador, Peru, June 2, 2015.

300 **younger sister**: Interview with Martha Moyano, Villa El Salvador, August 10, 2016.

300 **"An odious crime"**: "Repudio," *Sí*, February 24, 1992, 8.

301 **"murderous hunger"**: ACMFT, Gustavo Gutiérrez, "Sus semillas de vida será esparcidas," *Signos*, undated.

301 **"We killed her"**: Luis Escajadillo C., "Lo mató el narcotráfico," *La República*, February 21,1992, 17.

301 **"The gesture is what counts"**: Kirk, *The Monkey's Paw*, 8.

301 **opposed the military's war crimes**: See Burt, "Accounting for Murder," 69–98.

302 **"hooked like a gambler"**: Bertolt Brecht, *Mother Courage and Her Children*, trans. Tony Kushner (London: Methuen, 2009), 8.

302 **"So That Peru Might Live":** Sunday supplement cover of *El Comercio,* February 23, 1992.

302 **a bicycle for his birthday:** Interview with Diane Miloslavich, Lima, June 2, 2015.

302 **"Guzmán's Great Mistake":** "El gran error de Guzmán," *La República,* February 20, 1992, 17.

302 **"Closing Ranks":** "Cierran filas contra sendero," Sunday Magazine, *La República,* February 23, 1992, 1.

303 **"Imperialist Agent":** Movimiento Clasista Barrial, "!Viva la justa sanción de la agente del imperialismo M. E. Moyano!," unpublished flyer. Villa El Salvador, Peru, March 2, 1992.

303 **"anything to do with that situation":** CVR, Interview with Abimael Guzmán and Elena Iparraguirre," January 27, 2003.

303 **"agent of the Armed Forces":** Ibid.

304 **Rain never falls in Villa:** Guido Sattin, *Il desierto fiorito.* n.d., unpublished manuscript.

Chapter Nineteen: The Wolf and the Whale

305 **"fewer María Elenas":** Gustavo Gorriti, "El Leviatán y la Heroína," *Caretas,* March 2, 1992, 25, 87.

306 **no such romance:** See Cecilia Méndez G., "Incas, Sí, Indios, No: Notes on Peruvian Creole Nationalism and Its Contemporary Crisis," *Journal of Latin American Studies,* Vol. 28, No. 1 (February 1996), 197–225.

306 **furious, loving obituary:** Gustavo Gorriti, "El Sensei Inamine," *Caretas,* July 30, 1991, 40–1.

306 **Even generals feared** *El Doctor*: See Bowen and Holligan, *The Imperfect Spy.*

307 **Gustavo chatted with officers:** Interview with Gustavo Gorriti, Lima, October 4, 2016.

308 **camping in an empty apartment:** Interview with Elena Iparraguirre, Piedras Gordas, August 20, 2017.

309 **"Let Strategic Equilibrium":** CCPCP, *¡Que el equilibrio!.*

309 **"I was shocked":** Interview with Carlos Incháustegui, July 30, 2016.

310 **Marxists lived in the attic:** The arrangement became the subject of a later novel, Nicholas Shakespeare's *The Dancer Upstairs,* and John Malkovich's film of the same title.

310 **hardcore punk scene:** See Shane Green, *Punk and Revolution: Seven More Interpretations of Peruvian Reality* (Durham: Duke University Press, 2017).

310 **Carlos sometimes cooked:** Interview with Carlos Incháustegui, Lima, December 19, 2016.

311 **He was brought to the hideout:** Jiménez, *La Captura,* 305-6, 318.

312 **An** *autogolpe*: See Sally Bowen, *The Fujimori File: Peru and Its President, 1990–2000* (Lima: Peru Monitor Publications, 2000).

313 **"an authentic transformation":** Alberto Fujimori, "Mensaje a la nación anun-

ciando el autogolpe," April 5, 1992, https://www.youtube.com/watch?v=xmj4a AfLzB4.

313 **"genocidal traitor"**: CCPCP, *¡Que el equilibrio!*.

313 **the doorbell rang:** Gorriti wrote in *El Pais* about his arrest, April 8, 1992, www.elpais.com/diario/1992/04/08/internacional/702684001_850215.html.

315 **"We are very concerned":** "Difunden conversación entre George H. W. Bush y Alberto Fujimori" *La República*, April 8, 2017, www.larepublica.pe/politica/863294-difunden -conversacion-entre-george-bush-y-alberto-fujimori-luego-del-autogolpe.

316 **"thick-skinned pachyderm":** Quoted in Conaghan, *Fujimori's Peru*, 46.

316 **"a bribocracy":** Bowen, *The Fujimori Files*, 119.

316 **launched their uprising:** A few Canto Grande prisoners were survivors of the 1986 massacre.

317 **spotted Janet Talavera:** Gargurevich, "Janet, La Última Periodista Senderista."

317 **a stone-faced Fujimori:** Bowen, *The Fujimori File*, 129.

317 **"the wolf and the whale":** Gorriti, "El Leviatán," 87.

318 **stocks and whippings:** Starn, *Nightwatch*, 75–76.

318 **70 percent:** Some claimed, perhaps correctly, that the polls may have been manipulated. Regardless of the exact numbers, a majority of Peruvians supported the *autogolpe*.

320 **Tarata Street:** CVR, *Informe final*, Vol. 1, 702–708.

Chapter Twenty: Fat Cheeks, Affirmative!

322 **"I've seen this woman":** Quoted in Jiménez, *La Captura*, 340–41.

323 **"Garbage speaks an eloquent language":** Ibid., 167. It is not clear if Eco actually wrote this.

324 **"They're fucked":** Quoted in Ibid., 326.

324 **"dyed their blond hair dark":** Malcom Coad, "Terror Grips Peru's Capital," *The Guardian*, August 17, 1992, 8.

324 **testified before the US Congress:** Bernard Aronson, "Peru's Brutal Insurgency: Sendero Luminoso." *US State Department Dispatch*, 236–240, No. 3, Vol. 12, March 23, 1992, 36.

324 **"bleeding Peru to death":** Quoted in Bowen, *The Fujimori Files*, 134.

325 **"created a political vacuum":** Quoted in Ibid., 133.

325 *Cholo Sotil*: Interview with Marco Miyashiro, Lima, August 20, 2017.

325 **"a mangy reactionary dog":** Quoted in Jiménez, *La Captura*, 52.

326 **"The last time I saw Chairman Gonzalo":** Quoted in Ibid., 295.

326 **faked expense receipts:** Interview with José Luis Gil, Lima, August 22, 2017.

326 **recognizing his mistake:** "El Vigía Terco," *Caretas*, September 6, 2012, 14.

326 **"Lola is on the patio":** Tipe, *Abimael*, 180; Jiménez, *La Captura*, 60; Idealterna Perú, 1509: *Operación Victoria*.

327 **hoping to seize Guzmán:** Jiménez, *Inicio*, Vol. 2, 750–752; Jiménez, *La Captura*, 60.

328 *"El negro* is a wizard": Quoted in Jiménez, *La Captura*, 80.

328 "We had been anxious": Interview with José Luis Gil, Lima, June 10, 2015.

329 "Someone's head will roll": Quoted in Jiménez, *Inicio*, Vol. 2, 752.

329 find themselves in a firefight: Tipe, *Abimael*, 190–194; Jiménez, *La Captura*, 355–358, 364.

329 "talking about Quyllurit'i": Interview with Carlos Incháustegui, Lima, August 24, 2017.

330 Abimael sat calmly: Tipe, *Abimael*, 194.

330 "I was terrified": Interview with Elena Iparraguirre, Piedras Gordas, June 7, 2015.

331 "lovesick devotion": Jiménez, *La Captura*, 360.

331 Vidal introduced himself: Idealterna Perú, *1506: Operación Victoria.*

331 "to immortalize ourselves": Quoted in Paredes, *La caída*, 14.

331 Elena hovered: Poder Judicial, *Proceso contra Abimael Guzmán y otros.* Videos de exposición [video file]; Jiménez, *La Captura*, 366–368.

332 "We thought there'd be blood": Interview with Marco Miyashiro, Lima, August 20, 2017.

332 Butch Cassidy and the Sundance Kid: See Kim MacQuarrie, *Life and Death in the Andes: On the Trail of Bandits, Heroes, and Revolutionaries* (Simon and Schuster: New York, 2015), 315–342.

332 "You can kill a man": Poder Judicial, *Proceso contra Abimael Guzmán y otros.* Videos de exposición [video file].

Chapter Twenty-One: The Silence of the Lambs

334 this had been his idea: *The Fall of Fujimori*, 2005, directed by Ellen Perry.

334 "last stage of Communism": Andrei Codrescu, "Picking the Flowers of the Revolution, *New York Times* Magazine, February 1, 1998, 33.

334 *display us like animals*: Interview with Elena Iparraguirre, Lima, August 20, 2017.

335 "beheaded the brains": *The Fall of Fujimori.*

336 Vidal's own checkered past: Carlos Paredes, *La caída del héroe: La verdadera historia del general Ketín Vidal* (Lima: Planeta, 2006).

336 "this is unjust": Quoted in Jiménez, *La Captura*, 381. See also Bonilla, *Golpe Mortal*, 185–6.

336 exiled Miyashiro: Miyashiro, "Hoja de Vida."

337 "We won't be going home": Interview with Gustavo Gorriti, Lima, August 4, 2016.

338 "Peru is a problem": Jorge Basadre, *Meditaciones sobre el destino histórico del Perú* (Lima: Huascarán, 1947), 105.

338 "multiplied human experiences": Mario Vargas Llosa, "In Praise of Reading and Fiction," Nobel Lecture, December 7, 2010, www.nobelprize.org/nobel _prizes/literature/laureates/2010/vargas_llosa-lecture_en.html.

339 strode into Abimael's cell: Tipe, *Abimael*, 200–201.

339 **"Who killed Augusta?":** Interview with José Luis Gil, Lima, August 22, 2017.

339 **"You think I know everything":** Guzmán, " 'Exclusive' Comments" 57.

339 **"politically and ideologically incapable":** Guzmán, *De puño*, 62.

339 **Abimael stopped:** Tipe, *Abimael*, 203.

340 **"love in Communism":** Quoted in Roncagliolo, *La Cuarta Espada*, 182.

340 **"loved each other deeply":** Jiménez, *La Captura*, 162.

340 **"a child by her side":** Ibid., 161.

340 **"fundamental human rights":** Guzmán, *De puño*, 60.

340 **"It was awful":** Interview with Elena Iparraguirre, Piedras Gordas, February 20, 2017.

341 **the Zapatistas:** See Gloria Muñoz Ramírez, *The Fire and the Word: A History of the Zapatista Movement*, trans. Laura Carlsen with Alejandro Reyes Arias (San Francisco: City Lights Books, 2008).

341 **"their end is near":** PCP, "Sobre la captura del siglo," September 16, 1992, https://huellasdekantu.wordpress.com/tag/captura-del-siglo/.

343 **Montesinos nodded:** Latina.pe. *Abimael Guzmán y Vladimiro Montesinos, video inédito y completo* [video file], September 20, 2015. Retrieved from www.youtube.com/watch?v=fhcXs91WbcA.

343 **a peace agreement:** Montesinos, *Sin Sendero*, 207–208.

344 *What an idiot:* Interview with Elena Iparraguirre, Piedras Gordas, August 20, 2017.

344 **a televised statement:** Comveli. *Paz Perú y Sendero Luminoso Comité Central 3 Dic 1993* [video file], July 2, 2008. Retrieved from www.youtube.com/watch?v=eKQkCBvSQVo.

345 **broke away from the party:** Degregori, *How Difficult*, 28–36.

345 **unfulfilled hope:** Bowen and Holligan, *The Imperfect Spy*, 150.

346 **Vladivideos:** Alberto Kouri and Vladimiro Montesinos, "Bribing a congressman" in *The Peru Reader*, Starn et al., eds., 476.

347 **"We have not forgotten":** Alejandro Toledo, "Mensaje a la nación," November 8, 2004, in Guzmán, *De puño*, 93.

348 **"never liked to play games":** Interview with Elena Iparraguirre, Piedras Gordas, August 20, 2017.

348 *"después de tantas palabras":* César Vallejo, *Poemas Humanos* (Barcelona: Laia, 1985), 62.

Epilogue

350 **"unquiet souls":** Robert Herz, *Death and the Right Hand*, trans. Rodney and Claudia Needham (Glencoe, IL: Free Press, 1960).

350 **"Lie Commission":** Caroline Yezer, "Who Wants to Know? Rumors, Suspicions, and Opposition to Truth-Telling in Ayacucho," *Latin American and Caribbean Ethnic Studies* Vol. 3, No. 3 (2008), 271–289.

351 **"Tradition is alive":** José Carlos Mariátegui, "Reflections," in *The Peru Reader*, Starn et al., eds., 240.

352 **"Our work . . . is over":** Guzmán, *De puño*, 352.

352 **a caustic speech:** Perú21. *Abimael Guzmán amenazó procuradores* [video file], May 12, 2017. Retrieved from https://peru21.pe/politica/abimael-guzman-amenazo-procuradora-mete-video-387144.

353 **Gustavo excused himself:** CMFT, "Viudo de María Elena Moyano recuerda su afán de darse a los demás," *El Comercio,* May 3, 1992, no page number.

354 **villagers do not like discussing the war:** See Yezer, "Who Wants to Know?"

354 **sang a sad ballad:** Interview with Narciso Sulca, Huanta, Peru, February 8, 2016.

INDEX

Page references in *italics* refer to the map.